3-23-60

MEANING
AND
EXISTENCE

By the Same Author

THE METAPHYSICS OF LOGICAL POSITIVISM

PHILOSOPHY OF SCIENCE

MEANING
AND
EXISTENCE

Gustav Bergmann

THE UNIVERSITY OF WISCONSIN PRESS
MADISON 1960

Preface

BOOKS are books and essays are essays. Some collections of essays are just that. Some others in all but form are books. This volume, I submit, is of the latter kind. The essays gathered in it were written within a span of five years. They were all written with such a gathering in mind. Taken together, I believe they display a unity which is almost monolithic. The first business of this Preface is to give some reasons for that belief.

Titles ought to be accurate, expressive, and as short as possible. I have long hesitated between two titles. Eventually my love of brevity prevailed. The title rejected is *Meanings, Minds, and Logic*. But I shall make use of it, as well as of the one I eventually adopted, in stating the promised reasons by means of a thematic analysis.

There are many philosophical questions. They tend to cluster. A philosophical problem so-called is such a cluster. These clusters, too, have a way of clustering. Among the members of a problem cluster, one usually is more fundamental than the others. To understand what that means, consider that the solution a philosopher proposes for one problem more often than not imposes certain conditions on the solutions he may consistently propose for some others. (Such "consistency" is literal consistency as well as one of "style.") Call the number of problems so affected by (the solution of) one problem the scope of the latter. Very roughly, then, the larger its scope, the more fundamental a problem is. Call the most fundamental problems basic. They are but few. The most basic among them, if I may so express myself, is the analysis of mind; or, in the classical phrase, mind and its place in nature. This is also true historically. Moreover, the task seems to be the most difficult of all. The classical analysts, for all their spectacular achievements, did not even face it. (How I use that label, the classical analysts, is explained in Essay II.)

v

The main theme of this book is the analysis of mind. But even the basic problems fall into each other's scopes. Thus other themes had to be sounded, some of them rather fully. Foremost among these is the basic problem of ontology, that is, the search for a complete inventory of the several kinds of existent. An analysis which denies mind the status of an existent, in the full ontological sense of 'existent', is patently inadequate. That shows the connection. Yet, all attempts to place mind in any of the less extravagant ontological schemes available led to consequences which flaw the over-all pattern. That shows the difficulty. The book propounds how I propose to conquer it.

The characteristic feature of minds is their intentionality. That makes "Intentionality and Ontology" an accurate two-word title. "Meaning and Existence" sounds less formidable. Ontology asks what exists. This justifies the substitution of 'existence' for 'ontology'. That of 'meaning' for 'intentionality' will be justified in a moment.

What a philosopher takes a question to be as well as the sort of answer (rather than, which specific answer) he considers a (possible) solution depends on his conception of the philosophical enterprise. Or, what amounts virtually to the same thing, it depends on his method. That is why philosophers always were method conscious. At the beginning of this century analytical philosophy took what has been called the linguistic turn. The issue, and it still is an issue, is one of method. That is why our generation is even more method conscious than some of its predecessors. My work is in the linguistic stream. Inevitably, therefore, the basic theme of method runs through the whole book. One essay develops it in considerable detail.

The linguistic stream has several currents. I philosophize by means of one of the schemes known as ideal languages. My being in this current in part determines the content of the book. Analyticity, every one agrees, is a very fundamental problem. For a practitioner of my method it is basic. (I am even prepared to grant that the adequate explication of analyticity is the one and only major task for which the method is indispensable.) Moreover, there is a very close connection between the problem of analyticity and the analysis of mind.

To whatever current a linguistic philosopher may belong, the analysis of mind is for him virtually indistinguishable from that of the various ontological and logical aspects of meaning. (This justifies the substitution of 'meaning' for 'intentionality' in the two-word title.) If he belongs to my current, then the core of the problem is to construct an ideal language into which the relevant uses of 'to mean' can be adequately transcribed. I propose such an ideal language. Not surprisingly for anyone familiar with the course of analytical philosophy in this century, it turns out that this proposal requires radical re-examination and eventual modification of the classical analysts' explicit or implicit notions of analyticity. The connection of my main theme with this major subtheme is thus close indeed.

Replace 'method' by 'ideal languages', a tag quite reasonably applied to my method, and you obtain "Minds, Meanings, Ontology, Analyticity, and Ideal Languages" as a fully expressive title. Titles that long are monstrous. So I let the third constituent be absorbed by the first two and replaced the last two by the single 'logic'. No one conversant with recent developments will either quarrel with or be misled by these condensations. Hence the three-word title, "Meanings, Minds, and Logic."

That much for a thematic analysis. The fourteen essays are arranged in three blocks, not chronologically but by content. That calls for a structural analysis as the second business of this Preface. I shall dispatch it by indicating how in the arrangement I have chosen the themes weave in and out of each other.

The first block consists of four long essays (I–IV). The first, one of the two longest, introduces the main theme and presents the proposed solution. The remaining three center around the three major subthemes, method, analyticity, ontology, in this order.

Philosophy is dialectical. This means, among other things, that a critical examination of the positions he rejects is an important part of a philosopher's argument for the one he adopts. Essay II is dialectical in this sense. It builds the argument for my method around the examination of another, also in the linguistic stream, which at the moment has quite a few practitioners. The strategy also causes the other themes to appear, which makes this essay, too, rather long.

Nominalism versus realism, logical atomism, elementarism, individuals, continuants, substances. This is the small but formidable array of the great ontological issues. Essay IV centers on the ontological theme. It, too, is dialectically built around an examination of the views of some philosophers who are more or less in my current but who, unlike myself, are nominalists and who reject the distinction between the analytic and the synthetic.

The second block consists of five essays (V–IX). They are all very short and they all pick up loose ends, as it were. In the proposed explication the primary units of meaning are propositions, not terms. Essay V, which solves the problem this creates, thus supplements Essay I. Essay IX continues the examination of the new nominalism. Thus it relates to Essay IV and, because of the issue specifically involved, to Essay III. Essays VI, VII, VIII deal with the subjects men-

tioned in their titles, all fundamental ontological topics not immediately connected with the analysis of mind. Yet, in all three of them
essential use is made of the ideal language (and the ontology it reflects) which I was led to propose in the course of my efforts to arrive at
an adequate analysis of mind. This is the sort of thing I have in mind
when I claim that this book, though an essay collection in form, is in
substance almost monolithic.

The concluding block consists of five essays (X–XIV), none very
short, two very long. Its inner structure differs from that of the opening
block. None of the four essays in the latter strikes just one theme. Yet,
in each of them a different theme is in the center. The essays of the
concluding block are held together by a common theme, what I just
called the small but formidable array of the great ontological issues.
To this persistent theme the others are added in a progression of widen-
ing scope. The order of the progression is Essays X, XIII, XI, XII,
XIV. The reason that I did not arrange them in this order is that all
but the concluding essay are also studies in what I like to call structural
history. And I simply could not resist the temptation to arrange Essays X to XIII in the order this circumstance suggests.

Essays X and XIII continue the case against nominalism. The use of
the method, of course, is essential in both. Their common subject is the
basic dichord nominalism-realism. Essay X is almost puristically narrow. In Essay XIII all themes appear; but all except the basic ontological one remain very much in the background. In Essays XI and XII
analyticity has reached the foreground. This is so because in these
essays, particularly in the rather long Essay XI, the basic dichord is
being complicated by the trichord individual-continuant-substance.

Of all the specific existents, mind is the most crucial in that its analysis is the most fundamental as well as the most difficult. Of all other
existents the most crucial, in exactly the same sense, is time. The problem of time, though by no means the whole, is yet the core of that of
substance. (This is not to belittle the connection with analyticity. Substance is in fact one of the most nodal problems. I have long sensed
that. But I was rather slow in grasping the insight firmly and holding
on to it consistently. Probably this is part of the price I had to pay for
having started as a logical positivist in the classical style.) Naturally,
therefore, a good deal is said about time in Essay XI. Taken jointly,
the first four essays of the last block thus sound all the subsidiary
themes, though not the main theme of mind; and they progressively
focus attention on time. It remains to relate the analyses of mind and
time. This is the task I set myself in the concluding Essay XIV. I cannot be sure that I accomplished it. Of course not. But I am very certain
that one cannot accomplish it without paying almost equal attention to

all four themes, making them weave in and out of each other contra-puntally, as it were. This I have tried to do.

In sum, the structure of this book suggests to me the image of a chain suspended by its first and last link. (The first and the last essays are also the longest.) The first link introduces the main problem as well as the solution I propose. As the chain descends through the next three links, the three major subsidiary themes receive successive attention. Where the chain is lowest, in the five short essays of the middle block, matters of relative detail are taken care of. As it begins to ascend again through the next four essays, time, the other crucial existent, comes to the fore. The last link is the polyphonic finale.

That much for a structural analysis. I turn now to some matters that are traditionally taken care of in a Preface.

This is the second essay collection I publish. *The Metaphysics of Logical Positivism* (1954) was the first. Since the public for anything of this sort is rather limited, quite a few prospective readers of the second will have either read or at least heard of the first. I shall therefore answer a question which is likely to occur to such readers. What, if any, is the connection between the two books? The central thesis of this book is the proposed analysis of the act (I use the classical term). Its central idea is clearly stated in the first book. However, there is an important difference between a full statement and its central idea, just as there is such a difference between even a full statement and the ex-ploration of its consequences. (Remember what was said about the scopes of philosophical problems.) In the Preface to the first book I promised to apply myself to the tasks I had thus set myself. This book fulfills that promise. In this respect, and I believe also in some others, the first book stands to the second as flower stands to fruit. Whether the fruit was worth gathering is not for me to say.

Like *The Metaphysics of Logical Positivism* this book is not literally a collection; rather, it is a selection, although a very ample one, from the essays I have published since 1954. Some of those excluded simply are not relevant to the theme (or themes) of the book and, therefore, need not be mentioned. Four others might have been included by this criterion. These I think I should mention, if only in order to indicate why I excluded them. One, rather long, called "The Philosophical Sig-nificance of Modal Logic," is scheduled to appear in *Mind*. Not so long ago, the view that the modal calculi are indispensable tools for the ex-plication of (the philosophical uses of) 'analytic', 'necessary', and so on, was held by many. A few still hold it and still write in its defense. The paper, which argues that it is radically wrong, thus has a place in a journal. Even so, this view is not getting too much attention right now. I saw no point in perhaps helping it to get some by putting between hard covers a paper with a purely negative thesis. "Dispositional Properties and Dispositions" (*Philosophical Studies*, 6, 1955, 77–80) has been excluded for two reasons. It makes a point in the philosophy of psychology, which is connected with the current discussion of counterfactuals. This is another discussion which I don't think worth continuing. That is one of the reasons. The philosophy of psychology (as I use the phrase) certainly is relevant to the main theme of the book; but it is so only within the limits of the so-called philosophy of science. I mean this to be a book in first philosophy and in first philosophy only. That is the other reason for excluding the paper. Again, "The Contribution of John B. Watson" (*Psychological Review*, 63, 1956, 265–76) has been excluded because it is essentially a study in the philosophy (and history) of psychology. "Propositional Functions" (*Analysis*, 17, 1956, 43–48), finally, is merely an obvious or nearly obvious corollary of the later Essay XIII.

Essay V was written jointly with Herbert Hochberg, once a student of mine, by now a valued collaborator. I wish not only to thank him for permitting me to include this joint piece but also to call attention to a group of three papers of his own which is relevant to the themes of this book ("The Ontological Operator," *Philosophy of Science*, 23, 1956, 250–59; "Professor Quine, Pegasus, and Dr. Cartwright," *ibid.*, 24, 1957, 191–203; "On Pegasizing," *Philosophy and Phenomenological Research*, 17, 1957, 551–54). Among more recent students from discussion with whom I have benefited, I should like to mention Reinhardt Grossmann and Edwin Allaire. Grossmann's "Propositional Attitudes" and Allaire's "Tractatus 6.3751" are both relevant. The former is scheduled to appear in *The Philosophical Quarterly;* the latter, in *Analysis.*

W. V. Quine kindly called my attention to a blunder in Essay VI. I have added a footnote which I hope corrects it.

Aside from a few editorial changes the papers are reprinted as they originally appeared. A table indicating where each piece originally appeared will be found at the end of the volume. The necessary permissions by editors and publishers have been granted and are gratefully acknowledged.

If a detailed and intelligent index is important for a book, it is even more so for a collection of essays. May Brodbeck put the readers in her debt by constructing such an index. My debt to her is by now so great that I do not know how to acknowledge it.

My wife skillfully and faithfully read the proof.

G. B.

Iowa City, Iowa
Spring, 1959

Contents

xi

MEANING
AND
EXISTENCE

Intentionality*

A BOOK on botany mentions plants, but it need not mention botany. A zoological text mentions animals, but it need not contain the word zoology. Intentionality is like botany or zoology, not like plants or animals and their kinds. That is why I shall hardly mention it in this essay. The things I shall mention are awareness, meaning, truth, and, my method being what it is, inevitably also language, particularly language about language. Concerning my philosophical method and my views on some philosophical problems, I am in a quandary. I do not wish to proceed as if they were known and I do not quite know how to proceed without assuming that they are. So I shall compromise. I shall not explain once more either the notion of an ideal language, which is not really a language to be spoken, or how, speaking commonsensically about it and what it is about, one philosophizes. For the rest, I shall tell a connected story. I realize, though, that in order to grasp it fully some readers may have to turn to what I said elsewhere.[1] One device I shall employ to provide as many connections and as much context as I possibly can are some "historical" passages about the recent as well as about the more remote past. These should be taken structurally, not as excursions into scholarly history; for I do not pretend to be a scholar living in history. Only, I wouldn't know how to philosophize without the history, or the image of history, that lives in me. For another, I shall not be able to avoid the use of symbols; but I shall keep it at a minimum; nor do I wish to pretend that I could do much better. For, again, I am not a mathematician any more than

---

* Semantica (*Archivio di Filosofia, Roma: Bocca, 1955*), *177–216. Reprinted by permission.*

[1] A collection of eighteen of my essays has been published under the title *The Metaphysics of Logical Positivism* (New York, London, Toronto: Longmans, Green and Co., 1954). I shall quote these essays as MLP, followed by the number under which they appear in the volume.

I am a historian. Fortunately, certain matters can be left safely to the mathematicians, just as some others can be left to the historians. Every now and then, though, the philosopher who, since he is a philosopher, finds himself short of time and taste to emulate the achievements of these specialists, does need their services. Things would probably go more smoothly if those specialists were not all too often like miners who cannot tell the raw diamonds from the philosophical pebbles in the materials they bring to light. Some of the confusions I shall try to unravel can indeed be traced to the mathematical logicians. But, then, it may be fairer to lay them at the doorsteps of those philosophers who, admiring the mathematicians too much, knew too little of what they actually did.

Here is an outline of what I propose to do. *First*, I shall try to convince my readers that when we say, speaking as we ordinarily do, that *there are* awarenesses, what we say is true. If, then, there are awarenesses, one may ask whether they also *exist*, in the philosophical sense of 'exist'. (In its ordinary or commonsensical use 'exist' is expendable, since it can always be replaced by 'there are (is)'.) Awarenesses do exist. By this I mean three things. I mean, first, that instances of awareness are particulars in exactly the same sense in which a tone is a particular. I mean, second, that there are certain characters, among them at least one that is simple, which are in fact exemplified by those and only those particulars I call awarenesses, in exactly the same sense in which the simple characters called pitches are in fact exemplified by those and only those particulars that are called tones. An awareness may, for instance, be *a* remembering, i.e., an instance of remembering, just as a tone may be *a* middle *c*, i.e., an instance of middle *c*. The third thing which I mean I shall mention presently. Like everybody else, philosophers are sometimes aware of their awarenesses. Many philosophers nevertheless deny that they exist. One very important one, Ludwig Wittgenstein, spent the second half of his life trying painfully to convince himself, not only that they do not exist, but even that there are none. Such persistent refusals to admit the obvious are so strange that one must try to explain them. That will be my *second* step. Philosophers did not see how they could consistently hold that there are awarenesses without also holding that there are interacting minds, i.e., mental particulars causally interacting with physical objects in exactly the same sense in which the latter interact among each other. Thus, when the belief in interacting minds became less and less tenable, some philosophers denied, with the intellectual violence that is so characteristic of all of us, that there are awarenesses. This is the story of the classical act and its later vicissitudes. In its final stages one kind of concern with language came to the fore. Another kind lies at the root of all analytical philosophy. I shall turn in my *third* step to some aspects of this second concern with language. Each of the two different concerns produced some confusions; there were also some illegitimate fusions between the two. The fusions and confusions support each other. To clear up the latter and to undo the former is one half of the analysis which vindicates awareness. *Fourth*, I shall propose what I believe is the correct form of those sentences in the ideal language that mention awarenesses. This is the other half of the analysis which, in the nature of things, involves the analysis of meaning and truth. It is also the heart of the essay. All the latter amounts to, in a sense, is therefore a proposal for transcribing such sentences as 'I see that this is green' in the ideal language. The transcription will show that awarenesses and, in fact, only awarenesses exemplify certain peculiar characters, which I call *propositions*. (This is the third thing I mean when I say that awarenesses exist.) Because of these characters statements about awarenesses are, loosely and ambiguously speaking, statements about statements. To tighten the looseness and to eliminate the ambiguity is virtually the same thing as to clear up the confusions and to undo the fusions of which I just spoke. This is the reason for my expository strategy.[2]

I

I stand in front of a tree, look at it, and see it. As we ordinarily speak, we say that the situation has three constituents, myself, the tree, and the seeing. Ordinarily we let it go at that. Upon a little reflection, still safely within common sense, we notice that 'myself', 'tree', and 'seeing' may be taken in either of two contexts. In one of these, the first two words, 'myself' and 'tree', refer to two physical objects, namely, my body and the tree, while the third, 'seeing', refers, not to a third physical object, but to a relation between such, namely, the relation exemplified whenever one says truly that someone sees something. About this very complex relation physicists, physiologists, and behavioristic psychologists know a good deal. In the other context, 'seeing' refers to something mental, as we ordinarily use 'mental', and this mental something is again distinct from myself, the seer, as well as from what is seen, the tree. This seeing is an awareness. An awareness is thus something mental, distinct from what, if anything, is aware

---

[2] The fundamental ideas of this essay are first stated, very badly, in two papers that appeared over a decade ago: "Pure Semantics, Sentences, and Propositions," *Mind*, 53, 1944, 238–57; "A Positivistic Metaphysics of Consciousness," *Mind*, 54, 1945, 193–226.

as well as from what it is aware of. That much is evident and to that much I commit myself therefore without hesitation. To three other beliefs one is, I think, not committed by common sense. I, for one, hold all three to be false. One of them is crucial. Whether the other two are, in fact, false makes no difference for what I intend to say. Even so, I shall briefly mention all three; for it is well to grasp clearly what does and what does not depend on what.

I do not believe that an instance of seeing, or of any other awareness, is merely the exemplification of a relation, or of any other character, between two "things," as indeed the physical seeing is. I believe, instead, that an awareness is itself a "thing." I say thing rather than particular because it makes no difference for what I want to say right now whether or not the other two terms do or do not refer to particulars. (Presently we shall see that the content of an awareness could not possibly be a particular.) This is crucial. The second belief which I hold to be false is that there is a mental thing referred to by 'myself'. To make it quite clear that nothing I shall say depends on whether or not this belief is in fact false, I shall eventually transcribe, not 'I see that this is green' but, instead, '(It is) seen (by me) that this is green' without paying any attention to the problems connected with the two words in the second parenthesis. Third. Some philosophers believe that the object or, as one also says, the content of an awareness is, in some cases, a physical object. According to these philosophers, my illustration is such a case; the content in question is of course the tree, or, perhaps more accurately, something that is in some sense a part of its surface. To these philosophers I grant that when we use 'see' as we ordinarily do in such situations, we certainly mean to mention a physical object. Some other philosophers insist that the content of an awareness is always a mental object; in my illustration, a tree percept. To these philosophers I grant that there is a perfectly plain sense of 'directly apprehending' or of 'being directly acquainted with' such that what we directly apprehend, even in a so-called perceptual situation, is a mental object. But, again, nothing I shall say depends on which side one takes on this issue, even though at one place I shall *seem* to side with the second view. (To dispel the appearance of this seeming is one of the things I cannot take time to do in this essay.)

Sometimes I shall find it convenient to speak of an awareness as a mental state of the person who, as one ordinarily says, has it or owns it. In fact, I do not know what one could possibly mean when, speaking literally, one says that someone has or is in a certain mental state if not that he has an awareness of a certain kind. But I shall ordinarily not call an awareness a mental content. The reasons for this caution as well as for the qualification, ordinarily, are, I think, fairly obvious. Since I shall use 'content' to refer to what an awareness is the awareness of, and since I have committed myself to the distinction between the two, it is prudent to avoid expressions that may tend to blur it. The reason for the qualification is that one awareness is sometimes the content of another. (How would we otherwise know that there are any?) When I am aware of something, then I am aware of this thing, not of the awareness through which I am aware of it. But I may also, either at the same time or at some other time, be aware of that awareness. In this event the first awareness is the content of the second. Notice, though, that the second awareness is not, either directly or indirectly, an awareness of the content of the first, just as it is not, if I may so express myself, aware of itself.

Perceiving is one kind of awareness; directly apprehending, remembering, doubting whether, thinking of, wondering are others. The analysis of some of these kinds is very complex. For what I intend to do I can, happily, limit myself to direct apprehension. When I speak in the rest of this essay without further qualification of awareness I should therefore be taken to speak of direct apprehension. Similarly, when I speak of *an* awareness, I should be understood to speak of an instance of directly apprehending. Again, the difference really makes no difference. But I wish to make as clear as I can which problems I shall not discuss without, however, either belittling them or denying that they are problems.

Ordinarily we say 'I see this tree' but we also say 'I am aware of this being a tree', 'I know that this is a tree', 'I wonder whether this is a tree', and so on. If we choose, we can rephrase the first of these sentences: 'I see that this is a tree'. A statement mentioning an awareness can always be so rephrased that its content is referred to by a sentence. Grammatically this sentence appears in our language either as a dependent clause or as a participial phrase (e.g., 'this being a tree'). This is what I mean by the formula: *The content of every awareness is propositional.* If, for instance, I see (or directly apprehend, or remember; the difference makes no difference) a red spot, the content of my awareness is a state of affairs or fact, namely, a certain particular being red.

If one asks the proper question of one who has an awareness while he has it, one elicits a certain answer. If, for instance, somebody points at the tree while I am looking at it and asks me what it is, I shall say "This is a tree." This statement is the *text* of my awareness. This and only this sort of thing is what I mean by the text of an awareness. In many cases it is not easy to hit upon the right question or to be sure that the answer one receives is what one was asking for. In some cases the difficulties are very great. But, no matter how formidable they may be, they lie always within the limits of common sense and its long arm, science; in no case are they philosophical difficulties. The notion of a text is therefore itself entirely commonsensical. Three things about texts are worth noticing, though. Notice first that the text of an awareness states its content and only its content, without mentioning the awareness itself. This jibes well with what I said in the second to the last paragraph. Notice next that this is the first time I mention language in a certain way. More precisely, this is the first time I mention linguistic behavior as such. Notice, third, that the connection I thus establish between an awareness and its text is purely *external*. This means, first, that I am not dealing with the awarenesses one may have of the words he utters or hears uttered; and it means, second, that I am at this point not concerned with the question whether or not and in what sense one's inner speech is a "part" of his awarenesses. (These comments lay the ground for the unraveling of some of the fusions and confusions I mentioned in the outline.)

Let us return to my awareness of the red spot. The situation involves two particulars, the spot and the particular awareness. It also involves *at least* two states of affairs or facts, referred to by statements, namely, first, the spot being an instance of red and, second, the awareness being an instance of perceiving or, perhaps, of directly apprehending. The first of the two states of affairs is the content of this particular awareness. I said at least because the analysis is patently still incomplete. What it omits to mention is, in fact, the very crux of the matter, namely, that the one particular, the awareness, is an awareness *of* the state of affairs of which the other particular, the spot, is an ingredient. This third constituent fact of the situation is, I submit, not (1) that two particulars exemplify a relation, nor (2) that the one particular, the awareness, and the state of affairs of which the other is an ingredient exemplify a pseudorelation, but, (3) that the awareness exemplifies another nonrelational character, of the sort I call a proposition, which I shall specify in good time when I shall state my proposal. Alternatives (1) and (2) bring us to the classical act and thus to the development I wish to consider in my second step. In this development the difference between (1) and (2) was not always clearly seen. Nor shall I bother to distinguish between them in my quasi-historical account of it. However, we shall need the distinction later on, in the fourth step; so I shall state it now. A (binary) relation obtains between what is referred to by two terms. A (binary) pseudorelation obtains either between what is referred to by a term and what is referred to by a sentence or between what is referred to by two sentences. Symbolically, in the usual notation: 'xRy', 'xPp', 'pPq'. Connectives are, of course, not pseudorelations but truth tables. Logical atomism is the thesis that the ideal language contains no pseudorelations.

II

Draw on a sheet of paper two circles outside of each other; mark the two points, one on each circle, that are closest to each other; draw an arrow from one of them to the other. Replace, if you wish, the tip of the arrow by a sling or loop surrounding the circle at which the tip points. What you have drawn is, in either case, a graphic schema of the classical act, or, more precisely, of as much of it as belongs to my story. The seeing, which is the act, is the arrow or loop. Its being a loop or arrow, not a circle like the other two constituents, shows that an act is not a third thing but an exemplified relation (or pseudorelation). The circle from which the arrow issues represents me; the second circle, the tree. So far, so good; but there remains a question. We saw that, by our common sense, the situation involves two contexts. Which of the two does the diagram represent? Or does it represent them both indifferently? As long as one answers at all, the most nearly correct answer is that it represents them both, but inseparably, not indifferently. The best reply is that within the Aristotelian tradition, from which the act pattern stems and from which it has never really been freed, the question cannot even be asked. This is one reason why trouble brewed when it was asked. Clearly, the diagram does not do justice to some other peculiarities of the form-matter accounts of perception. The reason for this neglect is that my concern is really only with the post-Cartesian mind-matter distinction, which is of course quite different from the Aristotelian form-matter distinction. But it is worth noticing that according to the form-matter accounts of perception the perceiver is "active" in extracting from the perceived object its form even though perception is in a sense the least "active" of all acts. Only in "pure sensation," whatever that means, is he completely "passive."

To an act philosopher the analysis of 'meaning' offers no problems. An act was said to intend its content. The linguistic connection between 'meaning' and 'intending' is familiar. Instead of saying that an act intends its content I could have said that its content is its meaning. A thought's meaning, for instance, was said to "exist intentionally" in it, as its content. The act pattern is thus the archtype of the contemporary accounts of meaning according to which the meaning of a sentence is its referent. (Nor is this surprising in view of the often quite naïve realism of the proponents of these so-called reference theories of meaning.) As for the meaning of sentences, not of acts, within the classical pattern itself, one must remember that, broadly speaking, language enters into this pattern only externally, in exactly the same sense of 'external' in which I called external the connection between an awareness and the text I coördinated to it. A sentence is therefore for the classical act philosopher merely a physical object or event, or perhaps, a kind of such. It has meaning only derivatively or, as I believe it was sometimes put, it signifies only by eliciting an act which intends what, as we now say, it refers to.

Upon the classical view, awarenesses are acts. Thus, when the classical act ran into difficulties, the place of awareness in the scheme of things seemed to be threatened, too. To understand what happened, we must briefly inquire into those difficulties.

Brentano and G. E. Moore, the last two of the great protagonists of the act, are both direct realists. This did not happen by chance. The classical act is a relation exemplified by things in space and time. In this respect my seeing the tree is not at all different from its being to the left of, say, a rock. This is one of the two features that determined the course of events. The other pertains to a difference between seeing and, say, being to the left of. The thing from which the act issues is in issuing it spontaneous or "active." Neither of the constituents of an instance of, say, a spatial relation "acts" in this categorial sense upon the other merely by exemplifying the relation. Because they are patently incompatible with the ideas that reached their first culmination in Newton, these two features were, more than any others, responsible for the decline and eventual downfall of the act. In Newton's world the realm of physical objects, which includes our bodies, is causally closed; its physical constituents can therefore not in the old categorial sense be "acted upon" by anything else; otherwise the physical realm would not be causally closed. The difficulties one creates by introducing into this world mental constituents that "interact" with the physical ones are insuperable. This is not to say, though, that any or all of the constituents, physical or otherwise, of a Newtonian world are "passive." The point is, rather, that in their old categorial sense neither 'active' nor 'passive' can be sensibly applied to them. To insist in such circumstances on applying that half of a dichotomy that *seems* to fit better is to court philosophical trouble. The troubles that ensued in this case are notorious.

At this point I had better say what I should not need to say. I believe as a matter of course that the world is Newtonian. That is to me just common sense. Or, if you insist, it is scientific common sense; I shall not quibble; for to tilt even against scientific common sense is quixotic. This, however, is only half of what needs to be said. The other half is that common sense, including science, never answers the philosophical questions. It merely sets them to us. Awareness is a case in point. The classical act secured its place in the world. As the act became indefensible, that place was threatened. This proves that something was wrong; it does not prove that in order to defend awareness one must defend the classical act. To do that would be merely quixotic. The task is, rather, to disentangle awareness from the act so that its place may again be secure in a world that is, scientifically, Newtonian. I believe that my analysis does just that. This, however, I shall not show in this essay, since to show it I would have to analyze in its entirety the tangle which is known as the mind-body problem[3] and not only, as I proposed, a single strand of it.

I continue the schematic account, representing the next step by a modification of the diagram. Let the two circles stand for two spheres and make the sphere from which the loop or arrow issues hollow. Erase the tip or loop and let the remaining line represent all sorts of relations (and processes) among the material constituents of either sphere. The absence of the loop or arrow indicates that these are all Newtonian relations (and processes); their constituents are thus neither "active" nor "passive." Assume next that, as part and parcel of these Newtonian processes, all sorts of configurations appear, as on a screen, on the wall of the cavity of the hollow sphere. Finally, put in the center of the cavity a small sphere from which arrows issue toward the configurations on its wall. The structure represents a Lockean kind of world; an "inner" arrow, a Lockean kind of act; the inner sphere, a post-Cartesian Self or, as Hartley put it, "an eye within the eye." For what we are interested in, the decisive difference between the old and the new schema is that in the latter the arrows have been withdrawn into the cavity. Does this alteration suffice to make the schema fit Newton's world? The answer is clearly No. A schema that fits must not contain any arrows. Thus the "inner" arrows would have to be "withdrawn" once more. This shows what Hartley's admirable metaphor illuminates in a flash, namely, that the new schema merely starts its proponents on an infinite regress. The configurations on the wall cause no trouble, at least not for what we are interested in. (I am here not concerned with the perplexities of indirect realism.) The sphere inside the sphere may or may not have to go. (That is why I didn't even bother to mention that Locke does not have this sort of Self.) The one thing needful is to get rid of the arrows. To understand how that was done one must understand what the classical British philosopher-psychologists meant by "the analysis of the phenomena of

[3] See also MLP6.

the human mind." So I must next explain the idea of this sort of analysis or, as we would now say, of analytical introspection.[4] The way in which its original proponents explained it is full of difficulties. As I shall explain it, the idea is quite commonsensical. Since it is commonsensical, it can in principle be considered as the outline of a scientific research program. I say in principle because in practice it led to the impasse that was Wundtian psychology. This, however, is entirely beside the point; for the causes of that impasse were not philosophical.

Assume that someone, call him a psychologist, who has become very skillful in eliciting from people, call them his subjects, the texts of their awarenesses, engages in the following project. First he selects a limited vocabulary. Then he gives his subjects the following tripartite instructions: "(a) Familiarize yourself with this limited vocabulary. (b) I shall continue to ask you questions as before; continue to answer them as before, speaking as you ordinarily do, without any limitation on your vocabulary. (c) Having given me your answer, answer my question once more; in your second response use only the limited vocabulary." Assume that the game, or experiment, is carried on for a while and that in each case our psychologist writes down the subject's responses, the first on the white front of a card, the second on its pink back. His purpose is to discover empirically from his cards a set of rules (empirical laws) R that will enable him in each future case to infer what is written on the white front of a card from what is written on its pink back. This is the idea of analytic introspection. The way I explained it avoids many of the classical difficulties by bringing out two points. The first response is the text of the "original" awareness; the second certainly is not; it may be, and in fact is, that of another; but that need not concern us. This is the first point. All that could be meant by saying that the original awareness, whose text is the first response, "consists of" or has been "introspectively decomposed (analyzed)" into those of which the second response is or would be the text, is that the first text can by a set of empirical laws be inferred from the second. This is the other point. For about 150 years, roughly from 1750 to 1900, one of the major issues, if not perhaps the major issue, of psychology was whether a set of such rules R can be found; and if at all, for how limited a vocabulary (of the second response).

It is easy to see how this program, *if* it succeeds and *if* one is not too clear about what one means by 'consisting of', can be used to get rid of the act or, if you please, of the arrows and, incidentally, the inner sphere. Since awarenesses are sometimes the contents of others, the texts (first responses!) of some of the awarenesses of our psychologist's

[4] See also MLP17.

subjects will contain act verbs, such as 'thinking about', 'wondering whether', and so on. If, now, his experiment succeeds with a vocabulary so limited that it contains none of these expressions, that is, if he can for such a vocabulary (of the second response) find a set of laws R, then our psychologist will probably say that "there are no acts." This, at any rate, is what two generations ago the "content" psychologists, led by Wundt, said to the "act" psychologists, who gathered around Brentano. Their claim is thus that "introspective analysis" of any awareness yields only "contents," i.e., what the other side calls the contents of those acts whose contents are not themselves awarenesses. (This shows how 'content' is used in that literature. Whenever I shall use it in this sense I shall surround it by double quotes.)

By 1900 it was beyond doubt that Wundt's program—or should I say Hume's?—would never succeed. Its failure led, during the first decade of this century, to the rebellion, led by Kuelpe, of the so-called school of Wuerzburg. The ideas which the men of Wuerzburg propounded are still important. Also, they are, in substance, patently right. So I shall next explain these ideas in a way that will help my story along in other ways, too.

Assume that I and another person who does not know English both hear the sound of what I know but he doesn't know to be the English word "bell." Will our awarenesses have the same text? Wuerzburg's answer is No; and it is, at least for some such occasions, beyond all reasonable doubt. The way they put it, in the style of all introspectionists, the difference shows in the analyses (second responses) of the two awarenesses. The analysis of the other fellow's awareness will consist of that of his auditory percept of what he didn't know to be a word *and of nothing else*. The analysis of mine will have corresponding constituents but, *in addition*, a further one. Some of the Wuerzburgers called this additional constituent, which according to them is introspectively unanalyzable, "the meaning of 'bell' " or, also, "the awareness of the meaning of 'bell'." Take another case. Assume that both I and another person hear a sentence which we both understand but which I, unlike him, do not know to be true so that, hearing it, I wonder whether what it refers to is the case. Again, Wuerzburg claims, self-evidently I think, that there will be a difference between our two awarenesses. The analysis of mine will reveal a constituent which will not appear in that of the other person, namely, a "wondering about . . . ," which, according to Wuerzburg, is again introspectively unanalyzable. Rather remarkably the Wuerzburgers insisted that these unorthodox unanalyzable constituents are not "acts," but "contents." In terms of our diagram this means that the "inner" arrow appears now among the configurations on the wall. Whether the Wuerzburgers spoke as they did merely in order to limit the extent of their anti-Wundtian heresy is an historical question. Whatever the answer may be, the fact that they could consistently so express themselves shows that awarenesses can in principle be fitted into a Newtonian world. That, though, is a line of thought which I am not pursuing in this essay; I turn instead to two others.

For one, we have again encountered 'meaning'. The one thing to be grasped firmly and above all is that what we encountered is only in a peculiar sense a philosophical analysis of what we mean when we speak of the meaning of a sentence or, as in my illustration, of a word. What we are offered is, rather, a psychological analysis of how meaning, whatever it may turn out to be, is carried, or grasped, or represented in our minds. I prefer Titchener's phrase, carried, but I would not argue about the word. The point is that this piece of psychology becomes a philosophical analysis of meaning only if it is joined to the assertion that the psychological phenomenon in question is all that could be meant whenever we speak, in any context, of meaning. Since this assertion is patently false, any philosophical analysis of meaning of which it forms a part is certainly peculiar.

Notice, for another, that linguistic behavior enters the Wuerzburg account of awareness in a new way. I call it new because it appears here for the first time in our story, though, to be sure, not for the first time in history; but that is beside the point. In the introspectionists' peculiar sense of 'consisting of', the awareness itself consists, according to Wuerzburg, at least in part of verbal "contents," e.g., of the auditory percepts which both I and one who does not know English have upon hearing an English word. To distinguish this kind of connection between linguistic behavior and awareness from others, which I have mentioned before, I call it *internal*. A verbal "content" may be either an auditory percept or image (of speech), or a visual percept or image (of writing), or some kinaesthetic equivalent. Which it is in any given case may be of interest to psychologists; it is of no moment to us. I merely notice that the notion includes so-called inner speech. The thing important for what I am interested in is that the new twist makes the case against awareness appear sound. The appearance is deceptive. To understand why it is deceptive we must understand why it deceived some. What happened was, I believe, that a certain statement, which is true, was mistaken for another one, which is false. The truth is that many of our more abstract awarenesses—I use deliberately a vague word, abstract, for a vague idea—are indeed awarenesses of words. The decisive point is that on such occasions we find ourselves not just having verbal "contents" but knowing them, wondering about them, entertaining them, and so on, as the case may be. To assert the true statement is therefore not to assert that awarenesses do not exist. To assert the latter, in the language of Wuerzburg, is to assert that those unorthodox constituents, which according to Wuerzburg are unanalyzable, do in fact yield to introspection with the result that they, too, turn out to consist of verbal "contents." This is the false statement I mentioned a moment ago. As to its falsehood, I can only say that I, for one, do sometimes have awarenesses which upon introspection (if it be necessary) yield the critical unanalyzable constituents. In the texts of these awarenesses 'knowing', 'wondering about', 'entertaining', and so on, do of course occur. This, however, is a different matter; for the connection between an awareness and its text is external.

Titchener, the one first-rate mind among the Wundtians, gave Wuerzburg a consistent reply. Somewhat quixotically he insisted that whenever those critical "contents," awarenesses and meanings, occur, they can be introspectively decomposed into more orthodox ones. But he added that in many cases they do not occur at all. Take meaning, on which he was more explicit, and consider again a person who both hears and understands (the meaning of) the word bell. Titchener then says three things. 1. More often than not such a person has on such occasions no other "contents" than, say, auditory ones. 2. These events, namely, the occurrences of the auditory "content," are among the causes of other events, among which are, as a rule, (the occurrences of) other *orthodox* "contents" of the person in question. 3. This latter fact, 2, is what a psychologist means, or ought to mean, by 'meaning'. Titchener's formula was: The meaning of a content is not another content but its *context*. Since I believe that there are (to speak with Wuerzburg) unanalyzable awarenesses (though not meanings!), I object to the qualification, orthodox, which I italicized. Otherwise Titchener's is the correct analysis of *one* of the commonsensical (and scientific) meanings of 'meaning'. Very admirably, he distinguished it from a philosophical or, as he said, logical analysis. Again I agree, although I wouldn't put it this way. I would rather say that a philosophical analysis of 'meaning' must not only explicate *all* its important uses but that it must be particularly careful not to omit the philosophical ones, i.e., those that point, however confusedly, at genuine philosophical problems.

Titchener's meaning of 'meaning' contains implicitly another. Take again our illustration. In trying to specify the very complex causal pattern or, if you please, context of the case, one will certainly have to mention circumstances, of the kind called psychological, that pertain to people. But it will also be necessary to mention what the word refers to, namely, bells. If one disregards the psychological circumstances, one arrives at a *second* commonsensical (and scientific) meaning of 'meaning'. In this sense, the meaning of a (kind of) linguistic event, say, of a sentence, is what it refers to. When an anthropologist tells us that, as he discovered, in a certain aboriginal language a certain kind of noise means tree, he uses 'means' in this sense. Notice, though, that by acknowledging this meaning of 'meaning' we do not embrace a philosophical reference theory of meaning; for we know, first, that this is just one of the uses of 'meaning' and, second, that it is not even a philosophical use. I submit, finally, that all scientific uses of 'meaning' involve either reference in the sense of my anthropologist or context in Titchener's sense, and nothing else.

In substance, Titchener's view became dominant. It still is dominant. Those who made it so, in a different form, were the behaviorists. Metaphysical behaviorists, who deny that there are mental things, talk nonsense so manifest that nobody needs to pay any attention to them. Scientific behaviorists, who make eminent sense, merely insist for their own particular reasons on speaking about mental things in their own particular way, namely, as states of the organism which are defined, or, more realistically, in principle definable in terms of actual and potential behavior. Since their particular reasons do not belong to our story, I shall state the behaviorists' idea in the introspectionists' language. Thus stated, the idea is that a state of an organism is an awareness if and only if it contains either actual verbal "contents" or momentary dispositions to have such "contents." Scientifically, the idea is sound. Commonsensically and not at all scientifically and even less philosophically, the notion of a text acknowledges what is sound in it. This, however, is beside the point. My concern here is exclusively with the impact of the behaviorists' views on the philosophy of awareness. This impact is, I think, by now quite clear. Imagine a philosopher who, whether or not he knows it, is overly impressed by the behaviorists; who is not benighted enough to be a metaphysical behaviorist; and who therefore speaks without qualms the language of the introspectionists. Such a philosopher might hold, *first*, that there are no "contents" of the kind I called unorthodox; that, *second*, all there is to meaning is context; and, *third*, that so-called awarenesses are merely verbal "contents" in their contexts. Assume, furthermore, that my imaginary philosopher also suffers from the futilitarian or nihilistic delusion according to which all philosophical uses are not only, as I agree, always confused but also that there are no genuine philosophical problems which these confused uses indicate as smoke indicates fire.

Then he will also hold that, *fourth,* the first three sentences contain in principle everything anybody could possibly say about meaning and awareness.

The philosopher about whom I spoke is not at all imaginary but the other Wittgenstein, that is, the author of *Philosophical Investigations.* Negatively, this unfortunate book is nothing but a belated attempt to refute Wuerzburg. Positively it is, in dialectical disguise, a behavioristic-Titchenerian account of awareness and meaning. The words are of course not always those of the scientists. *Context,* for instance, becomes *use,* or perhaps, *rule* of use, or perhaps, *habit* conforming to a rule of use. Since I, for one, am willing to leave psychology to the psychologists, I naturally do not think that such distinctions are philosophically important. The author of the *Tractatus* is nevertheless one of the most important philosophers. That is why *Philosophical Investigations* marks a new low in the philosophical career of awareness. I am confident that this low is also the turning point.

There is still another reason why I introduce Wittgenstein at this crucial point of my exposition. Some futilitarians sometimes do propound philosophical doctrines—in the circuitous way that is forced upon them by their futilitarianism. The *Philosophical Investigations* propound the strange and erroneous doctrine that (*A*) awarenesses do not exist. I suggest that *A* is the one visible end of a hidden thread that connects the *Investigations* with one of the flaws of the *Tractatus.*[5] Its other visible end is the doctrine of the *Tractatus,* equally strange and erroneous, that (*B*) language cannot or must not speak about itself. In the next section I shall analyze some of the confusions that led some to accept *B.* In the fourth section I shall show that in some vague and confused sense statements mentioning awarenesses belong to language about language. That is the thread or, if you please, the hidden continuity between *A* and *B.* Since I am certain that this pattern illuminates some structural connections, I have patterned my exposition after it. Whether it contains also a biographical truth about Wittgenstein is a moot question. Perhaps it doesn't.

III

Linguistic events, whether they are mental or noises, are events among events. Linguistic things, such as marks on paper, are things among things. Talking about either, one talks about language as part of the world. This is the way scientists talk about it. Philosophers look at language as a pattern, that is, as a picture of the world rather than as a part of it. Event vs. pattern, part vs. picture; the formula is sug-

[5] For an analysis of some other flaws see MLP3.

gestive. That is why I begin with it. Yet, like all formulae, it needs unpacking. The following three propositions and five comments state what is sound in it. Propositions and comments are both very succinct. If I went into detail, I would do what I said I would not do, namely, explain once more the method of philosophizing by means of an ideal language.

There is of course nothing that is not part of the world. Clearly, then, the negative half of the metaphor must not be taken literally. The following propositions unpack it. (1) The construction of the ideal language L proceeds syntactically, i.e., as a study in geometrical design, without any reference to its interpretation. A schema so constructed is as such not a language; it becomes one, at least in principle, only by interpretation. (2) The philosopher interprets L by coördinating to awarenesses not their actual texts but ideal texts, i.e., sentences of L. (3) Having so interpreted L, he can, by speaking about both it and what it refers to or speaks about, first reconstruct and then answer the philosophical questions. This is the meaning of the positive half of the picture metaphor, according to which the ideal language is a picture, or, in the classical phrase, a logical picture of the world. These are the three propositions. Now for the five comments. (a) Notice that in (2) 'sentence' is used proleptically. Only by interpretation of L do certain of its designs become "sentences." (b) The connection between an awareness and its ideal text is as external as that between it and its actual text. (c) In coördinating his ideal texts to awarenesses the linguistic philosopher acknowledges in his own way the Cartesian turn. (d) The text of an awareness refers to its content. Some texts, whether actual or ideal, refer therefore to awarenesses. But a text does not refer to an awareness merely because it is coördinated to one. (e) Familiarity with the traditional dialectic shows that the undefined descriptive constants of L must refer to what we are directly acquainted with, in the sense in which the classical phenomenalists maintained that we are not directly acquainted with physical objects.[6]

The picture metaphor also misled some, among them the Wittgenstein of the *Tractatus*. One of the several errors[7] it caused is the belief that the ideal language cannot "speak about itself." Let me first show how this confused idea came to seem plausible. Change the metaphor slightly, introducing a mirror instead of a picture. Take an object and let it stand for the world. The mirror may mirror the object; it does not and cannot mirror its own mirroring it. One may, of course, place

---

[6] This is the issue mentioned earlier on which I *seem* to side with the classical phenomenalists. The appearance is dispelled in MLP.

[7] For an analysis of some others see MLP3.

a second mirror so that it mirrors the object, the first mirror, and the latter's mirroring of the former. But now one who understood what was said before might remark that when this is done then the first mirror and its mirroring have themselves become part of the world (of the second mirror). The remark is not yet the analysis, but it points at the crucial spot. The source of the confusion is an unnoticed ambiguity of 'about'. This ambiguity is not likely to be noticed unless one distinguishes clearly between the two ways of looking at language, once as part of the world, once as its picture.

Commonsensically we say that a sentence (or a word) *refers* to, or is *about*, a state of affairs (or a thing). This makes sense if and only if what is said to refer to something, or to be or speak about something, is a linguistic event or a kind of such. Notice, first, that in the two comments (d) and (e) above I myself used 'refer' and 'about' in this sense. In fact, I never use them otherwise; for I do not understand any other use of them. Notice, furthermore, how well all this fits with what was said earlier. What a linguistic event or a kind of such refers to is also its meaning, in one of the two commonsensical and scientific meanings of 'meaning'. And when scientists speak about language they speak of course always about linguistic events. What one asserts, then, when one asserts, with this meaning of 'about', that language cannot "speak about itself" is that there cannot be kinds of noises which, as we use them, refer to other kinds of noises. The assertion is so implausible that I hardly know how to argue against it. The best one can do if one wishes to dispose of it as thoroughly as possible is what I am doing in this section, namely, analyze the major sources of the illusion. But let me first dispose of what is even more obvious. If we use a language in which reference is not univocal, we will eventually get into trouble. This is just common sense. Thus, if we use a certain kind of noise to refer to a certain kind of animals, say, dogs, we had better not also use it to refer to something else and, in particular, not to itself, i.e., to this particular kind of noise. Any adequate language will therefore distinguish between the two kinds of design on the next line:

dog   'dog'.

This is the origin of the quoting device. In any language that is not on grounds of sheer common sense foredoomed, the linguistic events about linguistic events, or, if you please, the part of the language that is "about itself" are therefore those and only those that contain single quotes or their equivalents, e.g., the phrase 'the word dog'.

What, if anything, could be meant by saying that the ideal language speaks about itself? Every awareness has an ideal text. Let '*b*' be the name of (refer to) an awareness and let '$gr(a)$' ('This is green') be its text. From what was said earlier we know that the name of an awareness, in this case 'b', could not possibly occur in its text, in this case '$gr(a)$'; for the text of an awareness refers to its content, which is always distinct from the awareness itself. But consider now another awareness, c, whose content contains b. Since c is about b, its text contains at least one clause that predicates some character of b; for otherwise it wouldn't be about b. Let ' . . . (b)' be this clause, with the dots marking the place of the name of that character. Assume next that L contains as the name of the character the predicate expression ' '$gr(a)$' '.[8] Then the text of c *contains* ' '$gr(a)$' (b)'. L, therefore, contains an expression of its own between single quotes. This is the exact point at which the illusion arises that the ideal language may speak about itself *in the same sense* in which language as event may do so. Or, to put the same thing differently, this is the only clear sense in which the ideal language as a pattern could be said to "speak about itself." Moreover, this is, as we now see, *not* the sense in which language as a part of the world may speak about itself. After one has seen that, one may if one wishes continue to use the phrase, as I occasionally shall, and say that *in this sense* the ideal language may and must "speak about itself." Only, and this is my real point, or, rather, this is the point that matters most for my story, there is again no reason whatsoever why in this sense the ideal language should not or could not "speak about itself." Again, the assertion is not even plausible. One of two apparent reasons that made it seem plausible is, if I may so express myself, the grammar of the picture metaphor. This, I believe, is the reason why Wittgenstein propounded the dogma in the *Tractatus*. The other reason, which probably did not sway Wittgenstein but which seemed a good reason to some others, is that the mathematicians proclaimed they had proved that language cannot both be consistent and say certain things "about itself." The mathematicians had indeed proved something. They usually do. Only, what they had proved was not by any stretch of the imagination what they mistook it for. It took indeed all the philosophical clumsiness and insensitivity which mathematicians sometimes display to make this mistake, just as it took the wrong kind of awe in which some philosophers hold mathematics to believe them. In the rest of this section I shall analyze the mistake; partly in order to dispose of the strange dogma as thoroughly as I possibly can; mainly because this is the best place to introduce the notion of *truth* into the story. For the philosophical analyses of awareness, meaning, and truth belong together.

[8] These are not double quotes but one pair of single quotes within another.

The mathematicians thought they had proved that a schema syntactically constructed cannot (a) be consistent[9] and upon interpretation contain (b) arithmetic as well as (c) a predicate with the literal meaning of 'true'. To be a plausible candidate for the role of ideal language, a schema must obviously satisfy conditions (a) and (b). As to (c), one of the things one would naturally want to say in a language that "speaks about itself" is that its sentences are true or false (not true), as the case may be. Thus, if the mathematicians had proved what they thought they proved, there would be a difficulty. In fact, they proved that no schema can simultaneously fulfill (a), (b), and a third condition, (c'), which they mistook for (c).

In order to fix the ideas I speak for the time being about language as part of the world. Sentences, then, are kinds of linguistic events (or things). Literally, only sentences are true or false. Explicitly, 'true' is therefore a linguistic predicate in the sense that it is truly predicated only of the names of certain linguistic kinds. This, by the way, is the only meaning of 'linguistic' that is clear and does not stand in need of explication. Implicitly, truth involves more than the linguistic events themselves. *A sentence is true if and only if what it refers to (means) is the case.* Let me call this sentence (A). It is a truism: yet, firmly grasped, it has three important consequences. *First.* Some linguistic properties are syntactical properties. In the case of marks on paper, for instance, a property of a sentence or of any other expression is syntactical if and only if it is defined in terms of the shapes and the arrangement of its signs and of nothing else. Truth is obviously not a syntactical property of sentences. *Second.* Introducing 'true' into a schema means two things. It means (α) introducing into the schema a sentence which upon interpretation becomes (A). It means (β) that this sentence ought to be a "linguistic truth," in a sense of the phrase, linguistic truth, which is by no means clear and must therefore be explicated. It follows, *third*, that if all this is to be achieved, the schema must contain certain expressions, one which can be interpreted as 'refer' and others that can be interpreted as names of sentences. In the nature of things, these expressions must be descriptive.

The property mentioned in (c') *is a syntactical property of sentences; truth, the linguistic property mentioned in* (c), *is not.* Not to have seen this is the mathematicians' major mistake. They also made two subsidiary ones. One of these is that, accurately speaking, the property mentioned in (c') is not even a syntactical property.

Goedel, who did not make any of these mistakes, invented a method that allowed him to use arithmetic in speaking commonsensically about

[9] Consistency can be defined syntactically.

an uninterpreted schema. Specifically, he invented a rule by which to each expression of the schema[10] one and only one integer is coördinated in a manner that depends only on the shapes and the arrangement of the signs in the expression itself. (This is, in fact, the least achievement of that great mathematician.) In speaking commonsensically about the schema we can therefore use the number (n_A) which by the rule corresponds to an expression 'A' as the "name" of this expression. By the same rule, a class of integers corresponds to every syntactical property, namely, the class of all the integers coördinated to expressions which have the property. The name of a class of integers is called an arithmetical predicate. (E.g., 'square' is the name of the class [1, 4, 9, . . .].) Now remember (b). By assumption our schema contains number-signs (not numbers!), i.e., expressions we intend to interpret as referring to integers, and arithmetical-predicate-expressions, i.e., expressions we intend to interpret as referring to classes of integers. Assume now that one of these latter expressions, 'pr', upon interpretation becomes an arithmetical predicate that is coördinated to a syntactical property. In this case the mathematicians say that the schema contains the "name" of the syntactical property, just as they say that in the number-signs it contains the "names" of its own expressions. This use of 'name' is inaccurate. For one, an uninterpreted schema does not contain the name (or the "name") of anything. For another, in the intended interpretation 'pr' obviously refers to a class of integers and not to a syntactical property just as the number-signs refer to integers and not to expressions. Assume, third, that we actually use the (interpreted) schema as a language. We could not *in* it state what the mathematicians say *about* it unless it contained further expressions, namely, those which upon interpretation become the names of expressions and of their syntactical properties, and, in addition, the means to state *in* the schema the rules by which, speaking *about* it, we make integers and classes of integers the "names" of linguistic things and characters. This is the reason why, as we shall presently see, the property mentioned in (c') is, accurately speaking, not even a syntactical property. Not to have seen that is one of the two subsidiary mistakes. Its root is the mathematicians' special use of 'name'. For their own special purposes it is, as it happens, quite harmless. Philosophically, it is disastrous to believe that one can state *in* the interpreted schema what can only be stated *about* it. Why this is so is obvious. The one and only schema which interests the philosopher is that which upon interpretation be-

[10] More precisely, the rule works only for schemata of a certain kind; all plausible candidates for the role of ideal language belong to that kind. This is but one of the many omissions I shall permit myself on more technical matters.

comes L, the ideal language. And in L one must in principle be able to say everything nonphilosophical.

I am ready to state what the mathematicians did prove. Let 'A' be a sentence of a schema that satisfies (a) and (b) as well as some other conditions, of a purely technical nature, which every plausible candidate for the role of L must satisfy. Let n_A be the number we have coördinated to 'A'; let 'N_A' be the number-sign of the schema which upon interpretation transcribes n_A; let finally 'pr' be an arithmetical-predicate-expression. What has been proved is this.[11] The schema contains no 'pr' such that

(T) $$pr\ (N_A) \equiv A$$

is *demonstrable* for all (closed) sentences of the schema. But I see that I must again explain, first what demonstrability is, then why anybody should think that (T) ought to be demonstrable.

Analyticity is a syntactical property of sentences. More precisely, what philosophers mean by 'analytic' can and must be explicated by means of a syntactical property. Demonstrability is another syntactical property of sentences. Every demonstrable sentence is analytic, though not conversely. (The second half is one of Goedel's celebrated results.) Thus, while there is no 'pr' for which (T) is demonstrable, there could conceivably be one for which it is analytic. That there actually is none is a purely mathematical matter which does not interest me here at all. The question that interests me is: Why should one who believes, however mistakenly, that an arithmetical-predicate-expression could ever transcribe 'true', also believe that the transcription is adequate only if (T) is demonstrable? The answer is instructive. Remember the condition (β), which requires that (A) be a "linguistic truth." (T) was mistaken for the transcription of (A); demonstrability was implicitly offered as the explication of the problematic notion of linguistic truth. This is the second subsidiary mistake. It is a mistake because in the light of Goedel's result demonstrability is not at all a plausible explication of 'linguistic truth'. Analyticity might be. In the next section I shall propose what I believe to be the correct transcription of (A) in L; and I shall show that this transcription is analytic.

IV

The sentence I proposed to transcribe in the ideal language is 'I see that this is green'; or, rather, in order to sidestep the issue of the Self, '(It is) seen (by me) that this is green'; or, still more precisely, since I

[11] D. Hilbert and P. Bernays, *Grundlagen der Mathematik* (Berlin: Springer, 1939), Vol. II, pp. 245 f.

wish to limit myself to the indubitably simple character of direct acquaintance, 'direct acquaintance with this being green'. Let the undefined descriptive constants 'a', 'aw', 'gr' name a particular and two simple characters, direct acquaintance and greenness, respectively. Consider '$aw(gr(a))$'; call it (1). On first thought one might hit upon (1) as the transcription of our sentence. A little reflection shows that for at least two reasons we are already committed to reject (1).

To be a direct acquaintance, or an imagining, and so on, are, as we saw, characters of particular awarenesses. Let 'b' be the name of the awareness whose text I wish to transcribe. 'aw' must then be predicated of 'b' and not, as in (1), of '$gr(a)$', which refers to the content of b. This is the first reason why we must reject (1). 'gr' and 'a' refer to a character and a particular with both of which I am directly acquainted. Speaking as we ordinarily do, what they refer to is thus called mental. (This is my "point of contact" with the phenomenalists.) Change the example; consider '$kn\ (p_1)$'; call it (1'); let 'kn' and 'p_1' stand for 'known that' and 'This stone is heavy' respectively. 'p_1' refers to a physical state of affairs; to say that it refers to anything mental is to fall into the absurdities of the phenomenalists. 'kn', on the other hand, names a character which, speaking as we ordinarily do, we specifically and characteristically call mental.[12] It follows that (1') mixes the physical and the mental in the manner that leads to the interactionist catastrophe. Perhaps this becomes even clearer if for a moment I write, relationally, '$aw(self,\ p_1)$', which is of course the pattern of the classical act. However, the difference between the relational and non-relational alternatives makes no real difference so far as mixing the physical and the mental goes. This is the second reason why we must reject (1). But now a critic might insist that when somebody knows or sees something there is indeed a transaction[13] between what is known or seen and the knower or seer. Quite so. Only, this transaction is properly spoken of as the scientists speak about it, that is, in principle, behavioristically. (This is my "point of contact" with materialists and epiphenomenalists.) Notice that, in spite of the "phenomenalistic" feature of my ideal language, I can say all this and even find it necessary to say it. This alone should go a long way toward convincing anyone that I avoid the absurdities of the various classical positions.

Let us take stock. Negatively, we understand why (1) cannot be

---

[12] So used, 'knowing' refers to a character of awarenesses. To insist on that one need not deny that there are other uses of the word, e.g., those of which Ryle now makes too much.

[13] I use this clumsy word in order to avoid 'relation', which would be syntactically false since the "transaction" is a pseudorelation.

the transcription. Positively, we see that the transcription must contain the clause '$aw(b)$'. In this clause, by the way, 'aw' is a predicate and therefore, strictly speaking, the name of a character. In (1) it is a nonrelational pseudopredicate and therefore, as I use 'character', not really the name of a character. Of this presently. For the moment we notice that '$aw(b)$' could not possibly be the whole ideal text of our sentence since it does not say what b is an awareness *of*. Thus, there must be at least one more clause. To provide it, I make use of an idea I introduced before. That an awareness is an awareness of something I represent in the ideal language by a character of this awareness which is *in some sense* (I shall presently explicate it) a simple character; in our instance, call this character ' '$gr(a)$' '[14]; generally, I call it ' 'p_1' ', where 'p_1' refers to the content of the awareness or, what amounts to the same thing, is its (ideal) text. The transcription of our sentence becomes then

(2) $aw (b) \cdot$ '$gr(a)$'(b)

Undoubtedly there is something peculiar about ' '$gr(a)$' '. For one, the expression itself is very complex, even though it names a character that is simple. For another, the expression is not, as a syntactically introduced undefined descriptive predicate ought to be, wholly innocent of its interpretation. One can, of course, as I presently shall, syntactically construct a schema that contains it. But that in itself means nothing. Even so, ' '$gr(a)$' ' is innocent of the intended interpretation in that (α) it remains fully indeterminate as long as 'gr' and 'a' are. But it is not so innocent in that (β), after 'gr' and 'a' have been interpreted, if I am to achieve my purposes, ' '$gr(a)$' ' must be interpreted as the name of the character which an awareness possesses if and only if it is an awareness of what '$gr(a)$' refers to. On the other hand, we would like to say that (β) is "merely a linguistic matter" or, as I once put it, that to be an awareness of a certain kind and to have a certain content (and, therefore, text) is one thing and not two. Let there be no illusion. In so speaking we ourselves use 'linguistic' philosophically, i.e., in a problematic way that needs explication. The point is that what I am saying in this section is, among other things, the explication. The following are three salient points of it. (a) I introduce into the ideal language the sentence ' '$gr(a)$'$Mgr(a)$' as the transcription of what we *sometimes* mean when we say that the proposition (or sentence) this is green *means* that this is green. (b) I so extend the notion of a logical sign that 'M' becomes logical and not descriptive. (c) I so extend the notion

---

[14] Again, these are not double quotes but one pair of single quotes within another.

of analyticity that ' '$gr(a)$'$Mgr(a)$' and all similar sentences become analytic.

Sometimes, when we assert such things as, say, that the proposition (or sentence) this is green means that this is green, we would be dissatisfied if we were told that in asserting it we use 'means' in the sense of either reference or context. The cause of the dissatisfaction is that we feel, however confusedly, that we did not say anything, or did not want to say anything, about linguistic events. Or, if you please, we feel that what we really wanted to say is something "linguistic" in some other sense of this problematic term. 'M' transcribes this meaning of 'means'. I am tempted to call it the hidden or philosophical meaning; hidden, because it got lost in the development I described in the second section; philosophical, because I believe that it is what the philosophers who were not sidetracked by that development groped for. However, I ordinarily call meanings (or uses) philosophical if and only if, remaining unexplicated, they produce philosophical puzzlement. So I shall resist the temptation and call this third meaning, transcribed by 'M', the *intentional* meaning of 'means'.

This is as good a place as any to introduce a fourth meaning of 'means' (and 'meaning'). This I call the *logical* meaning. But first for two comments that might help to forestall some misunderstandings. (a) I have mentioned four meanings of 'means'. Two of them, reference and context, I called scientific; one I call logical; another I was at least tempted to call philosophical. There are good reasons for choosing these names; but one must not let the names obscure the fact that *'means' occurs with each of these four meanings in ordinary discourse,* sometimes with the one, sometimes with the other, sometimes with some combination. As long as one speaks commonsensically one does not get into trouble. As soon as one begins to philosophize in the traditional way about "meaning," the fourfold ambiguity begins to produce the traditional philosophical troubles. (b) There are quite a few further meanings of 'meaning'. They occur in moral, esthetic, and scientific discourse and in discourse about such discourse. I know this as well as the next man, even if that man should hail from Oxford. The four meanings I single out are nevertheless those which through fusion and confusion have produced one of the major tangles of first philosophy. Compared with the task of untying this fourfold knot the explication of the other meanings of 'meaning' is not very difficult.

Logicians often say that two sentences of a schema, 'p_1' and 'p_2', have the same meaning if and only if '$p_1 \equiv p_2$' is analytic. This is the logical meaning of 'means'. In logic the idea is important; hence the adjective, logical. Nor is there any doubt that it explicates *one* of the ordinary uses of 'means'. Technically, the basic notion in this case is not meaning but having-the-same-meaning; so the former must be explicated in terms of the latter, say, as the class of all sentences having the same meaning. These, however, are mere technicalities with which we need not bother.

I am ready to put the last touch to my main proposal. One may wonder whether

$$(2') \qquad aw(b) \cdot {}'gr(a)'(b) \cdot {}'gr(a)'Mgr(a)$$

is not preferable to (2). (2') has the advantage that, since its third clause mentions the content of the awareness whose text it transcribes, one can be quite sure of what in the case of (2) one may conceivably doubt, namely, that nothing essential has been omitted. Interestingly, one need not choose. The third clause of (2'), the one which makes the difference between it and (2), is, as I mentioned before, analytic. (2) and (2') are thus like 'p_1' and '$p_1 \cdot p_2$', where 'p_2' is analytic. In this case '$p_1 \equiv p_1 \cdot p_2$' is also analytic. (2) and (2') have therefore the same logical meaning. The meaning transcription must preserve is logical meaning. It follows that the difference between (2) and (2') makes no real difference.

Consider everything I have said so far in this section as preliminary, merely an exposition of the main ideas, to be followed by the more formal presentation and argument on which I am about to embark. First, though, I want to attend to two related matters.

The predicates of the ideal language L which I form by surrounding sentences of L with single quotes name those characters which I call *propositions*. Propositions are therefore not kinds of linguistic things or events in the sense in which certain marks on paper, certain sounds, and certain visual and auditory "contents" are linguistic things or events. And this latter sense is, as we know, the only clear and un-problematic sense of 'linguistic'. It is therefore a mistake, or, at least, it is confusing to say that what I call a proposition is a linguistic character. If a qualifying adjective must be used at all, I would rather say that propositions are mental or psychological characters. But then again, it would be another mistake to think that I propose what is traditionally called a psychological theory of propositions. To under-stand why it is a mistake one merely has to remember that, as the term is traditionally used in philosophy, propositions are a peculiar kind of entity of which some philosophers claim they are the real con-tents of awarenesses. I do not believe that there are propositions in this sense. So I would not propose a theory, either psychological or otherwise, to provide some status for these chimaeras. Why then, one

may wonder, use a word that invites mistakes and confusions. I hold
no brief for the word. I needed a name. This one came to mind. It is,
I think, as good as any other. Also, I welcome the opportunity it provides to cast new light on certain kinds of mistakes and confusions.
This is one of the two matters to which I wanted to attend.

Some particulars are tones. This does not imply that L must contain
an undefined predicate interpreted as 'tone'. If, for instance, L contains
the undefined names of the various pitches, middle c, c sharp, d, and so
on, one could try, in L, to define a tone as anything that exemplifies a
pitch. The technicalities of this business need not concern us here.[15]
Similarly, since awarenesses are in fact those particulars which exemplify propositional characters, one may wonder whether L must
contain undefined descriptive predicates, such as 'aw', which are interpreted as the names of different modes of awareness, in the sense
in which direct acquaintance, wondering, remembering, doubting, and
so on, are modes of awareness. There are undoubtedly such modes,
just as there are shapes, tones, smells, and so on. The only question is
whether, omitting from L all undefined names for any of them, one
can in L still account for the differences among them; that is, whether
one can in principle account for these differences in term of "content"
and of "content" alone. I have pondered the question for years. (Hume
threw out a casual suggestion concerning it when he distinguished
"ideas" from "impressions" by their "faintness.") I am not sure what
the answer is, though I am now inclined to believe that it is negative.
That is why I proceed as if it were negative. But it is also important to
see clearly that whatever it is does not make much difference for anything else I have said and shall still say in this essay. The only difference
is that if the answer were positive then propositions would be the only
characters that are in fact exemplified by awarenesses alone. This is
the other matter to which I wanted to attend.

Russell and the Wittgenstein of the *Tractatus* were the first who
practiced the method of philosophizing by means of an ideal language.
Since then quite a few philosophers, whether they knew it or not, have
more or less consistently employed this method. With two exceptions,
they all proposed essentially the same syntactical schema. This schema,
I shall call it the conventional schema or L_c, is of the *Principia Mathematica* type. The New Nominalists are one exception; the other, for
over a decade now, has been myself. The New Nominalists, who do
not belong in our story, believe that L must be syntactically poorer

---

[15] See also MLP12 and "Undefined Descriptive Predicates," *Philosophy and
Phenomenological Research*, 8, 1947, 55–82.

than L_c.[16] I believe that L_c is in one respect and in one respect only not rich enough to serve as L. My reason should now be obvious. I do believe that L_c can serve as a clarified language to be spoken, in principle, about everything which, as one usually says, is an object of mind—including mind itself, as long as we speak about it scientifically, that is, in principle, behavioristically. But I also believe that L_c does not provide adequate transcriptions for many statements we make about minds or mental things when we speak commonsensically. It follows, on my conception of philosophy, that one cannot, by talking about L_c and what it talks about, solve some of the philosophical problems concerning mind and its place in nature.[17] Hence L_c cannot be the ideal language. Positively, I believe that L_c becomes the ideal language if it is supplemented by two further primitive signs, namely

$$M \quad \text{and} \quad ' \cdots \cdots ',$$

i.e., the relational pseudopredicate which I interpret as the intentional 'means' and the quoting operator. We have incidentally come upon another reason why the question whether L must contain 'aw' and other undefined names for the several modes of awareness is not as fundamental as it might seem. 'aw' and its cognates are predicates; thus they exemplify a syntactical category provided by L_c. 'M' is a pseudopredicate. Thus it belongs to a syntactical category unknown to L. As it happens, it is also the only primitive sign that represents this category in L_c. And what holds for 'M' in these two respects also holds for the quoting operator. Presently I shall make much of these points. But I see that I am once more illuminating basic ideas when the ground for a more formal presentation has already been laid. So I shall proceed as follows. *First,* I shall very concisely describe those features of L_c that matter most for my purpose. *Second,* I shall construct syntactically the schema I believe to be L. It contains the two syntactical categories represented by 'M' and by the quoting operator. This feature requires a redefinition of the syntactical notions of *logical sign* and *analyticity*. The two new notions are broader than the conventional ones in that every primitive sign logical in L_c and every sentence analytic in L_c are also in L logical and analytic respectively, but not conversely. *Third,* I shall state explicitly what is implicit in this essay as a whole, namely, that the enriched schema can be made to bear the burden of the philosophy of mind.

[16] For an analysis of the New Nominalism see MLP4, MLP5, and "Particularity and the New Nominalism," *Methodos,* 6, 1954, 131–47, and also pp. 91–105 of this book.

[17] See also MLP6.

The primitive signs of L_c fall into two classes, logical and descriptive. The logical signs are of two kinds. There are, first, two signs, each individually specified, each belonging to a syntactical category of its own, each the only primitive representative of its category in L_c. These two signs are, of course, a connective and a quantifier, interpreted in the familiar fashion as, say, 'neither-nor' and 'all'.[18] The second kind of logical signs, not individually specified, consists of an indefinite number of variables of each of the several types. Each type is a syntactical category; but they are all categories of "terms." The essence of a term is that it combines with terms to form sentences. L_c contains no pseudo-terms, i.e., no category (except connectives) whose members combine either with sentences or with terms and sentences to form sentences. The primitive descriptive signs or, as one also says, the undefined descriptive constants of L_c are distributed over the various types of "terms." If a sentence S of L_c contains descriptive terms, then replace them all according to certain rules by variables. Call the resulting sentence the "form" of S. The syntactical definition of analyticity is so constructed that whether or not a sentence is analytic depends only on its "form." The syntactical significance of the distinction between the two kinds of signs lies thus in the role it plays in the syntactical definition of analyticity. The philosophical significance of the latter, and thus of both syntactical distinctions, lies in the circumstance that *in all cases but one* it can serve as the explication of what philosophers mean when they say that a sentence is "analytic," or a "formal" truth, or a "linguistic" truth. The exception where the conventional definition of analyticity is not adequate for this purpose is, as one might expect, the case of such sentences as "The sentence (proposition) this is green means that this is green," when 'means' is used intentionally.

That the definition of analyticity in L_c achieves its philosophical purpose depends of course on its details; they are specified in what is technically known as validity theory. I cannot here state the definition accurately; but I shall recall its nature by means of two elementary illustrations. Take the two forms '$p \lor \sim p$' and '$(x)f(x) \supset (\exists x)f(x)$'. The first is analytic because its truth table is tautological; the second is analytic because if '$f(x)$' is read 'x is a member of f', then it becomes a set-theoretical truth for all subsets of all nonempty sets. The definition of analyticity (validity) is thus combinatorial; arithmetical in the simplest case, set-theoretical in all others. What makes it philosophically significant is, first, the combinatorial feature, and, second, the

---

[18] If, as strictly speaking one must, one is to dispense with definitions, then a third logical primitive, the abstraction operator, is necessary. This is another of the omissions and simplifications for which I must take the responsibility.

circumstance that as far as we know all analytical statements are in fact true.[19]

Technically, validity theory is a branch of mathematics with many difficult problems. So it is perhaps not surprising that it, too, provided the philosophers with an opportunity to be misled by the mathematicians. The following two comments will show what I have in mind. (a) For all philosophical purposes (with the one notorious exception) our definition is an adequate explication of what philosophers mean by 'analytic'. Mathematically, it is not as interesting. It would be, if we knew a procedure which, applied to *any* sentence S of L_c, after a finite number of steps yielded an answer to the question whether S is analytic. There is and there can be no such procedure. (That there can be none even if one restricts S to the so-called lower functional calculus is the famous result of Church.) This is the reason why mathematicians are not very interested in validity; unfortunately, their lack of interest has blinded some philosophers to the philosophical significance of this explication of 'analytic'. (b) In speaking about a schema we always speak commonsensically. In framing the explication of analyticity in terms of validity we use set theory "commonsensically." Yet it is a matter of record that "commonsensical" set theory itself got into difficulties that had to be straightened out by the construction of schemata. Mathematicians may therefore feel that the explication of analyticity in terms of validity uncritically takes for granted what is in fact uncertain and problematic. For some mathematical purposes that may indeed be so. Yet, we must not allow the mathematicians to persuade us that we, as philosophers, ought to strive for certainty, or constructivity, or decidability, in the sense in which the finitists among them do. We seek, not certainty of any peculiar noncommonsensical kind, but, rather, the clarity achieved by explications framed in terms of common sense, that common sense of which science and (nonformalized) mathematics are but the long arm. If yesterday's "common sense" got us into trouble that had to be straightened out by the construction of schemata, we shall today still use this "amended common sense" to construct "commonsensically" the schemata of today. And if tomorrow we should get into trouble again, we shall start all over again. For what else could we possibly do?

One more feature of L_c must be mentioned. Let 'F_1' and 'F_2' be predicate expressions of any type, 'X' a variable of its subject type, '$\Phi(F_1)$' any sentence containing 'F_1', '$\Phi(F_2)$' a sentence made out of '$\Phi(F_1)$' by replacing at least one occurrence of 'F_1' by 'F_2'. It is a consequence of our definition of analyticity that

---

[19] See also MLP4, MLP14.

(E) $$(X)[F_1(X) \equiv F_2(X)] \supset [\Phi(F_1) \equiv \Phi(F_2)]$$

is analytic. Thus, if the antecedent of (E) is true, so is the consequent; and if the antecedent is analytic, so is the consequent. This feature is called the extensionality of L_c. I turn to the syntactical description of L. With the qualification entailed by 1 it contains L_c.

1. Only closed expressions are sentences of L. (This is merely a technical detail, necessary to avoid undesirable consequences of the quantification rules for expressions containing 'M'.)

2. L contains sentential variables. (Since L contains no primitive sentential constants, this modification has, upon my conception of ontology,[20] no untoward ontological consequences.)

3. L contains two additional primitive signs, the relational pseudo-predicate 'M' and the quoting operator, with the following formation rules:

a. Every sentence of L surrounded by quotes becomes a nonrelational first-order predicate (type:f) with all the syntactical properties of a primitive descriptive predicate.

b. Every sentence of the form 'fMp' is well formed. Call these sentences the simple clauses of 'M'.

These are the formation rules of L. Now for the definition of analyticity.

4a. Every sentence analytic according to L_c is analytic.

4b. Every simple clause of 'M' is either analytic or it is contradictory, i.e., its negation is analytic. It is analytic if and only if the predicate to the left of 'M' is formed by the quoting operator from the sentence to the right of 'M'.

The part of L that contains 'M' is not extensional. To see that, let 'A' be a constant of the same type as 'X' and assume that '$(X)[F_1(X) \equiv F_2(X)]$' is true. If L were extensional, then ' '$F_1(A)$'$MF_1(A)$' $\equiv$ ' '$F_1(A)$'$MF_2(A)$' ' would have to be true. In fact, this sentence is not only false, it is contradictory; for by 4b its left side is analytic and its right side is contradictory.

I call 'M' and the quoting operator, together with the two primitive logical signs of L_c, the four primitive logical signs of L. But then, one may ask, are the two new signs "really" logical? I can of course call them so. Yet, obviously, I do not wish to argue merely about words. The only real argument consists in stating clearly the similarities and the differences between the old and the new "logical" signs. I shall present this argument or, as I had better say, these reflections in three steps. *First.* Each of the four signs, both old and new, is individually

[20] See also MLP4, MLP13, and "Particularity and the New Nominalism."

specified. Each of the four signs, both old and new, belongs to a syntactical category of its own. Each of the four signs, both old and new, is the only primitive member of the syntactical category to which it belongs. These similarities are impressive. Nor is that all. *Second.* Consider the role the four signs play in the definition of analyticity. If in view of the three similarities just mentioned one accepts the two new signs as logical, then one can in view of 4a and 4b again say that whether a sentence of L is analytic depends only on its "form." This similarity, too, is impressive. But there is also a difference with respect to analyticity which I do not at all intend to minimize. For philosophy, as I understand it, is not advocacy, least of all advocacy of uses of words, but accurate description. The difference is that 4b is not a combinatorial criterion in the sense in which 4a is one. On the other hand, though, the "new" analytic sentences, i.e., those which are analytic by 4b, have a unique feature which in its own way is just as sweeping as any combinatorial one. They are all simple clauses of 'M' and each of these clauses is either analytic or contradictory. *Third.* Sentences which are analytic in the "old" sense of L_c (or 4a) are also called "formal" or "linguistic" truths. These are of course philosophical and therefore problematic uses of 'formal' and 'linguistic'. Analyticity in the old sense is their explication. Now we know that such sentences as "The sentence (proposition) this is green means that this is green" are sometimes also called "linguistic" truths and that this use of 'linguistic' is equally problematic. L transcribes these sentences into those that are analytic by 4b. Our "new" notion of analyticity thus clarifies two of the problematic uses of 'formal' and 'linguistic'; it exhibits accurately both the similarities and the differences between them; and it does not tear asunder what in the structural history of philosophical thought belongs together.

I have not, I shall not, and I could not in this essay show that L is the ideal language. What I have shown is merely this. *If* $(\alpha)L_c$ is an adequately clarified language which one can in principle speak about everything except minds, and if $(\beta)L$ provides in principle adequate transcriptions for what we say, commonsensically and not behavioristically, about minds, *then* L is the ideal language. Furthermore, I have shown (β) by showing, at the beginning of this section, that L contains adequate transcriptions of such sentences as 'direct awareness of this being green'. With this I have accomplished the main task I set myself in this essay. Again, if this is so, then the differences between L and L_c must provide us with the accurate description, or, in the classical phrase, with the logical picture of the nature of minds and their place in the world. Let us see. In the world of L_c there are tones, shapes, colors, and so on. That is, there are particulars such that *in fact* they and they alone exemplify certain simple characters, say, in the case of tones, the pitches. In the world of L there are in addition also awarenesses. That is, there are particulars such that *in fact* they and they alone exemplify certain additional simple characters, those I called propositions and, probably, also some among those I called modes of awareness. These, to be sure, are important differences; yet they are not as radical as the one I saved quite deliberately for the end of the list. This difference is that L requires two new logical primitives. For what novelty, I ask, could possibly be more radical than one which cannot be spoken about without new syntactical categories. Notice, finally, that the two new primitives determine *in a minimal fashion* that part of L which is, in a technical sense I explained, nonextensional. So far I have avoided the use of 'intentional' for 'nonextensional'. Now we might as well remember that philosophers, speaking philosophically, have insisted that "intentionality" is the differentiating characteristic of minds. Since they spoke philosophically, one cannot be completely certain what they meant. Yet, I am confident that my analysis is the explication of what they reasonably could have meant.

It will pay to reflect briefly on why I used the phrase 'in fact' at the two italicized places above. Interpret 'bl' and 'a' as 'blue' and as the name of a particular which is a tone. Let ' 'p_1' ' stand for the name of a propositional character. Both '$bl(a)$' and ' 'p_1'(a_1)' are well-formed sentences; all one can say is that they are *in fact* false. To say anything else, such as, for instance, that they are ill-formed or, even, that they are contradictory, amounts to accepting some form of the synthetic *a priori* and, probably, also some form of substantialism. I, for one, accept neither.[21]

In the third section I told one half of the story of truth. I am now ready to tell the other half. Then I shall be done.

In an unforgettable metaphor G. E. Moore once called awareness diaphanous or transparent. What he wanted to call attention to was that, because we are so prone to attend to their contents, the awarenesses themselves easily elude us. Intentional meaning is, as we now understand, closely connected with awareness. Not surprisingly, then, it is similarly elusive. That is why, when I first mentioned it, I proceeded negatively, as it were. Remember what I did. I selected a sentence to serve as illustration: "The sentence (proposition) this is green means that this is green." Then I insisted that we sometimes so use such sentences that we do not speak about either the contexts or the referents of linguistic events, in the only clear sense of 'linguistic

[21] See MLP3, MLP8, MLP11.

event'; but, rather, about something "linguistic" in a sense of 'linguistic' which is problematic and therefore in need of explication. The explication, as we now know, is this. (a) The sentence is transcribed by ' '$gr(a)$'$Mgr(a)$', which is analytic. (b) ' '$gr(a)$' ' refers to or names a proposition, i.e., a character of awarenesses. (c) '$gr(a)$' refers to a state of affairs. (d) 'M', being a logical sign, does not refer to or name anything in the sense in which descriptive expressions refer to something. (a) and (d) are the source of the problematic use of 'linguistic'. (b) and (c) show that intentional meaning is a logical pseudorelation between a propositional character and a state of affairs; they also show accurately in which respects it makes no sense whatsoever to say that intentional meaning is "linguistic."

When I spoke in the third section about truth, I spoke about language as event—with some reservation, or, as I put it, merely in order to fix the ideas. The reason for the reservation was that 'true', like 'means', has an intentional meaning. Or, to say what corresponds exactly to what I said before and just repeated in the case of 'means', sometimes, when we say "The sentence (proposition) this is green is true if and only if this is green," we speak neither about the contexts nor about the referents of linguistic events but, rather, "linguistically" in a problematic sense of 'linguistic'. I shall now explicate this sense by first proposing a definition of 'true' in L and then commenting on it.

A defined sign or expression is logical if and only if all the primitive signs in its definition are logical. Defined logical signs, like primitive ones, do not refer to anything in the sense in which descriptive ones do. 'True', as I explicate it, is a defined logical predicate of the second type with a nonrelational argument. Thus 'true', or, as I shall write, 'Tr', like 'M', does not refer to anything in the sense in which 'a', 'gr', ' '$gr(a)$' ', and '$gr(a)$' all do. The idea is, as one might expect, to define 'Tr' in terms of 'M' and of other logical signs, i.e., variables, quantifiers, and connectives. The actual definition is

1129767

(D)   '$Tr(f)$'   for   '$(\exists p)[fMp \cdot p]$'.

Notice that although 'Tr' can be truly predicated only of the names of characters which are propositions, its definition is nevertheless in terms of the variable of the appropriate type. '$Tr(gr)$', for instance, though it is false, is therefore well formed. To proceed otherwise amounts to accepting some version of the synthetic a priori. This is the same point I made before. Now for four comments to establish that (D) is in fact an adequate transcription of the intentional meaning of 'true'.

I. Remember the sentence I called (A): A sentence is true if and only if what it refers to (means) is the case. Since we are now dealing with intentions, I had better amend it to (A'): *A proposition is true if and only if what it means is the case.* Consider next that in view of (D)

(D')
$$Tr(f) \equiv (\exists p)[fMp \cdot p]$$

is analytic; for our notion of analyticity is of course so arranged that every sentence that stands to a definition in the relation in which (D') stands to (D) is analytic. (This is just one of the many details I skipped.) Now read (D') in words: Something is true if and only if there is a state of affairs such that it means this state of affairs and this state of affairs is the case. The only verbal discrepancies between this sentence and (A') are due to the greater precision which the formalism forces upon us. We must say 'something' instead of 'proposition'; and we must make the existential quantification explicit. (D'), being analytic, is thus an adequate transcription of (A'). A little reflection shows that 'Tr' is and is not "linguistic" in exactly the same senses in which 'M' is. I don't think I need to repeat the distinctions I just made under (a), (b), (c), and (d).

II. Ordinarily we think of true and false as contradictories. I define 'Fs', to be interpreted as 'false', by

$$\text{'}Fs(f)\text{'} \quad \text{for} \quad \text{'}(\exists p)[fMp \cdot \sim p]\text{'}.$$

It follows that 'Fs' and 'Tr' are not contradictories, or, what amounts to the same thing, that '$(f)[Tr(f) \vee Fs(f)]$' cannot be shown to be analytic. On first thought this may make our transcription look less than adequate. Closer examination reveals that we have come across one of its strengths. We do not really want to say that "everything" is either true or false. What we want to say is, rather, that "every sentence" is either true or false. Technically, this means that '$Tr(\text{'}p_1\text{'})$ $\vee Fs(\text{'}p_1\text{'})$' ought to be analytic for every proposition. And that this is so is easily shown. For those who care for this sort of detail I write down the steps of the demonstration: 'p_1'Mp_1; 'p_1'$Mp_1 \cdot (p_1 \vee \sim p_1)$; $(\exists p)[\text{'}p_1\text{'}Mp \cdot (p \vee \sim p)]$; $(\exists p)[\text{'}p_1\text{'}Mp \cdot p)] \vee [(\exists p)\text{'}p_1\text{'}Mp \cdot \sim p]$.

III. We are in a position to dispose of a question over which recently more ink has been spilled than it deserves. Do 'p_1' and '$Tr(\text{'}p_1\text{'})$' have the same meaning? To ask this question is, as we know, to ask four. With respect to *context*, we do not care and we need not bother. Take the two sentences 'Peter died' and 'It is true that Peter died'; and assume that a person hears once the one and once the other. Whether what he does is the same and whether his mental states are the same on the two occasions is a question for psychologists and psychologists only. As a matter of common sense, though, the answer will vary, depending on many circumstances, from sentence to sentence, from person to person, and, for the same person, from occasion to occasion. The attempt to answer this question by constructing schemata and trying to discern in them something that corresponds to this meaning of having-the-same-meaning is thus patently absurd. Unhappily, Carnap and some of his students have recently spent a good deal of time and effort on this goose chase. With respect to *reference* the answer is obvious. The two sentences do not refer to the same thing. The same holds for *intentional* meaning. To see that, one merely has to consider that while ' 'p_1'Mp_1' and ' 'Tr('p_1')'MTr('p_1')' are analytic, ' 'p_1'MTr('p_1')' and ' 'Tr('p_1')'Mp_1' are contradictory. There remains *logical* meaning, or, what amounts to the same thing, there remains the question whether '$p_1 \equiv Tr$('p_1')' is analytic for every proposition. This, I believe, is the question which most of those who recently dealt with the issue wanted to discuss. The answer is affirmative. Upon our broader conception of analyticity the sentence is analytic. Some will probably consider that another strength of our transcription. For those who care for this sort of thing I again write down the steps of the demonstration. For the proof that '$p_1 \supset Tr$('p_1')' is analytic they are: p_1; 'p_1'$Mp_1 \cdot p_1$; ($\exists p$) ['p_1'$Mp \cdot p$]; $p_1 \supset (\exists p)$['p_1'$Mp \cdot p$]. To prove that 'Tr('p_1') $\supset p_1$' is analytic, the definition of analyticity in L must be technically implemented with what is intuitively obvious. I add then to 4a and 4b a third clause 4c: If '$\Phi(p)$' is an expression such that when a sentence of L is substituted for the variable the sentence it becomes is analytic for every sentence of L, then '$(p)\Phi(p)$' is analytic. Now the proof proceeds as follows. '('p_1'$Mp_1 \cdot p_1$) $\supset p_1$' is obviously analytic. For every other p_i, '('p_1'$Mp_i \cdot p_i$) $\supset p_1$' is analytic because the first factor in the antecedent is contradictory. Hence, by 4c, '(p)['p_1'$Mp \cdot p$) $\supset p_1$]' is analytic. This sentence is equivalent to the one to be proved.

IV. Everybody is familiar with the Liar paradox, that is, with the difficulties one can produce by supposing that a sentence "says about itself" that it is false. When the mathematicians proved what I explained in the third section, they drew part of their inspiration from this conundrum. Assume 'pr' to be an arithmetical-predicate-expression that can be interpreted as 'false'. We know this assumption to be absurd; but that is not the point now. If there is such a predicate expression then one can by using Goedel's ideas show that there is an integer, n, such that if 'N' is the number-sign interpreted as n, the number coördinated to '$pr(N)$' is n. Speaking as inaccurately as the mathematicians do, one could then say that '$pr(N)$' says about itself that it is false. That is why, by a pattern taken from the Liar paradox, the mathematicians drew their conclusions from this sentence. Under the circumstances it is worth noticing that L could not possibly contain a sentence which literally "says about itself" that it is false, or, for that matter, anything else. Assume that S is such a sentence and that, written down, it is a sequence of, say, 17 primitive signs. Its name is then a sequence of 18 primitive signs, the 17 original ones and the quoting operator. Since this name is a predicate and not itself a sentence, any sentence containing it is a sequence of at least 19 primitive signs. S, which is a sequence of only 17 primitive signs, cannot be such a sentence and can therefore not literally say anything about itself. It follows that no sentence of a clarified language can literally say anything about itself.[22] The belief that there are such sentences is one of the illusions created by the logical deficiencies of our natural language.

[22] As I recently discovered, this idea can be read into prop. 3.333 of the *Tractatus*. Wittgenstein made an essential mistake, though. He omitted the quotes.

The Revolt Against
Logical Atomism*

Explaining metaphysics to the nation—
I wish he would explain his explanation.
Byron, *Don Juan.*

PHILOSOPHICAL movements rise and fall, not excluding those that set out to end all movements or even philosophy itself. Having run its course, a movement is either found wanting or judged to have made a contribution. In either case, it is vigorous while the clever young men gather around its banner. And, of course, there are always many clever young men eager to enlist. Oxford is now the center of a vigorous movement. Surely it is not the whole of contemporary British philosophy. Yet hardly anyone now philosophizing in Britain or, for that matter, in this country, is unaware of it.

Urmson's[1] recent book hails from Oxford. For at least two reasons it makes an excellent text for a critical study. One reason is that it is very good of its kind. The other is its major theme. Urmson tries to show, successfully I think, that the two main slogans of Oxford are reactions against certain ideas of the classical analysts. The word 'slogan' is his. The phrase 'the classical analysts' is mine. I shall use it to refer to the members of the movement or movements over which Russell and Wittgenstein[2] presided, with G. E. Moore as the most important figure in the near background.

* The Philosophical Quarterly, *7, 1957, 323–39, and 8, 1958, 1–13. Reprinted by permission.*

[1] *Philosophical Analysis: Its Development Between the Two World Wars* (Oxford: Clarendon Press, 1956).

[2] I.e., throughout this essay, the author of the *Tractatus*, not of the *Investigations*. In another long essay, I traced the tragedy of the second book to a fundamental shortcoming of the first. See "Intentionality," *Semantica* (Archivio di Filosofia, Roma: Bocca, 1955), pp. 177–216, and also pp. 3–83 of this book.

Urmson presents the case for Oxford. I shall take the other side. When I call his book good I therefore do not mean that I agree with everything he says. Far from so. But with a good deal of it every analytical philosopher can agree. This is to his credit. Also, he attends to what is important and does not niggle about what is not. He gives the other fellow a fair run for his money and doesn't wear him out by elaborating the obvious. These are rare virtues.

Logical Atomism is the metaphysical system at one time propounded by Russell and Wittgenstein. Among its numerous propositions, its several parts (theories), and the method by which it is established there are many structural connections. Its two major parts are the *picture theory of language* and the *verification theory of meaning*. Its method is reductive analysis by means of an *ideal language*. The structural connections between the whole, its two major parts, and the method are such that if one of the latter three is overthrown, all four collapse. Thus, even the method does not make sense unless one accepts some of the propositions it is designed to establish. The two major theories have in fact been overthrown. *Reductive analysis* has been shown to be unfeasible even if disengaged from the ideal language method. Logical Atomism thus collapsed. The two new slogans point in the direction of the right theory of meaning and the right method. In broad strokes, this is Urmson's argument. I shall now block out my own.

As it stands, the doctrine in question is indeed untenable, if only because it is an *unreconstructed* metaphysics. Properly reconstructed, its propositions fall into three classes. Some would seem to be true. I say 'seem' because one should never be too certain about propositions as sweeping as these. Some are almost certainly false. Some others become mere explications of philosophical uses. As such they are neither true nor false but, rather, adequate or inadequate. The ideal language method is philosophically neutral. The programme of reductive analysis has not been shown to be unrealizable. I have argued all this before.[3] In this paper I propose to supplement the argument by defending those parts of the doctrine which I believe to be sound against the criticisms Urmson marshals against them. It will be best if I first get two general matters out of the way.

The ideal language is not really a language but merely the skeleton of one. Some dismiss the method on this ground alone. Urmson has not joined their tedious company. One good turn deserves another. I shall keep out of this study a point which goes rather deep, namely, that the

---

[3] See "Intentionality" and *The Metaphysics of Logical Positivism*, hereafter cited as MLP, with Arabic numerals referring to the numbers of the essays in this volume.

ideal language must not even be thought of as the skeleton of what is called the inner monologue.[4] Perhaps it is worth noticing that a last-ditch defender of the notion goes (in the right direction) much further than its most scornful critics.

Urmson not only examines structural connections, he also suggests historical ones. With many of these no one need quarrel. Every now and then I disagree with his emphasis. Some historical connections I think he overlooks. In either case I shall say my piece without, however, offering much, if anything, in the way of evidence. So, perhaps, a historical connection I believe he missed is merely a structural one I see. Little harm will be done. Happily, neither Urmson nor I are primarily interested in philology, not even in Wittgenstein philology.

I

All physical objects consist of atoms. An atom, being a simple, does not itself consist of anything. This shows how 'atom' is used in (classical) physics. All other uses are controlled by the ideas of simplicity and consisting. In the proposition 'The world consists of simples' the words 'simple' and 'consist' are used philosophically. That makes it a philosophical proposition. It may be taken to state somehow, at its barest, the thesis of Logical Atomism. As it stands, it makes no sense. No unreconstructed philosophical proposition does. But this is not to say that one cannot recover the sense it is intended to make. The result is an explicated or *reconstructed* philosophical proposition. Explication and result must both be free from philosophical uses; otherwise we would be weaving a Penelopean pall. Philosophical (metaphysical) propositions are reconstructed by the ideal language method (hereafter, briefly: the method). I shall begin by describing it, most concisely to be sure and only selectively for my purpose, yet in sufficient detail to show that even in the most detailed description no word would be used philosophically. If I can show this, then I shall also have shown that the method does not commit its practitioners to any philosophical proposition, either reconstructed or unreconstructed. First, though, four comments on what has been said already.

A reconstructed philosophical proposition says something about the world and is, therefore, literally either true or false. In spite of all the other huge differences, in this one respect there is no difference between a philosophical proposition and, say, 'Peter is tall'. This I believe. According to Oxford, a philosophical proposition, neither true nor false, is at best a confused way of calling attention to the "logic" of non-

[4] See "Intentionality," especially pp. 7–8, 12–13 of this book.

philosophical uses occurring in propositions that are not, in my sense, the reconstructions of philosophical ones. This is the first comment. 'Confused' is the cue for the second.

All philosophical problems, or, as they say, puzzles are the result of linguistic confusion. The formula, very fashionable at Oxford, is but another way of saying that there are no philosophical propositions. I find this use of 'confusion' very confusing. To use ordinary language, to speak commonsensically, not to use any word philosophically, are one and the same thing. To confuse two or several things is either not to distinguish among them or to mistake one for another. Depending on occasion of utterance and grammatical context, some words and phrases of ordinary language have different "ordinary" meanings. The play of words that permits has, I believe, often called attention to philosophical problems. But this is not to say that the classical philosophers confused the "ordinary" meanings. Attempting to say what is very difficult to say, they rather groped for new meanings. Whatever linguistic confusion there was, and there was plenty, is the effect rather than the cause of such gropings.

When is a word used philosophically? Some philosophers maintained that bodies do not exist. Either they were raving mad or they used 'exist' in the peculiar way I call philosophical. This is a clear case. We all know many clear cases, through experience and from the tradition. If in doubt, explore. The question must be faced each time it arises. But there is no need to answer it once and for all, by a definition. This should be obvious to the men of Oxford, committed as they are to the two propositions (these are not the two new slogans) that we can only start from common sense and that some things cannot and need not be argued directly. This is the third comment. It leads to the last.

Ordinary language is not just small talk. Scientific and moral (not, ethical!) discourse are part of it. In such areas the establishment of and the distinctions among several nonphilosophical uses are often crucial. Call this the task of nonphilosophical linguistic analysis. It can be performed without the sharp tool of an ideal language. One does not cut butter with a razor. Nor need one be concerned with drawing a razor-sharp line between nonphilosophical linguistic analysis and philosophy. It suffices again that there are clear cases of either. Also, the former is often of propaedeutic value for the latter (and therefore quite properly done by philosophers). At Oxford they think that there is no such thing as the latter. So they overdo the former, a good thing in itself, until it becomes trivial and boring.

Language has many uses. We ask questions and issue commands. There is poetry. Some sentences are descriptive or, as one says, statements of fact. ('Fact' is also used philosophically. I speak, as always, commonsensically.) There is no doubt that philosophical propositions are meant to be descriptive. Lest this sound highhanded, consider ethics, where there is a good deal of talk about imperatives. Whatever the philosopher's position,[5] the sole purpose of such talk is to describe the facts involved in imperatives. Thus we are led to restrict our attention to descriptive statements. This the method does. *If* it should fail of its purpose, we can always return to inquire whether the restriction was the cause of the failure.

In unimproved languages unreconstructed philosophical statements are grammatically correct. This suggests the idea of an improved language. Notice the distinction between *improved* and *ideal*. An improved language is called ideal if and only if it is thought to fulfill *three conditions:* (1) Every nonphilosophical descriptive proposition can in principle[6] be transcribed into it; (2) No unreconstructed philosophical one can; (3) All philosophical propositions can be reconstructed as statements about its syntax (see below) and interpretation (see below). (3) is the heart of the matter. (1) and (2) are auxiliary; if they were not fulfilled, one could not possibly know that (3) was. Any attempt to "prove," directly and separately, as it were, that an improved language is the ideal one is patently absurd. This one "proves," indirectly, as well as one may by using it as a tool in philosophizing. All one can and need show is that the *four improvements* on which the method insists are not on commonsensical grounds impossible of achievement and that their being achieved does not depend on any philosophical proposition being true. This I shall now do.

First. Whether the *sentence* 'It's raining' is true or false depends on when and where it is *asserted*. The sentence 'It rained in Iowa City on October 12, 1956' is (as it happens) true whenever or wherever it is uttered or asserted or what have you.[7] Call it for the moment complete. Every scientific report is complete. The method requires that every sentence of an improved language be in this sense complete. *Second.* Consider the ellipsis 'We are far'. Sometimes, when I utter it, it is understood that I mean 'We are far from Iowa City'. (Had I driven instead of walked, I might on the same occasion have asserted its negation.) The convenience is achieved by using 'far' once as a one-term, once as a two-term predicate. This makes for "loose" grammar. Part

---

[5] One who asserts that 'This is good' is not a statement of fact uses 'fact' philosophically. For the explication of this use see Section Two.

[6] The phrase *in principle* refers as usual to the "skeleton" feature of ideal languages.

[7] "Vagueness" so-called is a different issue.

of the price paid for the looseness is that not only unreconstructed philosophical propositions but also some unquestioned nonsense is in natural language grammatically correct. Remember Russell's 'Quadruplicity drinks procrastination'. Thus we are led to the idea of a (written) language in which grammatical correctness depends only on the shapes and the arrangement of the words. An improved language must fulfill this requirement. It is, as one says, syntactically constructed. *Third.* Consider two men speaking the same natural language. The first utters a sentence containing a word or phrase not familiar to the second. The second asks to be enlightened. The first, without pointing or resorting to any other nonverbal means, produces another sentence, with the same meaning,[8] in which the critical word or phrase no longer occurs. This can be done in many cases. Without either circularity or an infinite regress it obviously can not be done in all cases. This leads to the following requirement. Each word of an improved language is of one and only one of two kinds, called *primitive* and *nonprimitive* respectively; for each sentence containing words of both kinds there is one and only one, with the same meaning, containing only primitive ones. *Fourth.* The second and the third requirement bring us up against the fact that a system of marks, to be a language, must be "tied" to what it is about. Call this "tying" interpretation. An improved language must be interpreted by interpreting either (1) all of its primitives, or (2) all of the sentences that contain only primitive words, or (3) by a procedure combining (1) and (2). This is the fourth requirement. It is a consequence of the third. Also, it is the only limitation which the method as such imposes on interpretation. In particular, it is not required that an improved language be interpreted by interpreting separately all, or even any, of its primitives.

No practitioner of the method ever interpreted his improved language by assigning *all* its primitives to things according to the rule *unum nomen—unum nominatum.* On the other hand, *all* interpretations ever proposed consist in part in assigning *some* primitives (they are called *nonlogical*) to things. That could not be done unless the following were true.

P. *There are* several *things with which we become acquainted if they are* once *presented to us. If* one *such thing is presented to us again, we recognize it.* Construe 'thing' and 'being presented to us' as 'physical object' and

---

[8] I know as well as the next man that in *one* of the *several* meanings of 'meaning' no substitution leaves meaning unchanged. See "Intentionality" and, for an elaboration, "Concepts" (jointly with Herbert Hochberg), *Philosophical Studies*, 8, 1957, 19–27, and also pp. 106–14 of this book.

'being perceived by us' and P becomes a truism. Notice, though, that P contains no such specification. Provided only that he stays within the limits of common sense (uses no word philosophically), the kind of presentation on which a philosopher insists for the things to which he assigns his nonlogical primitives as labels is still his choice. The choice is of course determined by what he thinks is required by his purpose of reconstructing all philosophical propositions, or, what amounts to the same, solving all philosophical problems by means of his improved language. Of this later.

According to one very influential philosophy, namely, Hegel's, P is "really" false; commonsensical belief in its truth, an illusion. Since Dewey's instrumentalism is merely a scientific version of Hegelianism, it is not surprising that he, too, rejects P. But P is also the "metaphysical presupposition" Oxford implicitly attacks whenever it attacks either the method, which as we just saw does not imply it, or the classical analysts, who indeed "presupposed" it. This, at the deepest level, is the "atomism" against which the movement rebels. *Pluralism*, I think, would be more accurate. In Urmson all this is relatively explicit. That is one of his merits. To another structural connection between Oxford and Hegel I shall attend later. For a historical connection, it comes to mind that not so long ago Oxford was a center of Hegelianism.[9] As far as P itself is concerned, I find myself at the limits of "direct" argument. A world in which P is false is beyond my imagination.

All practitioners of the method insist that *some* primitives, they call them *logical*, are *not* the names of anything and must, therefore, be interpreted differently. The connectives, for instance, they interpret by truth conditions (the so-called truth tables). This was in fact of tremendous importance to them. So I am not a little surprised by Urmson writing at least once (p. 95) as if he didn't know that. Perhaps it is merely a slip of the pen. Even so, it is significant. What it signifies is that Oxford has either repressed or forgotten a philosophical problem that was to all classical analysts of burning interest, namely, the ex-

---

[9] Confirmation of this diagnosis comes from Italy, where a keen and intelligent interest in recent and contemporary British and American philosophy is part of a remarkable cultural recovery. As far as I know, the bulk of this literature appears in three journals, *Rassegna di filosofia*, *Rivista di filosofia*, *Rivista critica di storia della filosofia*. With the historical astuteness that is part of their heritage, these newcomers discover similarity upon similarity between instrumentalism and Oxford. Some also stress the continuity with Hegel, perhaps in the hope of making the importations more palatable. Most recently still another twist, depressingly foreseeable, has been added. Oxford's casuistic approach and its emphasis on "ordinary language" are said to secure *la storicità e l'umanità* that are so dear to Italian philosophers.

plication of the nature of deductive logic (analyticity), i.e., of logic in the traditional sense, not in the all-comprehensive sense in which 'logic' is now used at Oxford. The matter will come up again. For the rest, since I must limit myself and since Urmson ignores the problem, I too shall ignore it in this study.[10]

The primitives of an improved language are in an obvious sense its simples. There is in each language still another kind of simplicity. Some sentences remain sentences if one omits from them one or several strings, each consisting of one or several consecutive words, without changing the order of the remaining ones. Sentences not remaining sentences if a word is omitted are called *atomic*. If, as in all known cases, an improved language contains both logical and nonlogical words, two kinds of atomic sentences can be distinguished. Call an atomic sentence that contains only nonlogical words *atomic in the narrower sense;* one that contains at least one logical word, *atomic in the broader sense.* Consider as illustration an improved language of the *Principia Mathematica* (PM) kind. Let 'a', 'b'; 'f_1', 'r_1'; 'F_1' stand for nonlogical primitives of type zero, one, two, respectively. '$f_1(a)$', '$r_1(a, b)$', '$F_1(f_1)$' are all atomic in the narrower sense. '$(x)f_1(x)$' is atomic in the broader sense. To understand the last example, one must understand that '$f_1(x)$' is not a sentence. In the formalisms mathematicians study, such expressions are often called sentences. This is technical jargon by which one must not be misled. In a language only closed expressions are sentences. It will be expedient and save words if in the sequel I replace 'atomic in the narrower sense' and 'atomic in either the narrower or the broader sense' by 'atomic' and 'atomic₁', respectively.

II

Urmson knows of course that, as he uses the phrase, Logical Atomism is not one proposition but many. Yet he misses some distinctions which he might have noticed had he used the phrase less freely. I shall now without either asserting or denying any of them state several propositions, investigate their connections or lack of such, then base a string of explications (reconstructions) on them. Since they are all involved in "Logical Atomism," I shall guard against the dangers of the phrase by avoiding it, except occasionally for demonstration purposes. Instead, I shall associate each of these propositions with a letter symbol. It will save bulk if I write 'L' for 'ideal language'.

---

[10] As I introduced them here, the appellations 'logical' and 'nonlogical' are mere names. Their justification lies in the role they play in the classical analysts' admirable but not quite adequate attempts to explicate analyticity, which I decided to ignore in this study. For the inadequacy of Wittgenstein's attempt, see MLP3; for the role it plays in his ontology, Section Four below.

A_1. *L contains no primitive pseudopredicates.*
A_2. *L contains no nonlogical primitive pseudopredicates.*

Let 'p_1' and 'p_2' be any two sentences of L, 'α' and 'β' two primitives such that 'αp_1' and '$p_1 \beta p_2$' are both sentences. 'α' is called a modifier; 'β', a connector of sentences. A pseudopredicate is, by definition, a modifier or connector of sentences that is not a connective. A_1 is obviously stronger than A_2.

A_3. *Every sentence of L is a truth function of atomic sentences.*
A_4. *Every sentence of L is a truth function of atomic$_1$ sentences.*
A_5. *Every sentence of L is a truth function of every sentence occurring in it.*

A_3 is stronger than A_4 which is in turn stronger than A_5 which is equivalent to A_1. '$(x)f_1(x)$' and '$(\exists x)f_1(x)$' are not truth functions of atomic sentences. A_3 is therefore false for all L that contain the lower functional calculus. More interestingly, perhaps, A_4, too, is false in this case. To see that, consider (1) '$(\exists x)[f_1(x) \cdot f_2(x)]$', (2) '$(\exists x)f_1(x)$', (3) '$(\exists x)f_2(x)$'.[11] Since (1) *contains* both (2) and (3), it is not atomic$_1$. Yet it is not a truth function of atomic$_1$ sentences. On the other hand, neither (2) nor (3) *occurs* in (1). Because of this difference between occurring and being contained, A_5 holds not only in the lower functional calculus but in any language, call it PM′, obtained from *Principia Mathematica* (PM) by adding nonlogical primitives.

The next three propositions assume that every atomic sentence of L is of the subject-predicate form. (As I use the term, predicates may be relational.) It would be easy to weaken this condition, but the game is not worth the candle. In case A_1 holds for L the parenthetical clauses in A_7 and A_8 can be suppressed.

A_6. *L contains particulars.*

Unless it is a pseudopredicate, a nonlogical primitive of L occurs either in subject or in predicate places. If nothing else has been said, it may therefore, either in different sentences or even in the same, appear in either place. Or, L may be so constructed that it contains nonlogical primitives which occur only in subject places. A particular is, by definition, a nonlogical primitive of this kind. Notice, first, that I use 'particular' syntactically, not philosophically. Notice, second, that the definition does not presuppose a Russellian theory of types in L. Notice, third, that one could be an "atomist" in the sense of using the method,

---

[11] Assume the operator to be primitive.

"accepting" P, and asserting A_1 and yet consistently deny A_6. An example of such an L is easily constructed. The type hierarchy of PM' is of the order type 0, 1, 2, ... Supplement PM' with variables and nonlogical primitives so that the hierarchy is of the order type . . . -2, $-1, 0, 1, 2,$ . . . . Since what matters logically in PM is not the absolute order numbers but merely the "width" of a sentence, i.e., the difference between the highest and the lowest type occurring in it, this addition requires no change in logic (in the narrower, not Oxford's sense of logic). It is worth realizing how different from ours a world could be in which both P and our logic hold. One who does realize that will not easily use 'atomic' as broadly as Urmson.

A_7. (*Unless they are pseudopredicates*) *the nonlogical primitives of L are all particulars.*

A_8. (*Unless they are pseudopredicates*) *the nonlogical primitives of L are all either particulars or occur only in predicate places taking particulars as subjects.*

A_7 and A_8 require no explanation. The first is of course stronger than the second. There are no deductive connections, either jointly or singly, between the two classes A_1, A_2, A_3, A_4, A_5, and A_6, A_7, A_8. I turn to the promised string of explications, associating each with a letter symbol and marking each philosophical use to be explicated by italicizing the word or phrase on its first occurrence.

E_1. A *fact* (*state of affairs*) is what is referred to by a sentence of L. An *atomic fact* (state of affairs) is what is referred to by an atomic sentence of L. 'State of affairs' has the virtue, if it be a virtue to make philosophical uses sound less strained, that in the case of a false sentence it grates less to speak of states of affairs not being the case or not prevailing. E_2. An *existent* is what *exists*. The proposed explication: An existent is what is or could be named by a nonlogical primitive of L. To explain first the 'could', what could be so named depends of course on how the philosopher construes, with an eye on his purpose, the 'presented' in P. This I deliberately left open, stipulating only that he remain within the limits of common sense. His purpose, to repeat, is to show that his improved language is ideal. As to the adequacy of the explication,[12] the philosophical uses of 'exist' are ontological. Ontology is above all the search for "simples," simples that are "things," neither

---

[12] As Russell knew, who invented this reconstruction but did not hold fast to it, it illuminates most strikingly the realism-phenomenalism controversy. For the mind-body tangle, see MLP6. One may wonder whether it works equally well for ontologies containing subsistents (eternal things, nonexistents). It works in the case of Leibniz. See "Russell's Examination of Leibniz Examined," *Philosophy of Science*, 23, 1956, 175–203, and also pp. 155–88 of this book.

too broadly facts nor too narrowly individuals (see below). The non-logical primitives of an improved language are those of its primitives that name things. To say about a thing that it is or could be named by a linguistic simple of the ideal language is to explicate the ontological use of 'simple' and, at the same time, say something about this thing.[13] E_3. There are no *internal relations*. Reconstructed, this thesis asserts A_2. E_4. An *individual* is what is or could be named by a particular. The explication adds weight to what has been said about A_6. The method, P, and A_5 jointly do not imply that there are individuals, or, as is often said with a philosophical use of 'particular', that there are "particulars." E_5. Only individuals exist. This is the thesis of "nominalism." I reconstruct it as asserting A_7. "Elementarism" reconstructed asserts A_8.

III

So far I have not asserted a single philosophical proposition. Now I shall state what I believe to be true. This gives me two opportunities; the opportunity, first, of saying what I shall presently need in the way I shall need it; the opportunity, second, of demonstrating in a case I know rather intimately the several senses in which one can consistently be a "logical atomist" without being one in others. According to the method, this statement, like any such statement, must answer two questions. Which things are named or could be named by the nonlogical primitives of my L? What is the syntax of this L? The first question naturally divides into two. How do I construe the 'presented' in P? Which things do I find thus presented to me?

'Presented' I construe as 'wholly presented in an act of direct acquaintance'. In this sense of the phrase, we are directly acquainted only with mental or, as one says, phenomenal things, such as percepts, but not with physical objects. Oxford demurs. Who mentions mental things speaks philosophically and not, as I insisted one must when specifying P, commonsensically. I disagree. Does one who mentions a memory image speak philosophically? Of course not. Oxford retorts that one can in the language of seeming and appearing speak about mental things without ever mentioning a single one. Of course one can.[14] This

---

[13] Concerning the objection from a plurality of ideal languages, see below, Section Four.

[14] This is the sort of thing which it is now fashionable at Oxford to prove with the utmost of care and circumstantiality. That is part of what makes for the tedium. Besides, philosophical analysis of the "logic" of seeming and appearing leads very quickly to the common sense root of the realism-phenomenalism issue. Moore, Broad, and Price knew and explained that very well. (It will have been noticed that when I use 'logic' as it is used at Oxford I quarantine the word by double quotes.)

is wholly beside the point. He who eliminates by nonphilosophical linguistic analysis the nonphilosophical uses of words that have also been used philosophically merely prevents himself from discovering the philosophical problems. Nothing illustrates more strikingly the nihilism of Oxford.

I am directly acquainted with such things as, e.g., sensa and some of the characters they exemplify; roughly and briefly, with all those things the *left* wing of the empiricist tradition claimed to be directly acquainted with. But I also find among the things wholly presented to me individual awarenesses and, among the characters these individuals exemplify, knowings, doubtings, rememberings, meanings, and so on. Only the *right* wing of the empiricist tradition claimed to be directly acquainted with this sort of thing. Urmson, very deplorably, uses 'empiricist' so that only the left wing would be empiricist, thus excluding, on this ground alone, Locke, the Scotch school, Brentano, and G. E. Moore. In this he follows uncritically the persuasive use of the classical analysts.[15]

Among the things wholly presented to me are characters. For instance, when I have a green sensum, two things are wholly presented to me, namely, first, an individual, the sensum, which I name by a particular, and, second, a character exemplified by this individual which, since I recognize it from a previous presentation, I call by the name I gave it before. Notice, though, that in any improved language (one could say, in any language) the nonlogical primitives are all "mere labels." In this respect it makes no difference whatsoever that the things named by the particulars of my ideal language do not happen to recur.

I turn to the syntax of my L. From what has just been said it is clear that I accept A_6, reject A_7 (nominalism). I also believe that A_8 (elementarism) is true. This, however, is not important. More precisely, if I found that I had to abandon A_8, I would not on this ground alone have to change any other of my views. That is perhaps of some importance, since it reveals a structural connection, quite independently of who believes what. I reject A_1, assert A_2. Specifically, my L contains one and only one logical pseudopredicate. It transcribes the meaning 'means' has in such sentences as 'the *proposition* . . . means . . .', uttered on occasions when we do not wish to mention either

---

[15] There is rhyme to this unreason. To run with the left wing, we shall presently see, prevents one from having an adequate philosophy of mind. Thus one is pushed toward philosophical behaviorism. Oxford, too, is implicitly behaviorist. The false radicalism of the left wing springs, in an intriguingly complex yet lucid pattern, from the Epicurean root of the empiricist tradition. See MLP17.

psychological matters or what the *sentences* of a natural language refer to. Sentences of L containing this logical pseudopredicate are not truth functions of all the sentences that occur in them. This is why I must reject A_5. These sentences, however, are the only ones which violate A_5. On the other hand, the pseudopredicate occurs only in the transcriptions of what one says when speaking *non*behavioristically about minds. It follows that A_5 holds for "almost all" of my L. In a formal sense, the difference is thus small. Philosophically, I submit, it is the difference between an adequate and an inadequate philosophy of mind.[16]

Now for the promised demonstration of the dangers of the phrase "Logical Atomism." As Urmson uses it, I am a "logical atomist" because (1) I practice the method; (2) I accept P, whatever it may mean to accept the obvious; and assert (3) A_2, (4) A_6, and (5) A_8. I am not a "logical atomist" because I reject (a) $A_5(A_1)$, (b) A_3, (c) A_4, and (d) A_7. With one exception, Urmson ignores all these distinctions. He recognizes the difference between A_3 and A_4, though none too clearly, since he misses that between A_4 and A_5.

The classical analysts all suffered from four grave weaknesses. They invented the method and on occasion practiced it superbly. But they did not see it either steadily or whole. The fully articulated idea of reconstruction escaped them. This made them all unreconstructed metaphysicians; either overtly, as in Russell's case; or paradoxically, as in Wittgenstein's before he threw away the ladder. This is their first weakness. Urmson agrees that they were metaphysicians. As metaphysicians, virtually all of them were or tended to be phenomenalists. In other words, they chose for what I believe were on the whole the right reasons, the construction I put on P. Urmson thinks that a weakness. I don't. But, since they could not hold on to the glimpse they had of the method, they were at times tempted to say such things as that physical objects did not exist or were logical constructions without remembering that in such statements 'exist' and 'logical construction' are used philosophically. This both Urmson and I consider a weakness. It is of course but an example of the first weakness.

In the style of the left wing the classical analysts all arbitrarily ignored some of the things that are wholly presented to us. This is their second weakness. I rather doubt whether (given their frame of reference) Urmson agrees. Very probably not; for this weakness is structurally related to and, I suggest, a partial cause of a third, to which Oxford fell heir. The classical analysts all either were or tended to be

---

[16] For details see MLP, *passim*, and, at considerable length, "Intentionality."

metaphysical behaviorists.[17] This is their third weakness. They were pushed into it by, among other things, excluding from what is wholly presented to us everything that pertains specifically to mind. Urmson agrees that their metaphysical behaviorism is a weakness. But since Oxford itself, as I shall presently show, is implicitly behavioristic, he naturally misses the structural and historical connection I suggest. So he must cast about for another. He finds it in the classical analysts' commitment to an L not richer than PM' and, therefore, to A_5, which prevents one from transcribing, except behavioristically, such non-truthfunctional statements as 'Peter knows that it rains'. Urmson has a point. There is undoubtedly a structural connection as well as a partial cause. But I think he overestimates it, partly because he misses the one I suggest, partly because of the Oxford distaste for symbolic logic, which tempts him into making PM the scapegoat for all the analysts' sins. One need not share this distaste to insist, as I do, that some of the classical analysts eventually became the servants of the symbolisms they mastered.

The classical analysts all suffered from implicit nominalism. This is their fourth major weakness. They inherited it from both the left and the right wing of the empiricist tradition. Presently we shall see that Urmson points at two sore spots which, as I shall then show, are symptoms of this secret malady. But I shall also argue, from what he says on these two occasions, that he himself is affected by the ailment.

Price[18] in a charming essay once proposed a witty formula. Logical Positivism is Hume plus mathematical logic. Let me say it differently. Classical analysis is Hume's data, an incomplete "ideal" language, and, perhaps most important, the vision of the method. As I see it, the formula for the next step in the empiricist tradition is: all the data, a complete ideal language, and a firm grasp of the method. The men of Oxford did not see this step. That is why they rebelled against the tradition.

IV

Urmson comments specifically and in detail on Wittgenstein's ontology, on his picture theory of language, and on his views about the na-

---

[17] A metaphysical behaviorist asserts that there are no minds without realizing that he is using 'there are', as 'exists', philosophically. The almost pathetic clash between the philosophical behaviorism (materialism) and the phenomenalism of the classical analysts should by now be obvious to everybody. Carnap escaped from it into an implicit realism (physicalism). Russell's waverings are notorious. For some distinctions between the eminent scientific sense and the egregious philosophical nonsense in "behaviorism," see "The Contribution of John B. Watson," *Psychological Review*, 63, 1956, 265–76.

[18] *Horizon*, 1939, no. 109, p. 69.

ture of universals. Following suit, I shall examine Wittgenstein's views on these matters as well as what Urmson says about them. To do that effectively, I must first briefly attend to Wittgenstein's logic or, what amounts virtually to the same thing, the syntax of his L.

What was the L Wittgenstein proposed? A precise answer is not easy. Everyone agrees, though, that his L contained the lower functional calculus. He therefore ought to have rejected A_3. Again, everyone agrees that he nevertheless embraced A_3 and tried to gloss over the difficulty by "construing" *all-* and *some*-sentences as infinite conjunctions and disjunctions, respectively. Urmson rehearses the obvious objection to this dodge. Every sentence of L is of finite length; yet there might be an infinite number of individuals. Two other objections, which Urmson does not mention, go deeper. Granting, for the sake of the argument, that a complete enumeration, finite or infinite, has been achieved, how could we ever know that it was complete? Even granting that we know it to be complete, mere conjunction or disjunction does not, as 'all' and 'some' do, either state or imply this completeness. In the circumstances, one must search for the structural reasons and intellectual motives behind Wittgenstein's strange insistence on A_3. Urmson finds them in Wittgenstein's ontology. Presently I shall examine the merit of his diagnosis. First, though, I want to suggest another reason (and probable motive) which he misses.

As I mentioned before, the classical analysts were *all* greatly preoccupied with finding a satisfactory interpretation for the logical primitives of their L; a satisfactory interpretation being one that permits an adequate explication of the nature of analyticity or logical truth (in the narrower sense). All details of execution apart, in the case of the connectives Wittgenstein had hit upon the heart of the matter, namely, the truth tables. In the case of the quantifiers, the key is what is now known as validity theory. When the *Tractatus* was written, validity theory was as yet unborn. This alone suffices to account for Wittgenstein's reluctance to admit quantifiers as logical primitives. As I also mentioned before, Oxford has lost sight of the classical analysts' preoccupation with logic. Small wonder, then, that Urmson misses this reason and, very probably, motive. So he must cast about for others. He finds them in an interpretation of Wittgenstein's ontology which, as I shall now try to show, is in itself questionable, to say the least. I say questionable rather than wrong, because this is not the place for detailed textual criticism and exegesis. I grant that Urmson could quote some passages in support of his view. A massive preponderance of evidence, I believe, favors mine.[19] This, I said, I shall not show. But

[19] E.g., 2.01, 2.02, 2.027.

I also believe that my view, unlike Urmson's, agrees with the spirit of the *Tractatus* as well as with that of the ontological enterprise. About this, naturally, I shall have something to say.

Ontology, we remember, is the search for simples, in some philosophical sense of 'simple', of which "everything else" consists, in some philosophical sense of 'consist'. Urmson's explication of Wittgenstein's ontology has two parts. (*a*) A "simple" is an atomic state of affairs which is the case, or, what amounts to the same thing, what a *true* atomic sentence (of *L*) refers to. (*b*) "Everything consists of simples" means that every statement of fact, either true or false, is a truth function of atomic statements, either true or false. Upon this explication A_3 is indeed crucial. The explication I propose, in agreement with E_2, has no parts. A "simple" is what is named or could be named by a nonlogical primitive (of *L*). Upon this explication A_3 becomes ontologically irrelevant. (Wittgenstein, we remember, had another plausible reason for clinging to A_3.) Also, I can do without a separate explication of 'consist'. "Everything consists of simples" will naturally be taken to mean that no logical word (of the proposed *L*) names anything.

Now for three nontextual reasons why I consider Urmson's explication inadequate. *One*. According to Wittgenstein, Urmson agrees, even atomic states of affairs have "constituents." The referent of 'ar_1b', for instance, has three, two individuals and one (relational) character. Whatever has constituents patently is not simple! *Two*. Notice the jarring necessity of introducing the qualifying 'true' into (*a*), though not into (*b*). Urmson agrees that it jars; so I shall not explain why it does. But, alas, he also blames Wittgenstein for a shortcoming that is merely one of his own inadequate explication. *Three*. The "simples" ontologists look for always were and still are "things" and not "facts." I conclude that in explicating Wittgenstein as he does, Urmson imputes to him three grave and implausible lapses of style. My admiration for the author of the *Tractatus* leads me to plead that even if the evidence Urmson could adduce were much stronger than I believe it to be, he should be given the benefit of the doubt. Generally, I find no satisfaction whatsoever in putting the most unfavorable of all possible constructions upon any classical text. But then, I do not have to prove, as they do at Oxford, that all metaphysics is nonsense.

A sentence (of *L*) shows, by sharing it, the *logical structure of the state of affairs* to which it refers. This is the gist of Wittgenstein's *picture theory*. Urmson's statement of it is admirably to the point. So is his diagnosis of the intellectual motive behind it. "What metaphysicians try to say is ineffable; it merely shows itself. In particular, they try in vain to describe the world's structure. This structure shows itself in

L; but, since one cannot properly speak about L, it remains ineffable."[20] Urmson rejects the theory as metaphysical. Again, I agree that as it stands it needs reconstruction. Against this helpful background of triple agreement I shall now show four things. First. Properly explicated, the theory becomes in one respect tautological and, therefore, ontologically trivial. Second. It has a core which is true and neither tautological nor trivial. Third. Urmson partly misses, partly misunderstands this nontrivial core. Fourth. Accurate understanding of the theory leads to the refutation of a criticism of both it and the method in general. Urmson, who rehearses the criticism, thinks it unanswerable.

First. The phrase italicized in the first sentence of the last paragraph is used philosophically. Thus it must be explicated. I explicate it to mean the syntactical structure of the sentence referring to the state of affairs in question. To understand the notion of syntactical structure, consider once more 'ar_1b'. It is a sequence of three marks, from left to right; a mark whose shape makes it, by definition, a particular; followed by a mark whose shape makes it, by definition, a two-term predicate of the first type; followed by a different particular. This and nothing else is the syntactical structure of 'ar_1b'. The notion is thus commonsensical, not philosophical. It refers to a (kind of) physical pattern; in the case of a written language, to a geometrical design. Thus explicated, the "theory" becomes tautological.

Second. Take any sentence (of L) containing nonlogical primitives, say, Hume's paradigm of a law, '$(x)[f_1(x) \supset f_2(x)]$'; replace all its nonlogical primitives ('f_1', 'f_2') by variables of the proper types ('f', 'g'); define '$R_1(f, g)$' as '$(x)[f(x) \supset g(x)]$'. 'R_1' refers to a logical relation[21] of the second type. What has been done in this case can be done in all cases. It follows that the *constituents of two states of affairs exemplify the same logical relation if and only if the sentences referring to them exemplify the same syntactical structure.* This is the nontrivial core of the theory. I don't think that Wittgenstein himself saw it clearly.

Third. Urmson characteristically bases his comments on a sentence (3.1432) which, as I read the *Tractatus*, is merely an isolated and accidental blunder. Assume the particulars to be blocks; the two-term relational predicates, flat discs; make the linear order vertical downwards; replace consecutiveness by contiguity. In this peculiar language

[20] These are, in spite of the quotation marks, my words, not Urmson's. But I have no doubt that he would concur.

[21] A logical relation is a defined relation in the definiens of which no nonlogical primitive occurs. For simplicity's sake I limit myself here to sentences that contain only primitives. The limitation is easily done away with. Nor is there in all this any limitation to atomic sentences.

we have, instead of 'ar_1b', the sentence: block resting on disc resting on block. Urmson claims, first, that the "sentence" does not exemplify the logical structure of the fact, and, second, that this structure would be exemplified by one block resting on (or being in a certain direction at a certain distance from) another. In this he makes two related mistakes. He confuses the character ordinarily named by 'r_1' and, in our peculiar language, by the disc, with a syntactical (geometrical) character exemplified by our peculiar names. And he confuses a character of this latter kind, namely, a syntactical (geometrical) relation exemplified by the names, with the logical relation exemplified by the things named. His mistakes are interesting for two reasons. For one, if I may for once speak allusively, they show that the ghost of Bradley's famous conundrum still walks in Oxford. For another, the reluctance to have characters named by nonlogical primitives ('r_1', or the disc), thus putting them in this respect on a par with individuals, betrays symptomatically an implicit nominalism.

Fourth. If there are several ideal languages, the "structure" of which among them is that of the "world"? This is the root of the criticism Urmson thinks fatal. *Mutatis mutandis* it can be directed at the method as such. Assume for the sake of the argument that there are several L.[22] Since they can all serve as ideal languages, they all have the same expressive possibilities. Hence certain isomorphisms must obtain among their syntactical (geometrical) structures. This use of 'isomorphism' is commonsensical (geometrical) and not philosophical. The detailed exploration of the isomorphism involved can therefore safely be left to the mathematical logicians. Philosophically relevant are of course only those syntactical features of *an L* which, as one says, are invariants of this isomorphism. The objection thus suggests a certain mathematical sophistication in the formulation of the method. After the sophistication has been introduced,[23] the objection collapses.

Wittgenstein's individuals are rudimentary Aristotelian substances. This is Urmson's third major comment on Wittgenstein. He has a point. His argument is based on Wittgenstein's claim that some such sentences as 'Nothing is (at the same time all over) red and blue' are analytic or, as one so misleadingly says, linguistic truths. Again, Wittgenstein does make this claim. It is, as I believe I can show, inconsistent with the

[22] There obviously are, at least in the sense that the sentences of two symbolisms which look at first sight quite different, such as PM and Quine's version of it in *Mathematical Logic*, can be put into one-one correspondence with all deductive connections preserved.

[23] MLP, p. 43; also "Two Criteria for an Ideal Language," *Philosophy of Science*, 16, 1949, 71–74.

bulk of what he says and therefore one of the major blemishes of the *Tractatus*, but it is certainly not merely an accidental blunder.[24] The issue is subtle; so I shall separate its strands. 1. A substance is or has a nature.[25] Its nature determines the characters it exemplifies and therefore, in particular, which characters are "incompatible" (e.g., green and red), which "necessarily" connected (e.g., being colored and being extended). 2. To insist on the analyticity of the statements in question may be taken for a roundabout way of asserting that individuals are or have natures. If so, then the particulars naming them are indeed not "bare particulars" or "mere labels." 3. Most classical analysts—though not, I think, Wittgenstein, except in those isolated but not accidental passages—fail to recognize a truth on which I insisted before, namely, that all nonlogical primitives, whether they name individuals or characters, are "mere labels." This failure puts them in double jeopardy. On the one hand, they are tempted either to ignore individuals completely[26] or to make them into rudimentary substances. On the other hand, they are prevented from realizing that some characters are sometimes wholly presented to us. This drives them to nominalism. That much for the issue. Urmson, though he senses its structure, does not make it explicit. One reason why he doesn't is that (given the frame of reference) he approves of Wittgenstein's lapse into substantialism. From where I stand the reasons for his approval are not hard to find. Urmson shares Oxford's implicit nominalism and its Hegelian commitment to the logical nature of such truths as that nothing is both red and blue. Of this later.

V

The silence that now virtually blankets Russell's name at Oxford, the failure or unwillingness to do justice to his epochal work shocks me profoundly. One wonders whether the somewhat frenzied revival of Frege is not merely the other side of the same coin.[27] Urmson's account is an honorable exception. Some of the criticisms he directs

[24] This is confirmed by the *Aristotelian Society* paper of 1929. For an analysis of four inconsistencies in the *Tractatus*, see MLP3. [Added in 1959: For a more accurate historical analysis see E. Allaire, "Tractatus 6.3751," to appear in *Analysis*.]

[25] By the difference between *is* and *has* there hangs a tale. For an analysis of the substance notion, see "Russell's Examination of Leibniz Examined."

[26] See the discussion of basic propositions in Section Five.

[27] This is not to deny Frege's historical significance, his ingenuity, and his occasional profundity. To do that would be foolish indeed. Incidentally, Frege was studied closely in Vienna a generation ago; quite properly so, since there was then much more to be learned from him than now.

explicitly against Russell I met implicitly in what went before. Presently I shall attend to what he says and doesn't say about the very peculiar use Russell makes of definite descriptions. First, though, I shall examine two broader issues; the nature of *basic propositions* and the problems of *reconstruction*. Russell thought and wrote about them as much as anyone; yet they are not specifically Russellian. On both of these issues the classical analysts ran into difficulties they could not conquer. On this I agree with Urmson. He also argues that the difficulties are unconquerable. I disagree. To show cause I shall therefore in each case first state the problem and indicate its solution and only then turn to what the classical analysts and Urmson say about it.

'Basic proposition' was used philosophically. Thus it must be explicated. I explicate it to mean *atomic sentence of L*. The phrase, we see, is expendable. If I use it at all, it is only for the sake of continuity. 'Basic' provides the cue for what is involved. The classical analysts set themselves the task of "proving" that veridical basic propositions possess a peculiar and peculiarly excellent kind of "certainty." This was their mistake. The task is not to prove anything, but rather to explicate *one* of the *several*[28] philosophical uses of 'certain'. This can indeed be done by means of the atomic sentences of *L*. The explication has two parts. (*a*) No atomic sentence follows deductively from any other. (*b*) The constituents of an atomic state of affairs, if they are presented to us at all, are wholly presented in an act of direct acquaintance. The strictness of the construction put on P secures the adequacy of the explication. This is *one* of the *several* reasons why P must be so strictly construed. It is also one of the motives for the classical analysts' (unreconstructed) phenomenalism.[29] Urmson diagnoses this motive correctly. I would add that even though explication of the philosophical uses of 'certain' is part of the task, the quest for some superior sort of certainty, which is so prominent in our tradition, did and still does more harm than good. But this is not to say that one cannot avoid the

---

[28] In another philosophical use, certain is what is analytic. There are still others. Notice also that if certainty were a character of states of affairs rather than of acts, 'certain' would be a (nonlogical) pseudopredicate. This, however, is a finer point which I can safely neglect for my present purpose.

[29] This, as so much else, comes to a head in Russell's *Inquiry into Meaning and Truth*, which appeared shortly after the close of the period Urmson covers in detail. Such generalities as 'nothing is both blue and red' are neither atomic sentences nor deducible from such. In the *Inquiry* Russell wonders whether one who claims to know that this sentence is true is still an "empiricist." Thus he identifies empiricism with some sort of skepticism, which is one of the two silliest of all philosophies. (The other is materialism.)

errors caused by the preoccupation with "certainty" without going to the extreme of rejecting P.

The troubles the classical analysts ran into with basic propositions have a common root in their implicit nominalism. More specifically, their troubles can all be traced to *three themes*. 1. They worried about the "communicability" of basic propositions. 2. One attempt to secure "certainty" succeeded only too well by seeming to make these propositions into "tautologies." 3. Another attempt led to "doubt" about their certainty.

Ad 1. The language in which we communicate with each other consists (in the spoken case) of physical noises emitted by physical objects, i.e., our bodies, in the direction of other such objects, i.e., the bodies of those whom we address. Thus, even if L were what it is not,[30] namely (the skeleton of) the inner monologue, it could not conceivably be the language in which we communicate with each other. *About* this latter language we can "speak" in L, but only after reconstructing in L (see below) the world of physical objects and events, including behavioristic psychology. Once this is understood, the worry about the "communicability" of *any* sentence of L vanishes. The classical analysts did not understand this. Had they been consistent phenomenalists, they would therefore have worried about the communicability of *all* sentences of L. What then, one must ask, is the special feature of atomic sentences that caused them to worry just about these sentences? The answer is not difficult. Every atomic sentence contains at least one particular. The classical analysts thought that particulars were the only "mere labels." The idea of a label leads to that of pointing. Naturally one cannot point at phenomenal things for the benefit of others. So one cannot "communicate" about "particulars." I explained before the connections between nominalism on the one hand and, on the other, the error that only particulars are mere labels combined with an unresolved distrust of all mere labels. *Ad* 2. Assume that one who shares the illusion that 'a' is and 'f_1' is not a mere label starts from '$f_1(a)$'. Since he distrusts mere labels, he somehow suppresses the particular. The remaining predicate is of course no longer a sentence referring to a state of affairs but a mere label naming a character. Our friend, however, not too alert to any of these distinctions, thinks that he is still dealing with the sentence from which he started. The error leads to another. He now thinks of that sentence itself as merely a label attached to a state of affairs. This is absurd; states of affairs have no

[30] See note 4.

names. Again, our friend is not aware of the absurdity. Nor does he grasp firmly that whether or not a sentence is a tautology depends on its syntactical structure and on nothing else. But he remembers that in attaching a label one cannot possibly go wrong. So he "concludes" that what he still mistakes for the sentence from which he started cannot possibly be false and is therefore a "tautology." *Ad* 3. This theme is the converse of the second. Those who followed it accepted particulars as mere labels but felt that predicates were more than just that. Thus they were led to believe that an atomic sentence refers to something more than could ever be wholly presented in an act of direct acquaintance. This belief caused them, quite understandably, to question the "certainty" of basic propositions. Failure to recognize that some characters are wholly presented to us is of course a major source of nominalism.

These are the three themes. The classical analysts all made either one or several of the mistakes connected with them. Urmson very astutely senses the importance of the themes. He does not see how one can decline these gambits and thereby avoid the mistakes. So he argues that the difficulties the classical analysts could not conquer are unconquerable.

Reconstruction is what Carnap called *Aufbau*.[31] Consider physical objects, say, chairs. No physical object is ever wholly presented to us in an act of direct acquaintance. It follows that in an *L* such as the classical analysts' (or mine) nonlogical primitives cannot serve as the names of physical objects. The task of reconstruction is to design in *L* the definitions of terms that can so serve. Since Urmson falters on this occasion, let me recall that all reconstruction is schematic or, as one says, in principle only. Anything else exceeds our strength. For all philosophical purposes, though, i.e., for the explication and solution of all philosophical problems, the schema suffices. A reconstructionist might even turn the tables on certain of his critics by adducing, correctly I think, the very impossibility of reconstruction in detail as a partial explication of what they mean when, speaking philosophically, they insist that "a real chair is more than a collection of sensa." Be that as it may, even schematic reconstruction has more philosophically relevant features than I could possibly touch on in this study. Some of these features the classical analysts did not understand. Or they did not understand them very well. Thus they ran into problems they could not solve. Urmson thinks these problems are insoluble. My best plan,

---

[31] This use of 'reconstruct' and its derivations is of course different from that in 'a reconstructed philosophical proposition'.

therefore, is to select the features connected with these problems. It will save bulk if I stick to chairs and write '*ch*' for the definiendum whose definiens the reconstruction must provide.

First I shall introduce a few symbols (A); then attend to their interpretation (B); then propose a schematic definition of '*ch*'(C); then explore what can be learned from it (D). The schema (C) does not make explicit all the features that can, and for certain purposes must, be made explicit. Thus it is most schematic indeed. Yet, what can be learned from it will suffice to conquer the difficulties Urmson thinks are unconquerable. This must of course be shown. If I can show it, then I shall also have shown, in an instance, why reconstruction in principle suffices. And this is the sort of thing that can only be shown by exhibiting instances.

(A) Write '*a*' and '$(\exists x)$' as abbreviations for '$a_1, a_2, \ldots a_n$' and '$(\exists x_1, x_2, \ldots x_n)$' respectively. Similarly, let '*y*' and '$\{y\}$' stand for a series of *m* variables all different from $x_1, x_2, \ldots x_n$ though not necessarily all of type zero and for a prefix binding all these variables but consisting of both kinds of operators, respectively. Let '*chp*' and '*chl*' be molecular predicate expressions such that '*chp(a)*' and '$\{y\}chl(a, y)$' are (closed) sentences. It follows that '$(\exists x)[chp(x) \cdot \{y\}chl(x, y)]$' is also a (closed) sentence. (B) Let '*chp(a)*' be the sentence referring to what is called the sensory core of a (schematic) chair percept. Let '$\{y\}chl(a, y)$' be a generality stating (schematically) what other individuals there are and the relations in which they must stand to each other and to $a_1, a_2 \ldots a_n$ if what '*chp(a)*' refers to is (the sensory core of) a veridical chair percept.[32] (C) Define

$$\text{'}ch(x)\text{'} \quad \text{as} \quad \text{'}chp(x) \cdot \{y\}chl(x, y)\text{'}.$$

(D) 1. If '*ch*' transcribes in principle the English word "chair," then the transcriptions of "There are chairs" and "This is a chair" are '$(\exists x)ch(x)$' and '*ch(a)*', respectively. Notice, first, that '*ch*' *is a predicate*, and, second, that *L contains no terms, either primitive or defined, that refer to individual chairs*. 2. '*ch(x)*' is essentially the conjunction of a molecular and a law statement. The latter manages to state what it does only because it contains predicates referring to spatial and temporal relations.[33] 3. The second conjunction term of '*ch(a)*' thus states, as it must, that there are individuals it does not mention which stand in certain relations among themselves and to certain others which it

---

[32] '$\{y\}$' may contain predicate variables. If it does, it may not be possible to gather the operators into a prefix. This, however, is merely a technicality. For some details, see MLP7.

[33] Rather detailed analyses, about as detailed as one can reasonably expect, have been given by Price and Ayer.

mentions. But there is no reason whatsoever why it should also contain (the schematic reconstruction of) the statement that there are individuals with which I or Jones or anybody else will be acquainted or would be acquainted if certain conditions, in turn to be schematically reconstructed, were fulfilled.

Urmson rehearses quite a few of the usual objections. Two of them he thinks are unanswerable. He reminds us, first, that whether or not a physical object is ever perceived, or under certain conditions would be perceived, either by myself or by anybody else is wholly extraneous to its being what it is, namely, a physical object, and that, therefore, a reconstruction is not even in principle adequate unless it does justice to this feature. Quite so. He adds that every "phenomenalistic" reconstruction must in this respect be inadequate. Let us see. Berkeley's first crude sketch of the idea certainly was. Nor did the classical analysts know how to rid their reconstructions of the Berkeleyan flavor. As far as they are concerned Urmson therefore has a point. The reason why they did not know how to solve this problem is, once more, that, not having learned the lesson Moore tried to teach them, they did not know how to distinguish between there being something and this something being sensed or perceived by somebody. Thus they couldn't get rid of Jones. That the problem is in fact soluble I have shown in D2 and D3 above.[34]

Urmson's second major objection is more interesting. A chair, to put the matter with Berkeleyan crudeness, is a pattern exemplified by an infinity of individuals. Urmson believes that even if this kind of infinity could in principle be controlled by the quantifiers in the second conjunction term, there is still another kind to which no reconstruction, either "phenomenalistic" or otherwise, could possibly do justice. For this argument the differences between English and L make no difference; so I shall write 'chair' instead of 'ch'. There is an infinite (more precisely, indefinite) number of true generalities in which 'chair' occurs. Chairs do not talk. Chairs do not leave their places by themselves. And so on.[35] Now, so the argument begins, all these truths are part of the "meaning" of 'chair'. A reconstruction, it continues, is suc-

---

[34] Urmson expressed the opinion that even if 'ch' could be adequately defined, it would be impossible to transcribe the sentence "There is a chair in this room." Let 'rm(b)' be the transcription of "This is a room." Since it is analogous to that of "This is a chair," we may by hypothesis assume that it is adequate. Let 'sp' be a predicate of the first type stating certain spatial relations among its arguments. '$rm(b) \cdot (\exists x) [ch(x) \cdot sp(x, b)]$' reconstructs in principle the sentence which Urmson claims it is in principle impossible to reconstruct.

[35] Sentences stating that chairs are available for perception, either by myself or by Jones or by anybody else, are of course among these truths.

cessful if and only if the term proposed has by virtue of its definition the same "meaning" as the one it is to replace. Hence, so the argument concludes, what I call the second conjunction term would have to state all these truths; thus it would have to be of infinite length, which is impossible. The way to meet this argument is to challenge the philosophical relevance of this meaning of 'meaning' and to claim, as I do, that its study may safely be left to psychological and historical linguists. Obviously, it is for ever open and growing, and therefore by its very nature not reconstructible. Historically, we recognize in it the "meaning" of the flower in the crannied wall. More soberly, what Urmson wants us to reconstruct is the holistic meaning of the idealists. We have come upon Oxford's second major structural similarity with Hegelianism. The other, we saw, is the rejection of P. More of all this presently.

That much for the two major issues, basic propositions and reconstruction, which, though Russell thought and wrote so much about them, are not specifically Russellian. I turn briefly to the third issue I mentioned at the beginning of this Section, Russell's peculiar use of definite descriptions.

Definite descriptions, Urmson points out, are among Russell's favorite illustrations for what can be achieved by reconstruction. This is correct. Urmson believes that to be misleading. For two reasons this is also correct. *First*, definite descriptions are often employed in cases where what they refer to either could be labeled or is of a kind that could be labeled. Thus they are not good examples of what can be achieved by reconstruction. This reason Urmson sees. *Second.* Defined terms can without further ado be used like undefined ones. Without a familiar existential premise one cannot so use definite descriptions. If one does, he gets into familiar troubles.[36] In this major respect definite descriptions are thus not on a par with definitions; yet reconstruction proceeds by definition. This reason Urmson does not see. Since logic isn't much studied at Oxford, that is perhaps not surprising. It is surprising, though, that while he spends a good deal of time pointing at the mote, he does not see the beam in Russell's eye. So I shall, *third*, point at the beam. As every one knows and as I had occasion to mention, Russell throughout his career chafed against the (unreconstructed) phenomenalism he did not know how to escape. One of the

---

[36] Technically, the identity $'(\imath x)f_1(x) = (\imath x)f_1(x)'$ is not analytic as, of course, it is for all genuine terms. Notice also that, even in a nonextensional calculus, $'\hat{x}f_1(x) = \hat{x}f_1(x)'$ is analytic. By lumping both these cases under the common heading of incomplete symbols Russell fathered a confusion of which we still have to see the last.

false leads he followed again and again he found in definite descriptions. The physical object, though it cannot be named, can be referred to by a definite description. Now there is indeed no reason why, say, '*ch*' could not be replaced by a definite description.[37] This, however, is not what Russell meant. What he expected definite description to yield were substitutes for particulars naming individual physical objects. This makes no sense for two reasons. For one, physical objects are not the sort of things that could, in his *L* and upon his construction of P, be named by particulars. For another, we saw (D1 above) that *L* does not and need not contain any terms or expressions referring to individual physical objects.

VI

The classical analysts and their Oxford critics, including Urmson' all fail to distinguish among several uses, philosophical and otherwise' of 'meaning'. In the case of the critics this is profoundly ironical. For, do they not propound that meaning is use and therefore, varying with the latter, could not possibly be univocal? As to meaning itself, there is, first, the idea of a meaning *criterion*, i.e., of a criterion by which to decide which utterances *have* meaning. There are, second, the several *theories*[38] as to what meaning *is*, or, as I would rather say, the explications of the several uses of 'meaning'. There is, third, the claim made for one of these explications, the so-called reference theory, which, with a different emphasis, goes by the name of *verification theory*. This theory explicates quite adequately *one* of the several uses of 'meaning'. It does not explicate *the* meaning of 'meaning', for the very good reason that there is no such thing. Some classical analysts who thought that there was, also thought that the reference theory was its explication. For this they should be criticized. Oxford, however, whose theory of meaning is just as monolithic,[39] does not criticize them on this ground. Rather, it criticizes the reference theory as such. Its real target, though, is once more the "presupposition" I called P. This is the outline of my argument. Now for some details.

One who states a meaning criterion specifies, whether he knows it or not, the syntax and the nonlogical primitive vocabulary of an improved language which he claims to be ideal. Since the classical analysts knew this after a fashion, they did not really use 'meaning criterion'

---

[37] Of a higher type, as in 'the color of my daughter's eyes'.

[38] The use of 'theory' for both philosophical doctrines and scientific theories invites confusion and should therefore be avoided. But it will do no harm and simplify the exposition if I for once follow the practice.

[39] See Section Seven.

philosophically but, rather, commonsensically about philosophy. The confusion they nevertheless produced, in their own minds and others', by their use of the phrase stems for the most part from their failure to distinguish between a criterion and a theory. This is one thing. The inadequacy of the criterion, or, less confusingly, of the ideal language which the classical analysts proposed is another thing. This inadequacy, we saw, stems from their left-wing radicalism, which caused them to exclude everything specifically mental from the things named by the nonlogical primitives of their L. There is a hackneyed argument that refutes the "positivistic" criterion by showing that it is meaningless by its own standard. Of course it is. But why bother? Is it not much more telling that by this standard all statements about minds, our own and others', are also meaningless? Few victories are more demoralizing for the victor than those won with big guns over little sparrows. Urmson expounds with considerable zest and relish the hackneyed refutation.

There are many meanings of 'meaning'. Four of them are of special importance in first philosophy. Each of them occurs in ordinary as well as in (unreconstructed) philosophical discourse.[40] No classical analyst clearly grasped all four; all classical analysts failed at times to distinguish clearly even among those they knew. This was another source of their errors. Two of these four meanings I cannot and need not discuss in this study. One of them I call *logical*. In this use, two sentences (of L) have the same meaning if and only if they are analytically equivalent. The other is the *intentional* meaning I have mentioned before[41] and transcribe by the one logical pseudopredicate of my L. At the two remaining uses we must look more closely.

Meaning is *context*. This is the gist of the context theory. Upon this explication the meaning of a mental content, say, the percept of a word, phrase, or sentence, is the response it elicits in the perceiver. Among these responses there are or may be bodily states, overt bodily actions, and other mental contents, be they auditory images of other words or, perhaps, visual images of things and actions. This is the prebehavioristic variant of the theory. Berkeley, we are told, anticipated it. More recently its most distinguished expositor was Titchener. If you limit the responses which constitute the "context" to overt ones and behavioristically defined bodily states, then you have the behavioristic variant. The latter dominates, quite properly, contemporary psychol-

[40] This is therefore an instance of nonphilosophical blending into philosophical analysis. See Section One.

[41] See note 8. Notice also that, technically, the logical meaning of a sentence *is* a class of such.

ogy. There is no doubt that the theory describes correctly *one* use of 'meaning'. Psychologists, when they speak as psychologists, always use it this way. Notice, for later reference, that this kind of meaning varies with the context. Thus it makes no sense to speak of *the* (contextual) meaning of a word, phrase, or sentence.

Meaning is *reference*. This is the gist of the reference theory. Upon this explication the meaning of the English word "horse" is a certain character exemplified by all horses. The meaning of a sentence is the state of affairs to which it refers. Again, there is no doubt that we all sometimes use 'meaning' this way.[42] To see that the so-called verification theory amounts to the same thing, consider the familiar formula: The meaning of a sentence is the method of its verification. Or, less misleadingly, if we want to find out whether a sentence is true we must somehow make contact with the state of affairs to which it (or its negation) refers. The phrase "somehow make contact" is vague. Yet it will do. For my purpose the many niceties, some of which are very nice indeed, don't matter. It will even do if we limit ourselves to an atomic sentence of L, where there is surely no "method," since the verification is, as one says, immediate and direct. What matters is one thing and one thing only. The theory makes no sense unless one "presupposes" that every sentence of L has one and only one referent.[43] This "presupposition," though it is as we saw not equivalent to P, is yet, as we also saw, very closely related to it. *Oxford rejects the verification, or, rather, the reference theory of meaning because it rejects P.* Urmson makes this rather clear even though, from where I stand, his exposition suffers from two serious defects. He is not aware of any of the distinctions I made; and he feels bound to reject the obvious.

VII

Don't ask for the meaning, ask for the use. Every statement has its own logic. These are, in Urmson's words, the two new slogans. He thinks that they state, however concisely, two major ideas or guiding principles of the movement. I agree. Structurally as well as historically, he further tells us, they are both reactions against the ideas of the classical analysts. I again agree. I even believe that they epitomize

[42] So certainly does a teacher of German who tells us in English that he taught his pupils what "Pferd" means by pointing to a horse while pronouncing the word. *As far as communication is concerned,* his method has of course its limits. Thus its results must be checked by making sure that the pupils acquired the right "referential" contexts. Oxford, under the spell of the second Wittgenstein, makes a mountain out of this molehill.

[43] Remember what was said in Section One about 'It rained in Iowa City on October 12, 1956'.

very aptly all the guiding principles of the movement. There, however, agreement ends. I shall use the first slogan to show that what is being done at Oxford is not philosophy but a curiously twisted kind of psychology of language, even though a gifted follower may occasionally and accidentally, as it were, lapse into philosophy. A person's implicit metaphysics is one he holds and propounds without knowing that he is doing just that. For a philosopher it is, in an obvious sense, the worst of all. I shall use the second slogan to show that implicitly the movement embraces Hegelian idealism, which, even if explicitly held, is very bad metaphysics.

Meaning is use. This is but another current version of the first slogan. More explicitly, if you want to know what a word, phrase, or sentence means, don't look for an entity called its meaning, be it a referent or anything else, but inquire instead how it is used. Oxford thus propounds what I called a monolithic theory of meaning. Nor is there any doubt, from what Urmson says and from what is being said at Oxford, that this "new" theory is one we encountered before, namely, the old context theory. With some honorable exceptions, Oxford embraces the behavioristic variant. This explains why most of what it has to say about language is as tedious and trivial as most of what the behaviorists have as yet been able to say. The cause of this more or less explicit behaviorism is the dislike and distrust, so unhappily prevalent at Oxford,[44] of anything mental.

One who expounds the context theory expounds matters psychological and sociological and nothing else. That is obvious. At least it is obvious to the many philosophers who consider the movement a dead end. Urmson, who is well aware of their opinion, speaks of a breakdown in communication. To say the same thing more gently, we have once more arrived at the limit of "direct" argument. So I shall attempt only two things. First I shall show how my diagnosis fits with what was said before. Then I shall try to explain why the men of the movement do not recognize what they are doing for what it is. The explanation I shall propose will fasten on differences in environment and tradition. Anything else would be invidious. For there are usually brilliant men on both sides of such fences.

The thesis that there are no philosophical propositions is not easily expanded. What passes for its expansion is therefore not likely to be philosophy. Some nihilists among the classical analysts soon became nonphilosophical students of artificial languages with materialism

[44] This trait Oxford shares with some of the classical analysts. I cannot here trace it in detail. But there are some hints scattered through this study. See also MLP, p. 74.

(physicalism) as their implicit metaphysics. At Oxford one cultivates the psychological study of language. The only nihilist whose practice was better than his teaching was the author of the *Tractatus;* and even he succumbed. The contextual meaning of an English word, phrase, or sentence depends on the circumstances in which it is used. So may therefore, if it has one, its referent. This shows how Oxford's espousal of the context theory fits with its rejection of improved languages in which, as we saw, reference does not depend on context. It also fits with the rejection of the reference theory. Uncritically argued, this rejection leads in turn to the Hegelian rejection of P. These are some respects in which my diagnosis that Oxford propounds the psychologists' context theory as still another monolithic theory of meaning fits with what was said before. There are still others. But we need not tarry.

Those who complain that our age is hostile to philosophy merely whistle in the dark. First philosophy has not been the major intellectual concern of any age; it has always been hard pressed by the dominant nonphilosophical concern of the day; this concern has usually been mistaken for philosophy; the latter has usually been blamed for not being what it is not. For quite some time now psychology and, more generally, behavior science has been the dominant intellectual concern. A generation ago, under the influence of Dewey, they were in this country mistaken for philosophy. Instrumentalism is on the wane. Behavior science still dominates the American intellectual scene. Until most recently British academic culture strenuously ignored it.[45] Oxford was and still is the center of this resistance. An analogy comes to mind. Those who repress too long a natural appetite tend to debauch themselves when they finally succumb. Oxford, as I see it, now enjoys its debauch.[46] The style of the revelry is colored by the spirit of the place. This spirit is philosophical rather than scientific and the overt hostility toward behavior science still persists. That is why what is being done is not really science but a kind of armchair psychology which is mistaken for philosophy. The philosophical climate in Britain when the movement first found itself was not speculative but, rather, analytic with the accent on language. That is why what is done is nonphilosophical linguistic analysis. On the continent, where both spirit

---

[45] The only two theoretical psychologists of note Britain has produced since Alexander Bain, E. B. Titchener and William McDougall, both made their careers in this country.

[46] The direction of the export trade in old fallacies on which Broad so caustically commented is thus reversed for once.

and climate are different, the dominant interest takes the even more curious form of the "philosophical anthropology" of the existentialists.[47]

I made it plausible, I think, why Oxford does what it does. I still have to explain what Urmson calls the breakdown in communication by explaining why it cannot see that what it does is psychology. The explanation has two sides, one negative, one positive, as it were. Since *modern* psychology is still a humble newcomer on the British academic scene, the men of Oxford do not really know what it is and does. So they are incredulous when they are told that what they do is logically (I use the word as they do) the same sort of thing. The positive side is of some historical interest. The central problem of *classical* psychology is the so-called decomposition by analytical introspection of all mental contents into introspectively irreducible constituents. This is of course not what they do at Oxford. Yet classical psychology is the only psychology they really know. So they are once more incredulous if they are told that what they do is psychology. Thereby hangs a nice point in historical semantics. The introspectively irreducible constituents of classical introspection are, in an obvious sense, psychological atoms (simples). Some classical psychologists put some quite arbitrary and unrealistic restrictions on the kinds of atoms of which they claimed all mental contents consist.[48] Thus their psychological "atomism" fell into well-deserved disrepute. Probably this is one of the reasons why at Oxford 'atomism' is still a bad word. So it may well be that a lingering distaste for psychological atomism was one of the sources of strength for the revolt against "Logical Atomism."

Every statement has its own logic. This is the second slogan. Negatively, it rejects classical logic as too narrow and vitiatingly abstract. Positively, it claims that there is such a thing as logic, sometimes also called logical grammar. Its task is the clarification of "meaning." Oxford thus maintains the distinction between matters of fact and of logic. This is all to the good. The trouble is that, as Oxford wants to make it, the distinction cannot consistently be made. I shall show in two ways, first how the difficulty arises, then why it is unconquerable.

---

[47] This fits very well with the common Hegelian root of instrumentalism, existentialism, and Oxford. Hegel's greatness, such as it was, lay after all in his intuitive grasp of the socio-psychological (historical) process.

[48] For this they had (mostly implicit) philosophical reasons. See MLP17. The connection with left-wing empiricism (Hume, James Mill) is obvious. For the continuity between Wuerzburg, the last school of classical psychology (except Gestalt) and the Wittgenstein of the *Investigations*, see "Intentionality."

Sometimes, when asserting what is false, we still make sense; we know how to use the language[49] and are merely in factual error. On this we can all agree. But consider now the sentence 'There is something which is (at the same time all over) both red and blue'. Oxford observes that no one who knows (English grammar and) the meanings of (how to use) 'red' and 'blue' is likely to assert this sentence though he may, of course, mention it as a paradigm of nonsense, in some vague and unanalyzed sense of 'nonsense'. As long as not too much is made of the observation, we can again agree. Oxford, however, makes this improbability or "impossibility" (of assertion) its criterion of logical error. There the trouble starts. It becomes apparent as soon as one raises an obvious question. Where is the line that divides logical from factual error? Oxford does not face this question. So they do not notice that it has no answer. Or, rather (if one accepts the criterion) the only consistent answer is that every error, or at least, every error concerning a generality either is or with increasing knowledge (growing meanings) eventually becomes a logical error. Theoretically, therefore, *cadit distinctio*. Practically, Oxford engages in a kind of armchair observation of linguistic behavior. The psychologism of the practice is patent. Three comments will reinforce the point.

First. According to the view predominant among the classical analysts the sentence I chose as an illustration, even though patently false or, if you please, absurd, is not "contralogical."[50] This is so because upon that view, which despite all defects in execution I believe to be correct, whether or not a sentence (of L) is analytic depends on its syntactical structure and nothing else. The sentence I chose as an illustration is synthetic and therefore, in the relevant sense of 'factual', a factual falsehood. Also, the line between the analytic and the synthetic is sharp (in L). So the unanswerable question never arises. Second. From Oxford we hear on this point nothing but a good deal of hermetic talk about the essential openness and stratification of language. This talk is merely another string of psychological and historical comments. Its profundity is mostly specious and hardly justifies the aplomb. Historically, all this stratified hemming and hawing about "analytic-synthetic" reminds one of the relative *a priori* of the Neokantians. Third. We have come upon further evidence that the "meaning"

---

[49] This is short for: know how to use the words occurring in the sentence or sentences under consideration. Whenever there is no danger of confusion I shall use the shorter version.

[50] I use this barbarous word because I do not want to explain in detail what becomes apparent at this point, namely, that Oxford ignores the distinction between falsehood, contradiction, and syntactical nonsense.

Oxford proposes to clarify is the holistic meaning of the idealists. Remember what was said about Urmson's major criticism of reconstruction.

The second way of exposing the unconquerable difficulty starts from a scrutiny of the alleged criterion for the contralogical and, therefore, also the logical. I shall first restate the criterion, underlining the three expressions, two words and a phrase, that stand for the three crucial ideas. "A sentence is *contralogical* if and only if one who *knows how to use the language* would not *assert it*." This proposition, I submit, is so "fundamental," particularly if one construes 'knowing' and 'asserting' behavioristically, that upon the Oxford view it may reasonably be taken to encode (part of) the meanings of the three expressions. Still upon this view, it is therefore a "logical" truth of the kind some others, in a different version of the same confusion, call a (partial) implicit definition. Assume now, in order to simplify the exposition, what upon this view one really must not assume, namely, that we have an independent criterion by which to decide whether or not an utterance is an assertion. Assume next that someone asserts a sentence which strikes you as "absurd." There are two possibilities. Either the sentence is contralogical and he does not know how to use the language. Or the sentence is logical and he knows how to use the language. The "criterion" does not permit you to decide which of these alternatives is the case. So it is not really a criterion. The unconquerable difficulty is that a "tautology" cannot do the job of a "statement of fact." It is essentially the same difficulty which the proponents of the (idealistic) coherence theory of truth encounter.

Every factual error is or eventually becomes one of logic. An analytic sentence must do the job only a synthetic one can do. These, we just saw, are two conclusions Oxford cannot escape. Structurally, they are the very heart of Hegelianism. The purpose of this philosophy, if I may so put it, is to enhance the role of the logical (rational) at the expense of the factual (empirical). Let me recall in three easy steps how the purpose is achieved. First. Every factual sentence is merely a most imperfect predication; apparently about an "empirical" referent; really about the one true subject, the Absolute. (*Hence the rejection of P.*) Second. Knowledge grows through the discovery of more and more adequate meanings. (Or, as I would rather put it, we gain knowledge by designing successively more and more adequate definitions.) Third. In the ideal limit knowledge consists of a system of "axioms" that are both synthetic and analytic. They are analytic because they are true merely by virtue of the ideally adequate definitions of the terms they contain. They are synthetic because somehow they comprehend all of factual truth. Nor need one worry about the apparent contradiction. In the Absolute, as in the God of negative theology, all contradictories coincide. This, such as it is, is Hegel's (and Dewey's[51]) way out. Made explicit, I don't think it is to Oxford's taste. Yet they have no other.

VIII

Some members of the movement are very clever. Of course. Mistakes made by clever people are often interesting, particularly in philosophy, partly because of the ingenuity of their authors, partly because they force us to grasp the truth more firmly and state it more neatly. Also, alas, they are at times rather influential. There is thus much, much more to be said about the mistakes of Oxford. But enough has been said to arrive at a judgment.

The movement's metaphilosophy is nihilistic. There are no philosophical propositions. In this respect they are no less radical than Wittgenstein and Carnap. Only, the author of the *Tractatus* fortunately did propound philosophical propositions. In its practice, tediously overdoing nonphilosophical linguistic analysis, the movement is futilitarian. Its implicit metaphysics is materialistic (behavioristic) in content and idealistic (Hegelian) in structure. The first to achieve this strange combination was Marx. From what I can tell, Sartre achieves it too. This profound similarity between Oxford and existentialism has struck me for quite some time. The two surfaces, of course, conditioned by vast differences of temper and tradition, are vastly different. At the two centers is the same failure of nerve, the same paralysis of that rarest of all gifts, the metaphysical genius.

[51] See also M. Brodbeck, "The New Rationalism: Dewey's Theory of Induction," *Journal of Philosophy*, 46, 1949, 781–91.

Analyticity*

M ANY philosophers believe that they can among all truths set aside the kind they call analytic; and they also believe that but for this distinction among truths some of the most pressing philosophical questions could not be answered. I share these beliefs. But I also believe that most of these philosophers use 'analytic' philosophically. Philosophical uses require explication. Their explication consists in talking commonsensically, that is, without using any word philosophically, about the syntax and interpretation of an ideal language (L). For, as they stand, philosophical uses make no sense. Yet in many subtle ways they direct, like guide posts, our efforts at explication. Otherwise there would be no philosophical problems. Nor would we know when to accept an explication as adequate. These are my beliefs concerning the proper method of philosophizing. Having explained and defended them before, I shall not in this essay either explain or defend them again but, rather, use the method to propose what seems to me an adequate explication of 'analytic' or, as I shall also say, of analyticity. More accurately, I shall attend to one part of it. The complete explication, it will soon transpire, is tripartite.

The philosophical uses of 'analytic' provide us with three guide posts. Each of the three italicized sentences in this paragraph stands for one of them. *Analyticity is a syntactical notion.* This implies that the explication proceeds in two steps. First one designs a syntactical definition of analyticity for the formalism proposed as L. Then one argues for its adequacy. *Arithmetic is analytic.* Or, to flex for once the muscles of the method, no one at all interested in analyticity would consider adequate an explication of this notion unless it comprehends

* Theoria, *24, 1958, 71–93. Reprinted by permission. For a dialectical rounding-out of the discussion of analyticity, see "The Philosophical Significance of Modal Logic" which was read at the meetings of the American Philosophical Association in Chicago, Spring 1957, and is scheduled to appear in* Mind.

all arithmetical truths, from the simplest to the most esoteric. *Descriptive words occur in analytic truths, if at all, only vacuously.* Less succinctly, every analytic truth is either a logical sentence or derived from one by specialization. In every likely candidate for L every primitive sign is of one and only one of two kinds, called logical and descriptive respectively. Among the former are the variables and their quantifiers. An expression is closed (not open) if and only if it contains no unquantified variable. Mathematically, it is often convenient to call open expressions sentences. Philosophically, it is confusing. A sentence is either true or false. An open expression, even of an interpreted formalism, is neither true nor false and not a sentence but merely, if well-formed, the schema of one. Sentences, as I shall use the term, are therefore always closed. A logical sentence is one that contains only logical signs. To understand what is meant by specialization, consider the five formulae[1]

(1) $(f)(x)[f(x) \vee \sim f(x)],$ (2) $(x)[f_1(x) \vee \sim f_1(x)],$

(3) $f_1(x_1) \vee \sim f_1(x_1),$ (4) $(f)(\exists g)(x)[f(x) \equiv g(x)],$

(5) $(\exists g)(x)[f_1(x) \equiv g(x)].$

(1) and (4) are logical sentences. (2) and (3) are derived from (1) by specialization; (5) from (4). Following this guide post, we can limit ourselves to the consideration of logical sentences.

Whether a practitioner of the method can come up with an adequate explication of analyticity depends upon his choice of a candidate for L. That is but another way of saying that this choice is his major gambit. The most prominent candidate for quite some time was the formalism of *Principia Mathematica* (PM); or, more precisely, the formalism, call it L', derived from PM by suppressing ramification on the one hand and, on the other, adding classes of undefined descriptive constants as well as the three axioms or, as I would rather say, the primitive sentences of extensionality (Ext), of infinity (Inf), and of choice (Sel). With it went more or less explicitly a definition of 'analytic'. A logical sentence is analytic if and only if it is either a primitive sentence or a theorem of L'. This gambit soon ran into triple trouble. *First.* If L' were L, Ext would be "analytic." In our natural languages Ext is false. It does not strictly follow that it must be false in L. However, certain considerations in connection with the analysis of 'meaning' and 'belief' make it more than likely that while Ext may be true for a very large part of L, it cannot be true for all of L. *Second.* If an arithmetical truth can be expressed in L', it becomes a logical sentence.

---

[1] Subscripts will be used to distinguish constants from variables; superscripts, when necessary, to indicate types.

That is as it ought to be. However, there are arithmetical truths expressible in L' such that neither they nor their negations are either primitive sentences or theorems of L'. That is of course Goedel's famous result. *Third.* Upon this definition elementary arithmetic is analytic only if Inf is, the rest of arithmetic only if both Inf and Sel are. Guided by the unexplicated notion they had of analyticity, not a few philosophers doubted whether Inf and Sel could reasonably be counted as analytic.

With the *third* objection I shall deal at some length; so I shall say no more about it at the moment. Goedel's result holds, broadly speaking, for every formalism which, as L undoubtedly must, contains elementary arithmetic. The *second* objection is therefore not just against L'. Its only force, though, is against the axiomatic method. All Goedel has shown is that an analytic sentence cannot be adequately defined as one which is either a primitive sentence or a theorem of L. There is no reason why it should be so defined. Thus there is no difficulty. The *first* objection, I believe, is unanswerable. That is why I proposed a different gambit. L'', my candidate for L, contains L' and in addition, two new logical signs, 'M' and the quoting operator. 'M' transcribes the intentional root meaning of 'means'. That is, if 'p_1' transcribes the English sentence P, then ' 'p_1'Mp_1' transcribes "the proposition P means P." The definition I propose proceeds in two steps. First one defines *analytic-in-L'*. This is of course not the definition Goedel has shown to be inadequate but the one I shall presently discuss. Let next ' . . . . . ' and '$\times\times\times\times$' stand for two different sentences, i.e., for any two sentences that are not, as one says, different tokens of the same type. A sentence is *analytic-in-L''* if and only if it is either analytic by the rules of L' or is of one of the two forms ' ' . . . . . 'M . . . . . ' and '$\sim$' . . . . . '$M\times\times\times\times$'. This is the second step.[2]

The complete explication of analyticity is tripartite. I shall number the three parts in a certain way, the reasons for which will soon be obvious. One part, saying what needs to be said because of the two new logical signs, concerns what I just called the second step of the definition of *analytic-in-L''*. This part I call the third. It may be found elsewhere. The other two parts deal with *analyticity-in-L'*. The first covers the truths known as sentential tautologies. It is so familiar that I shall assume it to be known. Its mathematical machinery is the

---

[2] The formulation *analytic by the rules of* L', rather than *analytic in* L', covers certain sentences which, since they contain the new signs, do not belong to L'. For a detailed description of L'' and the analysis mentioned at the beginning of the next paragraph, see "Intentionality," *Semantica* (Archivio di Filosofia, Roma: Bocca, 1955), pp. 177–216, and also pp. 3–38 of this book.

Boolean algebra of the truth tables. The remaining part, which I call the second, deals with the functional calculus contained in L' (and therefore also in my L, L''). Its mathematical machinery, to which I shall presently attend, is validity theory. These are the three parts of the complete explication. Calling every analytic truth a tautology,[3] one may say that the first part deals with the sentential tautologies, the second with those which are functional, the third with the tautologies of meaning. At this point some might object that since the complete explication has three parts, it establishes, if anything, three kinds of analyticity and not one. Nothing could be more wrong. But the objector may reasonably expect that the proponent of a tripartite explication identify in each of the three parts a feature shared by all three. To this task I shall attend at the very end. Now I shall only state accurately what I am about. *The subject of this paper is the second part of the complete explication.* To save words, I therefore stipulate that in the sequel, when speaking of the explication of analyticity, I shall mean the second part of the complete explication, and that, similarly, when speaking of a sentence being analytic, I shall mean its being analytic by virtue of the second part.

The tool of the explication is validity theory. In this theory nonformalized mathematics is used to talk about a formalism. The import of the qualifying adjective, nonformalized, is considerable and closely connected with one of the fundamental ideas of this essay. I shall next sketch this idea. A sketch, it should be kept in mind, serves its purpose best by purchasing lucidity and brevity at the expense of accuracy and detail.

Much of the trouble I hope to avoid stems from Inf. After the formalism has been interpreted and thus supposedly become L, Inf states, in substance, that there is an infinite number of things of a certain kind, namely, the kind that according to the rules for the interpretation of L could be named by its zero-level constants. Is that true? I have no opinion on the matter, though I am willing to grant that there is room for reasonable doubt. But can anything one may reasonably doubt be analytic? Certainly not upon the unexplicated notion of analyticity. Nor upon this notion would one be inclined, even if Inf were true beyond reasonable doubt, to call analytic the truth which in this case it states. But if one introduces the integers into L as Russell does and as, I believe, one must introduce them, then even elementary arithmetic is analytic only if Inf is. Or, to put it even more strongly (and with a deliberate inaccuracy), if there were only N things

---

[3] I find this use of 'tautology' very convenient. But since it is not very widely spread, I have not adopted it in this essay.

of the kind mentioned, there would be no integer $N+1$. Hence the distinguished chorus of worriers, led by Russell himself, who, in order to *secure* the *foundations* of mathematics, tried to count out the world. The two italicized words mark the source of the confusion. Of this presently. But that there is confusion is obvious. Something has gone radically wrong. Neither the truths of arithmetic nor their nature depend upon whether there is enough chalk in the world to write them down. And to count out the world is not the philosopher's job, but, if anybody's, the scientist's.

Validity theory avoids this difficulty, or apparent difficulty, by "interpreting" the sentences of L into such mathematical entities as infinite sets. This is a purely syntactical kind of interpretation, radically different from the "interpretation" that makes a "language" out of a formalism. One must not allow one's self to be misled by the use of the same word, which is, unhappily, quite common. (Sometimes the syntacticists speak of "models." That, too, is a very ambiguous word. 'Representation', which also occurs, has perhaps the fewest dangerous associations.) Even so, the procedure may seem circular. To understand why it is not is to grasp the fundamental idea I am trying to explain. Let us see.

A word may be used either philosophically or commonsensically. The distinction is the very heart of the method. A technical use, in the sense in which science and mathematics are technical, even of a very uncommon word is not on this ground alone philosophical. The most important philosophical uses are indeed of quite common words. As long as they go about their own business, the mathematicians do not use any word philosophically. A practitioner of the method may therefore in his explications without fear of circularity use all of mathematics, from elementary arithmetic to, say, the theory of infinite cardinals. But then, a critic will ask, what is the point or purpose of formalizing mathematics, that is, of building its "image" into the syntactical construction of L. The answer has two parts, one positive, one negative. Positively, the purpose is to explicate what is meant when, speaking philosophically, one says certain things about mathematics such as, most importantly, that it is analytic. In providing these explications the philosopher must, as it turns out, employ some results of the researches conventionally known as "foundations of mathematics." Negatively, the purpose of this particular branch of mathematics is not to provide a "secure foundation" for the rest of it. Most workers in the field, as well as some philosophers, think that it is. This is a philosophical view which I reject. But let there be no mistake. I do not of course reject that admirable branch of mathematics. I don't even know what it could mean to reject that sort of thing. I merely hold, *first*, that its very name, foundations of mathematics, invites confusion. I reject, *second*, the (philosophical) view about its (philosophical) significance which I just mentioned. I believe, *third*, that those who hold this view, philosophers and mathematicians alike, do so only because they have not seen through the twin follies of skepticism on the one hand and the search for an elusive kind of absolute certainty (an irrecoverable philosophic use of 'certain'!) on the other. These are but three ways of stating the fundamental idea I promised to sketch. So I shall let it go at that.

When Russell first set the course of these delightful investigations, validity theory did not exist. By now its more elementary part is widely known; expositions of it readily accessible.[4] Even so, I shall state its basic idea, which is simple enough. The theory applies to the calculi called functional. My choice of L being what it is, I shall, of course, apply to it PM (unramified, with Ext, Inf, and Sel), or, rather, to the functional part of PM. For it will simplify the exposition without slurring over any difficulty, if I assume that the formalism contains no sentential variables. Also, I shall use 'true' where mathematicians use 'valid', reserving the latter for another occasion.

The theory "interprets" the formalism into point sets, which in this context are called *universes*, as follows. '(x)', '$(\exists x)$', '(f)', '$(\exists r)$', '(f^2)', are read "for every point of the universe," "there is at least one point of the universe," "for every point set of the universe," "there is at least one set of ordered pairs of points of the universe," "for every set of point sets of the universe." This gives the idea. The interpretation of the connectives is standard. Given a universe, every logical sentence thus becomes a set-theoretical proposition about this universe. Whether it is true or false depends on the cardinality c of the universe (briefly, on c) and, in view of Ext, on nothing else. But it does depend on c. To see that, consider

$$(6) \qquad (f)(\exists x)(\exists y)(z)[f(x) \cdot f(y) \supset f(z)],$$
$$(7) \qquad (\exists x)(\exists y)(z)[z = x \lor z = y) \cdot x \neq y],$$
$$(8) \qquad (\exists x)(\exists y)(x \neq y).$$

(6) is true for $c \leq 2$; (7) for $c = 2$; (8) for $c \geq 2$.[5] The difficulty that worried Russell thus reappears, even more pervasively, though also with the important difference that since we are dealing with mathematical

[4] E.g., D. Hilbert and W. Ackermann, *Principles of Mathematical Logic* (New York: Chelsea, 1950).

[5] Notice that, because of the identity sign they contain, (7) and (8) are not closures of formulae of the lower functional calculus. I ignore the empty universe. See below and note 7.

entities, trying to resolve it by counting out the world is obviously futile. More precisely, the difficulty reappears provided there is some connection between the theory and the explication we are looking for. I shall next demonstrate this connection. That is best done by making, temporarily and for this purpose only, two assumptions which we already know to be objectionable.

Assume, first, that the world's cardinality is c, i.e., that the class of all things which could be named by the zero-level constants of L is of this cardinality. The objection is that we are not even sure the assumption makes sense; not to mention, in case it should, how we could ever know it to be true. Assume, second, that an adequate explication of 'analytic' may mention the world's cardinality. In the case of Inf, it will be remembered, the classical analysts, quite correctly I think, objected to this assumption. But then, I make it only for demonstration purposes. Waive therefore both objections and consider whether, if they are waived, the following definition would be adequate. A logical sentence is analytic if and only if it is true for c. I submit that the definition would be adequate. To me that is evident, just as evident as that in the sentential case (first part of the complete explication) the mathematical notion of a truth-table tautology shows what we mean by analyticity. I speak of "evidence," as I spoke of "demonstrating" the connection, because I am convinced that we stand here at the very limits of argument, in the strict sense of argument. This, however, does not mean that all talk must cease. Some comments may still serve a purpose. I shall make two. The first clears the ground; the second goes to the heart of the matter.

First. It is not the connectives that are explicated by the truth tables; for the very good reason that they need no explication. I don't even know what it could mean to explicate them. Rather, the tables explicate what is meant by calling certain sentences analytic, namely, I speak succinctly, those whose analyticity depends only on the connectives. Similarly, the definition which we now consider (for demonstration purposes only) does not help us to explicate 'all' and 'some'. Again, I do not know what it could mean to explicate them. Rather, it explicates what is meant by calling certain other sentences analytic, namely, those whose analyticity depends, I speak again succinctly, on the quantifiers. *Second.* Take a theorem of the lower functional calculus and close it universally for all variables. As is well known, it is true for all cardinalities (>0); hence also for c. In our demonstration world the original formula is therefore true for all possible predicates. My comment is that the idea expressed by the phrase "true for all possible predicates" is the heart of the unexplicated notion of analyticity. Some may grant that and yet balk at this point in case the prefix contains existentially quantified predicate variables.[6] I merely suggest that they replace '$(\exists f)$' by '$\sim(f)\sim$'. Call this feature the combinatorial core of the unexplicated notion of analyticity and, accordingly, the property a logical sentence must possess if upon our provisional definition it is to be analytic, *combinatorial universality*. I have no doubt that an explication, to be adequate, must contain this feature and, therefore, make use of validity theory. The connection I set out to demonstrate is thus close indeed. The task, as it now appears, is to preserve the feature of combinatorial universality and, at the same time, get rid of the dependence on c.

Under the circumstances one idea readily comes to mind. Perhaps one could arrive at an adequate explication by defining as analytic those and only those logical sentences which are valid in all nonempty universes. The qualification, nonempty, is perfectly natural. Mathematically, the case of the so-called empty universe is trivial, or very nearly so. Philosophically, it does not even make sense. It does make sense, of course, to speak of properties not exemplified in a world. But the notion of an "empty" world is an entirely different matter. It is, at any rate, beyond my grasp.[7] So I shall henceforth not bother to mention this obvious qualification. Now for the proposal. The primitive sentences of the lower functional calculus are true in all universes. That is familiar. Except for Ext, Inf, and Sel, the remaining primitive sentences of our formalism are obtained from those of the lower functional calculus by raising the type level. They, too, are therefore true in all universes. The derivation rules, by a familiar proof pattern, preserve this property. Ext is true in all universes by the very nature of the interpretation. All theorems, except those based on Inf, would therefore be analytic. Promising as that looks, Inf stubbornly remains. It is false in all finite universes. That stops us in our tracks. The attempt has failed. A new idea is needed. Before suggesting one, I want to reflect briefly on what a philosopher ought and ought not to do in situations like the one in which we find ourselves at this juncture.

The facts of science are what they are. Sometimes the philosopher must take them into account. Of course he must. But it is just as important that he know when to leave them alone. On this I spoke my mind quite bluntly when it came to counting out the world. What holds for science holds equally for mathematics. Stopped in our tracks

---

[6] An analysis of some reasons for this resistance may be found in "Particularity and the New Nominalism," *Methodos*, 6, 1954, 131–47, and also pp. 91–105 of this book.

[7] See Herbert Hochberg, "A Note on the 'Empty Universe'," *Mind*, 66, 1957, 544–46.

by the facts of mathematics, if I may so call them, we need a new idea. In some such situations we may acquire it by learning more mathematics. Of course we may. It may even pay to wait for new mathematical discoveries. But it is just as important to know when to leave mathematics alone, looking instead for the idea to turn up in a fresh examination of the philosophical problem. This is the course I shall take.

The connection between logic and analyticity is obvious. Thus it stands to reason that we may improve our chances by ridding the mathematical machinery we employ of all superfluity, that is, of anything not an accurate image of the fundamental ideas of logic, or, what amounts virtually to the same thing, of the syntactical structure of L. If my choice of L is correct, there are five such fundamental ideas, falling into three groups, each corresponding to one of the three parts of the complete explication of analyticity. The first, corresponding to the first part, contains the two ideas of *sentence* and *connective;* the second, which corresponds to the second part, those of *predication* and *quantification;* the third, corresponding to the third part, the single idea of *intentional meaning* ('M'). The first group has its accurate mathematical image in the machinery of the truth tables. Our concern is, of course, with the second. It does not contain the idea of individuality. To see why that is important, consider, *first*, the philosophical use of 'individual'. An individual is what is or could be named by the zero-type constants of L. Remember, *second*, that all that matters in PM are the arithmetical differences among the type numbers of the several signs contained in a sentence or a finite number of such. The absolute numbers do not. Take, *third*, the paradigm of predication, 'a is B'. If my choice of L is correct, 'a' and 'B' are of types n and $n+1$, respectively; but, again, the value of n does not matter. I conclude, *fourth*, that while the accurate image of predication is class membership,[8] the points of our universes are the image of individuality. The following definition gets rid of the superfluity thus revealed. A logical sentence is *valid for c* (i.e., valid in all universes of cardinality c) if and only if it as well as the sentences obtained from it by raising or lowering its type level in all possible ways are true for c. For instance, '$(f)(y)[(x)f(x) \supset f(y)]$' is valid in a given universe (it is in fact valid in all) because not only it but also '$(f^2)(g)[(h)f^2(h) \supset f^2(g)]$', '$(f^3)(g^2)(h^2)f^3(h_2) \supset f^3(g^2)]$', . . . are true in this universe. The definition exploits that feature of arithmetic, as reconstructed in PM, which is known as its systematic ambiguity. Mathematicians in their obsession with elegance dislike it.

[8] If anyone should wonder whether I can consistently say that, even though L'' is not wholly extensional, I would have him remember that 'M' is not a predicate but a pseudopredicate. See "Intentionality."

The authors of PM were almost apologetic about it. Exploring its philosophical significance, however, makes it not only appear perfectly natural but even yields a hint, namely, to build the explication of analyticity not on the notion of truth in a universe but, rather, on that of validity in a universe. To find out how far this idea will take us we must investigate the differences between the two notions.

Conventionally, the type hierarchy of PM is of the order 0, 1, 2, 3, . . . If a universe is of cardinality c, the totality of its point sets is of cardinality 2^c, the totality of sets of such sets of cardinality 2^{2^c}, and so on. By Cantor's theorem, each member of the progression thus obtained is smaller than the next. That yields the following results. (a) A logical sentence true for only one cardinality is not valid for any. Sentence (7) above will serve as an example. (b) If n is finite, a logical sentence true only for cardinalities $<n$ is not valid for any. Sentence (6) above will serve as an example. (b') To see that (b) does not hold for infinite n, one merely has to consider the negation of Inf, which is valid for all finite universes ($c<\aleph_0$), though of course not valid for any other. For a more elaborate example, take

(9) $(f^2)[N^3(f^2) \supset \{\operatorname{Post}^3(f^2) \vee f^2(\hat{x}(x=x))\}]$,

where 'N^3' and 'Post^3' stand for 'number' and 'posterity of zero' as defined in PM. (9) says materially that the universe is at most denumerable. It is valid for all finite universes. Unlike the negation of Inf it is also true for $\aleph_0$. But it is not valid for $\aleph_0$. (c) All primitive sentences of our formalism except Inf are valid in all universes. So are all theorems except, again, those based on Inf. (d) Inf is valid for all $c \geqq \aleph_0$. Let us take stock. (a) and (b) show that we got rid of two classes of bothersome sentences. (c) shows that we suffered no loss. This is progress. But validity, like truth, depends on cardinality. In particular, (d) remains bothersome. We must try again.

Call a sentence valid from c on if it is valid for all cardinalities $\geqq c$. Call it eventually valid if and only if there is a cardinality such that it is valid from this cardinality on. Consider the following definition. *A logical sentence is analytic if and only if it is eventually valid.* I believe that the definition is adequate. (More precisely, it is the definitional step of an adequate explication.) To show the adequacy of any explication is, in a sense, an unending task. But one may and one sometimes must begin what, in a sense, one cannot finish. I shall do three things. (I) I shall use elementary arithmetic to show that in spite of the substitution of eventual validity for validity in all universes the proposal achieves all one can reasonably expect. (II) By extending the conventional type hierarchy I shall so tighten the definition of validity that no logical sentence will be valid in any universe without being valid in some universes of cardinalities higher than any one arbitrarily selected. The negation of Inf will then not be valid in any universe. (III) I shall support my proposal indirectly by showing that an objection likely to be raised is without ground.

I. Building arithmetic into L is not to construct it but to *reconstruct* it. That is but a way of saying succinctly what was said earlier concerning the foundations of mathematics. But it will pay if we take another look. PM, everyone knows, purports to reconstruct arithmetic. "The class of all pairs," for instance, is offered as the reconstruction of "two." What is the nature and purpose of this enterprise? The answer has three steps. First. A reconstruction is *successful*, or, rather, it is a reconstruction only if, in some sense of 'meaning', it means what it purports to reconstruct. Is then the reconstruction of arithmetic in PM successful? I am prepared to argue that it is. This, however, is a long story and not the one I set out to tell in this essay. So I shall take it for granted. Second. A reconstruction is not an explication; if only because, once more, 'two', like 'and' and 'all', needs no explication. Third. The purpose of a reconstruction is to serve as a tool in the explication of philosophical questions about the things named by the terms reconstructed. If a (successful) reconstruction can so serve in an adequate explication then one may, derivatively, call it *adequate*. Again, the PM-reconstruction of arithmetic is the only adequate one I either know or can think of. There are several reasons for that. The only one that concerns us is that in this reconstruction arithmetic becomes analytic. Let us limit ourselves to elementary arithmetic. If (a) the PM-reconstruction of the integers is successful and (b) the proposed explication of 'analytic' is adopted, then elementary arithmetic can be shown to be analytic. Of course it can, since the only offender, Inf, is valid from $\aleph_0$ on. Nor need we worry about the details of the demonstration. They may be found in PM. The first premise, (a), I just said I would not argue in this essay. With respect to (b), though, I undertook to show, in the case of elementary arithmetic, that the critical substitution of eventual validity for validity in all universes is perfectly reasonable. I am now ready to do that.

There is an infinite number of integers and they are all things of the same kind, namely, integers. Taken commonsensically, these are truisms. Since I mean them commonsensically, I do not hesitate to use 'infinite', 'thing', and 'kind' in this manner. If L is what for quite a few reasons I believe it must be, namely, a subject-predicate language, then each integer must be reconstructed as a predicate. Their being all of the same kind can only be reflected by these predicates being all of the same type. Hence, since there is an infinite number of integers, L must contain an infinite number of predicates of at least one type. In validity theory a predicate becomes or "is" either a point set, or a set of such sets, and so on. Is it reasonable or does it even make sense to look for an infinite class of predicates (of any one type) in a finite universe? In every infinite universe, on the other hand, one can find (and Russell has found) the required infinite class (or, in view of the systematic ambiguity, classes). Each predicate of this class reconstructs one integer. The reconstruction of an arithmetical proposition is a logical sentence. If the proposition is true then its reconstruction can be shown to have the property of combinatorial universality in all infinite universes. Is it reasonable, I ask again, or does it even make sense to expect more by way of demonstrating the explicable core of the philosophical proposition that (elementary) arithmetic is analytic.

At this point one might wonder whether validity for an appropriate cardinality rather than, as I suggest, eventual validity is not perhaps the adequate explication. For elementary arithmetic, for instance, the appropriate cardinality would be $\aleph_0$. I don't think the proposal will do. I agree that for some logical sentences there are appropriate cardinalities. For such a sentence the idea of reconstructing it in universes of a cardinality smaller than the appropriate one simply makes no sense. That is indeed part of my point. But then, would we still want to call elementary arithmetic analytic if, *per absurdum*, it could be shown not to be valid in even one nondenumerably infinite universe?

II. Whenever in the last section I spoke of arithmetic I took care to qualify it as elementary. There was a point to that. As long as we are satisfied to reconstruct elementary arithmetic, the conventional type hierarchy $(0, 1, 2, \ldots)$ will do. In fact, a small part of it would serve that purpose. But it is very doubtful, to say the least, whether it will do when we wish the reconstruction[9] to comprehend the whole of arithmetic, including the theory of transfinite numbers. Conversely, it is more than plausible that this goal can be reached if we extend the conventional type hierarchy by means of the transfinite ordinals, of which there is no largest. So I shall do three things. (a) I shall extend both the hierarchy and the syntactical interpretation. (b) I shall inquire what the extension implies for validity. (c) I shall show on philosophical grounds which have nothing to do with arithmetic that this extension, however unconventional it may be, is yet quite reasonable.

(a) Assign to each transfinite ordinal a type of variables $'f^\omega'$, $'f^{\omega+1}'$, $\ldots$, $'f^{2\omega}'$, and so on. Add all these variables to our formalism (and to the L'' originally proposed). The addition produces no change in its logic. For, again, all that matters are the arithmetical differences among

---

[9] An axiomatization is as such not an adequate reconstruction. For how could one otherwise explicate the difference between arithmetic on the one hand and geometry or, for that matter, physics on the other?

the types of the signs occurring in a sentence. Notice that since some transfinite ordinals (e.g., ω) have no predecessor, signs of their types appear always as subjects and never as predicates. That is the cue as to how the conventional validity theory may be extended. Take a universe of cardinality c. The types of the conventional hierarchy (I speak concisely) are interpreted into its points, point sets, sets of such sets, and so on. The predicates of type ω we interpret into the points of a second set, which we adjoin to the first. The cardinality of the second set is the smallest larger than all members of the progression c, 2^c, 2^{2^c}, . . . (The cardinalities are well-ordered. Hence there is a smallest.) In the second set we proceed conventionally. For 2ω we adjoin a further set. And so on. Otherwise there is no change.

(b) A logical sentence is valid for c if and only if it as well as all the sentences obtained from it by raising or lowering its type level in all possible ways are true for c. This was our definition of validity in a universe. We need not change it. Or, rather, we need not change its wording. But the "raising and lowering" now ranges over the whole of the extended hierarchy. This material change has important consequences. To be valid in *any* universe, a logical sentence must now be valid in *some* of a cardinality higher than any one arbitrarily selected. The negation of Inf, in particular, is therefore no longer valid in any universe. Generally, as far as we know, each logical sentence belongs now to one and only one of three kinds. (α) Either it is not valid in any universe. (β) Or it is valid from a certain cardinality on. (γ) Or one can for each arbitrarily selected cardinality find two larger ones for one of which it is valid while for the other it is not. I said as far as we know in order to guard against the possibility that there are no logical sentences of the kind (γ). Of this presently.

(c) Some philosophers, including myself, believe that L need contain no descriptive constants but of type 0 and 1, i.e., those naming either individuals or characters exemplified by individuals. The vast majority of those holding this view do not therefore reject the conventional type hierarchy, presumably because they believe it to be needed for the reconstruction of arithmetic. If, therefore, one takes seriously the demand for the reconstruction of the whole of arithmetic and if I am right that in order to satisfy that demand one must extend the type hierarchy in the manner proposed, then the extension becomes inevitable. Perhaps I could let it go at that. But I promised to show, on philosophical grounds which have nothing to do with arithmetic, that however unconventional this extension may be, it is yet quite reasonable.

If the type hierarchy were of the order $\cdots -2, -1, 0, 1, 2, \cdots$, the logic of the formalism would still be the same. Take such a formalism; add to it undefined descriptive constants in such a manner that there is no lowest type to which they are assigned; and assume that, so supplemented, it becomes the ideal language of *a* world. In that world there are no individuals. This shows that there being some in ours is a matter of fact. (This, to be sure, is a philosophical use of 'fact'; but I don't think I need stop to explain it.) Consider next a world with an *L* otherwise like ours except that it contains undefined descriptive constants of type *ω*. (I limit myself to this case.) Since, as we saw, these constants appear always as subjects and never as predicates, the things they name would be of a peculiar kind and we might not inappropriately call them "higher individuals." The point of all this is obvious, I trust. Just as it is "merely a matter of fact" that there are individuals in our world, so it is also merely a matter of fact that there are in it none of the higher kinds. Thus it is not at all strange and in fact quite reasonable that our "logic" should provide for the possibility of there being some.

III. I started by erecting three guide posts to direct the search for an adequate explication of analyticity. Some classical analysts, notably Carnap, added a fourth. *Every logical sentence must be analytic or the negation of one that is analytic* (contradictory). Does our explication satisfy this condition? That depends on whether there are logical sentences of the kind, γ, or, briefly, γ-sentences. For, upon our explication, every analytic sentence is a β-sentence; its negation is an α-sentence, and conversely. But the negation of a γ-sentence is a γ-sentence. It follows that our explication fulfills Carnap's condition if and only if there are no γ-sentences. Among (the closures of) the logical sentences of the lower functional calculus we know that there are none. Every such sentence which is (upon our definition) valid in any universe is also valid from $\aleph_0$ on. That is the famous theorem of Loewenheim. So one may well wonder whether there is not perhaps for every logical sentence a cardinality *c*, depending on its type structure, such that if it is valid (as here defined, not just true!) for any universe, it is also valid from *c* on. I don't know. Nor do I know whether the question ever occurred to any mathematician. Or, if it occurred to one, whether he found it very difficult or could immediately think of counterexamples which are, to him, obvious and decide it negatively. Once again, we are up against the facts of mathematics. Should we try to learn more mathematics or, even, try to make a mathematical discovery? Some may think so. I prefer to examine the philosophical ideas that led to the erection of the guide post. So I shall next state them, in a capsule and in the form of an argument.

For a sentence to be analytic (or contradictory) and to be a *logical truth* (or falsehood) is one and the same thing. For a sentence to be a *logical sentence* (or derived from one by instantiation) and to be a logical truth or falsehood is one and the same thing. But every sentence is either true or false. Hence, every logical sentence is either analytic or contradictory. This is the argument. The gap which invalidates it lies between "logical sentence" and "logical truth." One may not notice this gap if, using the two words philosophically, one too facilely identifies the *logical* with the *linguistic* and believes, however implicitly, that logical signs are, if I may so express myself, linguistic *par excellence*. This, however, is not to deny that there are important differences between the two kinds of signs called logical and descriptive respectively. The differences appear in the syntactical and interpretation rules of the formalism. If one wishes, one may refer to them by calling the logical signs "linguistic," thus explicating one philosophical use of 'linguistic'. But then one must not in the same argument use the same word differently, as, for instance, in 'logical (linguistic!) truth'. For these reasons I reject Carnap's guide post, irrespective of what the facts of mathematics may be. If the Loewenheim theorem is generalizable for the higher types then our explication gains in elegance, simply because the world is that way. If not, it does as well as one can do in the face of the facts. Moreover, it would seem that any defensible purpose of Carnap's condition is just as well served by my third guide post, according to which in analytic truths descriptive signs occur, if at all, only vacuously.

I have made my proposal and supported it by three arguments or groups of arguments. Jointly they go a long way toward establishing that the proposed explication of 'analytic' is adequate, provided only that L'' is L. I say that they go a long way because to establish the adequacy of even a single explication is, in a sense, an unending task, just as it is an unending task to justify one's major gambit, the choice of a candidate for L. The only difference is that while one can and must argue directly every single explication, it does not even make sense so to argue for one's choice of L. That can only be done indirectly, by demonstrating the success of one's candidate in an ever increasing number of explications. Thus I have done what I set out to do. Three comments will round it out; first a few words about the axiom of choice; then a few more about reducibility; and, finally, redeeming a promise to identify the feature shared by the three parts of the complete explication of analyticity.

At the turn of the century, when what we now know as analytical philosophy was in its youth, the three primitive sentences, Inf, Ext, and Sel, were equally prominent in the discussion of the analyticity problem. To Inf I gave a good deal of attention. Ext, we saw, is guaranteed by the very nature of the syntactical interpretation; philosophical doubts about it are allayed by the recognition that L has a nonextensional part. The *axiom of choice* (Sel) was mentioned when I set the stage by a few remarks about the structural history of the problem; then I let it silently drop out of the discussion. It is now my business to explain this silence.

Sel is a truism. No one would either think of questioning its truth or, in nonformalized mathematics, try to prove it. Also, Sel is valid in all universes. That defines my task. What really needs explaining is not my silence but, rather, that there ever was so much commotion. Sel itself is trivial, to be sure. But what one can strictly deduce from it, after one has taken the trouble of explicitly stating it, is far from trivial and, even, surprising. (This is the only kind of surprise to be had in mathematics.) Among the nontrivial consequences of Sel and in fact equivalent with it is, for instance, the well-ordering theorem. Mathematicians thus had very good reasons and, if they work in certain areas, still have very good reasons for their interest in Sel. The philosophers' case is different. Mathematicians tend to lose interest in anything that cannot be axiomatized. In mathematics that is quite proper. In philosophy it isn't. At the beginning of this century, however, the most active philosophical students of logic were all under the spell of the axiomatic method. Some still are. Goedel, by showing that 'analytic' cannot be defined axiomatically (I speak succinctly), should have taught them better. Unhappily his work had the opposite effect. Some philosophers, taking from mathematics what was for them the wrong cue, lost interest in the problem of analyticity. Another bad effect of the axiomatic bias is over-concern with whether or not a certain tautology must be included among the primitive sentences of a (partial) axiomatization. One so biased does not see that any tautology is philosophically as good as any other. This is why some philosophers were quite concerned when it turned out that if certain parts of arithmetic are to be reconstructed, Sel has to be added to the primitive sentences of PM. Yet there was no good reason for either concern or surprise. On the one hand, it had long been known that, strictly constructed, those parts of arithmetic rested on Sel. On the other hand, Sel and Ext are the only primitive sentences of the (partial) axiomatization L' in which the types of the signs range over three steps (e.g., 0, 1, 2). In all others they range only over two. Small wonder, therefore, that the former could not be derived from the latter.

Like Inf and Sel, the so-called *axiom of reducibility* (Red) was for a time very prominent in the discussions of the analyticity problem. By now its interest is only historical or, in some contexts, mathematical. Yet I shall say a few words about it. For it may be instructive to see how the proposed explication trivializes what was once a weighty question. To explain what is involved, I shall brush aside all technicalities and limit myself to the first two subtypes (ramifications) of the first type. An expression '$\hat{x}[\ldots x \ldots]$' is called a predicate context (briefly, context) if and only if '$\ldots y \ldots$' is an (open) sentence; or, what amounts to the same thing, if and only if in '$f(y)$' the context can be substituted for 'f'. E.g., '$\hat{x}[g(x) \vee h(x)]$' is a context, yielding in this manner '$g(y) \vee h(y)$'. A context is impredicative if and only if it contains at least one quantified predicate variable. Otherwise it is predicative. Red asserts that for *each* impredicative context there is a predicative one which is formally equivalent to it. As it was stated, and as I restated it, Red is anything but clear. We know, though, that the question debated was whether Red was analytic. Thus there is no doubt that we must turn to the syntactical interpretation into universes. There, we know, two contexts are formally equivalent if and only if they are interpreted into the same point set. But then, which point sets are involved? Or, to say the same thing differently, what shall we make of the 'each' I italicized? There are two possibilities.

Given a universe, select from the set S of all its point sets a proper subset S'. Form the set S'' obtained by substituting for the predicate variables of all predicative contexts any member of S'. Consider next the set T whose members are the point sets obtained by substituting for all free predicate variables of all impredicative contexts any member of S'', stipulating at the same time that the predicate operators in these contexts range only over S''. One may take Red to assert that T is contained in S''. Given a universe *and a class* S', Red, so interpreted, asserts something definite. What it asserts obviously may be either true or false, *depending on the choice of* S'. This is one possibility. It would seem that it is what the authors of PM had in mind.

For the second possibility, distinguish syntactically two kinds (subtypes)[10] of predicate variables, '$f^{1'}$', '$g^{1'}$', $\ldots$; '$f^{2'}$', '$g^{2'}$', $\ldots$ Admit only predicative contexts within each subtype but let the closures of those of the first subtype be legitimate substitution instances for the free variables in those of the second subtype. Since the question of analyticity is involved, we must first of all look for an interpretation of the two subtypes into our universes. The discussions that went on leave no doubt that both must be interpreted into point sets. That leaves two alternatives. We may interpret the first subtype into a subset S' of S. (I use the same notation as before.) That leads back to a variant of the first possibility. Or we may interpret the first subtype into S. Then

---

[10] In view of the limitation to the first type, the superscripts can for the moment serve to indicate its subtypes.

the second subtype, too, must be interpreted into S and not into any proper subclass of it. To see that, one merely has to consider

$$(10) \qquad f(x) \equiv (g)(y)[f(x) \cdot \{g(y) \equiv g(y)\}],$$

which shows that every set can be written impredicatively. But if both subtypes are interpreted into S, Red becomes trivially valid in all universes and, therefore, analytic.

That much about the axioms of choice and reducibility. I am ready to turn to the last task I set myself. It will not take long.

Mere technicalities apart, an analytic sentence is of one of three kinds. Either it is a truth-table tautology. Or it is eventually valid. Or it is of one of the two forms ' ' . . . 'M . . . ' and '$\sim$' . . . 'M xxxxx'. If of the first kind, it is a sentential compound yielding the value "true" for *all possible* evaluations of its components in the two-valued Boolean algebra of "true" and "false." If of the second kind, it is true for *all possible* interpretations into the points, point sets, sets of such sets, and so on, according to type, of all universes from a certain cardinality on. The rules of L'' determine as either analytic or contradictory *all possible* specifications of the basic sentential pattern containing 'M'. The recurring phrase is "all possible." Analyticity is a combinatorial notion. *The feature shared by the three kinds of analytic sentences is combinatorial universality.* I introduced this phrase in connection with the second kind. But it fits the other two as well. The differences among the three criteria—all possible evaluations, all possible interpretations, all possible sentences—are fully accounted for by the differences among the sentences to which they apply. In other words, there are three kinds of analytic sentences and the complete explication is accordingly tripartite. But there is only one kind of analyticity.

Some, agreeing with all this as far as it goes, may yet feel that it does not go very far. I shall make bold to diagnose the source of their dissatisfaction. The crucial phrase, all possible, occurs over and over again in the unexplicated statements the classical philosophers made about analyticity. They spoke, for instance, of all possible worlds. To one in whose mind those statements reverberate the substitution of talk about all possible combinations in, say, a Boolean algebra for talk about all possible worlds may seem a comedown if not, even worse, a *quid pro quo*. I merely observe that in the last sentence 'possible' is used once commonsensically (all possible combinations), once philosophically (all possible worlds). And philosophical uses stand in need of explication. According to one such use of 'possible', a state of affairs is possible if and only if the negation of the sentence referring to it is not analytic. That closes the circle.

Particularity and the New Nominalism*

PHILOSOPHY has no surprises of the kind that abounds in science. This is by now commonplace. Yet philosophy yields a kind of novelty all its own. Philosophical analysis persistently pursued, in revealing ever more accurately the anatomy of the several philosophical positions, sometimes reveals connections among them that are surprising indeed. I, for one, was surprised when I first saw clearly that the rejection of "universals" by the new nominalists has its root in their rejection of "particulars," logically as well as, probably, historically. To bring out this connection, logically as well as in terms of what I like to call structural history, is the task I have set myself in this essay. Or, to speak for once as they do, I propose to show that what the new nominalists are so fond of calling their anti-Platonism is but a consequence of what may with equal propriety be called their anti-Aristotelianism.

The movement of thought I wish to retrace has three phases. The first culminates in *Principia Mathematica* (PM); the second in Quine's *Mathematical Logic* (ML) of 1940. The third may be thought to begin with Quine's essay "On What There Is," of 1948;[1] it comprehends his subsequent papers as well as Goodman's recent *The Structure of Appearance*. I shall first recall some of the views all these writers share and which I share with them. They form, as it were, a frame which I shall neither examine nor defend in this essay. I did that elsewhere.[2]

For one, we all agree, explicitly or implicitly, on a new method of philosophizing. Systematically, though of course not psychologically,

---

* Methodos, *6, 1954, 131–47. Reprinted by permission.*

[1] Reprinted in W. V. Quine, *From a Logical Point of View* (Cambridge: Harvard University Press, 1953).

[2] *The Metaphysics of Logical Positivism*, hereafter referred to as MLP.

we begin with the construction of a formalism, the sort of schema of
which PM, supplemented by a sufficiency of descriptive constants, is
the classical example. Not a language actually to be spoken, such a
schema is yet called an ideal language if it is supposed to contain, in
principle, the correlates of anything one could have occasion to say.
For another, we all agree, explicitly or implicitly, that philosophical
discourse is ordinary discourse, explicating the philosophical problems
by means of an ideal language, and that in these explications the syntax of the latter is of paramount importance. During the first two
phases there was also agreement on a third point. The interdependent
distinctions between logical and descriptive signs (of the ideal language)
and between analytic and synthetic propositions (of the ideal language)
were agreed to be philosophically significant. Since I still hold this view,
since it was within our movement of thought challenged only during
its last phase, and since the bulk of this paper deals with its earlier
phases, I shall take the two distinctions for granted without defending
them once more.

I

The issue or issues I propose to discuss are ontological. So I state
next the two relevant conceptions of ontology. The first, I shall call
it O_1, is, as I shall show, implicit in the first phase of our movement of
thought. The second, call it O_2, which is due to Quine, is characteristic
of the third. To show how O_2 grew during the second phase out of O_1 is
part of my purpose. The two conceptions are, as one might expect,
alternative explications within the shared frame of what the classical
ontologists could reasonably have meant when they asked what there
was or existed. But neither attempts to construct an actual list or
catalogue of (the names of) what exists. Their concern is, rather, with
syntactical kinds or categories.

O_1. *What there is or exists, in the sense in which ontology speaks of
existence, is shown by the undefined descriptive constants of the ideal
language.*

To explain, assume the ideal language to contain, in addition to connectives and quantifiers, two categories of signs, called individual signs
and property signs respectively. Assume, furthermore, that each of
these two categories contains variables, which are logical signs, as well
as undefined constants, which are descriptive. Because of the occurrence of the latter, one would upon this conception of ontology have to
say that individuals, i.e., the referents of individual constants, as well
as properties, i.e., the referents of the second kind of descriptive constants, exist.

O_2. *To exist, in the sense in which ontology speaks of existence, is to be the referent of what is in the range of a variable of the ideal language.*

To explain, assume the ideal language to be as above except that, though it contains undefined property constants, it does not contain the corresponding variables. Upon this conception of ontology only individuals would exist, properties would not. The position has two variants. Either the mere occurrence of a category of variables constitutes ontological commitment; or the quantification of these variables must also be provided for. The difference makes no difference for my purpose. So I shall assume that the schemata considered allow for the quantification of all their variables. This variant also helps one to understand one possible intellectual motive for adopting O_2 over O_1.

With quantification available the ideal language contains propositions whose idiomatic correlates begin with 'there is' or 'there are', e.g., 'There is a property such that . . . ', in PM-symbols,

$$(\exists f) \ldots f \ldots .$$

O_2 thus makes these so-called existential statements of the ideal schema itself the correlates of classical ontology; for O_1 ontology belongs to ordinary discourse about the schema. Only the latter alternative is consistent with what I believe to be the only consistent conception of the philosophical enterprise as a whole. But again, I do not intend to reargue in this paper this general objection to O_2. My intention is to analyze another intellectual motive, more specific as well as more technical, that could lead one to adopt, however mistakenly and unnecessarily, O_2 instead of O_1. I say could because, let that be understood once and for all, structural history is not concerned with the intellectual biographies of individuals. To do that sort of thing I should neither care nor presume. However that may be, one who holds, as I do, O_1, needs a special name for the so-called existential statements of the ideal language lest they be mistaken for correlates of ontological assertions. Borrowing from the familiar symbolism, I shall call such statements $\exists$-statements or sometimes, more fully, there-are-statements.

Both conceptions of ontology are purely syntactical. That has its dangers. One may be tempted to forget that philosophical discourse is not just about the ideal language but rather, by means of it, about the world. To see how this danger arises, assume that the ideal schema contains only one kind of variables but that the undefined constants within their range refer to quite different entities. Assume, for instance, that they refer among other things to particular animals such as my late cat Olaf, to zoological species such as cats and dogs, and to zoological genera. Even if these variables and constants be called individual, a world so constituted is still a far cry from what the classical nominalists believed ours to be. Thus it is rather misleading if a world so constituted is now on these purely syntactical grounds called nominalistic. Syntax counts for much. For how much is to me, though no longer a surprise, an inexhaustible source of intellectual delight. Yet syntax is not literally everything. Like the new nominalists', the concern of this essay is nevertheless almost exclusively syntactical. There is no danger in that as long as one knows what one is doing. Speaking for convenience' sake as they do, I state therefore next the syntactical core of what the new nominalists mean by their nominalism.

N. *The ideal language contains only one kind of variables.*

This, and nothing else, is what I mean by nominalism in this essay. For there is no point in arguing about names, except in the structural history of ideas where they so often provide bridges which are not, though they are mistaken for, deductive connections.

Particularity, as philosophers spoke and still speak about it, is not a purely syntactical notion. Its nonsyntactical core is the idea that there are entities which are, as it were, self-contained, though of course not in a causal way, and which cannot, upon any notion of analysis, be further analyzed. A particular dog or tree (not their properties!) are in the Aristotelian tradition taken to be particulars in this sense. In the empiricist tradition particular visual or auditory sensa (not their qualia!) play the same part. That goes to show how fundamental the notion really is. Some express it quasi-syntactically when they insist that only what is in fact a particular is properly referred to by those purely indexical signs which are the only ones that should properly be called "proper names." There is, as I just said, no point in arguing about words. Yet this particular phrase, proper name, is so compromised that I shall, since I easily can, avoid it in this essay.

Particularity has an important syntactical core. It is the structure of the simple clause. This clause may be conceived in analogy to such idiomatic propositions as 'Peter is tall' or 'Olaf is a cat'. Quantifiers lie outside of it; and relations may be temporarily disregarded, since they can be introduced later on, on a less fundamental level, by means of a familiar device due to Wiener and Kuratowski. Taking one's cue from the idiom one will then naturally envisage the possibility of the simple clause having two syntactically distinguished places or positions, namely, a *subject place* and an *object place*. With one exception, which I shall discuss only at the very end, the schemata I consider in this paper all allow the distinction. A first and, as it were, minimal component of the particularity thesis may thus be stated as follows.

P_1. *The simple clause has a subject place and a predicate place.*

It will be noticed that I omitted an obvious qualification, speaking of the simple clause instead of, more fully, the simple clause of the ideal language. I shall always do that from now on when there is no danger of confusion. P_1 means that the schema of the simple clause is asymmetrical. In Russell's notation, '$f(x)$', the predicate place is the first; in Quine's, '$x \, \varepsilon \, y$', the subject place precedes it. The parentheses of PM and the 'ε' of ML are logical signs, signifying no more and no less than that the terms are combined into a proposition or, if they are variables, into the schema of one. A pair of parentheses around the two terms, '(f, x)' or '(x, y)', would do as well. The point is that in PM as well as in ML the order of the two terms matters. In other words, PM does not contain the theorem or analytical truth '$f(x) \equiv x(f)$', just as ML does not contain the theorem '$(x \, \varepsilon \, y) \equiv (y \, \varepsilon \, x)$'. Yet there is also a difference. In PM the expression '$x(f)$' is not even well formed. In ML '$x \, \varepsilon \, y$' and '$y \, \varepsilon \, x$' are both well formed. To say the same thing differently, Quine, unlike Russell, rejects the distinction between the two syntactical categories of *subject signs* and *predicate signs*. The latter, one between two kinds of signs, is of course different from that between the two kinds of places in the simple clause. The Quine of ML can thus accept P_1 but rejects the following second component of the particularity thesis.

P_2. *There are at least two kinds of terms.*

Signs fall into two kinds. Each of the first is individually specified and they are all together very few. One of them serves to form the simple clause, the others are the connectives and the quantifiers. The signs of the second kind, usually letter symbols, are indefinite in number. They are called terms. A kind or category of terms may contain either only constants or only variables or both. The distinction between constants and variables permits one to state a third thesis.

P_3. *There are undefined constants which can in a well-formed sentence stand only in the subject place.*

Jointly P_1, P_2, and P_3 express the syntactical core of the classical particularity thesis. $\overline{P}_2$, as I shall sometimes call the rejection of P_2, entails of course the rejection of P_3. It also entails N. We notice that ML, if adopted as the logical skeleton of the ideal language, also realizes N. Thus, if the Quine of the third phase repudiates ML as not sufficiently "nominalistic," the reason or reasons must lie in other roots of his "nominalism," as he, but not I in this paper, uses the term.

If there were exactly two kinds of terms, one could, if one accepted P_3, call them subject signs and predicate signs respectively. There is, however, a complication which is inevitable *provided one accepts P_2.* Let

'Henry' be the name of a color spot. Then 'Henry is green' and 'green is a color' are both well-formed and even true propositions. Yet, 'green', presumably corresponding to an undefined descriptive constant of the ideal schema, stands once in the subject place, once in the predicate place. The difficulties to which that leads can only be overcome by introducing further syntactical distinctions among the various "predicate" signs and the variables that correspond to them. That is, as everybody knows, Russell's theory of types, which leads to an indefinite number of kinds of terms. The device is in turn the cause of certain formal inelegancies in the development of the logical apparatus, particularly in the formalization, to whatever extent it can be formalized, of mathematics within PM. Against these inelegancies mathematical minds like Quine's chafe. What price he had to pay for avoiding them will be seen presently. His great merit is to have discovered that if one wants to avoid them and yet construct a schema of the same expressive possibilities as PM, then one must reject not only the so-called higher types, which is one loose meaning of that loose label, anti-Platonism, but also, much more radically, P_2. How radical that really is will, perhaps, be seen only at the end, after I shall have shown that Goodman, pursuing further the same line of thought, arrives at a position which is most naturally construed as rejecting even P_1.

Secondly, it is well worth noticing that if the central role of P_2 is once realized, a point of which Quine has always made very much becomes trivial, if I may say so with due respect. Quine has told us again and again that, contrary to an old prejudice, the ideal language need not contain proper names. Obviously not, if one rejects P_2, whatever that phrase, proper name, may mean. Here is what I believe is actually meant. Remember that to be a particular is not a syntactical notion. Let 'a' be an undefined descriptive constant added to ML that refers to such an entity. Assume furthermore, that if ML, supplemented by a sufficiency of constants, is used as the ideal language, 'a' will occur at least once in the subject place, say, in '$a \, \varepsilon \, b$'. Since '$x \, \varepsilon \, a$' is well formed and since ML contains the machinery of description, one can form the incomplete symbol '$(\imath x)(x \, \varepsilon \, a)$' and replace '$a \, \varepsilon \, b$' by '$(\imath x)(x \, \varepsilon \, a) \, \varepsilon \, b$'. To repeat, using Quine's favorite illustration, it is a direct consequence of $\overline{P}_2$ that the verb 'to pegasize' can do the job of the noun 'Pegasus'. But consider now how misleading it would be if, seduced by the blur that surrounds the notion of a proper name, one were to express this truism by saying that, since in the ideal language an undefined constant need never occur in the subject place (which is as close as one can come to denying P_3 if one rejects P_2), there are, contrary to an old prejudice, no particulars. All one could say is this. If PM is to serve as the skeleton of the ideal language, then the old question whether there are particulars becomes, in part, the question whether at least one undefined constant needs to be added to a certain category of its terms. If ML is to serve as the skeleton of the ideal language, then it becomes, in part, the question whether there is among the constants that must be added to it at least one, say, 'a', such that the *synthetic* proposition '$(x)[(x \ \varepsilon \ a) \equiv (x = a)]$' is true. Or, to put the same thing still differently and as it is usually put when the simple clause is built by means of 'ε', the question would be whether at least one of the needed undefined constants refers to a unit class. Of course such undefined constants would be needed; and in this sense one would still have to say that there are particulars. This shows again very clearly that, all-important as it is, syntax by itself is not everything. One also needs a firm grasp of the old problems as well as of the nonformal aspect of the new method in philosophy.

II

Let me take stock. So far I have merely introduced the *dramatis personae*. Less metaphorically speaking, I have done little more than state and explain the six theses which I labeled O_1, O_2, N, P_1, P_2, P_3. They are merely the terms in which the story must be told, or, if you please, the drama acted. So let me here insert a scenario. We have already seen that the type theory, unavoidable if one accepts P_2, produces certain mathematical inelegancies which in turn have suggested $\overline{P}_2$. This is the seed of the plot. In the third section we shall see that in order to endow ML, in spite of $\overline{P}_2$, with the same expressive possibilities as PM, one must add to its primitive and therefore presumably analytic sentences *an* ∃-*statement which asserts that there are classes*. Classes, to be sure, are indispensable if there is to be mathematics. Thus everybody has them, one way or the other, or else he must be prepared to make the Herostratic sacrifices of the third phase. Yet everybody agrees, at least within the movement of thought with which I am dealing, that in the sense in which ontology speaks of existence, *classes do not exist*. Those primitive ∃-statements of ML which are made necessary by $\overline{P}_2$ are, therefore, a cause of understandable concern, particularly if one is not completely clear, on philosophical grounds, about the relative merits of O_1 and O_2. They are, I submit, the structural reason, that specific and technical intellectual motive of which I spoke before, which led the new nominalists first to adopt O_2 and then, because of what thus became an ontological commitment to classes, to repudiate ML. This is the beginning of the third or Herostratic phase. If this is so, as I believe it to be, then it becomes very important to grasp firmly what I shall show in this section. Within PM and upon O_1, which is implicit in what Russell says about classes, the latter can be introduced without ontological commitment (O_1) and without adding a special $\exists$-statement to the primitive sentences. So I shall in this section do three things. First I shall briefly state the class issue. Next I shall give a succinct account, adjusted to my special purpose, of Russell's theory of classes. Finally I shall show that the concern with primitive $\exists$-statements has its source in PM itself or, more generally, in a certain conception of analyticity. The last point makes the new nominalists' concentration on classes, which require in ML a special primitive $\exists$-statement, even more plausible. The denial of the existence of classes is indeed the second and, to my mind, the only sound root of their ontology. That makes it the more ironical that upon what I take to be the correct conception of ontology, namely, O_1, this goal had already been reached by the "Platonist" Russell. What kept the new nominalists from seeing this was, I believe, above all their craving for mathematical elegance. Einstein is reputed to have said that elegance of all kinds is best left to shoemakers and to tailors.

Ordinary speech distinguishes between a property, say, that of being green and the corresponding class, say, that of all green objects. We insist on the distinction, at least we are not willing to abandon it even in the ideal language without a thorough examination, because of the possibility of one class corresponding to more than one property. Yet we also feel that the phrase 'the class of all green objects' does not have a referent[3] in the sense in which 'green' has one. This is quite independent of how many syntactical categories one admits (in the ideal language) and into which of these one puts (the correlate of) 'green'. The reason is that, as we in fact use and wish to use 'class', there are also classes of objects that have nothing whatsoever in common except their being mentioned together, which is not in a relevant sense anything they share. Russell described this state of affairs by saying, first, that properties are epistemologically primary while classes are not, and, second, that classes do not, in the sense in which ontology speaks of existence, exist. They are, as he put it, logical fictions. Presently we shall inquire into the syntactical expression he gave to these ideas in PM. But let me first state a condition which the very nature of the

---

[3] Quine now uses 'naming' and 'referring' so that only what exists can be named or referred to. Thus, since he now denies the existence not only of classes but also of properties, he would now not wish to say that 'green' has a referent. But this is merely a decision about the use of 'naming' and 'referring'. Though at present a good deal of ontological discussion is carried on in "semantical" disguise, I do not propose to explore here this aspect of the current debate.

distinction between a property and the class it determines imposes on any formalism that intends to preserve it. PM preserves it. If, e.g., 'f_1' is a property constant, then '$\hat{x}f_1(x)$' is the corresponding class constant. That two properties, referred to by 'f_1' and 'f_2' respectively, determine the same class is obviously expressed by '$(x)[f_1(x) \equiv f_2(x)]$'. Now the point of the distinction is that two such properties may yet be different, that is, that there may be a context which is true of the one and false of the other. For if there were no such context, there would be no sense in distinguishing between them. But there being no such context is symbolically expressed by '$f_1 = f_2$'. This is exactly the meaning of the defined logical sign of identity. It follows that if

(E) $$(x)[f(x) \equiv g(x)] \supset (f = g)$$

were a theorem, there would be no point in distinguishing between the two kinds of signs. Formally expressed this means that

(1) $$\ldots f \ldots \equiv \ldots f(\hat{x}) \ldots ,$$

where the dots indicate any well-formed context, ought to be a formal consequence of (E). Conversely, a sign defined in terms of a property sign or, more generally, of a predicative context, will be properly called a class sign if and only if it satisfies

(2) $$(x)[f(x) \equiv g(x)] \supset [\hat{x}f(x) = \hat{x}g(x)].$$

We shall have occasion to note that (2) and $(E) \supset (1)$ are both theorems of PM. ML does not preserve the distinction between properties and classes. Any descriptive constant added to it refers to a class. At least, that is what one usually says. I find it clearer to say instead that a proposition (E') which corresponds to (E) is a theorem of ML. For to be a class sign and to satisfy (E) or whatever corresponds to it in another schema is one and the same thing.

PM realizes the idea that classes do not in the ontological sense exist by making every class sign a defined sign. If, e.g., 'f_1' is an undefined descriptive constant added to it, then '$\hat{x}f_1(x)$' is an expression defined in terms of 'f_1'. This is the reason why I am prepared to maintain that PM implies O_1. Whether Russell himself, presented with this observation, would have acknowledged it or would do so now, is a different matter. Specifically, he introduces

(3) $\quad$ '$\ldots \hat{x}f(x) \ldots$' $\quad$ for $\quad$ '$(\exists g)[(x)(f(x) \equiv g(x)) \ldots g \ldots]$'.

He calls class signs incomplete symbols. This, however, is merely another way of calling them defined, since (3) is nothing but a schema for definitions rather than a single one. As one might expect, (2) and $(E) \supset (1)$ both follow from (3). In the light of the later developments the crucial point is that while the definientia of (3) do contain an

∃-statement, no such statement and, therefore, in particular no such primitive statement is required in order to operate in PM with classes. This becomes even clearer by contrast with definite descriptions, the other kind of incomplete symbols in PM. These require the premise '$E!(\imath x)f(x)$' if they are to be used like undefined constants.

We see, then, that upon O_1 and with PM as the syntactical schema of the ideal language classes do not exist. Nor do ∃-questions literally arise in connection with them. What comes nearest is this. Given a predicate or a predicative context and another one in which it occurs, one may ask whether the ∃-statement in the definiens is true, or, loosely speaking, whether what is true of the class is true of the predicate. Even this question could be answered in the affirmative once and for all if (E) and the corresponding schemata for the higher types were added to the primitive apparatus of PM. Russell hesitated to do that, particularly since he did not need to do it in order to obtain unproblematic class signs. But there were two more reasons for his hesitation. (I am again, as always, speaking structurally, not biographically.)

One reason is that our natural language does not satisfy (E); that it is not, as one usually says, extensional. So one might well wonder whether the ideal language could be so radically different. Quine and Goodman are both extensionalists. So am I, with a qualification which does not bother and which certainly need not bother us here since it lies beyond the scope of this essay. It is only fair to add, though, that as of now this commitment to extensionality means less for them than for me. For they, unlike me, have in the meantime repudiated analyticity; and upon my conception of analyticity (E) is analytic. But whatever the state of this issue is now, it is well to remember that one of the purposes of PM—at a time when the discoveries of Goedel were still in the future—was to formalize the whole of logic and mathematics, thus producing a complete model of analyticity within the ideal language. Here lies the second reason why one might have hesitated to add (E) to the primitive rules and propositions (I do not here distinguish between the two) of PM. These rules and propositions fall into two kinds. One comprehends the propositional calculus and quantification theory. They and they alone were felt to be unproblematic, because they and they alone were felt to yield quite indubitably analyticity, in the philosophical sense the formalism was designed to reflect. They become problematic only if one raises the doubts and objections of the finitists or intuitionists; their ideas lie outside our movement of thought. Indeed, Quine and Goodman refer even now to the propositional calculus and to quantification theory as the "logical" apparatus, with a strange inconsistency which they cover up by making it a mere matter of convenience. Be that as it may, at the time of PM it had become clear that these rules and primitive propositions did not suffice. The theory of types may pass muster as a refinement of quantification theory. But further primitive sentences are needed to reconstruct mathematics, even within the Goedelian limits of the possible. *These were felt to be problematic simply because, I submit, they were additional ones.* (E) would be such an addition. Hence the hesitation. Even so, (E) is at least not an ∃-statement. On the other hand, we just saw that it is not needed. Two other primitive statements which are needed, the so-called axioms of infinity and of choice, are ∃-statements. More specifically, they both contain the clause '(∃f)'. To accept such statements as both primitive and analytic seemed then definitely too much. It certainly was too much for Russell. Yet he displayed what seems to me to have been the most admirable good sense. For as he saw it, the issue was one of analyticity, not one of ontological commitment in the sense of ontology implicit in his theory of classes. Or, as he put it, he wondered whether the two axioms stated matters of fact which may or may not be so. This is the situation from which the new nominalists inherited their concern for primitive ∃-statements. It is also the point where, moved by this concern, they turned a question of analyticity into one of ontology. Thus they were pushed toward O_2. ML marks the transition.

III

ML includes among its primitive statements one, (E'), which corresponds to (E). As we saw, that makes all its terms class signs. There remains therefore only the task of providing the corresponding class expressions for those predicative contexts, ' . . . x . . . ', which are not of the basic form '$x \, \varepsilon \, a$', 'a' being an undefined constant. Purely notationally, there is no reason whatsoever why class expressions '$\hat{x}$(. . . x . . .)' should not be introduced as incomplete symbols in analogy to (3). Yet there is a difference. In PM the type rule imposes on any context ' . . . x . . . ' a restriction that suffices to preclude the formation of those "classes" which produce the Russell paradox. In ML such a restriction must still be imposed. The most natural or, if you please, the most elegant way of doing that has two steps. First, one adds as a further primitive statement an ∃-statement which guarantees that there is a corresponding class in every case in which the context fulfills a certain condition, called stratification, whose specification need not detain us. This primitive statement reads, quite obviously,

(Q) $\qquad\qquad (\exists y)(x)[(x \, \varepsilon \, y) \equiv \; \ldots x \ldots],$

with 'y' not occurring in the context. One sees intuitively that (E') guarantees the uniqueness of the classes which (Q) asserts to "exist." In other words, (Q) corresponds, except for the uniqueness clause, exactly to '$E!(\imath x)(\;\ldots x \ldots\;)$'. Thus one introduces, secondly,

$$\hat{x}(\;\ldots\; x \;\ldots\;)' \quad \text{for} \quad '(\imath y)(x)[(x \;\varepsilon\; y) \equiv \;\ldots\; x \;\ldots\;]'.$$

Here mathematical elegance triumphs. One needs no longer, as in PM, two separate definitional schemata, one for definite descriptions, one for classes, for the two kinds of incomplete symbols. One of them, that for definite descriptions, will do. Nor is that all. Elegance scores two more victories. The so-called axiom of infinity becomes superfluous; the so-called axiom of choice can be replaced by certain modifications of (Q). This is the pattern. Details need not concern us. This particular pattern, by the way, is not literally that of ML but that of NF, a schema Quine outlined as early as 1937 in a remarkable paper, "New Foundations for Mathematical Logic."[4] The differences are minor and for our purposes without consequence. What matters is that ML, like NF, requires a primitive ∃-statement to the effect that there are certain classes, or, as I prefer not to say, that certain classes "exist."

Let me sum up. The theory of types is the cause of some inelegancies in the foundations of mathematics within PM. If one wishes to avoid these inelegancies and yet secure a schema of the same expressive power as PM then one must reject P_2. This leads to schemata such as ML or NF which satisfy N but contain a primitive statement that asserts, if one embraces O_2, the existence of classes. Historically, this latter circumstance was probably one of the causes for the emergence of O_2. On the other hand, we all agree that in the sense in which ontology speaks of existence, classes do not exist. It follows that if one holds O_2 and $\overline{P}_2$, one is forced to repudiate ML. This Quine and Goodman both did. The nonexistence of classes is, as I said before, the nonsyntactical root of what they chose, rather confusingly, to call their nominalism. It seems then that I have kept my promise. I have shown that $\overline{P}_2$, which is what I mean by the new nominalists' anti-Aristotelianism, is the syntactical root of the whole movement of thought. The one thing left is to understand what happened in the third phase. In this phase, there are important differences between Quine and Goodman. In explaining them I shall avoid the two words 'concrete' and 'abstract', which they both use profusely. I have two reasons for this.

---

[4] This paper, too, is reprinted in *From a Logical Point of View*, with corrections and a supplement. (E') and (Q) correspond in NF to P1 and R_3' respectively. In ML extensionality is *201, the primitive ∃-statement is *202. The schemata of ML corresponding to (3) are D9 and D12.

For one, it would take another essay at least as long as this to distinguish critically the several meanings of each of these two words. For another, and rather significantly I think, the ideas involved can be just as easily expressed without them.

Quine now is not willing to say that such things as colors exist. Let us inquire into the causes of his reluctance as well as into what it entails. One cause, I think, is again $\overline{P}_2$. Because of it the names of individual green objects and 'green' itself are constants of the same syntactical kind and lie, therefore, in the scope of the same variables. Their being of the same syntactical kind seems to suggest that their referents exist in the same way, that greenness is a thing like and different from green things. But this is exactly the kind of nonsense to which the extremists among the medieval realists owe their bad name. Thus we understand also why Quine does not hesitate to call a Platonist anyone who says that colors exist. Yet, since he embraces O_2, he would have to say just that as long as he insists on $\overline{P}_2$. For, with $\overline{P}_2$, to admit a constant at all is to admit it into the range of the one kind of variable there is. Thus he has but two choices. The one alternative is to expunge all such undefined constants as 'green' from the ideal language. Fortunately he does not do that. I say fortunately because to do this is to adopt some variant of the absurd doctrine that 'green' can somehow be defined in terms of the names of green objects. (This, by the way, is the core of the modern meaning of that ambiguous word, nominalism.) The other alternative is to accept P_2; to make 'green' and the names of other properties constants of the predicate variety; and either not to introduce at all or not to quantify the variables which correspond to them. Then one will not, even upon O_2, have to say that properties exist. This is apparently the alternative Quine chooses. I say apparently because he has not, since he repudiated ML and explicitly propounded O_2, actually given us the schema of an ideal language he could accept. Again, this is easily understood. If he reintroduces P_2, sticks with O_2, and continues to reject the theory of types, he limits himself in substance to the logical apparatus of the lower functional calculus. Thus he would have to give up most of mathematics. Unlike Goodman, he is not quite ready to go that far.

There is still another reason, which is not syntactical, why Quine does not want to say that such things as colors exist. If he used the term as I do in this paper, he would have to insist that only particulars and certain compounds of them exist. It is interesting to note, then, that upon the only explication of the nonsyntactical notion of particularity of which I can think, there is no good reason why, say, the color green should not be counted a particular. A particular, we remember, is an entity both simple and self-contained. Goodman, for instance, though he certainly uses his words most uncommonly, is therefore not unreasonable when he holds that colors actually are particulars. Accordingly, he admits such terms as 'green' among the undefined constants within the range of the variables of a schema that realizes N. I conclude that Quine's notion of particularity or, what virtually amounts to the same thing, his notion of existence has an additional ingredient or ingredients. One ingredient is, perhaps, localization in space and time. Properties of course are not so localized. But to introduce such relatively contingent features of our world as space and time into the analysis of a notion as fundamental as particularity would be in any world, is, to my mind, a categorial error. This does not mean that it is false. It is just not good philosophy.

Goodman in *The Structure of Appearance* (SA) constructs an ideal language, or at least a substantial part of one, which realizes N. He embraces O_2. His undefined constants refer, as we just saw, to things very different from what modern nominalism means by particulars. Among his primitive statements there are ∃-statements. One reason why that does not bother him is, perhaps, that he rejects the notion of analyticity. At least, this explanation fits the pattern I think I discovered within our movement of thought. I criticized Goodman's schema and what he says about it elsewhere[5] and I do not propose to repeat any of the points I then made. The one point I wish to make I had not seen when I wrote that paper.

As Goodman himself interprets his schema and as I then interpreted it, SA maintains P_2. It contains two undefined relational terms, 'overlapping (ov)' and 'being affiliated (af)'; and, say, '$x(ov, y)$' and '$ov(x, af)$' are not well formed. The two terms are therefore predicates in the full sense of P_2, in a syntactical category of their own and not within the range of the variables. But they are also the only two undefined "predicates" of the schema. More important, they are both symmetrical. In other words, '$ov(x, y) \equiv ov(y, x)$' and '$af(x, y) \equiv af(y, x)$' are both "theorems." (I put 'theorem' between quotation marks because without analyticity there is no difference left between the theorems of logic and any other presumably true proposition such as a law of physics.) This state of affairs suggests the following description of Goodman's ideal language. As in any schema likely to be proposed for this role, its signs fall into two major classifications. The one comprehends all terms, constants as well as variables; in this case, according to N, without further syntactical distinctions among them. The other consists of a

[5] "Two Types of Linguistic Philosophy," *The Review of Metaphysics*, 5, 1952, 417–38. The paper is reprinted in MLP.

few combinators, individually specified signs serving to combine terms into propositions. In SA there are, as usual, connectives and operators and, not so usual, *two* modes of combining terms into simple clauses. To emphasize this interpretation one could, if one wished, write '(x, y)' and '$[x, y]$' instead of '$ov(x, y)$' and '$af(x, y)$', respectively. The statements which, as one so misleadingly says, implicitly define the two "relations," become then simply a special set of primitive statements, coördinate with those of propositional logic and quantification. The point is, to repeat, that both '(x, y)' and '$[x, y]$' are symmetrical. This amounts to the rejection not only of P_2 but also of P_1. If his schema is looked at in this way, which is from a purely syntactical standpoint the most natural way of looking at it, the most radical anti-Platonist among the new nominalists becomes also the most radical anti-Aristotelian. Thus my thesis is again confirmed.

The idea of two syntactically different modes of combining terms into simple clauses is not entirely new. As far as I know, it was first proposed in a very different context by Storer; and it has since been taken up in the same context, analytical ethics, in a recent book by E. W. Hall.[6] But, to be sure, in all other respects the similarities, if any, are very superficial.

One may ask, in conclusion, whether our analysis permits one to arrive at a reasoned opinion about the significance and prospects of the new nominalism. Perhaps the material in this essay does not suffice by itself. Together with the criticism of Goodman which I presented elsewhere it leads, I think, to the conclusion that the new nominalism is but a passing fancy. For the time being this is obscured by the brilliance of its main representatives. Yet it was this very brilliance that made them succumb to the lure of mathematical elegance at the expense of philosophical significance. This, we saw, was how the whole thing began.

[6] *What Is Value? An Essay in Philosophical Analysis* (New York: Humanities Press, 1952). Storer's paper is "The Logic of Value Imperatives," *Philosophy of Science*, 13, 1946, 25–40.

Concepts*

A PHILOSOPHICAL position is characterized by its proponents' explicit or implicit ideal language. The classical logical positivists all claimed, explicitly or implicitly, that a certain syntactical schema, call it L_c, can upon interpretation serve as the ideal language. To obtain L_c, start with the schema of *Principia Mathematica*. Add certain classes of descriptive constants to its primitive signs and the so-called axiom of extensionality to its primitive sentences. Suppress ramification. The resulting schema is L_c. In a recent essay[1] one of us, having given some reasons why L_c cannot be the ideal language, proposed another schema, call it L, as a more likely candidate for this role. Our purpose in this note is to apply this new schema, L, or, rather, the "language" which it becomes upon interpretation, to some issues that are now widely discussed. Foremost among these is the nature of *concepts*. We shall explicate it in section II. In section III we shall inquire how the Russell-Leibniz analysis of *identity* fares in the new ideal language. This will enable us to answer, in section IV, some questions concerning the several meanings of *meaning*.

The argument of "Intentionality" as well as the description of L it contains are both rather detailed; so detailed that it would be neither possible nor proper to reproduce either. But it is possible, fortunately, since it is also necessary, to state their gist, or at least what we need of it for our purpose, rather succinctly. This background we provide in section I, which is divided into two parts. In the second part we give a selective description and interpretation of L. In the first part, hoping

* *Jointly with Herbert Hochberg.* Philosophical Studies, *8, 1957, 19–27. Reprinted by permission.*

[1] "Intentionality," *Semantica* (Archivio di Filosofia, Roma: Bocca, 1955), pp. 177–216, and also pp. 3–38 of this book.

to purchase simplicity at the price of a certain unguardedness of statement, we explain the basic idea.

I

1. Consider the two statements (1) 'This is green' and (2) 'I see (know, am aware, etc.) that this is green'. The undefined descriptive constants of both L_c and L all refer to entities of the kind called phenomenal. Assume, then, that both (1) and (2) mention only such entities, namely, a particular (this), a character (green), and an awareness (seeing). L_c and L both contain an individual ('a') and a predicate ('gr') constant such that upon interpretation '$gr(a)$' becomes an adequate transcription of (1). L_c provides no adequate transcription for (2). Or, to say the same thing more ornately, L_c is not an adequate tool for the philosophical analysis of mind.[2] This is the reason (and, as we believe, the only reason) why it cannot be the ideal language.

L is designed to remedy this deficiency. The basic idea that leads to its construction has four parts. (a) An awareness (we use the term generically) is different from its content. (b) Awarenesses are particulars. (c) An awareness is one *of* its content by virtue of exemplifying a character of the kind called *propositional*. (d) To each content, referred to by a sentence, corresponds accordingly a propositional character, named by a predicate. To grasp all this more firmly, consider an awareness the content of which is referred to by (2). It follows that the transcription of (2) must contain '$f_1(b)$', where 'b' (not 'a'!) is the name of the awareness the content of which is referred to by (1) and 'f_1' names the propositional character which, as specified in (d), corresponds to (1). Notice that we merely said the transcription of (2) must contain the clause '$f_1(b)$'. The question which further clauses, if any, it must contain is of course examined in "Intentionality"; for our purpose, we need not stay for the answer.

2. L contains L_c. After what has been said, that is not surprising. But it is, perhaps, surprising that the only additions to L_c that are needed, aside from descriptive constants, are, first, two new *logical* signs and, second, one new schema[3] for *analytic* sentences. L_c, we assume, is so constructed that only closed expressions are sentences and that it contains abstraction operators as well as sentential variables.[4] The two new primitive signs are

---

[2] This is not to say that L_c cannot accommodate behavioristic psychology.

[3] 'Schema' is here used as logicians use it when they say that the primitive sentences of a calculus may be given by schemata.

[4] These assumptions are mere matters of convenience. The second can be made because L_c is extensional. The third, since it involves only variables, has upon our view of ontology no ontological implications.

$$M \quad \text{and} \quad ‘ \ldots ’.$$

The first is a pseudopredicate, the second the quoting operator.

Formation Rules. F1. Every well-formed sentence of L_c is well formed in L. F2. Every sentence of L surrounded by quotes becomes a first-order nonrelational predicate with all the syntactical properties of a primitive descriptive constant. F3. Every sentence of the form 'fMp' is well formed. Call these sentences the simple clauses of 'M'.

Analyticity. A1. Every sentence analytic according to L_c is analytic. A2. Every simple clause of 'M' is either analytic or it is contradictory, i.e., its negation is analytic. It is analytic if and only if the predicate to the left of 'M' is formed by the quoting operator from the sentence to the right of 'M'.

Interpretation. L_c is interpreted as usual. ' ' $\ldots$ ' ' is interpreted as "the proposition $****$," where '$****$' stands for the interpretation of ' $\ldots$ '. For example, where we wrote a bit earlier 'f_1', L writes instead ' '$gr(a)$' '. 'M' is interpreted as "means." Sometimes, when we say such things as "The proposition this is green *means* that this is green," we speak neither psychologically nor about what 'this is green' refers to but, rather, "linguistically," in a problematic sense of the term that needs explication. 'M' transcribes this *intentional* root meaning of 'means'.[5]

Two comments will conclude this outline. (a) The above uses of 'logical' and 'analytic' are problematic. That is why we italicized them. That these uses fit with and are, in fact, part of the explication of the two terms must therefore be argued. This explication is, in turn, part and parcel of that of the intentional meaning of 'means'. Those arguments and these explications are of course to be found in "Intentionality." (b) According to L, an awareness is always distinct from its content. One is not aware of the former merely by being aware of the latter. Phenomenally, the "two" awarenesses are often inseparably one. Hence, some may argue, L cannot be the ideal language. We disagree. No schema could possibly fit the phenomena with that accuracy which is, quite properly, the ideal of those who describe the phenomenological material for its own sake. Philosophical analysis, however, is not phenomenological description; and its problems are such that the inevitable discrepancy between the phenomenological material and any schema whatsoever does not matter. That is why in philosophical analysis one can use schemata. These rest on the phenomenological

---

[5] There are of course other meanings of 'means'. See "Intentionality"; also below.

material, if we may so express ourselves, but they need not slavishly reproduce it.

II

Take the color green. L contains a predicate, 'gr', which names it. Thus, if there is also a concept green, which is a thing different from the color itself, then 'gr' cannot possibly name this thing, too. Historically, there have been attempts to identify a thing's concept with its name. Those who made them usually ended up by expounding, in reply to a philosophical question, a bit of speculative psychology, which as such is quite reasonable, namely, that concepts, *if* there are such things, are psychologically carried by either explicit or implicit verbal events. This surely will not do. Let us then inquire whether concepts can be accommodated in L without ontological expense, i.e., without adding, more radically, either to the syntactical categories it provides or even, less radically, to the constants in these categories. The answer is affirmative.

Thinking analogically and with one's pencil, as it were, one may be tempted to assert that a concept, e.g., the concept green, is a character which, like a propositional character, is sometimes exemplified by awarenesses and which is named by a new predicate, "'gr'". Yet a moment's reflection shows that, by F2, "'gr'" is ill formed. This proposal thus would put us to ontological expense, and of the more radical sort at that. Nor is this the only difficulty it encounters. Awarenesses, it is argued in "Intentionality," are all propositional. Syntactically, this means that a particular is an awareness if and only if it exemplifies a character named by one of the predicates mentioned in F2. This, we submit, holds also for the awarenesses of concepts. Consider one who is "thinking of green."[6] He may, for instance, imagine a green particular. But then, a particular being green is a content referred to by a sentence! This is where the proposal we are about to make rests on the phenomenological material. So we must also remember what was said about the limitation of schemata on the one hand and the nature of philosophical analysis on the other. We are not interested in all the various ways in which a concept may be carried psychologically. Our task is, rather, to represent them all by a single schema, provided only that this schema does not omit or distort anything but the phenomenal detail. The "proof" that our proposal meets this criterion lies, of course,

---

[6] This is *one* of the ways in which we refer idiomatically to contents of this kind. Depending on the circumstances, 'thinking' may be replaced by such expressions as 'remembering' or 'imagining'.

in what can be done with it. (The proof of all puddings is in the eating. In this respect philosophy is no exception.)

Let 'f_1' be a constant predicate of L, either defined or undefined.[7] Form the sentence '$(\exists f)(f=f_1)$', which, incidentally, is analytic. The "concept of f_1" is the propositional character named by '$(\exists f)(f=f_1)$'. The expression '$(\imath g)gM(\exists f)(f=f_1)$' is, as one easily sees, a definite description of it. Having thus without ontological expense located the concept of f_1 in L, we of course may and occasionally shall use 'f_1'' as an abbreviation of its name. This is the explication of 'concept' we propose.

With the customary notation 'f_1' belongs to the first type. It is easily seen that nothing we said depends on that. Call an expression a *term* if and only if it is either an individual constant or a (defined or undefined) predicate (of any type) or a definite description (of any type). Our method provides names for the concepts corresponding to all terms. '$(\exists x)(x=a)$'', for instance, transcribes "the concept of a." Notice that upon this explication of 'concept' the idea of an individual concept, which has recently been the cause of much puzzlement, offers no difficulty. The concept of a definite description, say, '$(\imath y)f_1(y)$', is '$(\exists x)(x=(\imath y)f_1(y))$'. The expression inside the inner quotes, being analytically equivalent to '$E!(\imath y)f_1(y)$', is of course not analytic. '$(\exists x)(x=a)$' and '$(\exists f)(f=f_1)$' are. This, too, is perhaps worth noticing.

III

Let 't_1' and 't_2' be two terms. We shall say that they are the same if and only if in writing them down we produce different tokens of the same type; otherwise we shall say that they are *different*. Introduce '$t_1=t_2$' as an abbreviation in the calculus for the schema[8] '$\ldots t_1 \ldots \equiv \ldots t_2 \ldots$' with the dots signifying any well-formed context. The Russell-Leibniz explication of *identity* proposes '$=$' as the transcription of 'identical'. Its adequacy has long been a much-debated issue. Let us inquire what light the new ideal language throws on it.

Assume 'f_1' and 'f_2' to be different. Can '$f_1=f_2$' ever be true? In L_c the answer is affirmative. Take two predicates that are different. Since L_c is extensional, '$(x)[f_1(x) \equiv f_2(x)] \supset (f_1=f_2)$' is a theorem. Some characters are coextensive with some others. For some characters the antecedent of the theorem is therefore true. For some it is even analytic. It follows that some characters, though referred to by different predicates, are

---

[7] Since L contains abstraction operators we need not distinguish. Strictly, we should therefore write metalinguistically, say, by means of Greek letters. Nothing untoward will happen, though, if we neglect this precaution.

[8] See note 3.

yet *identical in L_c* and that for some the statement of identity is even analytic. L_c is a very important part of L; otherwise it wouldn't have been mistaken for the ideal language and wouldn't be, as in fact it is, an adequate tool for the analysis of all philosophical issues except some of those that involve mind. L_c, then, is the bulk of L. Or, what amounts almost, though not quite, to the same thing, all contexts of L, except those containing 'M', are extensional. Identity in L_c is therefore an important notion. We shall abbreviate it by '$\sim$'. Yet, since we do not accept L_c as the ideal language, we naturally cannot accept '$\sim$' as an adequate translation of 'identical'. That is not to say, though, that there is anything wrong with the Russell-Leibniz idea. This idea we accept, apply it to L instead of to L_c, use '$=$' as an abbreviation for this notion and propose it as the transcription of 'identical'.

Let 't_1' and 't_2' be different terms of L. '$t_1 \sim t_2$' may well be true; it may even be analytic. But it is an analytic truth that the two are not identical. In symbols, '$-(t_1 = t_2)$' is analytic. To see that clearly, consider the four sentences (1) 'f_1'$M(\exists f)(f = f_1)$, (2) 'f_2'$M(\exists f)(f = f_2)$, (3) 'f_2'$M(\exists f)(f = f_1)$, (4) 'f_1'$M(\exists f)(f = f_2)$; and remember that, by F2, there is no substitution inside the quoting operator. By A2, (1) and (2) are analytic; (3) and (4) are contradictory. Yet (2) and (4) may be obtained from (3) and (1) respectively by substituting 'f_2' for 'f_1'.

Speaking with a deliberate blur, in the way that gives rise to the philosophical problems, one may summarize the last result as follows. Two expressions, if they are different, are never identical, even though they refer to the same thing; the reason for their not being identical is that "their" concepts are different; and the reason for the two concepts being different is that they "have" different meanings. This shows the connection between the analysis of 'concept' and that of 'meaning'.

IV

1. Wittgenstein in the *Tractatus* rejected the very notion of identity. Our analysis enables us to separate what is just from what is unjustifiable in his rejection. Since he argues the case of particulars, let 'a' and 'b' be two individual constants. '$-(a = b)$' is upon our analysis analytic. This reflects what is just in Wittgenstein's view. On the other hand, '$a \sim b$' may well be true, though it can of course not be analytic, the necessary and sufficient condition for its truth being that 'a' and 'b' name the same particular. This shows what is unjustifiable in Wittgenstein's view. For, as we mentioned earlier and shall elaborate presently, the notion transcribed by '$\sim$' is not only important; it also is, so to speak, very close to identity.

2. Assume '$t_1 \sim t_2$' to be true; 't_1' and 't_2' being two predicates, the

first undefined, the second defined and fully expanded into its undefined constituents none of which is 't_1'. It is one of the basic ideas of the
positivistic kind of analysis, and not of it alone, that in this case 't_1'
can without loss of expressive possibility or, as one also says, without
loss of "meaning," be dropped. Or, as it is usually put, the ideal language need not and does not contain 't_1'. This is, of course, the very idea
of reconstruction (*Aufbau*, definition by extensive abstraction). Objectors claim that there is, in fact, a loss of "meaning." Again, our analysis
separates what is sound from what is unsound in this claim. Its sound
core is explicated by the analyticity of '$-(t_1 = t_2)$'. In the "world" of
L_c, though, there is no loss and this world is indeed the whole world,
except for "mind" as represented by the logical(!) sign 'M'. Notice
that we say by 'M', not by 'M' and the *quoting operator*. There is a
reason for that. Technically, 'M' alone without the quoting operator
would do us no good. But the quoting operator alone and the primitive
predicates it engenders by F2, if added to L_c, would not yet introduce
the essentially "mental" nonextensionality produced by 'M' because of
A2.

Some years ago the issue was discussed under a rather confusing
heading. One spoke then of the paradox of analysis. We shall make up
a sentence to indicate how the puzzles arose. "A cube can be *defined*
either as a regular polyhedron with twelve edges (t_1) or as one with
eight corners (t_2). Yet, one may not *know* that '$t_1 \sim t_2$' is true; and,
whether or not he knows it, he may *perceive* the same object once as a
regular polyhedron with twelve edges, once as one with eight corners."
The words we italicized mark the trouble spots. The bearing of our
explications on the puzzles they engendered is obvious. Some of the
confusion stemmed from an improper concern with phenomenology.
The analyticity of '$-(t_1 = t_2)$' explicates the one sense in which there is
indeed no "analysis" of any content. Thus it brings out what is sound
in this concern. It also shows, incidentally, how we can do justice to
phenomenology, not by slavishly clinging to the phenomenological
material but, rather, by locating certain of its characteristics correctly
in our schema.

3. 'M' represents one of the idiomatic uses ("meanings") of 'means'.
There are quite a few others.[9] It will round out what has been said if we
group this "intentional" meaning with two of the others. (a) Inside as
well as outside the philosopher's study *explicans* and *explicandum* are
often and quite properly said to have the same meaning. This use, if

[9] See note 5.

correct, is represented by the synthetic truth of '$t_1 \sim t_2$'. (b) We say, in a different sense, that two terms and, in this case, also that two sentences have the same meaning if and only if a certain sentence is analytic. For two first-order predicates, for instance, this sentence is '$(x)[f_1(x) \equiv f_2(x)]$'. In "Intentionality" this is called the logical meaning of 'means'. Different expressions can, of course, have the same logical meaning. (c) Two expressions have the same meaning if and only if '$t_1 = t_2$' is true. This is the intentional meaning of 'means'. In this sense, we saw, different expressions never have the same meaning.

4. The New Nominalists now contribute to many discussions a twist or flavor of their own. In the case of "meaning" the contribution is Goodman's.[10] With a characteristically behavioristic foreshortening, he attaches "meaning" to actual utterances. As it happens, though, that makes no difference for our point. Here then is, as we understand it, what Goodman says. There are particulars. An utterance is a particular. A word or phrase or sentence, uttered several times on different occasions, is said to have the same meaning on each of these occasions. Meaning, if there is such a thing, would therefore have to be a universal. There are no universals. Hence there are, in the accepted sense, no meanings. The only way out is to say that every utterance has or is[11] its own meaning. Meaning thus is particular and unique. Surely, this is the counsel of despair. Yet, coming from a distinguished source, it echoes profound ruminations.[12]

Different utterances of the same (English) sentence may have different transcriptions in L. Take then, instead of utterances, contents, which do uniquely determine their transcriptions. Contents recur. Their "meanings," in one of the idiomatic uses of the noun, are the propositional characters, including, as we saw, those that are "concepts." These characters are universals. Not being nominalists, we do of course not shun universals. Propositional characters, though, like all characters, are exemplified by particulars, namely, those particulars which are awarenesses and which, being particulars, are like all particulars in

---

[10] N. Goodman, "On Likeness of Meaning," *Analysis*, 10, 1949, 1–7. For an examination of the New Nominalism, see "Particularity and the New Nominalism," *Methodos*, 6, 1954, 131–47, and also pp. 91–105 of this book.

[11] We say *has* or *is* because we are not told in that essay what sort of thing a meaning is. For the philosophical behaviorists, one will remember, the utterance or, rather, the noise, provided only it has certain behavioral effects, actually is the meaning.

[12] As I now realize, this is not quite fair to Goodman. For a more adequate analysis of his errors, see R. Grossmann, "Propositional Attitudes," to appear in *The Philosophical Quarterly*. [Added in 1959.]

a certain sense "unique." In this sense, speaking once more with a deliberate blur, meaning is indeed unique. Nor is that all. It is, as a universal, also unique in the sense that is explicated by the analyticity of '$-(t_1 = t_2)$'. Concern with this uniqueness is, we submit, the profound core of those ruminations. Very probably it was also one of the roots of Berkeley's nominalism. But then, we believe to have shown that one need not be a nominalist to do justice to this peculiar uniqueness of "meaning."

Elementarism*

C AN such words as 'color' and 'pitch' be replaced by circumlocutions in all contexts without loss of meaning? Elementarism is the affirmative answer to this question. Or, rather, this is what I would say if asked to explain the notion to one not familiar with the techniques of analytical philosophy. The precise explication uses the tool of an ideal language, L. With this way of philosophizing I assume the reader to be familiar.[1] Unless L contains either the type division of *Principia Mathematica* (PM) or one syntactically equivalent to it, the problem of elementarism does not arise. In the first two sections of this note I shall assume that L is the schema of PM, without ramification, with extensionality, supplemented by a class C of undefined descriptive constants. C, the elementarist claims, can be so chosen that all its members are of types zero or one, i.e., either individual constants ('a', 'b', . . .) or first-order predicates, including relational ones ('f_1', 'f_2', . . . 'r_1', 'r_2', . . .). To see the connection between this precise formulation and the vague one with which I started, one merely has to assume, quite plausibly, that some color words, say, 'green' ('gr') and 'red', are among the first-order predicates of C. Since we say 'green is a color', 'color' would then be of the second type; thus the elementarist would have to insist that its transcription ('Col') can be defined in terms of his C.

The thesis of elementarism has occupied me for quite some time and I have repeatedly expressed the opinion that it is *in fact* true. That is why I call it a thesis, using the label for factual assertions of so broad a

* Philosophy and Phenomenological Research, *18, 1957, 107–14. Reprinted by permission.*

[1] See *The Metaphysics of Logical Positivism.* For the analysis of determinism mentioned below, see *Philosophy of Science* (Madison: University of Wisconsin Press, 1957).

nature that they are felt to be "philosophical." (Determinism, as I explicate it, is another thesis.) Recently Weinberg and Palmieri have come to share my preoccupation. Weinberg[2] in a difficult paper suggests, if I understand him correctly, that elementarism may be true *on philosophical grounds*. Palmieri devoted two papers to the subject. The first[3] is a brilliant criticism of some points Weinberg made. In the second[4] he examines, among other things, a definition I once gave for 'pitch'. Stimulated by these three studies, I now propose to do three things. In Section One I shall show that the only philosophical reasons which one could with some plausibility adduce in favor of elementarism, or, rather, the only such reasons I can think of, are specious. In Section Two I shall show *on logical grounds* that except in a finite universe, where it is trivially true, elementarism, if true, cannot but be a factual truth of the kind I call a thesis. In Section Three I shall suggest a reason for what I think is a weakness in Palmieri's otherwise very penetrating second paper.

I

What does it mean to hold a proposition on philosophical grounds? Consider an example. Some hold that all undefined descriptive constants of L must refer to things with which we are directly acquainted, or, what amounts to the same, which are *wholly presented* to us in an awareness of the kind called direct acquaintance.[5] Those sharing this belief (including, probably, Weinberg and Palmieri as well as, certainly, myself) are said to accept the Principle of Acquaintance (PA). To accept a proposition as a principle is to refuse to defend it directly and to argue instead, first, that the things it mentions are all commonsensical, and, second, that without accepting it one cannot solve all the philosophical problems. (This, I submit, is what 'principle' means in philosophy.) A proposition is held on philosophical grounds if it is thought to follow deductively from one or several principles, either (α) by themselves or (β) in conjunction with some commonsensical truths about the things which they mention.

The example is not haphazard. Those trying to establish elementarism on philosophical grounds all believe, either explicitly or implicitly, that it follows deductively from PA in conjunction with two

---

[2] "Concerning Undefined Descriptive Predicates of Higher Levels," *Mind*, 63, 1954, 338–44.

[3] "Higher Level Descriptive Predicates," *Mind*, 64, 1955, 544–47.

[4] "Second Level Descriptive Predicates," *Philosophy and Phenomenological Research*, 16, 1956, 505–11.

[5] Remember that, with this meaning of the phrase, we are not acquainted with anything but phenomenal objects.

additional premises of the kind (β). Moreover, this is the only *prima facie* reason for their belief of which I can think. To show that it is specious I must expose the flaw in the supposed argument.

Awarenesses are *events*. Certain states of affairs, such as the one, call it S, referred to by '*Col*(*gr*)', are not. These are the two additional premises. *So far as they go*, I have no quarrel with them. 'Event', to be sure, is vague. In some contexts we call the French Revolution a single event; in some others we don't. In the present context, though, an event is, without doubt, what is *wholly contained* in a specious present. The fallacious argument has two major parts. In the first, one concludes from the first premise that what an awareness is the awareness of, or, as one says, its content, is also an event. In the second part one makes use of the second premise. If '*Col*' were undefined, its referent would on some occasions be wholly presented in a single awareness of the kind called direct acquaintance. So would or could therefore on other occasions S. Yet S is not what by this hypothesis it would have to be, namely, an event. One concludes that '*Col*' cannot be undefined. The flaw or gap is in the first part. An awareness and its content are two things and not one. Hence the latter need not be an event merely because the former is one. This is the heart of the matter. The error is facilitated by three subsidiary confusions. The first stems from a certain blur surrounding 'wholly contained', 'wholly presented', and 'event'. That is why I italicized them when they first occurred and inserted at the beginning of this paragraph the qualifying clause which I also italicized. The second subsidiary confusion stems from a faulty analysis of time; the third, from an inadequate explication of the notion of analyticity. I shall take them up in this order.

1. A particular is wholly contained in a specious present; a character (universal) is not. This use of 'wholly contained' is as unproblematic as is the truth of this proposition. It follows that if 'wholly contained' and 'wholly presented' were synonymous, no universal, whatever the type of "its" predicate, could be (part of) the content of a direct acquaintance. One who takes PA seriously and is not, though perhaps without knowing it, a nominalist must therefore insist on two points. First, to be wholly presented in a specious present and to be wholly contained in it are two things and not one; second, some characters are sometimes wholly presented to a direct acquaintance even though they are not wholly contained in "its" specious present or, for that matter, in any other. These, too, I submit, are commonsensical truths. The crucial blur beclouds them by blurring the distinction between being wholly presented and being wholly contained in a specious present. The haze that surrounds 'event' derives from it.

Events are a kind of states of affairs. A state of affairs is what is referred to (not "named"!) by a sentence. In our context, which "ties" events to a specious present, an event is a state of affairs referred to by a substitution instance of '$f(x)$', say, '$gr(a)$'.[6] But of the two constituents of this state of affairs only one, the particular, is wholly contained in a specious present; the other, which is a character, is not. In this sense no event is wholly contained in a specious present. That is why I spoke noncommittally of a tie. For most purposes the inaccuracy does not matter. In this argument, though, one may well wonder whether I have not merely shifted the blur by making as much as I did of each awareness being in a specious present. Happily, this is not so. Closer analysis[7] reveals that an awareness *as such* is a particular; it is an awareness *of something* by virtue of exemplifying a character of the kind called *propositional*. These characters, incidentally, have no adequate transcription in L. Thus L is not really the ideal language. Of this later.

2. 'Green is a color' is sometimes called an eternal truth. In order to dispel the second subsidiary confusion, I shall for the moment use 'truth' ambiguously, once as I just did, once for the states of affairs to which true sentences refer. Green being a color is then an eternal truth. To be eternal, if it means anything at all in analytical philosophy, is to be timeless. What, then, does it mean for a state of affairs to be timeless? Since there is of course no such thing as "time," it can only mean that no temporal characters (being earlier, later, simultaneous, and so on) are among its constituents. Notice that in this sense, which is the only literal sense of the term, a being green is just as timeless as green being a color. Nor is that all. Since the temporal characters are just characters, a being green and green being a color are both timeless in exactly the same sense in which they are also soundless and tasteless and in which, say, middle c being a pitch is colorless. The only difference is that we have no adjectives that are to 'soundless', 'tasteless', and so on, as 'eternal' is to 'timeless'.

The bearing all this has on elementarism is clear, I trust. The positions philosophers take on the several philosophical issues tend to fall into patterns. Quite a few patterns contain (a) PA as well as (b) the rejection of the very idea of "eternal truths." And, if there are none, we can of course not know any, let alone be directly acquainted with

---

[6] Extending this schema, as one easily could, e.g., to certain "molecular' states of affairs, yields nothing that is relevant to my purpose. The above explication of 'state of affairs' is, of course, Wittgenstein's in the *Tractatus*.

[7] See MLP, especially essays 3 and 6, and, in greater detail, "Intentionality," in *Semantica* (Archivio di Filosofia, Roma: Bocca, 1955), pp. 177–216, and also pp. 3–38 of this book.

some. The connection between (a) and (b) is, as we just saw, purely incidental or, if you please, historical. Structurally, we also saw, its major cause is a faulty analysis of time.

3. Consider the two states of affairs S and S' referred to by '$Col(gr)$' and '$\sim Col(gr)$' respectively. No character, of any type, is ever wholly presented to us without being exemplified. This is a part of PA which we have not yet attended to. Or, perhaps, it is a principle of its own; the difference makes no difference. It follows that for S to be the content of a direct acquaintance green itself must be exemplified, say, by the particular a. Similarly for S', the particular involved being b. The two particulars may be but need not be identical. If different, they need not be contained in the same specious present. Hence, so a certain argument runs, if 'Col' were undefined, S and S' could *conceivably* be the respective contents of two successive direct aware-nesses. This is thought to militate against the unquestioned analyticity of '$\sim[Col(gr) \cdot \sim Col(gr)]$'. One concludes that '$Col$' cannot be undefined. The fatal flaw of this argument arises from an inadequate explication of the notion of analyticity. The analyticity of the sentence I just wrote down depends on its being an instance of the form '$\sim(p \cdot \sim p)$' and on nothing else. 'Conceivably' marks the major source of the in-adequacy. That is why I underlined it.

II

In a universe with a finite number of individuals every descriptive predicate, of any type, can be defined by enumerating the things which exemplify it. In a finite universe elementarism is therefore trivially true. Consider next a universe of cardinality $\aleph_0$, i.e., with a denumer-ably infinite number of individuals. The class consisting of (1) all undefined logical signs of L and (2) the maximum number of individual constants, one for each individual, is then also denumerable. The class of all possible one-term predicates, however, being equinumerous with that of all possible subsets of a denumerable set, is of cardinality $2^{\aleph_0}(\aleph)$; and we know that, by Cantor's famous theorem, $2^{\aleph_0} > \aleph_0$. Since the classes of all ordered pairs, triples, and so on, of individuals are each also denumerable, the classes of all possible two-term rela-tions, three-term relations, and so on, are each also of cardinality $\aleph$. So is therefore, as is easily shown, the class of all possible constant predicates of type one. Assume now that L contains—as of course it need not, but this is the most favorable case—an undefined constant for each of the $\aleph$ different predicates of type one. Call the class of these constants (3). This makes the sum of classes (1), (2), and (3) of cardi-nality $\aleph$. It follows readily that the class of all finite sequences, with repetitions, of signs from this latter class is still of cardinality $\aleph$.

Every well-formed expression of L not containing undefined constants of types higher than one is such a sequence. It follows that even in the most favorable case one can in L form at most $\aleph$ formally different definitions for predicates of the second type. The number of all possible predicates of this type, though, is $2^\aleph$; and we have, again, $2^\aleph > \aleph$. This is just another application of Cantor's theorem. Now it may of course be the case that all the second order predicates, defined or undefined, which L must contain in order to be the ideal language are among those that can be defined. It *may* be the case. But since, as we saw, it is impossible to define all possible ones—there are, so to speak, too many for that—it *need* not be the case. This is the point. I have already shown that in a denumerable universe elementarism, if it be true (as I believe it is), is a factual truth, or, as I put it, a thesis. The proof is easily extended to universes of higher cardinality. But I shall not bother with what interests only mathematicians and is mathematically rather trivial at that. A philosopher may be puzzled by something else. In the introduction I said that this proof rests on logical grounds. Yet I introduced into it the number of individuals in the universe which, it is felt, is a matter of fact and not of logic. Quite so. The issue this question raises is important indeed; I hope to return to it on an early occasion.[7a] Here I can only say that I chose my words deliberately.

To insist that elementarism is a thesis is not to deny that one can, by means of logical (structural) properties, single out large classes of predicates of higher types, say, the second, which are, by virtue of these properties, definable in terms of certain others of lower types, say, the first. For a rather obvious example, consider a predicate 'F_1', of type two, such that (α) the empty class is not F_1, and (β) if f_1 and f_2 are different and both F_1, then there is no individual that is both f_1 and f_2. Define now

(1)   '$r_1(x, y)$'   for   '$(\exists f)[F_1(f) \cdot f(x) \cdot f(y)]$'

and

(2)   '$F_2(f)$'   for   '$(\exists x)(y)[f(y) \equiv r_1(x, y)]$'.

One proves easily

(3) $F_2 = F_1$

i.e., that 'F_1' can be defined, by (2), in terms of 'r_1'. I skip the proof, which is trivial, and make instead four points.[7b]

[7a] This I have since done in "Analyticity," *Theoria*, 24, 1958, 71–93, and also pp. 73–90 of this book. [Added in 1959.]

[7b] Add to the right side of (2) the conjunction term '$f \neq \Lambda$'. As it stands, '$F_2(\Lambda)$' would be true, in violation of (α), if the universe is not exhausted by the

1. (α) and (β) are of course the logical (structural) properties in question. Pitch and color (hue) are two among the many characters having these properties. If 'F_1' is interpreted as "pitch," then 'r_1' names the relation "equal-in-pitch."

2. Instead of (3) I could have written (3') $F_2(f) \equiv F_1(f)$. In other words, since L is extensional, there is nothing problematic about the '$=$' in (3).

3. *Formally*, there is nothing circular about the procedure outlined. Given 'F_1' as an undefined predicate, one can, by (1), define a certain relation. Because F_1 has the properties (α) and (β), this relation has certain others. Given 'r_1' as an undefined name for *this* relation, one can, by (2), define 'F_2' and then, by making use of those properties of r_1, prove (3).

4. *Philosophically*, one might feel there is some sort of circularity. He may argue, for instance, that even though 'equal-in-pitch' be a relation of the first type, to be directly acquainted with what it names is the same thing as to be directly acquainted with what is named by the type-two predicate 'pitch'. Or, to introduce another crucial word, he may insist that one cannot know the *meaning* of 'higher-in-pitch' without knowing that of 'pitch', and conversely.

Points 1 and 3 require no comment. Points 2 and 4 do; also, they are involved in the difficulties with which Palmieri wrestles in his second paper. So I shall comment on them in the next section.

III

Palmieri thinks that a definition of 'pitch' which I once suggested[8] is circular. The crucial predicate there is 'higher-in-pitch', not, as above, 'equal-in-pitch'. But this difference makes no difference, just as the other details of that definition do not matter. The supposed circularity is, I believe, of the kind mentioned in the last point of the preceding section. One reason for my believing this is that he explicitly accepts another feature, shared by all such definitions, which some may mistakenly think to entail another sort of circularity. Let me explain.

Suppose someone proposes two predicative contexts, 'Φ_1' and 'Φ_2', as definitions (transcriptions) of 'duck' and 'bird' respectively. How are

members of the members of F_1. W. V. Quine kindly pointed this out to me in a private communication. [Added in 1959.]

[8] "Undefined Descriptive Predicates," *Philosophy and Phenomenological Research*, 8, 1947, 55–82. Palmieri is also puzzled by my use of '$=$' in that paper. On this score I perhaps misled him by not being as clear as I should have been. Even so, I eliminated whatever doubt there might have been a year later in "Conditions for an Extensional Elementaristic Language," *Analysis*, 8, 1948, 44–47 (reprinted in MLP), which Palmieri has apparently overlooked.

we to judge their adequacy? The criterion is, very roughly, that such sentences as '$(\phi)[\Phi_1(\phi) \supset \Phi_2(\phi)]$', which transcribes "all ducks are birds," must be "true." I say very roughly for two reasons. First, there is much more to be said about the matter, e.g., as to which English sentences must and which need not satisfy the criterion. Second, what is really meant by 'true' is that the sentences in question must be deductive consequences of the two definitions *in conjunction with* some other sentences, containing only undefined descriptive predicates, which we have reason to believe are true.[9] In this note I am merely interested in the clause which follows the italicized phrase. For it seems to me that some think it involves some sort of circularity; the idea being, if I may so put it, that one merely gets out what one has put in and thus does not really achieve anything. As I see it, these objectors fail to grasp the very idea of definitional reconstruction (*Aufbau;* definition by extensive abstraction). On this Palmieri agrees with me; so I shall say no more about the matter. Also, he acknowledges that the procedure is not formally circular (point 3 above). I conclude that what bothers him is the supposed circularity of "meaning."

'Meaning' has many meanings. Three of them are here relevant. In the first sense, which is the weakest or broadest, two predicates have the same meaning if and only if they are extensionally equivalent, as in (3'). As long as the language as a whole is extensional, such expressions are also identical, at least if one accepts, as I do, the Leibniz-Russell explication of identity. In the second sense, which is stricter, two predicates have the same meaning if and only if the statement of extensional equivalence is analytic. In the third sense, which is the strictest, two expressions have the same meaning if and only if in writing them down we use the same tokens in the same order. In a sense, this third kind of meaning, called *intentional*, is thus unique. The reason for this uniqueness is that different expressions "belong" to different *concepts*.[10] Concepts, it turns out, are a special kind of the

[9] The conditions (α) and (β) are merely a special case of such sentences. Their only peculiarity is that they state *non*relational properties of a single character. In the general case the structural properties are relational. Concerning 'structure': Let 'P' be a (closed) sentence containing two descriptive signs of types m and n respectively $(m \geq n)$ and no other descriptive signs. Replace in 'P' the two constants by variables of the proper types. The resulting expression is the definiens of a *logical* relation of type $m+1$, satisfied by two constants if and only if 'P' is true for them.

[10] I use the noncommittal 'belong' advisedly. For details, see "Intentionality," and "Concepts," *Philosophical Studies*, 8, 1957, 19–27, and also pp. 106–14 of this book. Addition to L of the propositional characters still leaves it extensional. The only nonextensional contexts are those containing the transcription, by a new logical primitive, of the intentional meaning of 'means'.

propositional characters which were mentioned in Section One. More important, the intentional meaning of 'meaning' cannot be accommodated in L, which is therefore not really the ideal language. The latter, call it L', is no longer extensional; and no two different expressions are identical in L'. L is nevertheless the bulk of L'; and an even larger part of it remains extensional.

What stirs in Palmieri and, generally, in those who raise the objection of point 4 in the preceding section, is, I submit, the idea of intentional meaning. To see that, consider that the objection may be taken to assert that, loosely speaking, "equal-in-pitch" and "pitch" share the same or nearly the same intentional meaning. I say loosely speaking, because intentional meaning is, as we saw, unique. Informally, though, there is a connection of ideas which I can understand and appreciate. If I am right and this is indeed the heart of the objection, then it is, I believe, ill-founded. The reason why I believe this is that the proper criterion for definitional reconstruction is not identity in L' but, rather, extensional equivalence or, what amounts to the same, identity in all extensional contexts of L'. Again, a very good reason for this being the proper criterion is that identity of different expressions in L', which includes identity of "concepts," is, as we also saw, unattainable. This leads to what may well be the ultimate source of Palmieri's uneasiness.

The crucial objection may also be taken to assert that since "equal-in-pitch" and "pitch" have *phenomenally* the same or nearly the same meaning, definition of the former in terms of the latter is an entirely empty achievement. As far as phenomenological meaning is concerned, I agree and even insist. The above analysis explicates the sense in which intentional meaning is unique and this uniqueness reflects the sense in which the phenomenal material simply is what it is, neither analyzable nor reconstructible, either definitionally or otherwise. The reason why I believe the objection to be nevertheless ill-founded is that phenomenological description and philosophical analysis are two things and not one. The latter indubitably *rests* on the former. But that does not mean that it either should or could follow it in all details. For, if it did, would it not *be* the former?

Individuals*

INDIVIDUAL is one of a group of peculiar words. 'Property' and 'class' are others. As long as we use such a word commonsensically, we have no difficulty. When we use it philosophically, we get into trouble. The proper way of getting out of it, according to one conception of philosophy, is to explicate the philosophical use by means of talking commonsensically about an "ideal language." This conception or method is by now familiar. So I shall not in this note expound it again but, rather, use it in trying to make a contribution to the explication of (the philosophical use of) 'individual'.

An ideal language, it will be remembered, is an interpreted formalism or schema, fitting our world in certain ways, that can be put to certain uses. So understood, the phrase "the ideal language of a world" makes sense. Most practitioners of the method, including myself, believe that the ideal language L of our world either is or contains, as a very major part, a PM-like formalism with a type hierarchy of the order 0,1,2,3 · · · , supplemented by undefined descriptive constants (udcs) distributed over all or some of the types. Upon this view, which I shall not question, our world is a subject-predicate world. For what I am about, that is its most important feature. The order type of the hierarchy suggests the following explication.

(E_1) An individual$_1$ is what either is referred to by a zero-level constant of L or, according to the rules for the interpretation of L, could be so referred to.

E_1 is familiar. Implicitly, at least, it occurs in the early work of Russell. I have, explicitly, used it for quite some time. Yet I have become in-

* Philosophical Studies, *9, 1958, 78–85. Reprinted by permission.*

creasingly dissatisfied with it. The subscript I employed foretells what I now propose to do about this dissatisfaction. In each of the two main sections of this paper I shall suggest one other explication, calling them E_2 and E_3 respectively. To keep the ideas straight, I shall thus soon have to speak not only about individuals$_1$ but also about individuals$_2$ and individuals$_3$. Does this mean that E_1 is not adequate?

The answer is both No and Yes. For one thing, E_1 captures what I am still convinced is the most important single feature possessed by all those and only those things which philosophers, speaking philosophically, have called "individuals." For another, it will transpire that in our world every individual$_1$ is also an individual$_2$ and an individual$_3$; every individual$_2$, an individual$_1$ and an individual$_3$; every individual$_3$, an individual$_1$ and an individual$_2$. These are two very good reasons for calling E_1 adequate. On the other side of the ledger, E_2 and E_3 each articulates a characteristic feature of "individuals" in our world. Negatively, that exposes the root of my growing dissatisfaction with E_1. Positively, one would hope that such articulation yields analytical insight. I shall show that the hope is justified. E_2 leads to an explication of the *pointing* feature of individuality. What that means I shall explain in good time. E_3, it will be seen, involves a contribution to the analysis of *identity*. In a very subtle and very special sense E_1 may thus be called inadequate. But, then, this is merely another way of saying that the task of philosophical analysis is infinite. Or, if you please, its only limits are those of our ingenuity.

I

Let '$^i a_i$' be a udc of L. The superscript marks the type level. By E_1 all '$^0 a_i$' are individuals$_1$. Assume tentatively that '$^0 a_1$', '$^1 a_1$', '$^1 a_2$' refer to a continuant, say, a lobster, and two colors, say, green and red respectively. In L '$^1 a_1(^0 a_1)$', '$\sim^1 a_1(^0 a_1)$', '$^1 a_2(^0 a_1)$', '$\sim^1 a_2(^0 a_1)$' are all well formed. When the lobster was boiled, its color changed from green to red. The four sentences are therefore all true. This is logical catastrophe. It is also the root of a famous difficulty encountered by all philosophers who insist on calling continuants individuals. Whether the difficulty can be overcome we need not inquire. I note, instead, that one who embraces L must consistently hold that all individuals$_1$ are "momentary" things such as, say, sense data. But I do not wish to discuss sense data. I merely wave a familiar flag in order to call attention to the connection between individuality and time.

A subject-predicate world, i.e., a world whose ideal language L' either is or contains, as a very major part, a PM-like schema, need not contain time. "Time" is introduced into it by stipulating that L' contains two binary udcs, 'pr^{n+1}' and 'sim^{n+1}', of the same type $n+1$, ordering all constants '$^n a_i$' of type n in the same manner in which the two relations of being earlier and being simultaneous at least approximately order all momentary events. I shall not tarry to state once more the axioms for these two constants.[1] Rather, I notice that the order thus introduced among the '$^n a_i$' "attaches" each of them to what I shall call a "segment." Each udc of type n, and none of any other, "belongs" to a segment in the sense in which a stick belongs to a length. This suggests the following explication.

(E₂) An individual₂ (of a temporal world with 'pr^{n+1}' and 'sim^{n+1}') is what either is referred to by a udc of L' of type n or, according to the rules for the interpretation of L', could be so referred to.[2]

In our world, every individual₂ is an individual₁, and conversely. But consider now a world with an ideal language, L'', otherwise like L, whose type hierarchy is of the order . . . $-3, -2, -1, 0, 1, 2, 3, . . .$ with no lower limit for the level to which udcs are assigned. All that matters in PM are the arithmetical differences among the type numbers of the several signs that occur in a formula or a finite number of such. The absolute numbers themselves do not. The "logic" of this world is thus the same as that of ours. Obviously, it contains no individuals₁. It would seem that it may contain individuals₂. The assumption that it does creates a difficulty that is, as it were, the syntactical mirror image of the lobster catastrophe.

To speak about schemata, as I have done so far, is to talk ontology. To explain the difficulty in question one must talk epistemology. This one does by attending to the rules for the schema's interpretation. No udc may be introduced unless what it refers to is *wholly* presented.[3] This is a possible rule of interpretation. It has been proposed and defended, for example, as a Principle of Acquaintance. Some of its proponents would rather say "wholly presented in experience." They don't really add anything, just as one cannot really explain, except by examples, what it means to be wholly presented. But one can explore the connections of the phrase. The most important one is again with time.

One may hold that only "individuals" are ever wholly presented.

---

[1] Nor shall I inquire whether one constant with some other axioms would do instead. Similarly, I ignore as irrelevant for my purpose the questions that arise if one starts from overlapping "moments" rather than from "points" in time.

[2] The very need for the parenthetical clause in E₂ shows that E₁ articulates the more fundamental feature.

[3] See "Elementarism," *Philosophy and Phenomenological Research*, 18, 1957, 107–14, and also pp. 115–23 of this book.

Those who do also tend to say that only individuals exist. Or one may hold (as I do) that L contains udcs of at least two successive types, each referring to what is wholly presented. Those who do should consistently also hold that all udcs are mere indicators (names, labels) and use 'naming' where, noncommittally on this occasion, I use 'referring'. Just now, though, all this is neither here nor there. What matters is that where there is "time," it makes sense to speak of repetition. *Presentations and individuals$_2$ both belong to segments; nonindividuals$_2$ do not.* Thus it makes sense to say that an individual$_2$ is wholly presented only once while a nonindividual$_2$ may be so presented repeatedly. This is the major difference between individuals$_2$ and nonindividuals$_2$. If one explores what it implies, one comes upon the difficulty in question.

Turn to the world of L''. Assume that its individuals$_2$ are of type zero. Since the absolute type numbers do not matter and since there is no lowest level to which udcs are assigned, this is merely a notational convention. Consider the four sentences '$^0a_1(^{-1}a_1)$', '$\sim^0a_1(^{-1}a_1)$', '$^0a_2(^{-1}a_1)$', '$\sim^0a_2(^{-1}a_1)$'. In each the name of an individual$_2$ stands in the predicate place. At first sight that seems strange. Yet they are all well formed. In the picturesque language of the tradition one may express that by saying that in this world of my fancy a "temporal" thing may not only exemplify but also be exemplified by an "eternal" thing. Consider next that the four sentences may all be true. Not being an individual$_2$, the thing $^{-1}a_1$ can be wholly presented more than once. Assume it to be so presented twice, once exemplifying $^0a_1$, once $^0a_2$, two individuals$_2$ attached to different segments. Then the four sentences are all true and we are faced with a contradiction which is, syntactically, the mirror image of the lobster catastrophe. Syntactically, the only way out is to exclude as ill formed the negations of all sentences with type-zero predicates. To show what this apparently arbitrary ruling means I switch to L.

The "individuals" of our world are both individuals$_1$ and individuals$_2$. Thus they are attached to segments. This is often expressed in two ways. One says that individuals and only individuals can be pointed at. Or one says that, strictly speaking, the name of an individual can only be used while one is presented with it (i.e., the individual). On the other hand, when we are presented with, say, a sense datum, or, for that matter, with one of the many things common sense calls individuals, we never hesitate to predicate of it, negatively, a character which it does not exemplify. Pointing at a raven, for instance, we say "This is not white." Call that the Principle of Negative Predication. This makes the ruling for L'' which was forced upon us a Principle of Excluded Negative Predication.

Some philosophers wish to say that "individuals" are all those and only those things that can be pointed at. To speak of *pointing* is either to speak about communication or to use a psychological metaphor. Clearly, therefore, these philosophers speak metaphorically. Philosophical metaphors are often dangerous and always in need of explication. In this case the danger is that two issues will get improperly mixed up with each other. One issue is the explication of 'individual'; the other, whether only proper names (i.e., words referring to individuals) or also some words referring to characters are "mere labels." The verbal bridge between the two is the association between 'pointer' and 'label'. Nor is all this a minor matter; for the second issue is part and parcel of the nominalism controversy.[4] No doubt, then, the pointing metaphor is dangerous. But this is not to say that we may simply ignore it. The "individuals" of our world do possess a characteristic feature at which the metaphor aims. The thing to do, therefore, is to explicate the metaphor, or, what amounts to the same, to describe the feature by means of the method. This is done by pointing out that if one wants to make the world of L'' safe for individuals$_2$, one must adopt the Principle of Excluded Negative Predication. To grasp firmly that this is the answer, one merely has to remember three things. First, the "individuals" of our world are also individuals$_2$. Second, as they are often used philosophically, 'this can be pointed at' and 'this is wholly presented' have the same meaning. Third, the sentences the principle excludes are those asserting that a thing presented does *not* exemplify another thing which is *not* presented and which is an individual$_2$.

II

E_3 requires rethinking of the logic of identity. So I shall first attend to the latter, starting with a succinct summary of what I have done elsewhere,[5] and state E_3 only toward the end. Also, it will be best to assume until then that L not only contains PM but actually is PM, supplemented by the usual constants and, also, the primitive sentences of extensionality for all types,

(Ext) $$(\phi)[\phi(\alpha) \equiv \phi(\beta)] \supset \alpha = \beta;$$

where '$=$' is not a primitive sign but so defined, in the familiar manner, that '$\alpha = \beta$' says no more and no less than that 'α' and 'β' can be substituted for each other in all contexts.

---

[4] See "The Revolt against Logical Atomism," *The Philosophical Quarterly*, 7, 1957, 323–39, and 8, 1958, 1–13, and also pp. 39–72 of this book.

[5] See "The Identity of Indiscernibles and the Formalist Definition of 'Identity'," *Mind*, 62, 1953, 75–79, reprinted in *The Metaphysics of Logical Positivism*.

Now for the summary. 'Same' and 'different', as we ordinarily use them, need no explanation. I don't even know what it could possibly mean to explain them. Or, if the truism has to be stated elaborately, whenever we are presented with two things and not one, we can discern them from each other, and conversely. Nor am I aware of any philosophical uses of the two words, at least not within the analytical tradition, that require explication. The very tag of the classical issue, the identity of indiscernibles, is therefore misleading. Consider the following two propositions. (1) Ext is analytic. (2) '=' (and '≠') can serve as the transcription, in L, of 'same' (and 'different'). Exclude, for expository purposes, 'identical' from ordinary speech and read '$\alpha = \beta$' as 'α is identical with β'. Proposition (2) can then be reworded as follows: (2') 'Identical' can serve as the transcription, in L, of 'same'. Can both (1) and (2) be successfully defended? This and only this is the question. I take those who assert the so-called identity of indiscernibles to answer it affirmatively. This will do for the summary.

Virtually all the discussion has been in terms of "individuals." Those who use schemata discuss the issue in terms of individuals$_1$. But even they stick to this curious limitation. I call it curious because in the schema itself there is nothing either to warrant or even suggest it. Quite to the contrary. Curious as the limitation thus is, it is yet easily understood. There is a general and a specific reason for it. The general reason is the implicit nominalism of so much of recent philosophy, according to which "individuals" are the only existents, together with the proposition, often equally implicit, that "identity" cannot be predicated of anything but existents. The specific reason, which concerns us here, is that while no one really doubts the identity of indiscernibles in the case of individuals$_1$, there is ample ground for doubting it in the case of characters, i.e., in the case of things referred to by the non-zero-level descriptive constants of L. Or, rather, there *appears* to be such ground as long as the identity issue has not been analyzed completely.

Take the familiar illustration, the two characters of being a featherless biped and of being human. They are two characters, not one, and hence not the same (not: not identical). This is again a truism and we must not under any circumstances allow ourselves to be talked out of it.[6] Yet, the two characters satisfy the left side of Ext. Hence, if (1) holds, they are identical (not: the same). This is the apparent ground. The appearance vanishes if one distinguishes, as I did, between 'same' and 'identical'. To grasp that firmly, reintroduce 'identical' into ordi-

---

[6] The resistance against such talk is undermined by the kind of nominalism that "identifies," in the wrong way, a character with its extension.

nary speech but preserve the technical meaning which I assigned to it. Then one can say that, unlike individuals, two characters may be identical and yet be two and not one. Notice, incidentally, that the only illustrations available involve at least one character whose name in L is defined. And there are, of course, no defined zero-level constants.[7] This increases the plausibility of what has been said.

All this suggests the following explication.

(E₃) A thing is an individual₃ if and only if it is not identical with any other thing.

Or, as one says, rather confusingly, such a thing is not identical with anything but itself. It would be better to say that in this case '$\alpha = \beta$' is true if and only if 'α' and 'β' refer to the same thing. Catchy tags are often as dangerous as they are sometimes useful. Yet I cannot resist the temptation of providing one. One may say that while individuals are ruled by the identity of indiscernibles, in the case of characters we must recognize the *discernibility of identicals.*

One may grant that E₃ captures an important feature of "individuals" and yet wonder whether every individual₃ is also an individual₁. Take, for instance, phenomenal green, or, for that matter, any other character to which, according to some (including myself), an undefined descriptive predicate of L may refer. Is there in fact always a second predicate in L such that the left side of Ext holds for the two? The answer is Yes. The argument that must be made for it is more tedious than difficult. So I shall merely sketch it. Green sense data can in principle be characterized in terms of their physical and physiological causes. The transcription of this characterization into L will provide us with the predicate we are looking for.

Call the schema with which I have so far operated in this section L^*. L, though it contains L^* as a very major part, is not itself L^*. I cannot and need not on this occasion describe in detail the required addition to L^*.[8] It will suffice to say that one could not without it arrive at an adequate philosophy of mind and meaning. This has something to do with why, in conclusion, I must mention the matter. In L, '$\alpha = \beta$' is analytically false unless 'α' and 'β' are, as one says, different tokens of the same type.[9] Hence, being human and being a featherless biped,

---

[7] Definite descriptions, *if successful,* may of course be used like constants. But that does not make them, technically, defined constants. Nontechnically, the difference appears in the need for the italicized clause.

[8] See "Intentionality," *Semantica* (Archivio di Filosofia, Roma: Bocca, 1955), pp. 177–216, and also pp. 3–38 of this book.

[9] See "Concepts," *Philosophical Studies,* 8, 1957, 19–27, and also pp. 106–14 of this book.

though "identical" in L^*, are not strictly identical anyway. This, one might think, makes the analysis contained in this section superfluous. That is the lazy man's way out. It is even worse than that. It is worse because one taking it will probably be tempted to say that the two characters are indeed the same and that it is only their meanings which are different. Yet, the two characters are out there, in the world. Meanings are in the mind. One who says this sort of thing is therefore well along on the road toward some kind of philosophical subjectivism. Such subjectivism is unacceptable. What has been said shows that we need not accept it.

Sameness, Meaning, and Identity*

WORDS are used either commonsensically or philosophically. Some uses hover on the boundary. That does not make the dichotomy less important. Unexplicated philosophical uses make no sense. To explicate them is the business of analysis. Its method is to talk commonsensically about a schema, called the ideal language, which permits all ordinary but no philosophical uses. At least, this is one current conception. Since it happens to be mine, I shall on this occasion show the method at work by applying it to the three notions of sameness, identity, and meaning.[1]

To learn an ordinary use is one thing; to explain it is another. Some such uses can be explained. Others are basic. The latter must be learned, of course, but I do not know what it could possibly mean to explain them. The numeral '2', for instance, is basic. Russell in his

---

* *To appear in* Proceedings of the Twelfth International Congress of Philosophy. *Reprinted by permission.*

[1] This paper now appears to me as the conclusion of a development of ideas that has extended over several years. For its successive stages see the following papers: "The Identity of Indiscernibles and the Formalist Definition of 'Identity'," *Mind*, 62, 1953, 75–79, reprinted in *The Metaphysics of Logical Positivism;* "Concepts," *Philosophical Studies*, 8, 1957, 19–27, and also pp. 106–14 of this book; "Elementarism," *Philosophy and Phenomenological Research*, 18, 1957, 107–14, and also pp. 115–23 of this book; "Individuals," *Philosophical Studies*, 9, 1958, 78–85, and also pp. 124–31 of this book. During the last year I have benefited from discussion with Reinhardt Grossmann, who is preparing publications of his own on this and related topics. See, in particular, his "Propositional Attitudes," to appear in *The Philosophical Quarterly.*
Concerning intentionality and the analysis of mind, see the third and sixth essays in MLP and, in particular, "Intentionality," *Semantica* (Archivio di Filosofia, Roma: Bocca, 1955), pp. 177–216, and also pp. 3–38 of this book. Concerning Frege, see "Frege's Hidden Nominalism," *Philosophical Review*, 67, 1958, 437–59, and also pp. 205–24 of this book.

celebrated reconstruction neither explained nor, of course, explicated it. Rather, he transcribed it and the other numerals into his ideal language and by means of this transcription tried to explicate the philosophical use of 'analytic' in the proposition that arithmetic is analytic.

'Same' has two ordinary uses. One is basic, the other is not. In ordinary discourse the distinction may safely go unnoticed. It is so subtle indeed that I cannot state it without first explicating some philosophical uses. Many philosophers use 'name' and 'existent' so that an existent is what has or could have a name. Both uses, being philosophical, must be explicated. *Name* I explicate as: undefined descriptive sign of the ideal language, *L*. *Existent* I explicate as: whatever has or could have a name (in *L*). Since *L* is a subject-predicate schema, it follows that an existent is either an individual or a simple character. It is an *individual* if and only if its name is of type zero; otherwise it is a *simple character*.[2] In my world, sensa are individuals; some of the qualities and relations they exemplify are simple characters. These are not the only existents of my world. But they are all as elementary as these two kinds; they are all phenomenal things; and, if they are presented to us at all, they are wholly presented in a specious present. This adds credence to what I am about to say about sameness. But what I shall say does not depend on it. So I shall often skirt controversy by simply speaking of existents. Nor shall I deprive myself of such familiar paradigms as that of the morning star, even though Venus is not, in the sense explicated, an existent.

Some philosophers believe that '*a* is the same as *b*' makes no sense unless '*a*' and '*b*' both refer to existents. The phrase they actually mention is 'identical with', not 'the same as'. This has something to do with a blur to which I shall presently attend. That is why I make the substitution. Either way, I believe that these philosophers are wrong. Yet they provide us with the cue for distinguishing between the two uses of 'same'. Limit discourse to existents. A use of 'same' is basic if and only if it occurs in such discourse. Two existents are two and not one. One is one and not two. Nor, when I am presented with two, is there any doubt that I am not presented with one, and conversely. This goes for simple characters as well as for individuals. In the case of the former, an objector might cite the fallibility of memory and the circumstance that some simple characters, such as colors, shade into each other. The objection raises different issues. The analyst divides and conquers. This is the key to the basic use of 'same'. If you please,

---

[2] Henceforth 'name', 'existent', 'individual', and 'simple character' will be used only in this *explicated* philosophical sense.

that is all there is to it. In particular, it makes no sense to search for a criterion by which to decide whether or not two existents are the same. The decision, if it be one, is immediate. Notice, finally, that while 'same' is rather useless when it stands between names, such sentences as 'The evening star and the morning star are the same' serve a purpose.

Red-or-blue is a complex character. So is not-both-not-red-and-not-blue. We say intelligibly that they are one and not two. Generally, two complex characters are the same if and only if they are analytically equivalent. This is the second use of 'same'. In this case, there is a criterion and one may indeed wonder whether a statement of sameness, in this use, is true. But, then, is there not often grave or even irresoluble doubt about the truth of a statement and yet none whatsoever as to what it means?

As we ordinarily speak, we use 'same' and 'identical' synonymously. This leads to trouble. Its source is Leibniz's famous formula: Two things are identical if and only if whatever can be said of the one can be said *salva veritate* of the other. However intended, the formula was mistaken for a criterion of sameness. Yet, a criterion makes no sense for the basic use of 'same'. For the other use, we saw, the criterion is different. This is the cause of the trouble. So far I have avoided 'identical'. Henceforth I shall use it as if the Leibnizian formula were its definition. In view of the wording of the definiens one may wonder whether the relation defined obtains between expressions or between things. However that may be, the key phrase is "whatever can be said." What can be said depends upon the language. The one we are interested in is of course the ideal language. What the ideal language is like depends on what the world is like. We have come to a fork in the road. Consider a world otherwise like ours but without minds. Call it the truncated world. Its ideal language is not L but L_1. The logical skeleton of L_1 is *Principia Mathematica*, without ramification but with the axiom of extensionality. Let us for a while consider this truncated world, or briefly, L_1.

Is identity a relation between expressions or between things? In L_1 it is a relation between things. If "two" things are the same, are they also identical? In L_1 the answer is Yes. If two things are identical, are they also the same? Even in L_1 the answer is No. More precisely, it is Yes for individuals, No for characters. For individuals, therefore, 'identical' may in L_1 serve as the transcription of 'same'. That explains why the distinction between sameness and identity is so easily overlooked. With characters the matter comes to a head. Take the familiar paradigm, human and featherless biped. Patently, these are two characters. Yet, being coextensive, they are identical in L_1. That is why some philosophers felt compelled to maintain that they were one. This quixotic effort I trace to three roots; first, the failure to distinguish between sameness and identity; second, the belief, implicit or explicit, that L_1 is the ideal language; third, a tendency toward nominalism. With the first two, which go together, we are familiar. The third deserves a brief comment. Nominalists believe that no character exists; hence they identify each character with the class it determines; and coextensive classes are presumably the same. In this argument the notions of identification and class remain vague. Properly explicated, as for instance by Russell, a class expression is a defined predicate. In L_1 a character and its class are indeed the same. This is an instance of the second use of 'same'.[3] Human and featherless biped are thus each the same as its class. The two classes, however, since they are merely contingently coextensive, are merely identical. So therefore are the two characters. Nor is there anything paradoxical in this. What is expressed by saying, as one usually does, that two coextensive classes are one and the same is merely that even in languages where other predicates don't, class expressions do satisfy the axiom of extensionality. The rest is but another loose use of 'same', based on the image of a class as a heap of pebbles in a basket. I merely observe that being in a basket is a character.

Meanings are mental existents. To consider them, I therefore turn from the truncated world to ours. In connection with sameness and identity, meanings produce the problem Frege saw but could not solve. Take the familiar paradigm 'Smith knows that Venus is the morning star'. Upon a view, deeply grounded in our language, which Frege never questioned, each mental act, such as a knowing or a believing, exemplifies a descriptive relation of some sort between a mind and its content. If so, then the descriptive phrase in the paradigm refers to Venus. Frege also held that it was a name. Nor did he distinguish between sameness and identity. Hence, since the morning star and the evening star are one thing, he concluded that the paradigm and the sentence 'Smith knows that Venus is the evening star' must either be both true or both false. Yet, depending on what Smith knows, one may be true and the other false. In this perplexity, Frege's initial gambit, consistent with his determination to treat descriptions as names, was to decree certain nonmental existents, such as the meanings of 'morning star' and of 'evening star'. If these nebulous things really were existents, we would immediately know whether any "two" of them are or are not the same. Since they are merely the creations of a logician's

[3] This was pointed out to me by Grossmann.

fancy we don't. Thus the search for a criterion of sameness or, as it was put, of identity seemed plausible. Nor is that all. If the initial gambit is to serve its purpose, then the criterion proposed must solve the problem of Smith. Frege never proposed one that did the job. This is the measure of his failure.

There are two ways out. One is to abandon mind. That is what the philosophical behaviorists propose. The other is to replace the descriptive relation of the classical act by a logical nexus between a thought and its content. That is my proposal.

The behaviorists replace thoughts or meanings, which are mental things, by words, or, rather, by noises. Let me first take advantage of their gambit to get rid of the issue of descriptions which unnecessarily complicates the usual paradigm. Assume for the sake of the argument that 'round' and 'spherical' are two names for one existent. Consider 'Smith believes that the earth is round' and 'Smith believes that the earth is spherical'. If Smith's vocabulary is properly limited, the first will be true, the second false. Let us now see what the behaviorist can do. The names of his ideal language, L_2, refer to physical things. But its logical skeleton is that of L_1. It is, as one says, nonintentional. Consider 'Smith sees green'. In principle at least, the behaviorist can in L_2 define a predicate 'seeing-green', which is exemplified by a human body whenever, as one says, the mind inhabiting it sees green. So construed, however, 'seeing-green' is one inseparable predicate. 'Green', either in its physical or in its phenomenal use, does not occur in it, just as the word 'one' does not occur in 'stone'. What goes for colors goes for meanings. The behaviorist can, at least in principle, define the relational predicate 'x means round to y at t', where the letters stand for a noise, a human body, and a moment of time, respectively. But, again, this is one inseparable predicate and neither 'means' nor 'round' occurs in it, although the latter may and probably will occur in the definiens. If this were not so, not even the behavioristic meaning of 'means' could be reconstructed in the nonintentional schema L_2. What goes for 'means' also goes for 'believes'. There is no need to continue. Notice, though, that these characters are complex. Thus, if L_2 were the ideal language, they would not, in the relevant sense, exist. The behaviorists catch only the shadow of mind. For the science of psychology that will do. But it is clear that the behaviorists cannot answer philosophical questions about minds. Of these questions, that of meaning is but one.

In my world mental things are existents. Awarenesses are individuals. 'Awareness' I use generically. Just as a nonmental individual is a tone or a pain or a smell by exemplifying certain nonmental characters, so

an awareness is a remembering, or a doubting, or a believing, and so
on, by exemplifying certain mental characters. Some of these characters are simple. Hence they are existents. There are still others among
the mental furniture of my world. An awareness is always distinct from
its content. It is an awareness *of* its content by exemplifying a character I call propositional, or a thought, or a meaning. These characters
are all simples and, therefore, existents. To see that this is as it ought
to be, consider that while the contents of most thoughts are neither
phenomenal nor wholly presented to us, the thought itself, while we
are thinking it, is. But, then, what is the connection between a thought
and its content? In English, it is expressed by such sentences as 'The
thought Peter is blond means Peter is blond'. For the practitioner of
the method the crucial question is therefore how to transcribe this
sentence into his ideal language. 1. It cannot be transcribed into either
L_1 or L_2. 2. L, into which it can be transcribed, contains a new primitive
logical sign, call it 'M', which transcribes this use, call it the intentional
use, of 'means'. 3. In L, the phrase 'the thought Peter is blond' becomes
a simple predicate. 4. The transcription of our sentence is *analytic*. The
uses I just made of 'logical' and 'analytic' are not merely honorific but
carry the full philosophical meaning. In fact, their explication com-
pletes the explication of that meaning. All this has an important consequence. The (transcription of) the pattern 'The thought . . . means
. . . ' is analytic if and only if the dots stand for different tokens of
the same type. Otherwise it is contradictory. This is again as it ought
to be. Take the two thoughts Peter is blond and Paul is blond. Considered as existents they are two things, not one, even if 'Peter' and
'Paul' are two names of one boy. A thought is accurately and uniquely
determined by what I call its text. This is not to say, of course, that if
Peter and Paul are one boy, there are not many causal connections
among the occurrences of these two thoughts or that there are no logical
connections between their texts. These, however, are different matters.
The central issue is neither causal nor logical but ontological. That he
sensed this is the measure of Frege's greatness.

   This, then, is my world, or, briefly, my L. What happens in this
world to sameness and identity? It will be best to begin with the latter.

   The case of Peter and Paul is not different from that of round and
spherical. Remember that Leibniz's formula, taken as a definition, controls my use of 'identical'. Remember also the crucial phrase: whatever
can be said. In L, M-contexts are included in what can be said. It follows
immediately that the transcription of 'round is identical with round'
is analytic while that of 'round is identical with spherical' is contradictory. Generally, a statement of identity between two expressions,

even if they refer to one thing and even if they are names, is either analytic or contradictory, depending only on whether or not the two expressions are or are not different tokens of the same type. In L identity is a relation not between things, but, as it were, between expressions and a trivial one at that.[4] That is not to say, however, that Leibniz's formula is either trivial or useless. Identity in L_1, we shall see in a moment, remains a useful notion even in our world.

Now for sameness; first the thing, then its expression in L. Awarenesses are just individuals among individuals. Thoughts or meanings are just simple characters among simple characters. They are not, like Frege's nonmental meanings, nebulous entities of odd ontological kinds. Like sensa and their characters, they are phenomenal things and when they are presented to us at all, they are, like sensa and their characters, wholly presented in a specious present. Thus, unlike Frege, we need no criterion of sameness for them. The decision, if it be one, is still immediate. A thought, in particular, when we resort to words, is uniquely determined by its text.

The word 'same', we remember, aside from convenience, serves two functions. In its first use, it stands informatively either between a name and a description or between two descriptions of an individual. In its second use, it tells us something worthwhile about complex characters. Two complex characters are the same if and only if they are analytically equivalent. L_1 is a very major part of L. And analyticity in L is of course so defined that every statement analytic in or according to the rules of L_1 remains analytic in L. It follows that as far as the second use is concerned, nothing needs to be added to what has been said before.

Two individuals, finally, are the same if and only if every statement in which they are not referred to in an M-context and that is true of the one is also true of the other. Technicalities apart, that amounts to this. "Two" individuals are the same if and only if they are identical in L_1. That is one reason, though not the only one, why identity in L_1 remains even in our world, whose ideal language is L, an important notion. But suppose now that someone doubts whether all this is really so, that is, whether the M-contexts really make no difference. I shall conclude with what I would tell this doubter. If it were otherwise, then what a thing is would depend, as the idealists absurdly claim, on whether and how it is thought about.

[4] This very suggestive formulation is Grossmann's.

Professor Quine on Analyticity*

IN A recent issue of *Mind* Professor Quine[1] defended the reasonableness and usefulness of formal logic against some of Mr. Strawson's doubts and objections. With this defense I heartily agree. But there is more to Quine's paper. He distinguishes two views, labeling them (*a*) and (*b*), either of which may be consistently held by one who agrees with him in rejecting the sort of criticism Strawson's book exemplifies. Let me, then, for the convenience of the moment speak of A-theorists and B-theorists. The latter hold that the two related distinctions between logical and descriptive signs and between analytic (logical) and synthetic statements are even for artificial languages merely enumerative or, to put it baldly, arbitrary. They are, at best, a matter of convenience. A-theorists deny this. According to them, the two distinctions are anything but arbitrary or conventional, even within what they call pure syntax. If they are philosophers, then their main motive for insisting on this is their conviction that if artificial sign systems are used as tools in the nonphilological and nonpsychological study of natural language, then the two distinctions yield philosophical clarifications that could not be obtained in any other manner. About the propriety of this use of artificial languages in general Quine has no quarrel with the A-theorists. He also grants, very fairly, that some A-theorists are cautious. They know that the relation between a formalism and what it purports to formalize is delicate and that, therefore, a great deal of caution and sophistication is required when one applies the two distinctions in philosophical discourse.

Quine is a B-theorist. I am a cautious A-theorist. But I do not intend to reopen this very complex argument by attempting to restate the

* Mind, *64, 1955, 254–58. Reprinted by permission.*

[1] "Mr. Strawson on Logical Theory," *Mind*, 62, 1953, 433–51.

A-theorist's case.[2] All I propose to do is this. First, I shall try to show that at one crucial point Quine's argument against Strawson is less than cogent. More bluntly, I don't think Quine has a good reason for the position he takes against Strawson on one crucial issue. Second, I shall show briefly that the A-theorist has *at this point* no difficulty whatsoever. Third, I shall indicate why I think the argument Quine actually uses at this point against Strawson is wrongheaded in a way that goes far beyond the limits of the philosophy of logic.

The issue I just called crucial concerns the acceptance or rejection of the following three propositions. (1) Quantifiers are timeless. (2) The temporal relation words 'earlier', 'later', 'simultaneous' are in the same logical boat with such other nonlogical words as 'louder', 'brighter', 'beats (in football)'. (3) Let the first three lower case letters be the names of three short temporally nonoverlapping flashes of light. Then

(L) If a is earlier than b and b is earlier than c then a is earlier than c

is not a logical truth. (This is Quine's preferred name for truths others call analytic and which he singles out merely for the sake of convenience, in a manner ultimately based on enumeration and according to him devoid of philosophical significance.) I am prepared to die in the last ditch for these three propositions, if necessary, alone. It looks, though, as if I were to enjoy Quine's company. Let us see, then, what reasons a B-theorist could give for this stand. The one I can think of, instructed as I am by Quine's earlier writings, and which has at least a semblance of appropriateness is this. If in (L) 'earlier' and the three names are replaced by other words *of the same kinds*, then some of the resulting sentences, *e.g.*,

(F) If Harvard beats Yale and Yale beats Princeton then Harvard beats Princeton,

are not even true, let alone logically true. There are two reasons why this argument will not do. First, if 'earlier' were enumerated among the logical words, nobody, and Quine least of all, would think of applying any kind of substitution test. For, to use his earlier phrase, logical words do not occur vacuously in logical truths. Or does anyone expect 'It rains *and* it does not rain' to be true because 'It rains *or* it does not rain' is? Second, even if one grants for the sake of the argument that 'earlier' and 'beats' are both words to which substitutions are somehow appropriate, how do we know that they belong to the same kind in the sense that they may be substituted for each other? The only reason a

[2] For a statement, see several of the essays in *The Metaphysics of Logical Positivism*.

B-theorist could give is that the two words are grammatically similar in our natural language (though perhaps not in Afghan or in Tamil). Unfortunately, a defender of the philosophical use of formalisms against Strawson's kind of attack cannot afford to use this argument. Besides, whether we side with Strawson or with Quine, we all know by now how easy it is, with the door once opened to natural language in this manner, to discredit any attempt to generalize grammatical similarities as broadly as the formalist would have to generalize them for his purpose. Quine, of course, knows all that, though he does not bother to say it on this occasion. So he casts about for another argument, the one which I think is both bad and wrongheaded. But let us first inquire how an A-theorist would fare.

A philosopher may have *motives* for wanting to put such statements as (F) and (L) in the same boat with each other and not together with, say, 'It rains or it does not rain'. Probably he expects these groupings to be helpful when he tackles some philosophical questions that have been raised about, say, time and space. I certainly have this motive and so, I presume, at least partially and in some fashion, does Quine. For if he didn't, why should he bother at all to argue that (F) and (L) are in the same boat. Little as this can mean to him, it must mean something. As for myself, this motive is also among my motives why I should like to find *reasons*, independent of what I consider to be the right views on, say, space and time, for being an A-theorist. The point then is this. An A-theorist who knows what he is about has such independent reasons, which he believes to be good reasons, for the two distinctions, between logical and descriptive words and between analytic and synthetic truths. These reasons provide him with criteria by which he concludes, instead of legislating *ad hoc* by enumeration, that 'earlier' is descriptive, that 'earlier' and 'beats' are of the same kind, and that (L) is synthetic. This is what I meant when I said that an A-theorist has *at this point* no difficulties. For the rest, I did not undertake to make a complete case for the A-theorist. So I turn to Quine's reason for accepting the three propositions.

He takes them to suggest, or to be suggested by, or to fit better than others, I do not quite know how to put it, the "four-dimensional view of space-time" with its "notable technical advantages." This view and these advantages I understand to be of a scientific nature. The gist of the argument is thus, if I may paraphrase a now prominent statesman, that what is good for science is good for logic. Perhaps, even, what is good for science is good for philosophy. I demur. Whenever science is appealed to, covertly or overtly, in such manner and in such context, my suspicions are immediately aroused. In this one respect I think

Strawson is more likely to agree with me than Quine (or Carnap, or Dewey). Things just are that complex. Fortunately; otherwise the world would be even duller. Be that as it may, the reference to four-dimensionality and to hyphenated space-time creates the impression that one who rejects the three propositions could not "square" his logic with the theory of relativity. So I shall first show that this is not so.

Contrary to an impression produced by the wrong kind of advocacy of artificial languages, science itself, including theoretical physics, does not use what Quine calls the algorithms of formal logic, except occasionally, incidentally, and, if I may once use the phrase, for mere convenience. (Notice that I speak of science, not of mathematics, and that for an A-theorist mathematics is not science.) The algorithms theoretical physics actually uses are those of nonformalized mathematics. It is true, though, that if the theory of relativity is axiomatized, i.e., if it is treated as an uninterpreted scientific (not logical) calculus, then its basic relation term is what one calls, in pure or uninterpreted geometries, a four-dimensional interval. This, if I understand him at all, is the one fact Quine could adduce as a reason. So I shall give two reasons for my belief that this fact does not constitute a good reason for accepting the three propositions.

For one, if the axiomatic relativity calculus is to be of any significance in physics, it must be first interpreted. In the interpretation the four "components" of the "four-dimensional interval" turn out to be expressions defined in terms of *ordinary (three-dimensional) space* and *ordinary (one-dimensional) time*. Similarly, by the way, the events signified by proper names of the interpreted calculus are happenings among ordinary physical objects persisting in time and space. This is why one does not *have* to accept a sense data philosophy or any other sort of "eventism" in order to square one's self with modern science. For another, assume that a logical formalism with the three propositions both Quine and I accept were needed, as in fact it is not, to put the scientific relativity calculus in good order. Even in this case one could only claim that the formalism is useful in science, or perhaps in the philosophy of science (see below), but not in logic or in philosophy in general. An example should make this still clearer. Some people who are very competent in physics have claimed that a three-valued logical formalism is needed to straighten out the axiomatics of quantum mechanics, or, at least, that it is the tool best suited for the job. I believe that these people are wrong.[3] But there is of course no *a priori*

[3] For reasons see my "The Logic of Quanta," *American Journal of Physics*, 15, 1947, 397–408 and 497–508, reprinted in H. Feigl and M. Brodbeck, eds., *Readings in the Philosophy of Science* (New York: Appleton-Century-Crofts, 1953).

reason why they could not have been right. If, then, they were right, would Quine be prepared to conclude that the real logic of our world, whatever that may mean, is three-valued? This brings me to what I called the general wrongheadedness of his argument.

Historically, science and philosophy interact with each other in many ways. Logically, only two kinds of things can happen. Either science itself poses problems that must be solved by philosophical analysis. This is the limited task of the so-called philosophy of science. Or philosophers may have to discard some of their analyses, not because science has proved them wrong, but because it has discovered that the world is in some respect different from what the philosophers thought it was. Newly discovered facts have made their analyses useless, as it were. Consider the relational theory of space and of time in philosophy on the one hand and the scientific theory of space-time on the other. The latter implies the former. As Professor Broad has pointed out, the former does not imply the latter; and the former has been proposed on philosophical grounds long before science discovered the new facts which led to the formulation, as a mere scientific hypothesis, of the latter.

And now once more for our three propositions. I, too, believe that because it accepts them formal logic helps in solving some philosophical problems which could, perhaps, not be solved without it. Only, these problems and questions do not stem from the theory of relativity. They are the questions Parmenides and Plato asked when they first probed the notions of change and identity which have been with us in all sorts of disguises ever since. Generally, not all philosophical questions belong, as Quine seems to believe or to hope, to the philosophy of science. None of the fundamental ones do. Yet, to these latter a philosopher must refer when he argues for the usefulness of artificial languages. The appeal to science merely confuses the issue.

Some Remarks on the Ontology of Ockham*

T HE title of this paper is so wildly hyperbolic that it requires explanation, not to say apology. For one, I know only those fragments from Ockham which Professor Ernest Moody published
some years ago in his well-known book.[1] For another, even if the whole
text were easily accessible as, alas, it is not, a contemporary philosopher
could not hope to make sense out of it simply by reading it. Either he
must first devote many years to historical studies or he must, as I shall,
rely on such commentaries as Moody's. Neither philosophy nor history
have benefited from the cautious silence which for such reasons contemporary philosophers maintain about all but a very few of their more
remote predecessors. What I am offering here, very incautiously, are
therefore merely "Some Remarks on the Ontology Contained in the
Ockham Fragments Selected and Explicated by Moody." Titles that
long have gone out of fashion; hence the inaccurate one I chose. Yet
the fragments in question are so rich in content and the exegesis that
accompanies them is so painstaking and, virtually throughout, en-
lightening, that even this modest undertaking may be of some interest.
It could even be of some relevance to what was, in matter of historical
fact, the ontology of Ockham. So I shall, for brevity's sake, express
myself as if I were actually talking about the latter.

* Philosophical Review, *53, 1954, 560–71. Reprinted by permission.*

[1] *The Logic of William of Ockham* (New York: Sheed, 1935). All page references
are to this book, page references followed by footnote references to one of the
numerous and often very generous fragments.

I

The following three propositions express some of Ockham's ontological views.

(1) The only things that *exist* are *particular things*.

(2) The only things that *exist independently* are *individual substances*.

(3) Particular things are either individual substances or some *qualities*.

There are five technical terms in these propositions. I italicized each of them at its first occurrence. Three need little, if any, explanation. To be sure, in a discussion of contemporary issues I would be the last to suggest that 'to exist' and 'to exist independently' need not be closely examined. Here it suffices to say that they mean what all philosophers until about a generation ago meant when they used them to assert or deny such things as that physical objects exist, that numbers and propositions do not exist, or that what we now call a quality exists dependently and not, as do the physical objects that exemplify it, independently. As long as one restricts oneself, as I shall, to what the medievals called corporeal substances, individual substances are simply physical objects, this apple, that book, or, to use some of the old illustrations, *Plato, hic homo, ille asinus*. All this is as plain from the text and the exegesis as it is, to my knowledge, uncontroversial. The crucial term is 'quality'.

First, the qualifying 'some' in the third proposition requires comment. Not everything we now call a quality is one in this sense. There are, at the one end, as it were, the *differentiae*. As parts of (the definitions of) their species they do not, either dependently or independently, exist for themselves or, as the phrase was, *per se*. At the other extreme there are, roughly speaking, what many now call defined or nonsimple qualities, dispositional properties, and properties implicitly relational with respect to parts of the substance in which they are present (pp. 162–67). These three sorts of things are not qualities that exist in the sense of the third proposition. Typical of qualities that exist are the classical contraries, say, wetness-dryness, heat-coldness.

The fragments show conclusively, or so at least I am prepared to maintain, that for Ockham "quality" did not mean what it means to us but, rather, what we would call an *instance of a quality*, as when, pointing at a sheet of paper, I say, 'This is (an instance of) white (or whiteness)'. If that is correct then it amounts to this. Ockham was not trying to maintain that only physical objects exist outside of minds. Rather, he maintained that the only things which so exist are particular things, physical objects as well as the instances of the qualities that are present in them. The point has probably been blurred by a change in terminology. Most of us, or at least those among us who do not distinguish between 'white' and 'stone' and 'whiteness' and 'stoneness', call both 'white' and 'stone' universals. The medievals called universals only what they also called substantial forms, that is, for instance, stoneness, but not whiteness. Now everybody knows, of course, how vigorously Ockham denied the existence outside of the mind of "universals." Thus one may be puzzled if one finds that he admits the existence, however dependently, of "qualities" outside of the mind. The suggested meaning of 'quality' solves the puzzle. Ockham denied indeed the existence outside of the mind of particular things which are not either individual stones or instances of whiteness and which could serve as referents of either 'stone' or 'white'. But this does not commit him to deny the (dependent) existence as a *res simplex* and *per se una alia ab substantia* (p. 162, n. 1)[2] of an instance of, say, whiteness. Again, the particular acts of the mind (*conceptus*) which are the second intention referents of universals, in the new and broader sense of the word, are all alike in that they refer indifferently to every one of their respective instances, no matter whether they are qualities or, in the old and narrower sense of the word, universals.

It would seem that the fragment just cited furnishes by itself sufficient evidence for this explication of Ockham's use of 'quality'. For good measure I shall cite some more. (a) In one of the few fragments Moody gives in English, Ockham says that "of the essence of 'this whiteness' there are at the very least 'universal whiteness,' 'universal colour,' and 'quality,' which is the *genus generalissimum*" (p. 132). (b) Ockham argues vigorously against the existence, outside of the mind, of particular things other than (groups of or qualities of) individual substances that could serve as the first intention referents of terms in the eight predicaments different from substance and quality. With respect to numbers, for instance, which are in the predicament of quantity, he uses the illustration of a *trinitas canum*, that is, a trio of dogs, asking whether its threeness could exist *in re*. We notice first that, as Moody prettily explains by means of an analogy with modern ideas, what is involved is the threeness of this particular trio and not the class of all triples. Since this threeness, if it is to exist, must be a particular thing, it would either have to be present wholly in each dog or partly in the one, partly in the other, partly in the third. Neither alternative is possible for one particular thing (p. 148, n. 1). The analogy to quality is perfect. What Ockham here refutes is the existence of what we would call, not threeness, but an instance of threeness. Speaking of this would-be existent he calls it once, in a broader meaning of the term, an accident. We know, of course, that some qualities are accidents. Furthermore, the argument is exactly the same as that used

---

[2] See also "*haec res est calor*" in this fragment.

against universals in an English fragment (p. 80). If qualities were what we mean when we speak of a quality, it would, therefore, apply equally to them. If, however, the term signifies what we call an instance of a quality, then it applies no longer. For such an instance inheres always in one and only one particular substance. Thus this case lacks the plurality, e.g., in the illustration, the *trinitas*, on which Ockham's dialectical refutation rests.

In the remainder of this paper I shall use 'quality' and 'universal quality', the former for what I suggest Ockham meant by it, the latter for what we now mean by the former.

II

Nothing in Professor Moody's commentary indicates that when he wrote it he was aware of the suggested meaning of 'quality'. One crucial passage (p. 163) is incompatible with it. As one might expect, this is the passage in which Moody defends Ockham against those who are puzzled by his admitting the existence of "qualities." The defense fails, fundamentally, I suggest, because Moody speaks there about universal qualities, whose nonexistence is indeed the cornerstone of Ockham's ontology. So I shall support the suggested interpretation by attempting to show that this defense fails because it is incompatible with the fragments as well as with what Moody himself at other places says about them. This will require two preliminary remarks concerning Ockham's use of the terminists' distinctions.

(1) A thing, whether substance or quality, may have many names. Take again a white piece of paper. It has at least two, 'paper' and 'white', the one a universal,[3] the other an adjective. Of these two only the first, 'paper', can, as we would say, be substituted without a resulting change in truth value in every true sentence (of demonstrative science) for any other name of the substance involved, that is, for any other name of my piece of paper. Such names are said to signify *absolutely*. It is easily seen that a universal signifies absolutely each of the individual substances which it names indifferently. Not so an adjective. 'This is square', for instance, is true about my piece of paper, while 'White is square' is false. (The demonstrative pronoun is considered to be a name.) Such names are said to signify *connotatively*. This is, of course, the doctrine of supposition. Its distinctions are as natural as they are necessary if one starts, as the medievals did, from a very broad notion of name. This notion, strange as it seems to us, follows in turn quite naturally from the Parmenidean illusion, which

---

[3] From now on the term is used in its older and narrower sense. For its contemporary meaning I shall later use *character* and *character term*.

is at the root of so many strange things in philosophy, that every occurrence of the copula indicates an identity.

But then, how about the quality that is present in my piece of paper?
Since it exists, a *res una per se*, though of course dependently, there
should be a name to signify it absolutely. To serve as this name is the
function of the *abstractum*, 'whiteness', in contradistinction to the *con-
cretum*, 'white'. Furthermore, this is the only purpose of the distinction
between the abstract and concrete forms of quality terms (p. 56; p. 59,
n. 1; p. 162, n. 1). To convince ourselves how well all this hangs together, we notice that while in our illustration the adjective signifies
connotatively the piece of paper as well as its whiteness, there is nothing
at all for it to signify absolutely. In this sense 'white' is merely a word
and requires therefore a definition. Such a definition must of course be
nominal. So we understand why Ockham insists, strangely to us but
quite naturally from where he stands, that the concrete form of an
adjective must be nominally defined by means of the abstract; 'white',
for instance, as 'something that has whiteness' (p. 110, n. 1). We notice
finally, for later use, that such phrases as 'to exist absolutely' or 'a being
in the absolute sense' would make no sense at all to Ockham, except
perhaps in theology. For 'absolute' and 'connotative' refer only to
modes of the signification of terms. To distinguish the two modes of
existence in things, we had better stick to 'dependent' and 'independent'. For this latter distinction Ockham himself does not need special
terms. To him, as to all other medieval writers, *substantia* and *qualitas*
connote it beyond all doubt and ambiguity.

(2) Terms signify either *divisim* or *conjunctim*. The distinction is
needed in Ockham's analysis of the last eight predicaments. His thesis
is that there are no particular things outside of minds that are in any
of these predicaments, in that specific sense in which a thing can be
said to be in a predicament (p. 134, n. 2). For the corresponding terms
there are, therefore, two possibilities. Either they do not signify anything in the first intention,[4] or they signify *somehow* (*aliquo modo*)
groups of particular things (p. 122, n. 1). Take the predicament of relation and consider the proposition 'This is similar to that'. The two
pronouns refer to existents, either substances or qualities. (Characteristically, Ockham's illustration in this fragment operates with qualities,
hoc album and *illud album*. This is further evidence, if such were still
needed, for our explication of 'quality'.) But even in cases where the
demonstrative pronouns refer to two individual substances, neither of
the two is signified by the relation term, not even connotatively. For it

---

[4] This is the position of the modern "nominalists," e.g., Locke. See below and,
also, "The Problem of Relations in Classical Psychology," *The Philosophical
Quarterly*, 2, 1952, 140–52; reprinted in *The Metaphysics of Logical Positivism*.

does not make sense to say either 'This is similar' or 'That is similar'. The way out is to let the term signify *conjunctim*, that is, on each particular occasion that particular pair of particular things that is on this occasion said to be similar (p. 122, n. 1; p. 156, n. 2). The abstract term, 'similarity', as in the case of universals the abstract term, say, 'humanity', signifies nothing outside of minds. All this is completely analogous to the analysis of threeness. It seems to me that Ockham's analysis of numbers and relations offers indeed the easiest avenue, least encumbered by antiquarian rubble, to an understanding of his critique not only of the eight predicaments but of what one might call Porphyry and the Consequences.

Quality terms, whether abstract or concrete, and universals signify existents not in groups but singly. In this respect they are said to signify *divisim*. Consider now the case of a substance in relation and the corresponding relation term, say, 'father'. The term signifies the father conjunctively with the son—somehow. Strictly speaking it does not signify the father at all, not even connotatively,[5] though one may be tempted to believe that it does, since in this case 'This is *a* father' makes sense. It is even true. (Notice that the Latin '*Hic est pater*' misses the nuance of the indefinite article.) If one yields to the temptation, one's thought becomes blurred. By the way, I found no fragment in which Ockham himself says any such thing as, say, that 'father' signifies some men connotatively. The best protection against the temptation is, I believe, to realize the radical inadequacy of Ockham's theory of relations. But of this later.

Moody discusses in this context (p. 122) the distinction between *ens per se* and *ens per aliud*. Again, I found no fragment in which Ockham himself either explicates these terms or uses them with Moody's meaning. With the latter they mark distinctions in discourse and signification, not *in re*. If so, then their realistically sounding names are dangerously misleading. What Moody has in mind, if I understand him correctly, is the distinction between terms that signify absolutely on the one hand and terms that signify either connotatively or conjunctively on the other. This bracketing of the latter two modes of signification is the blur to which I just objected. The danger is that we may not realize that while relations do not literally exist according to Ockham, neither dependently nor independently, qualities do exist for him, though of course dependently. Again, things do hang together very satisfactorily. We understand now why Ockham insists that with

---

[5] Otherwise a son not himself a father would also be connoted by "father," which is absurd. Similarly for all nonsymmetrical relations. This is therefore obviously not, as Moody seems to believe, a case of *significare secundario*, as in the case of connotation (p. 55, n. 2).

respect to the last eight predicaments, but not for either substance or quality, 'ens' is used *equivoce* (p. 156, n. 2). That is, to repeat, substances as well as qualities literally exist. Instances of numbers, relations, and so on, do not exist at all.

I am ready to examine what I called Moody's "defense" of Ockham (p. 163). First the supposed problem or, as I put it, the puzzle is stated.

In view of the fact that Ockham calls abstract qualitative terms of this first kind, "absolute" terms, verifiable of individual things outside the mind which are *per se one* and distinct from individual substances, it might seem that Ockham was making the contraries *entia per se*, and thus positing them as *absolute principles* [italics added] distinct from substances, such that the *first principles of metaphysics* [italics added] would include contraries.

This is indeed what Ockham does. Only, and I take this on Moody's authority, the phrases I italicized signify for Ockham merely simple existents whose nature must be grasped by an intuition not itself demonstrable, which is the indispensable basis of all demonstrative science. Besides, Moody himself uses here 'absolute' equivocally, apparently without noticing it, once for a mode of signification, once ontologically.

Next he sets the stage by recalling what he has shown earlier, cogently and as far as I know quite uncontroversially, namely, first, that Ockham distinguishes sharply between metaphysics on the one hand and physics in the broad medieval sense of demonstrative science on the other and, second, that he considers logic the discursive instrument of physics and of physics only, not of metaphysics. So far, so good. But now the stage is set for the defense proper. Roughly speaking, its gist is that when Ockham speaks of qualities as particular things in his logical works,[6] he must be understood to be speaking logically, not ontologically. I do not know what that means. The illusion that it means anything at all is, I think, again caused by a loose use of the terminists' vocabulary. I quote:

Physics uses terms that signify substances not merely as *things which are* and which are *per se one*, but as things without which something else cannot be said to be. The "something else" is being in the qualified and equivocal sense, i.e., the *ens per aliud* which is a function of the conjunction or co-existence of two or more things which, considered separately, are beings in the unqualified sense.

In the light of the two preliminary remarks this reads as follows: "Physics signifies substances not only by universals, absolutely, but also by quality terms, connotatively. The something else the latter terms connote does not literally exist, it exists only *equivoce*, that is,

---

[6] Virtually all the fragments are from the two main logical works.

as a group of individual substances each of which exists independently."
Clearly this will not do. Or else I would have to be shown the two individual substances which 'white' as applied to my piece of paper
"conjunctively connotes."

I take it, then, that I have established the suggested meaning of
'quality' as well as the three propositions which I claimed express some
of Ockham's ontological views.

III

Consider the following two propositions.

(4) An individual substance *consists* of a *form* and of *matter*.
(5) A quality consists of a form and of the matter of the individual
    substance in which it is present.

Like the three propositions of the first section, these two are of the kind
commonly called ontological. The first three, we saw, Ockham explicitly
expounded. I am not prepared to maintain that this is also true of the
fourth and fifth. I shall merely try to show (a) that these two are
compatible with the first three and (b) that a position embracing all
five can meet certain criticisms which are fatal to one that accepts the
first three but rejects the last two. Thus, if one wishes to express (b)
more fancifully, one may say that Ockham *ought* to have held all five.
Both (a) and (b) are of course philosophical, not historical, questions.
What follows is therefore an intellectual experiment, not a historical
hypothesis gratuitously erected on fragmentary evidence. Its purpose
is to show how a limited doctrine of form and matter in the Aristotelian
style would permit Ockham to hold without inconsistency what is now
known as a realistic theory of perception.

(a) This time we cannot say that the three new technical terms,
'form', 'matter', and 'to consist', mean what they always meant in
philosophical discourse and let it go at that. For each of the two nouns
means more than one thing with Aristotle himself as well as in the
Aristotelian tradition. There is, first, the sense in which, say, an apple
would consist of the apple form and of that "piece" of matter, *materia
signata* as Aquinas called it, that partakes of the form while the apple
exists. 'Partake' is, as we would put it, Plato's undefined or basic
term; the medievals used *informare*. I chose 'consist' because it is symmetrical with respect to its two grammatical objects and, therefore,
perhaps less burdened by untoward connotations. There is, second, the
sense in which the two nouns stand for the actual and the possible, and,
not unconnected with it, a third in which form is the final cause or
agent, whatever that means, of the changes which, say, apples undergo
in time. That it may not be possible to find univocal explications which
make the Aristotelian doctrine consistent is, I take it, by now a re-

spectable opinion. There is, finally, the Platonic or essentialist variant, which was very influential during the middle ages. According to that variant, forms and forms only exist. (I realize that 'to exist' is here not the historically correct term. Yet I believe that I know what I am doing.) This makes 'to exist' and 'to be a form', if not synonymous, at least coextensive. Loosely speaking, that amounts to a fourth meaning. So we must make a choice. I stipulate, then, that in our two propositions "form" and "matter" occur with the first of these four meanings.

Individual substances and qualities do not "consist" of forms and (pieces of) matter in the sense in which, say, a knife consists of a blade and a handle, that is, of parts each of which is itself an individual substance. From this we may draw two conclusions. First, 'to consist' as it occurs in our propositions has a specific meaning different from its ordinary nonphilosophical one. Second, forms and (pieces of) matter are not themselves individual things. Taken together our five propositions exclude therefore the Platonic variant. According to the position they express, neither forms nor matter exist. This is why I do not see the slightest reason to suspect that the five propositions jointly yield a contradiction. Certainly, Ockham's characteristic argument against "universals," which rests on the first three, cannot be brought to bear on forms. This argument depends on what he considers the self-evident impossibility of an existent being at the same time at several places. But forms are not existents; hence he is not committed to deny that numerically one form may inform several pieces of matter. The one thing he is committed to is to insist that the "tie" between a form and the matter it informs is different in kind from that between a quality and the substance in which it inheres or is present. In other words, the "relation" between forms and matter ought to be different from that between predicables and their subjects. That there is such a difference follows directly from the last two propositions. According to them, for a quality to be present in a substance means, not that the former informs the latter but, rather, that their forms inform the same piece of matter.

Yet there is still a roughness. Since forms and matter do enter into the constitution of what exists (ens), one may not wish to say, however correctly, that they do not exist and let it go at that. At this point a word comes to mind. One may say that forms and matter *subsist*. Let us see where that leaves our technical vocabulary. Altogether it has now nine undefined terms. Five of them, those that occur in the first three propositions, have ordinary meanings which we may be assumed to understand and they are in these propositions used with these meanings. The remaining four, 'form', 'matter', 'to consist', and 'to subsist', either do not have such meanings or are in our propositions used with different ones which are by no means clear. Thus one may ask why a philosopher should want to erect upon the "empirical" basis of the first three propositions the "metaphysical" structure of the last two. This leads to my second point.

(b) Moody argues convincingly for important similarities between Ockham's and Aquinas' theories of perception. They are, he says, both realists in the modern sense of the term; they are both empiricists; and they are both firmly set against any sort of illuminism in the Augustinian fashion. This, I take it, means the following three things. First, whatever the mind grasps or extracts or abstracts when it perceives a particular object comes from the object itself, not from a further one, say, its form, which exists separately. Whether or not exemplars subsist in the mind of God, in some medieval sense of "subsist" that is different from ours, is not relevant as long as they do not participate in the process of perception. This is the realism. Second, the perception of individual objects is the only way in which we acquire knowledge about them. This is the empiricism. Third, in perceiving, the mind acts by itself unaided by any further agent. This is the anti-illuminism which corresponds on the side of the mind, as it were, to the realism. The one aspect of these theories that interests me at the moment is this realism, perhaps because I, too, hold it to be self-evident that when, looking at something, I see that it is a flower and not an old shoe, there must be something in or about what I see, rather than in me or elsewhere, that makes it a flower and not an old shoe.[7] Aquinas can take care of this piece of common sense. In his theory the mind extracts from the particular object the intelligible species which is, in some sense, in it. He pays his price when he meets the difficulties this account causes him on the side of the mind. These Ockham avoids by making the mind grasp its object directly. (In this respect the analogy to modern representative and direct realism, the former corresponding to Aquinas', the latter to Ockham's theory of perception, is, I think, striking.) His trouble lies on the side of the object. For if he actually held the first three and rejected the last two of our five propositions, then he could not, as he undoubtedly intended, explain in a "realistic" fashion how he or anybody else knows flowers from shoes. It is equally obvious that a position which includes all five propositions, whatever else its shortcomings may be, has in principle the means to answer this sort of question. This is what I had in mind when I said that Ockham ought to have held all five propositions.

Looking more closely, one sees that the last two propositions would save Ockham with respect to flowers and shoes, greens and blues—

---

[7] For what is here involved it makes no difference whatsoever whether the object of the mental act is or is not itself mental.

generally, with respect to qualities and individual substances. They would not save him with respect to relations. As will be recalled, he locates the referents of relational character terms in "groups" of existents, say, in the case of spatial contiguity indifferently in each of the pairs of individual substances that are contiguous. Thus, either there must be a relational form which informs each of these pairs or it cannot be explained how one knows two people who are contiguous in space from, say, a pair of siblings.[8] But our propositions, while they provide for the forms of qualities and individual substances, do not provide for relational forms. All this becomes completely plain if one considers that there is really no difference between Ockham's analyses of relations and of numbers. In the case of numbers he is, loosely speaking, on the right track, since what matters with them are, indeed, again loosely speaking, arbitrary groupings and nothing but such groupings. The groupings produced by a relation are not arbitrary. So what works for the one could not possibly by itself work for the other.

I have come to the end of my intellectual experiment. The view Ockham actually held was probably more like Abelard's. According to this view, individual substantial forms and qualities *in re* account by virtue of the *similarities* that do or do not obtain among them for the facts of perception. The consequences or, as I see it, the shortcomings of this opening gambit are familiar; so I shall not restate them. It is worth noticing, though, that in this schema, too, relations cannot be accounted for. Nor is that surprising. The problem of relations was not fully understood until several centuries after Ockham. More precisely, it was not understood that a "realistic" theory of perception requires that in each instance of a relation there be something *in re* which is not "localized" in space after the manner of individual substances and qualities. And it would seem unreasonable to expect a man even of Ockham's genius to have been so far ahead of his time in all respects. His main purpose in giving a great amount of attention to relations was to disprove the existence of such entities as number, length, and fatherhood, since according to the position he opposed, this special kind of universals enjoyed the same ontological status as those related to shoes and flowers. He had set out to prove that no universals exist; so he was forced to examine closely that special kind. In this task he succeeded completely. In carrying it out he stumbled, if I may so put it, upon the real problem of relations. He may even have felt that not everything was well with the solution he proposed. Why otherwise that curious *aliquo modo?*

---

[8] I chose a symmetrical relation for this illustration because it is not necessary to raise the additional difficulties of the general case. See note 5, above.

Russell's Examination of
Leibniz Examined*

R USSELL'S book[1] on Leibniz appeared in 1900. That it is important, because of its subject and because of its author, hardly
needs to be argued. An examination of it, or of parts of it, after
more than half a century is therefore in order. Yet the title I chose indicates only part of my intent. The other part is to examine certain ideas,
irrespective of what either Leibniz or Russell thought and of what the
latter thought about the thoughts of the former. The title best suited
to this part is *Individuals, Natures, Relations, and Change.* The mixed
form of presentation, analytic and quasi-historical, has very great advantages. For the nature of the philosophical enterprise is such that an
analyst is lost without some grasp or, at least, some image of "structural history." The danger is that only very few, if any, are masters of
two trades; in this case, logical analysis and historical scholarship. I,
for one, make no pretense whatsoever of being a scholar. Naturally, I
have read in Leibniz; and I did not skip or take lightly anything in the
letters to Arnauld and Clarke; but I have by far not read everything
that is available. Reading about Leibniz, aside from Russell, of which
I did but little, I found Latta[2] and, particularly, Joseph[3] sometimes

* Philosophy of Science, *23, 1956, 175–203. Reprinted by permission.*

[1] *A Critical Exposition of the Philosophy of Leibniz* (Cambridge: at the University Press, 1900). Page references are to this book, which is based on lectures
delivered in the spring of 1899. In the introduction to the second edition (1938)
of *Principles of Mathematics* (1903) Russell states that most of it was written in
1900. The striking differences between *Leibniz* and the *Principles* make it possible to date certain developments of Russell's thought rather precisely.

[2] *The Monadology,* etc., with introduction and notes by Robert Latta (Oxford:
Clarendon Press, 1898).

[3] *Lectures on the Philosophy of Leibniz* (Oxford: Clarendon Press, 1949).

helpful. More often, though, I felt that the former's Hegelianism and the latter's Aristotelianism had got between them and their subject.

There is one special reason why I yielded to the temptation of a mixed presentation. Russell's book, which most analysts now consider the best guide to Leibniz, is not only intensely interesting and sometimes profound, it is also often very confused and confusing. That this is so I expect to show; why it is so can be understood. For one, Russell's thought, though churning with momentous matter, was at that time still inchoate. For another, Russell attributed to Leibniz some of his own preoccupations or, perhaps, blamed him for not sharing them. Third and not unrelated, Leibniz is much closer to medieval ideas than the young Russell or anybody else at his time and place was likely to realize. (By now the pendulum has perhaps swung too far in the other direction.) Fourth and not least, when Russell delivered these lectures he did not yet have the tool which he later forged himself, the formalism of *Principia Mathematica* (PM). I shall use this tool.

Lest this essay be mistaken for an exercise in historical scholarship, I shall not quote Leibniz. The passages I would quote (though I could also quote a few others) are well known; most of them are in the letters to Arnauld and to Clarke and have been quoted repeatedly. Another precaution lies in the way I arranged my material. In the first two sections I ignore both Leibniz and Russell. In the third section I state what I take to be some of Leibniz's fundamental ideas. The next three sections take up the three issues I selected for this partial examination, namely, the meaning of the formula *predicatum inest subjecto,* space, and time. Throughout these sections there is, I hope, no doubt as to where I report, where I analyze either Russell or Leibniz, and where I speak for myself. A concluding section draws some lessons for a contemporary issue.

I

Ontology asks: What is there (what exists)? Common sense answers: Everything. Few, if any, philosophers accepted this answer. That alone shows that they used 'exist' and 'there is (are)' in peculiar ways, philosophically rather than commonsensically. Philosophical uses require commonsensical explications. My first business is to clarify the ontological query by explicating, in the proper order as I see it, some of the ontological vocabulary.

One often says, commonsensically, that a thing consists or is composed of others. This is our first cue. Ontology searches for *simples* (elements, constituents), which may be said to exist in a narrower sense, while the compounds (configurations, structures) will then be said to exist only in a broader sense or, even, in some philosophers'

usage, not to exist at all. Historical tags for the distinction are not hard
to find. *Unum, res,* and *ens* were held to be convertible. Multiplicity,
according to Leibniz himself, is grounded in unity. Like all metaphors,
that of consisting or compounding has its dangers. One must beware
lest one overlook and, by overlooking it, prejudge the question whether
in addition to those one might otherwise mistake for the sole constituents of a compound there are not some special kinds of simples which
provide the "structure." This danger, though, need not deter us now.
We must realize first of all that 'simple', used philosophically as I just
used it, is anything but simple. Our first explication thus calls for
another.

The philosophical uses of 'simple' are in the main controlled by three
ordinary ones. I shall call them psychological, physical, and linguistic.
Much bad philosophy stems from the unexamined belief that these
three kinds of simplicity must coincide or, in the case of the one which
is linguistic, must be made to do so. Psychologically simple is what
cannot be "decomposed" by so-called analytical introspection; the notion of analytical introspection itself is commonsensical.[4] Physical objects we often call simple if they have no parts. 'Part', however, even
if not used philosophically, is itself ambiguous. What seems to be the
dominant meaning is geometrical. Or, rather, philosophers tend to use
'part' as we use it when we say of two concentric circles that the smaller
is a part of the larger.[5] Again, we need not tarry; for the notion of
simplicity that left the deepest mark on philosophical thought is linguistic. Simple, upon this notion, is what is named by the undefined
descriptive signs of an ideal language.[6] Why this kind of simplicity

[4] See also "Intentionality," *Semantica* (Archivio di Filosofia, Roma: Bocca,
1955), pp. 177–216, and also pp. 3–38 of this book.

[5] Something is in this sense a part of something else if and only if the two
exemplify a descriptive (not logical) relation of a certain logical structure. If
that is not seen, one may well wonder how anything can exemplify a character
(e.g., extension) that is not exemplified by any of its parts (e.g., points). This, it
would seem, is the real monster that lurks, for Leibniz, in the labyrinth of the
continuum. Accordingly, he finds no difficulty in a continuum of attributes (e.g.,
hues); for he does not think of them as parts of a compound (e.g., color). Everybody agrees that biographically the continuity issue was the seed from which
Leibniz's system grew. No doubt this is so; yet I shall, because I think I safely
can, ignore the issue completely. If I am right in that then something is gained
for the understanding of the ideas themselves, both those considered and those
neglected, as well as for the structural understanding of Leibniz's thought.

[6] A broader meaning of 'ontology' may be obtained by omitting 'descriptive'
from this sentence. Since this meaning is neither interesting nor very important
historically, I shall ignore it and, for brevity's sake, use 'undefined' instead of
'undefined descriptive'. These notions are really syntactical, as is another distinction I shall presently introduce. But the ideal language is an interpreted
syntactical schema; that is why I prefer to call them linguistic rather than syn-

intrigued philosophers and, therefore, whether they knew it or not, affected their use of 'simple' is easily understood. Defined terms name compounds, and conversely. They are eliminable, i.e., they can be replaced by their definientia. (That is one reason why one may not wish to say that compounds "exist.") Also, the syntactical form of the definiens expresses the structure of the compound the definiendum names. (Or, rather, this is one clear meaning one may assign to the elusive 'structure'.) Conversely, terms that are undefined or, perhaps better, undefinable are opaque in a sense in which defined ones are not. They are "merely" names; and to attach mere names or labels is all one can do when referring to a "simple." So far, so good. A slight change in metaphor, from attaching labels to pointing at, provides the cue for another distinction.

Assume, for the sake of the argument, that physical objects and the colors they exemplify are all named by undefined terms. One can point at a physical object in a sense in which one cannot point at a color (though perhaps at an instance of it in a physical object). In one of the two senses of 'pointing' which we thus discern, one can point only at what is spatially and temporally localized. To be so localized is one important ingredient of the philosophical notion of individuality.[7] Presently I shall pursue this line; first, though, I want to consider a likely objection. My objector argues as follows. Whether spatial and temporal characters or, perhaps, places in space and time exist is itself an ontological question. Yet you attempt to clarify the very nature of ontology by means of spatial and temporal notions. Are you not, therefore, in danger of prejudging the ontological status of space and time and have you not, moreover, fallen into circularity? I reply by calling attention to the distinction between commonsensical and philosophical uses. I used 'spatially and temporally localized' neither philosophically nor metaphorically but commonsensically and literally in explicating, i.e., speaking *about* philosophical uses. Thus I have not fallen into circularity and did not prejudge what one who speaks philosophically or, for that matter, I myself speaking as a philosopher (though not, I hope, philosophically) may have to say about space and time. Yet, I agree, even insist, that the philosophical use of 'individual' which rests on the distinction between two kinds of "pointing" has been the cause of much bad ontology. Accordingly, I shall explicate 'individual' by

---

tactical. For the notion of an ideal language, its commonsensicality, and the distinction, within it, between descriptive and logical signs and expressions, see *The Metaphysics of Logical Positivism*, hereafter referred to as MLP.

[7] It is also an ingredient of the notion of concreteness. Let me say, then, that 'concrete' and 'abstract' are banned from this essay. For I have found not only that *they are a pair of troublemakers* but also that in philosophy *I can do nicely without them*. In the psychology of thought they are of some use.

means of another distinction. To take uncritically for granted that the two are coextensive or even identical may become a source of confusion.

In the ideal language which, whether they knew it or not, influenced the ontologists, some descriptive terms, call them predicate-terms, occur in some sentences as predicates, in some others as subjects. Some other terms, call them subject-terms, occur only as subjects. Notice that the distinction is one among terms and distinguishes, therefore, between 'subject' and 'predicate' on the one hand and 'subject-term' and 'predicate-term' on the other.[8] This linguistic distinction is the other major ingredient of the philosophical notion of individuality. I shall here make it the whole, calling an *individual* what is named by a particular, i.e., by an undefined subject-term of a philosopher's (explicit or implicit) ideal language. An individual is thus a simple, but not conversely. The notion is important because many philosophers want to use 'exist' so that only individuals "exist." But then, again, quite a few among these philosophers also want to say that individuals exemplify characters, i.e., those, according to them, nonexisting things which are named by predicate-terms. This produces a difficulty. One part of it is purely verbal and easily overcome; the other is more serious. To begin with the former, it might seem paradoxical that in speaking of what exists, namely, individuals, one should be forced to mention what does not exist, namely, characters. The paradox disappears as soon as one remembers that one deals with some very peculiar uses of 'exist'. I shall say, therefore, without fear of paradox, that some ontologists operate with two kinds of elements or building stones, namely, things that do and things that do not, as they speak, exist. The other part of the difficulty, the one I called more serious, stems from another distinction to which these philosophers have either implicitly or explicitly committed themselves. This is the distinction among characters as such and characters as exemplified (instantiated). I shall call the former *eternal things* (ideas, universals); the latter, *attributes*. Or, rather, these are the explications I propose for 'eternal thing' and 'attribute'. The difficulty itself has two sides. Most philosophers want to say something about exemplification or instantiation, i.e., about the "tie" reflected in the juxtaposition of a subject-term and a predicate-term, which makes them the subject and the predicate of a sentence. To distinguish eternal things from attributes is to double this task, because one then has to account not only for the "tie" between individuals and their attributes

---

[8] To say the same thing in the language of *Principia Mathematica*, which I shall employ in the next section, terms (and variables) are of different types; particulars are the undefined descriptive constants of type 0. The possibility of an ideal language without this (syntactical) distinction among terms has been considered only recently. See "Particularity and the New Nominalism," *Methodos*, 6, 1954, 131–47, and also pp. 91–105 of this book.

but also for that between eternal things and the attributes which are their instances. This is one side of the difficulty. The other is that most of these philosophers wish to say that while eternal things don't exist, attributes do. One cause of this desire is, perhaps, that attributes are spatially and temporally localized and can, therefore, be pointed at, at least after a fashion. However that may be, such philosophers face a dilemma. Either they must eventually give up the (implicit or explicit) idea that only individuals (i.e., what is named by particulars) exist; or they must be prepared to treat the names of attributes as particulars. Clearly, there is danger of confusion and, even, of absurdity. One way out was, for many, to introduce a distinction among existents. Those who take this way say that individuals exist independently, attributes dependently. This, however, is only one of the major uses to which the pair 'dependent-independent' has been put in ontology. The other is even more problematic. It is also our cue to introduce the notion of substance.

Some philosophers maintained that only *substances* exist. The explication of 'substance', so used, has four components. S1. Substances are individuals. S2. Substances are continuants. S3. Substances are capable of existing independently. S4. Substances have natures. S1 and S2 are plain enough; S3 and S4 require explanation. By making substances individuals, i.e., simples, or one kind of simples, S1 excludes so-called complex substances. Yet it excludes nothing but a phrase and, perhaps, a derivative use of 'exist', without thereby barring us from speaking, with our vocabulary, about the "compounds" in question. To be a continuant is to persist in time. The common sense root of this component is obvious. Physical objects and minds, which many substance philosophers want to be substances, do so persist. Notice that once more a temporal notion is used to explicate an ontological one. But this, we saw, does no harm as long as commonsensical and philosophical uses are kept apart. Historically, there was a rather notorious difficulty connected with S2, namely, how God, who according to the classical substance philosophers is a substance, stands to time and eternity. This difficulty I disregard.

An attribute, to exist, must, as it was put, inhere in a substance. In this sense, which we encountered before and which I shall henceforth take for granted without further mentioning it, substances exist independently, attributes exist dependently. The independence mentioned in S3 is not of this kind. The traditional formula was that a substance, in order to exist, needs only the support of God. To see what is involved, assume once more physical objects to be substances and remember that we hold, commonsensically, some characters of physical objects to be caused by other physical objects. In other words, physical objects depend causally upon each other. This is the common sense notion which controls the philosophical use of '(in-)dependent' in S3.[9] Consequently, S3 leads to two extreme positions. The one holds that, philosophically speaking, there is only a single substance. The other denies so-called transeunt causation or interaction. Thus one may well wonder whether we have hit upon a plausible explication of S3. In the next section I shall propose one that does not mention causes. But this is not to say that S3 does not, upon either explication, sooner or later lead to catastrophe.

Consider once more a physical object or, for that matter, a thing of the kind called a sensum. Both have been called individuals (S1), although sensa, as far as I know, have never been called substances, probably because they are not continuants (S2). Each exemplifies several characters, the sensum simultaneously, the physical object simultaneously and successively. The *nature* of an individual, as philosophers use 'nature', is the tie, or what accounts for the tie, that presumably connects several characters if and only if they are exemplified by one individual. The analysis of this notion is delicate; so I begin with two preliminary comments. *First.* I used the metaphor of a tie once before when I spoke of exemplification. This is the tie that presumably connects an individual with any of its characters. An individual's nature is the tie, presumably "grounded" in the individual itself, that binds its several characters together. To grasp the difference firmly, consider that, had the words been so used that each individual could be said to have one and only one character, the issue of natures would never have arisen. *Second.* Historically, the dialectic of our notion is almost inseparably intertwined with that of time (change) and force. Logically, a crucial part of it can be freed from the entanglement. To do that is indeed one of my major purposes. Accordingly, I shall first consider a world without change or, as one also says, a timeless universe.

Assuming that there is something to be accounted for, one inclines to say that the tie consists of the several characters being exemplified by the same individual and let it go at that. This answer makes the individual itself the nature, as it were. It was not acceptable to the classical substance philosophers because (by their implicit reasoning) a nature ought to be a character, i.e., what is named by a predicate-term and not, like an individual, by a particular. To understand that,

---

[9] This is why it is worth while to distinguish two meanings of the pair 'dependent-independent'. By collapsing them one commits one's self, perhaps unnecessarily and certainly prematurely, to calling a substance the cause of its attributes. As will be seen in the next section, this use may, without one's noticing it, prejudge the explication of 'cause'. Notice also that wherever change is mentioned, so is, implicitly, time.

one must understand what they meant by "accounting." To account for something is to make it "intelligible." Intelligible is what can be seen with the mind's eye. (This metaphor is fundamental.) The only things that can be so seen are eternal things (ideas, concepts). If they are simple (i.e., if their names are undefined) the mind's eye sees them directly (intuitively); if they are complex, it retraces their definitions. The close connection between characters and eternal things we noticed before. By this line of thought the nature of an individual is a second-type character, namely, a character shared by all and only those characters the individual exemplifies. There is a difficulty, though. A nature, so conceived, connects the characters exemplified by an individual. But how is it, the nature, connected with ("grounded" in) the individual? It only makes the difficulty more obvious if one raises a question that might have been raised earlier. Are natures individual or specific, i.e., does each individual have a nature of its own or do several share the same nature? If natures are to be characters, then the latter alternative, natures being specific and not individual, would seem more plausible. The pity is that it widens the gulf between an individual and "its" nature. The difficulties to which it eventually leads are, in one form or another, those of a hylomorphic scheme with matter as *principium individuationis*. Let us then look at the other alternative. An individual, which is an existent and named by a particular, cannot literally *be* a character, which is perhaps an eternal thing and is named by a second-type predicate. Thus it is as well as one can do to assign to each individual its own (individual) nature and then connect the two in some way one finds somehow "intelligible." This is what Leibniz did. But of that later. Let us now look at the alternatives open to those who conceive of natures as generic characters.

  I simplify without essential distortion by assuming that an individual exemplifies only two characters, f_1 and f_2. Then the second-type character which is its nature may be written as a relation, $R_1(f_1, f_2)$. There are two possibilities. 'R_1' is either (a) descriptive or (b) logical. (a) 'R_1' may be either defined or undefined. If it is defined, then what I shall say holds for its undefined constituents; so I assume it to be undefined. Whoever asserts that he is acquainted with such an undefined character clearly takes the line of those contemporary philosophers who defend what they call nonlogical entailment.[10] This is the structural connection between a contemporary view and the philosophies of substance. (b) Since logical terms do not name anything either existent or eternal, 'R_1', if it is to name a "nature," cannot very well be logical. To see that clearly, remember that '$(x)[f_1(x) \supset f_2(x)]$' can

<hr>

[10] See also "On Nonperceptual Intuition," *Philosophy and Phenomenological Research*, 10, 1949, 263–64; reprinted in MLP.

equivalently be written '$R_1(f_1, f_2)$' with 'R_1' as a defined logical rela-tion.[11] And '$(x)[f_1(x) \supset f_2(x)]$' represents indeed the Humean tie, that is, in the view of the substantialists, no tie at all.

These are some of the difficulties in the notion of nature, and there-fore of substance, which do *not depend on their connection with change* (*time*). To introduce time opens up a new possibility. One may think of an individual's nature as a force (agent, entelechy) "producing" its characters or, if one wants to distinguish, its attributes, thus through this common origin providing the sought for tie among them. But there is also a limitation imposed by the philosophical uses of 'produce'. Sub-stance philosophers would not wish to say that an existent can be "produced" by anything that does not itself exist. If characters are said to exist, forces could therefore be characters, which is, in a tem-poral world, the alternative we just examined. But if characters are said to be eternal things, then forces must be either attributes or indi-viduals. Since in a temporal world attributes change while natures pre-sumably don't, forces cannot be attributes. Thus they must be indi-viduals. This looks hopeful. For now one could perhaps say that an individual is, literally, its nature, namely, a force. But then we are back where we started, at a nature which is what, upon one of the ideas implicit in this dialectic, it ought not be, namely, an individual.

II

Let 'a' be a particular of a formalism. Reconstruction in the properly chosen formalism of the phrase 'the nature of a' yields further insight into the nature of "natures." The formalism I choose for this purpose is the standard one, namely, the noncontroversial parts of PM. And I hold the familiar notion of analyticity or logical truth that goes with it. Upon this notion, the sentence

$$\sim (\exists x)[f_1(x) \cdot f_2(x)],$$

where 'f_1' and 'f_2' are undefined predicates, transcribing the English 'Nothing is (at the same time all over) red and green', is synthetic. Both

(I) $\qquad (\phi = \psi) \equiv (\alpha)[\phi(\alpha) \equiv \psi(\alpha)] \cdot (\Phi)[\Phi(\phi) \equiv \Phi(\psi)]$

and

(E) $\qquad (\alpha)[\phi(\alpha) \equiv \psi(\alpha)] \supset (\Phi)[\Phi(\phi) \equiv \Phi(\psi)]$

are analytic. In these formulae 'ϕ' and 'ψ' are of the same type, 'α' is of the type of the subjects they take, 'Φ' of that of their predicates. E.g., if 'ϕ' and 'ψ' are of type 2, then 'α' and 'Φ' are of type 1 and 3 respec-tively. For the lowest type (I) becomes

---

[11] The definition is: '$R_1(f, g)$' for '$(x)[f(x) \supset g(x)]$'. 'R_1' is logical because the definiens contains no descriptive constants. As is customary, I distinguish con-stants from variables, which are logical signs, by subscripts.

(I′) $(x = y) \equiv (f)[f(x) \equiv f(y)]$.

(I) is said to state the identity of indiscernibles;[12] (E), extensionality.
Consider the following attempt at a definite description

(N) $(\imath X)(f)[X(f) \equiv f(x)]$.

Because of (E), the attempt succeeds;[13] and, since (E) is a logical truth,
it succeeds on purely logical grounds. There is one and only one defined
character exemplified by all and only those characters which are exemplified by an individual. (N) thus reconstructs one conception of nature.
To minimize the machinery I shall from now on use 'A', 'B', and so on,
as names for the natures, thus understood, of a, b, and so on.

Let 'f_1' be an undefined[14] predicate-term of type 1. '$f_1(a)$' and '$A(f_1)$'
are both synthetic; but

(1) $f_1(a) \equiv A(f_1)$

is analytic. This is an immediate consequence of (N). I inquire next
whether natures, so explicated, are generic or individual. One easily
convinces one's self that

(2) $(a = b) \equiv (A = B)$

is analytic. I omit the elementary proof, merely observe that only (E)
is needed to derive the right side of (2) from the left; in the derivation
of the left side from the right (I′) must also be used. It follows that
our natures are individual, i.e., to each individual corresponds one and
only one nature, and conversely.

The issue of substance and nature is connected with that of relation.
To analyze the connection as closely as possible is one of my purposes.
So far I have ignored relations. Now I shall introduce them, though
not as yet the specific ones of space and time. The formalism contains
relational variables of all types; (undefined) descriptive relational
predicate-terms may therefore be adjoined to it. Let 'r_1' be such a term
of the first type. The predicative context '$r_1(\ldots, b)$'—abbreviate it
'$f_{r_1,b}$'—falls within the range of the variable 'f' in (N). This does not
at all affect what has been said so far in this section. It follows that
natures (S4) and undefined descriptive relations among individuals are
compatible. Or, to say the same thing in a certain way which, though a
bit exuberant, is suggestive, they can live together in the same (timeless) world. Undefined descriptive relations are, however, incompatible

---

[12] More accurately, if (I) is considered as a definition of '$=$', this (defined logi-
cal) sign can be shown to be an adequate transcription of the English 'identical'.
See "The Identity of Indiscernibles and the Formalist Definition of 'Identity',"
Mind, 62, 1953, 75–79; reprinted in MLP.

[13] More accurately, it is sufficient that (E) hold for 'ϕ' and 'ψ' of type 2.

[14] The qualification excludes such predicates as 'ϕ_1', where '$\phi_1(x)$' stands by
definition for '$(x = a) \vee (x = b)$'. '$\phi_1(a)$' is of course analytic.

with S3. To see that, assume '$r_1(a, b)$' to be true. Then '$A(f_{r_1,b})$' is also true; '$r_1(a, b)$' is therefore among the atomic sentences one has occasion to assert when one specifies or describes the nature of the substance a. But this sentence mentions the substance b; the notation, '$f_{r_1,b}$', is just one way of calling attention to that. I promised earlier to provide an explication of S3 that does not mention causes. What I just said suggests such an explication. Substances being capable of existing independently may be taken to mean that no atomic sentence specifying or describing the nature of one substance need mention any other. If this explication of S3 is adopted, then substances, in any sense of 'substance' comprehending S3, are incompatible with undefined descriptive relations among individuals. But they are not so incompatible if 'substance' is used in a sense comprehending only some or all of the three other components, S1, S2, S4.

The proposed explication of S3 permits one to keep apart two questions which I believe ought to be kept apart. The one is whether undefined descriptive relations and substances with or without natures can inhabit the same world. The other is whether causal "relations" (in time) and the "relations" obtaining among characters by virtue of their being lawfully connected (either in time or in a timeless world) are logical or descriptive.

To continue with relations. How about undefined descriptive relations among characters of the first type, $R(f, g)$, and of the second type, $R^3(X, Y)$?[15] A little reflection shows that they cause no difficulties whatsoever. Characters of these two types may exemplify undefined descriptive relations. It follows immediately that substances could be "ordered" by such relations among their natures. Whether and, if at all, under what conditions relations of either the second or the third type could be used to introduce space and time is a question I shall examine later. Leibniz, who rejected all undefined relations, did of course not consider this question.

So far I have limited myself to analysis. Now I shall for the first time offer a criticism. (1) is analytic. Hence, whatever can be said in the first three types (0, 1, 2) by mentioning natures can be said equivalently without mentioning them. Concerning contexts in which the names of natures occur as subjects, consider the schema

(3) $\phi(x) \equiv \Phi^3((\imath X)(f) [X(f) \equiv f(x)])$.

Given a constant 'Φ_1^3', (3) can be made the basis for the definition of a uniquely corresponding 'ϕ_1', and conversely. It follows that this reconstruction of 'nature' does not at all increase the expressive possibilities

---

[15] As with 'A' and 'B', I use capitals for type 2 and add superscripts to them to mark the higher types.

of our formalism. If one assumes, as I do, that it must be possible to explicate philosophical uses by the method I use, this criticism is very weighty. Let me state and refute one likely objection. The objector says, quite reasonably, that my result is an obvious consequence of having construed natures as defined characters; for defined terms are expendable. Assume, then, that natures are intuited simples, or, as I would have to put it, that my formalism contains for each 'a' one and only one undefined 'A^*' such that (1), with 'A^*' put in the place of 'A', is a synthetic truth. The fact remains that I can still define 'A' as I did and that A and A^* are coextensive and, therefore, in an extensional schema identical. The objector may now challenge the analyticity of (E). I reply that if the contexts in which the names of natures ('A^*', 'B^*', and so on) occur are not all extensional, then the nature of an individual is not uniquely determined by the characters it exemplifies. This, I believe, is incompatible with my objector's intended use of 'nature'.

III

The inventory of Leibniz's ontology consists of individuals (monads) which exist, of characters (eternal things) which do not exist, and of attributes corresponding to these characters which exist dependently. The "tie" between a character and "its" attributes has not, as far as I can make out, occupied his thought to any great extent or with very striking results. Eternal things are either simple (undefined) or complex (defined) but they are, emphatically, all nonrelational.[16] The distinction between simple and complex characters is logical rather than ontological; naturally, since neither of the two kinds "exists." Leibniz's individuals *are* forces and *have* natures. They are forces since their "essence" is, as he says, activity. This use of 'essence' is idiomatic and must not be taken in the technical medieval sense, in which 'essence' and 'nature' are synonymous. An individual's nature is an individual nature or, as he also says, an individual concept; i.e., to each individual belongs one nature, and conversely. If Leibniz, *as he did not*, had used a symbolism like mine, he would, I think, have named individuals by particulars. How he named natures I am not yet ready to say, though he could certainly not have named them as I did ('A', 'B', and so on), since the type distinction was of course quite unknown to him. But there is not the least doubt that an individual concept or nature is for him an eternal thing. To distinguish between the two, an individual and its (individual) concept, is therefore of the essence. The gulf between them can be bridged only by a free decree of the divine will, i.e.,

---

[16] I refrain deliberately from mentioning at this point "perceptions" and ideal things (*entia rationis*). See note 29 and Section Five.

by creation. What is thus created is only the existent and its attributes.[17] Eternal objects, uncreated, are the objects of God's understanding, not the product of his will. Let me at this point interrupt the
exposition in order to explain why I called Leibniz's thought medieval
in some fundamental respects.

Not counting Locke who (as I do) rejected the problem, there were
before Leibniz three ways to "account" for individuals. In the hylomorphic way of Aristotle generic natures inform prime matter. In the
second way, generic natures or essences, composed, except in the case
of spirits, of both form and matter, are by divine acts endowed with
"being." This is Aquinas' way or, as M. Gilson has taught us to call it,
the existentialist way. The third way, essentialist, is Scotus'. There are
individual natures or *haecceitates;* I use, as Leibniz occasionally did,
the term for the whole individual nature. For the rest, *simpliciter
falsum est quod esse sit aliud ab essentia.* Leibniz invented a fourth way,
a synthesis, rather grandiose in its simplicity, between Thomas' and
Scotus'.[18] In his world individual natures are by a divine act endowed
with existence (being). The logical advantage he thus gained was tremendous. Rather notoriously, Aristotelian essences perform several
functions, one of them dynamic (forces), another definitional (natures).
Since Leibniz separates the two, his world can accommodate natures,
which is his medievalism, as well as forces, which is his modernism,
since these forces become the subjects of his mathematical dynamics.
But it is worth noticing that his basic distinctions would stand in a
timeless world, although in such a world, which he himself never considered, he would probably not call forces what I (but not he) name
by particulars. But I am throughout this essay not concerned with the
finalistic features of his system. I return to exposition.

Every truth (true proposition) *is* of either of two kinds, necessary[19] or
contingent; and we *know* it, if we know it, in either of two ways, *a
priori* or *a posteriori*. Knowing a truth not itself self-evidently necessary

---

[17] That the existent itself produces or creates, in a lesser sense of 'create', its
own attributes is here beside the point.

[18] It seems to me that *haecceitates* are not the only Scotist feature in Leibniz's
thought. He also holds, for instance, that every created monad, including spirits,
has primary matter. The attributes corresponding to primary matter are, in
bodies, inertia and impenetrability. Do not then the eternal things which correspond to these attributes jointly constitute a *forma corporeitatis?* And is there
not some structural similarity between the evolution and involution of immortal
monads and the doctrine of *rationes seminales*, which, if not Scotist, is at least
Franciscan? Ignorant as I am, I say these things with great hesitation; but it
might be worth a scholar's while to trace the cues. One wonders how many
Scotist works the young Leibniz devoured in his father's library.

[19] I am aware of the ambiguity of the unqualified term in Leibniz and shall
therefore soon replace it by 'analytic'.

without being able to deduce it from others is to know it *a posteriori*. Who can so deduce it knows it *a priori*. All necessary truths are about eternal objects and nothing else, and conversely. They all follow, as Leibniz puts it, from the principle of noncontradiction. All contingent truths are about existents and nothing else, and conversely. Their "sufficient reasons" lie ultimately in free decrees of God, though we can and must search for proximate reasons from which we may deduce them, thus coming to know them *a priori*. I interrupt the exposition for exegesis.

In intent, *though not in detail nor in all conclusions he draws from it,* Leibniz's notion of necessary truth is the contemporary one of analyticity with which I operate. I shall show how I would defend this thesis against all objections by first raising and then answering one that is representative. Consider 'red and green are incompatible'. Since colors are for Leibniz eternal things, this sentence is for him analytic. We (though not he) transcribe it '$\sim(\exists x)[f_1(x) \cdot f_2(x)]$', '$f_1$' and '$f_2$' being undefined, making it synthetic for us. This is the apparent difficulty. The point is that while for some (including myself) 'green' and 'red' are undefined, they are not undefined for Leibniz. *Quoad nos*, he grants, they may be. *Quoad se*, or as they are in the understanding of God, they are not. His paradigm of definition is conjunction. What he says, then (I symbolize it as he would not), is that, *first, quoad se* 'green (x)' and 'red (x)' are definitional abbreviations for, say, '$\phi_1(x) \cdot \phi_2(x) \cdot \phi_3(x) \ldots \phi_m(x)$' and '$\psi_1(x) \cdot \psi_2(x) \cdot \psi_3(x) \ldots \psi_n(x)$' respectively; and, *second*, one of the 'ϕ_i' is the negation of one of the 'ψ_j'. I don't believe that this is so; but, if it were so, then our transcription of the critical sentence would, upon our notion of analyticity, indeed be analytic.

To ask whether Leibniz believed that (I) and (E) are analytic makes no sense. Since he did not know the type distinction, the question could not have occurred to him. But it can and must be asked about (I'), which transcribes what he meant by the identity of indiscernibles. There is no doubt that he held it to be true; but he did not, as I shall now show, hold it to be analytic. Let us look at the proof which he offered for its truth. I present it in five steps. 1. Every (created) individual is at a "place"; no two at the same. 2. Assume that there are two individuals, a and b, of the same nature, A. 3. It is an analytic truth that in an indifferent situation no act of will (choice) can occur. 4. God, in creating a and b, would have been in an indifferent situation when deciding which to put at which of the two places they actually occupy. 5. This refutes 2. Let us not question 3.[20] As we shall see pres-

---

[20] One may well wonder, even if 3 is granted for human choices, whether the *via affirmativa* carries that far. The medievals distinguished more nicely in such matters.

ently and as is generally agreed, the proof introduces "places" in a manner not consistent with Leibniz's analysis of space and is, therefore, merely a plausible argument. Even so, it provides the opportunity for saying all that is needed. *First*. Even if 1 were analytic, the argument would not have the slightest tendency to show that (I') is, unless 'God exists' and 'God created the world' also are analytic. Leibniz accepts the first of these two missing links; but he couldn't possibly accept the second; otherwise his whole system (and his case against Spinoza) would collapse.[21] *Second*. It is generally agreed that for expository reasons Leibniz sometimes gave merely plausible arguments when he could, or thought he could, have given cogent ones. But I know of no instance of his doing so when he thought that the proposition to be proved was analytic; provided only one distinguishes probable arguments from frankly speculative ones, like the one in the last paragraph, about colors. *Third*. Notice that, even to state Leibniz's argument, one must distinguish between individuals $(a, b, \ldots)$ and natures $(A, B, \ldots)$. Nor is it by chance that the proof operates with places. It seems that every intelligible use of 'individual' contains what I called the "pointing" ingredient.

I turn for the first time to Russell. He recognizes that for Leibniz necessary truths are those and only[22] those that mention only eternal objects (p. 30). But he believes (a) that this is false and (b) that it leads to absurdity. One of the reasons he gives, without argument, for (a) is that geometric truths, while eternal (which is correct), are yet synthetic (which is also correct) and, in some unanalyzed sense, necessary (pp. 16, 17). His notions of analyticity and necessity at the time were thus Kantian. For (b) he offers an argument. He observes, correctly, that Leibniz, as he consistently must, held (b1) that all characters which are really simple are mutually compatible. From (b1) he infers, invalidly, that (b2) any two complex characters are also compatible, which Leibniz did not hold and which is indeed absurd (pp. 19, 20). To grasp firmly that (b2) does not follow from (b1) it suffices to remember what has just been said about Leibniz's *speculative* analysis of 'red and green are incompatible'. The point is that for Leibniz, though neither for Russell nor myself, 'green' and 'red' are not simple

[21] I dodge, as expendable for my purposes, the essentially theological issue of the nature of the principle of sufficient reason as such. Yet my argument sides with Latta and Joseph by rejecting implicitly Russell's contention that any part of it, except possibly that embedded in 3, is analytic. If the principle itself were held to be analytic, as it well might by one who combines Leibniz's arguments with Spinoza's theology, the distinction between the two kinds of truth would disappear. At one point (p. 24) Russell, because of another misunderstanding, says that it might disappear. See note 25.

[22] I neglect here and subsequently statements mentioning God.

quoad se. What goes for 'red' and 'green' also goes for 'point', 'straight line', and so on. Thus Leibniz could without absurdity and, within his speculative pattern, even plausibly maintain that geometry is analytic. That, as it happens, he was wrong does not improve the quality of Russell's analysis.

Russell also recognizes that Leibniz calls contingent those and only those propositions that mention only existents. He himself calls them (p. 24) propositions "asserting existence." The phrase probably reflects his own preoccupation at that time (p. 27) with the predicate 'exist'. Yet it is misleading, since to mention an existent is not to assert that it exists. Even more misleading, for at least two reasons, is his attempt (pp. 24, 29) to explicate the notion of contingency as involving reference to "time." For one, the distinction, as Leibniz intended it, between the two kinds of truths holds, as we saw, also in a world without time. For another, we shall see presently, Leibniz's world contains temporal characters, which are eternal things, as well as temporal attributes, which are existents. Propositions mentioning the former are therefore for Leibniz analytic, not contingent; yet they involve reference to "time." Clearly, then, Russell, though he occasionally mentions (e.g., p. 10) the distinction between a character and "its" attributes, does not appreciate its importance.

Russell admits that Leibniz's plausible argument for the truth of (I′), the one I reported in five steps, has no tendency to show that (I′) is analytic. Yet, he asserts, Leibniz probably did regard and, at any rate, should have regarded (I′) as analytic (p. 55). The gist of the "proof" which he puts into Leibniz's mouth (p. 57) is that since a substance *is* nothing but the sum (correctly: class) of its attributes it makes no sense (is contradictory) to speak of two substances exemplifying the same characters. Leibniz, we saw, did not hold that a substance *is* a nature; for him, as for any careful analyst, a substance is an individual (S1) that *has* a nature (S4). Thus the "proof" collapses.[23] Strangely, Russell also believes that his "proof" depends on there being no relations in Leibniz's world (p. 58). All he shows, rather trivially, is that in a world with relations two individuals may exemplify the same nonrelational characters. That Leibniz's notion of substance comprehends S3 and is therefore, as we saw, incompatible with undefined relations among individuals is completely irrelevant. To sum up. (I′) and (2) are in fact analytic. This we have since learned from PM. But

---

[23] Russell does, in fact, glimpse the distinction (p. 59) or, rather, he comes close to the notion of an individual which, as such, cannot be a nature. But he concludes, rashly and wrongly, on this score alone, not only that there are no substances, but that the substance notion is irremediably confused.

Russell gives no good reason, and there is none, for his assertion that Leibniz either did believe or consistently should have believed that they are analytic.

IV

Few passages in the philosophical literature move me more deeply than the one in which Arnauld,[24] having finally accepted Leibniz's thesis, musingly repeats it: *predicatum inest subjecto*. Russell takes it to assert that the sentences which he himself, *after* PM, would transcribe '$f_1(a)$' are analytic.[25] Nothing, we shall see, could be further from the truth. To understand what is involved, we must first acquire some ideas about Leibniz's logic and his ideal language.

Leibniz's logic is much more limited and traditional than is usually realized, probably because of his anticipatory vision of the syntactical method in the *characteristica universalis* and the keen linguistic insights contained in his proposals for a *langue universelle*.[26] Like Aristotle's and the medievals', his schema contains, in addition to syncategorematic words, only one type of signs.[27] These signs or, rather, the constants of this single type all refer to concepts (eternal things). *His* sentential schema is, therefore, 'α is β', corresponding to what *we* would write '$(x)[f(x) \supset g(x)]$'. Accordingly, his paradigm of an analytic sentence, is '$\alpha\beta$ is α', which corresponds to our '$(x)[f(x) \cdot g(x) \supset f(x)]$'. For the connection between species ($\alpha\beta$), genus (α), and difference (β), this is again the classical account. There are only two differences. In addition to generic and specific concepts,[28] Leibniz, in what I called his Scotist vein, emphasizes individual concepts; and he analyzes the latter in a manner peculiarly his own. Of this more presently.

A philosopher's explicit or implicit ideal language is a syntactical

---

[24] Letter of September 28th, 1686.

[25] And, therefore, all (noncontradictory) sentences? See note 21.

[26] This judgment is based on the report of Couturat (*La logique de Leibniz*, 1901) and the logical fragments he edited (*Opuscules et fragments inédits de Leibniz*, 1903). Nowhere in these two volumes have I found the slightest hint that Leibniz (or, for that matter, Couturat; see also his own *L'algèbre de la logique*, 1905) realized the need for a schema containing *both* subject (x, y, . . . ; a, b, . . .) and predicate (f, g, . . . ; f_1, g_1, . . .) variables and constants. Nor, I judge, in spite of some most intriguing anticipations (pp. 17, 60), did Russell himself realize it at the time he delivered the Leibniz lectures. Notice, incidentally, that *la langue universelle*, not being designed for philosophical purposes, is not in the current sense an ideal language.

[27] Leibniz usually employs Latin capitals; I use Greek letters in order to avoid confusions with the notation of Section Two.

[28] Quite consistently within his pattern, Leibniz brushes aside the distinction between accidents and attributes.

schema which, upon suitable interpretation, contains in principle the transcription of everything nonphilosophical that can be said about his world. Leibniz himself of course did not speak of ideal languages, although in the *ars combinatoria* he comes closer to the idea than anyone before Russell and Wittgenstein. Three points then are crucial. (1) Any schema adequate to accommodate Leibniz's official[29] ontological inventory must, like our own, contain at least three categorematic types, for the names of individuals, of attributes, and of natures, respectively. (1′) It must distinguish between the name of a character, say, 'f_1', and the names of "its" attributes, say, 'f_1″', 'f_1‴', 'f_1⁗', and so on. (2) A philosopher's ideal language depends, among other things, upon his logic. Leibniz is no exception. Thus his ideal language is inadequate for at least three reasons. It contains only one categorematic type, which, as we just saw, corresponds to the first-order predicates of PM. It provides no names for individuals. It constructs the names of natures or individual concepts (not: of individuals!) as first-order predicates. (3) While thus too weak in one sense, his ideal language is too strong in another. To speak for once metaphorically, it is, perhaps, God's language but it is, alas, not ours. I shall explain that in a moment. No doubt these defects are serious. One can but admire how rarely they affected Leibniz's thought. But they did at times affect his presentation and are, I think, the cause of many misunderstandings, including some of Russell's.

The key to what Leibniz meant by his thesis, *predicatum inest subjecto*, lies in the way in which he restates and restates it in his letters to Arnauld: the *concept* of the predicate is contained in the *concept* of the subject. That is, the sentence he asserts to be analytic is the one we (but not he) transcribe '$A(f_1)$' and not either '$f_1(a)$' or, correctly, '$f_1'(a)$', neither of which even occurs in his (implicit) ideal language. So I ask next: Why did he believe that?

Consider the sentences he writes '$\alpha\beta$ is α', '$\alpha\beta\gamma$ is α', '$\alpha\beta\gamma\delta$ is α', *and so on*. They are all analytic, in fact and according to Leibniz. Consider next '$\alpha\beta\gamma\delta$ *and so on* is α', or, as one usually writes, '$\alpha\beta\gamma\delta$ . . . is α'. Leibniz infers, invalidly, that it, too, is analytic. The error shows in the positional shift of 'and so on'. More precisely, Aristotle's schema does not even contain the crucial sentence, '$\alpha\beta\gamma\delta$ . . . is α'. Nor for that matter does ours or any other. A second-order predicate may be defined or undefined. The natures of our own schema are, as it happens, defined. But no such predicate, provided it is exemplified by an *infinite* number of first-order predicates, can be defined by enumeration. Leib-

---

[29] I say official because his inventory is upon his own account incomplete. See note 16 and Section Five.

niz thus makes two mistakes, the type error and the error of "definition by infinite enumeration." Making the first may facilitate making the second;[30] yet they are two and not one. This is half of the analysis. To complete it, one merely has to remember that for Leibniz an individual concept is the conjunction, in principle infinite, of all the simple characters the individual exemplifies. But he also insists that to perform the analysis into simples is, in the case of individual concepts, in principle beyond our power. (In the case of generic and specific concepts we might, at least in principle, succeed.) This is what I meant when I said that Leibniz's ideal language, though perhaps God's, is certainly not ours.

I conclude that Leibniz's thesis, *predicatum inest subjecto*, is false, even within his own Aristotelian frame. But we understand now accurately not only how he came to hold it but also two other things that are important. *First.* One can, as he did, consistently assert that of the two sentences which we (though not he) transcribe '$A(f_1)$' and '$f_1'(a)$' the first is analytic while the second is synthetic. *Second.* The *inesse* with which Leibniz is concerned is neither the "nexus" between form and matter that preoccupied the hylomorphic tradition nor the "tie" of exemplification between an individual and its characters that has puzzled so many moderns. For this different *inesse* Leibniz accounts differently: the individual, being a "force," "produces" its attributes.

The mistake of definition by infinite enumeration is interesting, not only because the great Leibniz made it long ago but also because it has been made at least twice and with considerably less excuse in this century. Once it was made by Wittgenstein in the *Tractatus* when he tried to dispose of generality as a primitive logical idea by writing '$f(a) \cdot f(b) \cdot f(c) \ldots$ ' for '$(x)f(x)$'. More recently it is being made by those who maintain that in view of the identity of indiscernibles we can, in principle, do without particulars (zero-type constants). Even though the class of all characters exemplified by an individual "determines" the latter uniquely, it does not follow that we either have or can construct a single predicate on which to base the definite description by which, according to these students, the individual's name, i.e., the particular, could always be replaced. Nor, if by chance we had such a predicate, could we ever be certain that it is one. Thus the pointing feature of particularity would be lost in the clouds of induction.[31]

[30] Let 'a', 'b', 'c' be the names of particulars which, as it happens, are green. A "nominalist" who purports to define 'green(x)' by

$$'(x=a) \lor (x=b) \lor (x=c) \ldots '$$

makes, at a lower type level, the same mistake.

[31] See also "Particularity and the New Nominalism."

Let us for a moment look at Leibniz's thesis as it is in itself. Correctly stated, it becomes: '$A(f_1)$' is analytic. Remember now the sentence in Section Two which I called (1). '$A(f_1) \equiv f_1(a)$' is in fact analytic. Thus it seems that if one asserts, in the spirit of Leibniz, that '$A(f_1)$' is analytic, which is false, one would consistently have to assert that the *corresponding contingent sentence, '$f_1(a)$'*, is also analytic, which is absurd. The appearance is deceptive. The point is that the corresponding contingent sentence is not '$f_1(a)$' but, rather, '$f_1'(a)$'. Thus everything still depends on the nature of the "tie" between f_1 and f_1'. This tie, involving creation, is contingent. Notice, furthermore, that there is no connection whatsoever between the alleged analyticity of '$A(f_1)$' and the identity of indiscernibles. The latter merely assures, for Leibniz, that there are individual concepts just as, in our schema, it assures the definability of 'A' by (N) and the analyticity of (2).[32]

I am about to turn to Russell. First, though, I wish to consider an obvious criticism which, characteristically, did not occur to Russell. Assume *per impossibile* that we could show our schema to Leibniz and then ask him whether '$f_1'(a) \lor \sim f_1'(a)$' was analytic. As a logician, he would undoubtedly wish to say that it was; yet he would immediately notice that, since the sentence mentions only existents, he would by his own principles have to regard it as synthetic. In his own schema he would, of course, transcribe it 'α or not α', thus avoiding the embarrassment. But this merely shows once more that his own (implicit) ideal language was only a fragment of what it should have been.

Russell's criticism of the thesis *predicatum inest subjecto* can be stated as follows. 1. Leibniz, "holding a substance to be defined by the class of its predicates," confounds erroneously and inconsistently a "substance" with its nature (p. 50). 2. If a substance is the "sum of its predicates," then "the necessary connection of predicates and subject" amounts to nothing but the identity of indiscernibles (pp. 28, 46).[33] 3. But then "predications concerning actual substances would be just as analytic as those concerning essences or species," which is absurd (p. 50). 4. Hence the notion of substance itself is absurd.

Now for criticism of this criticism. *Ad* 1. Leibniz, we saw, did not hold that individuals (S1) which are substances (S1, S2, S3, S4) because, among other things, they *have* natures (S4), *are* natures. Rather, it is Russell who confuses individuality, substantiality, and nature. *Ad* 2. Because of 1, Russell believes that Leibniz's thesis is a deductive con-

---

[32] Unaware as he was of the type distinction, Leibniz did of course not realize the role of (E) which is explained in Section Two.

[33] The passage on p. 28 reads "amounts to little more than the law of identity"; but the context leaves no doubt about its meaning.

sequence of (I'). We saw that this is not so. (I') merely guarantees that there are individual natures (concepts). *Ad* 3. Not recognizing that he uses 'subject' once as the name of an individual ("actual substance"), once as that of an individual nature, Russell wrongly identifies the two sentences we transcribe '$A(f_1)$' and '$f_1'(a)$'.[34] Thus he takes Leibniz to assert the analyticity of the latter, which is indeed absurd. *Ad* 4. Since Russell holds (I') to be analytic, which is correct, though, as we saw, he gives no good reason for this view and ascribes it wrongly to Leibniz, it seems to him that the absurdity of 3 is implicit in the very notion of substance. This is the heart of the matter. Now for some detail.

Why does Russell think that the identification of a "substance" with its nature is, from Leibniz's own viewpoint, erroneous and inconsistent? He asserts, not unreasonably, that the notion of a term which functions only as a subject (S1) is the most fundamental ingredient of the substance notion (p. 42); and "if subjects were nothing but collections of predicates," *cadit distinctio* (p. 50). This is why he considers the view he wrongly attributes to Leibniz erroneous. It is inconsistent because, as Leibniz also holds, activity is "the very substance of things" (p. 44). So Leibniz does. Only, there is no difficulty whatsoever since, according to him, the activity is, literally, the individual itself, not its nature. Russell does not see that. So he asserts that for Leibniz activity is a special character or, more reasonably, a special kind of characters, different from those whose "sum" allegedly is the individual (p. 45).[35] This alone is sufficient evidence that at that time Russell, not yet understanding either individuality or its syntactical image, particularity, could not possibly do justice to Leibniz. Another piece of such evidence shows how tantalizingly close he already was to his later insights. At one point (pp. 49, 50) he arrives at the conclusion that the only proper way to refer to individuals—he, of course, says substances—is by 'this'. But then he proceeds to reject it because he doubts, with Lotze, that such a term, being a mere pointer and thus "destitute of all meaning can be logically employed."

I selected from Russell's argument against the thesis of which Leibniz convinced Arnauld only what I take to be its gist. The full argument extends through four chapters of his book and contains many more

---

[34] The error is facilitated by Leibniz's writing '$\alpha\beta\gamma\delta$ . . . is α' for the first and having *no* transcription for the second.

[35] One contributory cause of this error was Russell's preoccupation with the relations issue. For he ascribes to Leibniz at this point the desire to get rid of the causal *relation* which connects two successive states of a substance by replacing it, in the earlier state, with an *attribute* of activity. The realism issue also interferes. The attributes other than activity are referred to as "phenomenal." See Section Five.

errors, concerning both Leibniz and the issues themselves. But it testi-
fies throughout, in the errors selected as well as in those omitted, to his
preoccupation, logically and metaphysically, with particularity, relations, and existence. His labors were gigantic indeed. Their eventual
fruits are a matter of record. Without them this essay could never have
been written.

V

Places and moments are not "absolute" beings (individuals). Space
and time are therefore merely relative, the former an order of coexist-
ence, the latter an order of successions. This is, virtually in his own
words, the gist of Leibniz's view. More often than not he treats of space
and time together, perhaps because he is so intent on combatting the
"absoluteness" Newton claims for both of them. The association obscures a fundamental difference between them. So I shall separate the
two, dealing in this section only with space, in a timeless universe as
one says. But one cannot intelligently discuss Leibniz's views on either
space or time without first attending to another feature of his system.

Assume that I watch, in our temporal world, a physical object change
its color. What really happens, according to Leibniz, is this. As certain
attributes of the individuals which really are the object change, so do
simultaneously certain others of the individual that is I. At each moment, the latter "express" the former without, however, being "caused"
by them. Rather, they are caused (produced) by the activity which is,
as we saw, quite literally, I; just as the attributes they express are produced by the individuals which are the object. This remarkable con-
comitance (preëstablished harmony) among the attributes of the several individuals was built into the latter when, at creation, they were
endowed with their natures.[36] An individual's acts (activity) are, in *all*
cases, conceived as something *like* awarenesses. *Some* acts of human individuals (Selves) *are* awarenesses. However, what a Self is aware of is
not, literally, what it produces. Just as a stone in itself is not "really"
a stone but an assemblage of soul-like agents, so the qualities of my
stone percept are not the attributes of my Self which the latter produces when, as one ordinarily says, I perceive a stone. This is crucial.
To the modern mind Leibniz's system appears no doubt quaint in its
entirety. Such quaintness, however, is not incompatible with structural
excellence. Here we have come upon what I consider a grave structural
weakness. To grasp it firmly, try to place my stone percept in Leibniz's
ontological inventory. Surely, it is neither a substance nor an eternal
thing. Nor is it, as we just saw, an attribute. What, then, is it? There

---

[36] This is, within the system, the major function of natures.

is within the system no satisfactory answer. This is why I called Leibniz's official ontology incomplete even upon his own account.[37] About the cause of the defect one can only speculate. Perhaps it was that for Leibniz "percep*tion*" covered ambiguously what can and must be distinguished, namely, both the act of perceiv*ing* and the thing perceiv*ed*.[37a] Nor is the distinction limited to percepts. What holds for them holds equally for all contents, including those Leibniz sometimes calls ideal things and *entia rationis*, such as numbers and mathematical space.[38]

Consider now the question whether, for Leibniz, space is "real." In the light of what we just learned it must be restated as follows. Are there, according to Leibniz, existents which establish *objectively* among individuals[39] an order "corresponding" to what *subjectively* we perceive as space? The answer has three parts. L1. Places are not individuals. L2. There are "spatial" attributes. Hence, there are also spatial characters, i.e., eternal things "whose" attributes the spatial attributes are. L3. Since there are no relational characters and attributes at all, there are in particular no spatial ones. Now for some comments.

(a) L1 is the sound root of the assertion that for Leibniz space *is not real* but merely relative or relational. 'Absolute', instead of 'real', would be less misleading. (b) L2 is the sound root of the assertion that for Leibniz space *is real*. (c) Space being relative or relational in sense (a) is not incompatible with L3. (d) I hold no brief for the pair 'objective-subjective'. What I use it for is clear, I trust; probably it is preferable to 'real-phenomenal', which seems to blur or even to condone the gap in Leibniz's ontology. (e) One or several attributes, say, f_1' and f_2', "corresponding" to, say, a perceived instance of being-to-the-left-of or being-contiguous-to means that a human individual (Self) has this percept on the occasion of producing those attributes of his own, $^cf_1'$

[37] See notes 16 and 29.

[37a] This is a crucial point of contact between Leibniz and the tradition that reached its last peak in Hegel. Remember G. E. Moore's classical "The Refutation of Idealism," which, though manifestly and perhaps rather unfortunately built around *esse est percipi*, is above all an argument against Hegel. [Added in 1959.]

[38] Ideal things are not ideas. The latter are the eternal things; for the former Leibniz has no official place. But he was of course aware of them and even has a name for them. The point is that he didn't do anything decisive about them in a "systematic" way, just as in the case of the "tie" between a character (eternal thing, idea) and "its" attributes. (Perceived relations, too, are sometimes called ideal. Like all "rationalists" Leibniz struggles with the concept-percept dichotomy.)

[39] Limiting one's self, as I do, to relations among individuals and thus sidestepping the issue of extension, just as I sidestepped that of continuity (see note 5), does not affect what I wish to discuss.

and $^ef_2{}'$, which "express" $f_1{}'$ and $f_2{}'$. In Leibniz's words, $^ef_1{}'$ and $^ef_2{}'$ are the *foundation* of the perceived relation.

Is the objective part of Leibniz's analysis of space adequate? To ask this question is to ask whether the spatial structure of our world can be introduced into the world of Section Two by introducing into it a special class of characters of the first type but without introducing into it undefined relations of any type. The answer is negative. The spatial relations cannot be defined in terms of nonrelational characters. The point is by now as familiar as it is noncontroversial.[40] Even so, it may help if I rehearse it in context. Assume, then, that there is a class of undefined characters, p_1, p_2, p_3, . . . , such that each nature contains one and only one of them. Assume, furthermore, that, in particular, '$A(p_1)$', '$B(p_2)$', '$C(p_3)$', '$D(p_4)$' or, what amounts to the same thing, '$p_1(a)$', '$p_2(b)$', '$p_3(c)$', '$p_4(d)$' are all true. It is easy to define a relation r_1 such that it holds between two individuals if and only if they exemplify p_1 and p_2 respectively. Correspondingly for r_2, p_3, p_4. Assume, finally, that a is contiguous to b and that c is contiguous to d. Obviously, contiguity cannot be defined in terms of any finite number of such defined relations as r_1 and r_2. Equally obviously, it could be defined if we were allowed to add to our vocabulary an undefined relation of the second type which obtains between two "spatial" characters if and only if the individuals that exemplify them are contiguous. In Leibniz's world L3 prevents us from making this addition. We may nevertheless ask whether space as we know it can in some such manner be introduced into the (timeless) world of Section Two. Or, what amounts to the same thing, we may ask whether space is compatible with S3 and S4.[41] There are three possibilities.

First. We may introduce undefined "spatial" relations of the first type among individuals. This, we saw in Section Two, is compatible with S4 but not with S3. *Second.* We may introduce undefined "spatial" relations of the second type in the manner just indicated, e.g., a relational predicate of contiguity, C, such that $C(p_1, p_2)$ if and only if a and b are contiguous. As we also saw in Section Two, this is compatible with both S4 and S3 provided the latter is given the explication I proposed for it. *Third.* We may introduce undefined "spatial" relations of the third type among natures. Again, this is compatible with S4 and,

---

[40] I disregard the Wiener-Kuratowski method of replacing relational predicates by nonrelational ones of a higher type. Within logic this possibility is important and not merely, as Russell once called it, a trick. But to take it into account in a discussion like this is merely to burden one's self with a lot of verbiage without adding anything to the substance.

[41] This is clearly a philosophical question, not one about Leibniz.

upon my interpretation of it, with S3. Notice, though, that this procedure does not permit us to dispense with the p_i. These peculiar "spatial" characters are still needed to prevent two individuals which agree in all nonspatial characters from collapsing, by (I) and (E), into one.

To sum up. Leibniz's space is, in the sense of the terms I explained, both real and relative. His actual analysis of space is, because of L3, inadequate. Yet there is not the least doubt that he thinks of space as an assemblage of relations.[42] His error is logical, as it were. He claims that all these relations can be defined in terms of nonrelational predicates. As far as the thing itself is concerned, though, individuals with natures (S4) can consistently live in a space like ours; and, with the explication I proposed for S3, they may even "exist independently."

That much for the objective part of Leibniz's analysis of space. Only very little needs to be said about the *subjective* part. The inadequacy of the latter follows from that of the former. To see this clearly, assume that $^ep_1{}'$, $^ep_2{}'$ are the two attributes of a Self which express the two spatial attributes $p_1{}'$ and $p_2{}'$. Just as objective contiguity cannot be defined in terms of p_1 and p_2 alone, so perceived contiguity cannot be defined in terms of $^ep_1$ and $^ep_2$ alone. Perceived contiguity has thus no adequate foundation in the attributes of the perceiver. There is, finally, within Leibniz's account, the question of mathematical space. But since for him mathematical space with all its denizens is merely an *ens rationis*, I shall say no more about it.

I turn to Russell. Again, as in Leibniz's case, one cannot intelligently discuss what he says about either space and time or Leibniz's analysis of them without first attending to a more general matter. Throughout this book, as throughout his life, Russell is intensely preoccupied with the realism issue. Thus he takes great pain, in a special chapter and elsewhere, to show that upon Leibniz's own account no individual could from his own perceptions infer with "certainty" that there are other individuals. Quite so. I quarantined 'certainty' between double quotes only because this use, however familiar, is yet philosophical. For the rest, I share Russell's preoccupation. Virtually all analytical philosophers since Descartes have shared it. Leibniz is the spectacular exception. (This is another reason why I think he is closer to the medievals than is generally realized.) Reading Russell, one gains the impression, not only that he was irritated by the absence of this preoccupation in Leibniz, but also that the irritation at times affected his judgment. I find it more profitable to enjoy Leibniz's many insights

---

[42] See, for instance, his famous analysis of 'being at the same place' in the fifth letter to Clarke.

and to take his philosophy as a whole for the speculative system it is. By calling it a speculative system I mean, first, that, *if* true, it would account for the "phenomena," or so at least its author believes; and I mean, second, that the author does not share our concern as to how we could ever know *that* it is true.[43] Notice, finally, that as I use 'objective' and 'subjective', and as Russell himself often uses them in this book, particularly in the chapter on space and time, the former is synonymous with 'real', in the sense in which modern realists assert that, say, physical objects are real.[44]

Before turning to Russell's specific arguments about space, I shall restate two unsupported assertions which dominate the whole chapter on space and time. *First.* He claims that (a) space is objective but that (b) "there is plainly something more than relations about space" (p. 121).[45] In other words, Russell agrees with Newton. In support of (b) he cites Kant's opinion that while we can never imagine that there should be no space we can quite well think that there are no objects in it, observing, correctly I think, that Kant's space, while subjective, is thus absolute rather than relative (p. 119).[46] One who believes, as I do, that while (a) is true, (b) is false and that, therefore, Leibniz is right while Russell is wrong, will not be surprised to find that the latter misunderstood the former's analysis of space. *Second.* At the end of his discussion (p. 130) Russell admits that Leibniz may confusedly and inconsistently have held the views on space I attributed to him. 'Confusedly' is his own word (p. xiv). 'Inconsistently' I added, drawing the conclusion from the specific arguments we are offered, those I shall examine as well as those I shall disregard. But, Russell adds, the objective space and time which (according to an inconsistent Leibniz might) exist after creation are, *of course*, still relational. If 'relational' means 'irreducibly relational' then I should say: *of course not.* For this detail we are offered an argument which leaves no doubt about the crucial short-

[43] This is not to deny that Leibniz, who anticipated so much, also anticipated one part or version of the early positivists' so-called meaning criterion when he argued against Clarke that there can be no such thing as absolute space since, if the world were displaced in it, we could not know it. His own subsumption of this argument under the identity of indiscernibles and the principle of sufficient reason is mistaken.

[44] One who reads this essay *as if* I were a realist will not be misled. This is not the place to present my analysis of the realism issue. It may be found in MLP.

[45] The context makes it clear that this something more is not extension (see note 39).

[46] This appeal to Kant's authority fits well with the Kantian view Russell then held on geometry (see Section Two). The other German whom he then knew best and who influenced him most was probably Lotze, who was notoriously a great student of Leibniz.

coming of Russell's analysis. He did then not realize that some spatial relations, *whether subjective or objective*, are undefinable or, as he says, irreducible, i.e., that they cannot be defined in terms of nonrelational characters. This is why he did not spot Leibniz's crucial error, namely, the belief that all spatial relations are reducible. Now for the argument I just mentioned. We are told that objective relations would have to be irreducible *because* they are "between monads, not between the various perceptions of one monad" (p. 130). Yet, the situation with respect to $^ep_1$, $^ep_2$, as far as the relations which can or cannot be generated from them are concerned, is exactly the same as with respect to p_1, p_2. (I use the earlier notation.) It follows that the difference Russell believes to be decisive is in fact irrelevant.

I turn now to two specific arguments. The first merely makes more explicit one facet of what has just been said. So I shall state it but not comment on it. The second is perhaps more interesting.

1. Space, for Leibniz, is relational. "Spatial relations do not hold between monads, but only between simultaneous objects of perception of one monad. Thus space is properly subjective" (p. 122). Properly, I presume, means: if Leibniz wants to be consistent.

2. The second argument (pp. 118–19) has three steps. 1. If space were *absolute*, there would be an irreducible relation of occupancy exemplified by an individual and a place if and only if the former is at the latter. 2. A substance philosopher must reject all irreducible relations. 3. Hence, "it is essential for a philosophy of substance to disprove the *reality* of space" (p. 119). Now for criticism. *Ad* 3. The conclusion warranted is merely the necessary rejection of *absolute* space, not of *real* (objective) space. In other words, Russell confuses the two dichotomies objective-subjective and absolute-relative. This is a glaring mistake, the more surprising in view of his penetrating comment about Kant's space being both absolute and subjective. It illustrates what I had in mind when I said that at times Russell's preoccupation with the realism issue gets the better of his judgment. *Ad* 2. Leibniz did in fact reject all irreducible relations. But we have also seen that a "substance philosopher" need not do that. *Ad* 1. The proposition is interesting, if only because the introduction of such a relation seems to raise interesting structural questions.[47] However, a substance philosopher has the alternative of making places or, in a temporal world, continuing places the only substances. Russell recognizes this structural possibility,[48] at

---

[47] Some of these questions are explored in C. D. Broad, *The Mind and Its Place in Nature* (Chap. 4).

[48] Twenty-five years later Broad (see note 47) examined it, very interestingly, on its own merit. See note 53.

least indirectly, by detailing, quite correctly, those features of Leibniz's system which exclude this alternative.

VI

Leibniz's analysis of space fails because he rejects undefined relations. Yet one could by adding such relations add space to his world without otherwise interfering with its structure. I showed this by introducing "spatial" relations into the world of Section Two, which is in all relevant respects a Leibnizian world except that it does not contain either space or time and does not distinguish between a character and "its" attributes. The latter distinction I disregarded because, as is easily seen, it would have made no difference for the business at hand (i.e., the introduction of space). In what follows I shall for the same reason again disregard it. What I propose to show is that while for space Leibniz's system can be repaired (if I may so express myself), it breaks down for time. So does every substance philosophy. The only way out, such as it is, is to accept absolute time or, what amounts to the same thing, to accept moments as individuals.

On space Leibniz goes to great length; but I know of no passage that contains a thorough discussion of those problems of time which are not also problems of space. Russell, after a very careful search of the texts, assures us that there is none (p. 127). If, as I claim, the system breaks down for time, then there can't be one, otherwise Leibniz would have become aware of the breakdown. Russell, very remarkably, did not notice it. Under the circumstances I shall change my procedure, deal next in two paragraphs with Leibniz's view and Russell's criticism of it and only then examine the matter on its merits. First, though, I want to get one fairly obvious point out of the way. If time could be added to the world of Section Two, then space, too, could be added by introducing it into its "temporal cross sections." The one thing we could no longer do, since the spatial relations among individuals change in time, is to transcribe these relations by (relational) predicates of the first type. But we saw that there are other ways to transcribe them provided only one keeps Leibniz's nonrelational spatial characters p_i. If, on the other hand, space is first added, which as we know can be done, then time cannot be added afterwards. To consider this difference is one way to impress upon one's self the difference between space and time.

Just as there are, in Leibniz's world, spatial characters (p_i) and attributes (p_i'), but no spatial individuals (places), so there are temporal characters and attributes, call them t_i and t_i' respectively, but no temporal individuals (moments). Time, like space, is thus for Leibniz both objective (real) and relative. Unlike Russell, I think that in this he was right. It is also what interested him above all in his polemic against the Newtonians, which helps, perhaps, to explain why he let it go at that. The relations of succession and simultaneity are, he claims, definable in terms of the t_i. This is the same mistake he made in the case of space. The difference, we shall see, is that in the case of time the error cannot be "repaired" by adding an undefined second-type relational predicate establishing a linear order among the t_i and whatever else might be needed.[49]

Russell, much more explicit about space than about time, himself follows the pattern to which he calls attention. Even so, he insists that there is a difference; space as we ordinarily think of it being an "order" among individuals while "the time-order consists of relations among predicates" (p. 128). But there, unfortunately, he stops. For the rest, he holds that time, like space, is objective and absolute (p. 127) as well as that Leibniz cannot consistently maintain it to be both relative and objective. *Mutatis mutandis* the arguments are, in the nature of things, those I examined in the preceding section. So I shall say no more about them.

Let 'a' and 'f_1' name an individual (S1) which is a continuant (S2) and a character, respectively. Continuants (substances) do at times exemplify characters which they don't exemplify at others. Assume f_1 to be such a character of a. Then '$\sim f_1(a)$' and '$f_1(a)$' are both true. This is logical catastrophe; so the system breaks down. The point is as simple as it is old, really as old as the arguments of the Eleatics. Why, then, one must ask, did Leibniz and Russell overlook it. Taken biographically the question is moot. Taking it structurally, I shall venture an answer. One who grasps fully the nature of both individuality and its syntactical image, particularity, thus realizing the need for at least two categorematic types, is not likely to overlook the point. One who does not possess these insights may not notice it. Leibniz and Russell, two thinkers of the highest rank, did in fact not notice it. That is why in Section Four I took such pains to show that they did not possess those insights. Russell, of course, gained them, for all of us, almost immediately after he had delivered those lectures.[50]

If one writes '$f_1(a, t_1)$' instead of '$f_1(a)$' the predicament disappears.

---

[49] E.g., in order to say that a nontemporal character f_1 is exemplified at a certain time, a relational second-type predicate of coincidence ('Co') such that '$Co(f_1, t_1)$' transcribes 'f_1 coincides with t_1'. A little reflection shows that this relation does not at all have the properties of simultaneity. Notice also that the indices I used ($t_1, t_2, \ldots$) are merely parts of the names of the temporal characters. Only after a linear order has been introduced among these characters by means of an undefined relation may the indices be used to indicate position in this order.

[50] See notes 1 and 26.

To Leibniz this way out would have been unacceptable for at least two reasons. 1. It makes time absolute by making the 't_i' names of individuals (S1).[51] 2. It makes all predicates of individuals relational. One may ask what happens if one accepts either one or both of these consequences. Since it is impossible to get around 1, there are two possibilities. One may accept either 1 or both 1 and 2. Let us see what happens in either case. It is clear, I trust, that in asking these questions I am no longer talking about Leibniz but, rather, about how any substance philosopher could account for time.

If there is only one "substance" in the world, or, rather, if there is only one thing of the sort we originally decided to call a substance, then the 'a' in '$f_1(a, t_1)$' serves no particular purpose. Thus one may try to write '$f_1(t_1)$' instead of '$f_1(a, t_1)$'. This avoids 2; but it also makes moments the only individuals (S1). Now moments are of course not continuants (S2). But if one adds, as one must, an irreducible ordering relation among them, then one may say that "time" is, at least in an attenuated sense, a continuant. The only substance (S1 and an attenuated S2) of this "monistic" world is thus time. Its "nature" (S4) is, obviously, the class of all characters ever exemplified, which makes it pointless to speak of its nature. Is it possible to introduce into this world things, such as physical objects, of the sort substance philosophers ordinarily want to call "substances"? The answer is affirmative provided one accepts Leibniz's spatial characters p_i, some undefined "spatial" relations among them, and, in addition, an irreducible ternary predicate of coincidence ('Co') of type (1, 1, 0) such that '$Co(f_1, p_m, t_n)$' signifies 'f_1 is at moment t_n exemplified at place p_m'. Some may balk at such a relation. This, however, is not the point. The point is that even if one accepts it the things substance philosophers ordinarily want to call substances would still lose their "natures." For, the only way to single them out by gathering their characters would be to impose conditions on their space-time trajectories (p_i, tj).[52] Ever since Berkeley, this is what the antisubstantialists have done.

[51] I assume thus that the 't_1' in '$f_1(a, t_1)$' is of type zero. Formally one could assign it to type one. However, the victory would be hollow, not necessarily because 'f_1' would then be of the rather complex type (0, 1) but, rather, because it would still be true that the 't_i' occur always as subjects and never as predicates. A predicate being always exemplified by an individual would be transcribed by '$(x)[ti(x) \supset f_1(a, x)]$'. The character '$ti$' (being a moment) could be defined in terms of the order relation that obtains between any two of these peculiar "individuals" and no others.

[52] A little reflection shows that it would not do to make the 'a', 'b', ... into attributes. I say attributes rather than characters because the word may, perhaps quite properly, remind some of Spinoza. Again, the "world" I consider in

One who accepts '$f_1(a, t_1)$' and thus both undefined relations and absolute time still has three possibilities. *First.* If he also accepts Leibniz's peculiar spatial characters p_i, some irreducible relations among them, and, in addition, an irreducible order relation among moments, then he can continue to use particulars as the names of those things which substance philosophers ordinarily want to call substances. That they satisfy S1 and S2 goes without saying; and even their natures (S4) can be defined by introducing time into the schema (N) of Section Two. The pattern is clear; so I shall skip the details. This is, in a sense, as well as a substance philosopher can do. The one price he must pay is absolute time though not, as we see, absolute space. This shows once more the essential difference between space and time. *Second.* Another possibility is to make the 'a', 'b', and so on, stand for places. This makes places in absolute space persisting in absolute time the only substances (S1 and an unattenuated S2). Again, I shall skip the details.[53] *Third.* Giving up S2, one may interpret the 'a', 'b', and so on, as the names of "places at a moment." With respect to the "natures" of, say, physical objects one is then reduced to the methods of the antisubstantialists. This, by the way, is also the case on the alternative I considered second. The difference is that now no continuant is left. All that remains are "positions" in a four-dimensional manifold which are considered as "individuals." Thus any incentive to cling to these peculiar individuals has vanished. One may just as well replace them by the individuals of a "sense data philosophy" or by "temporal cross sections of physical objects." The latter is what thoughtful physicalists such as Carnap have done.[54] In either case space and time become relative and no trace is left of substance.

VII

A lesson for a contemporary issue may be drawn from this analysis. For the last two hundred fifty years or so a certain kind of philosophy has been with us. I shall call it the sense data philosophy. The name, it will soon transpire, is misleading. I use it only because it is popular with opponents of this kind of philosophy and because sense data in particular have recently received a good deal of unfavorable attention. For the sense data philosophy is being vigorously attacked right now.

---

this paragraph may remind some others of Whitehead. But, again, not being a thorough student of either Spinoza or Whitehead, I say these things only with hesitation.

[53] This is the alternative C. D. Broad explored. See note 48.

[54] Thoughtless ones say that the particulars of their ideal language refer to physical objects. Thus they inherit, without knowing it, the greatest difficulty of all substance philosophies.

Naturally, it has been attacked before. Any kind of philosophy has its vicissitudes. Flourishing in one generation, it must defend itself in another. But few, if any, have been so solemnly pronounced dead so often. I am nonetheless confident about its future. But even if I were wrong in this, two hundred and fifty years are a respectable span of survival. Any kind of philosophy which is so durable must have some strengths, that is, it either answers at least *some* questions or avoids at least *some* difficulties more effectively than its competitors. The sense data philosophy has three major sources of strength. As philosophies go, this is an excellent score. That is why I am confident about its survival. Two of these sources have always been drawn upon by its proponents. The third has not been fully exploited during the last fifty years or so. Let me explain.

A philosopher ought to start from what he is directly acquainted with. The formula, like all formulae, needs unpacking. 'Start' is used metaphorically; 'direct acquaintance' is used in a special sense. One who has looked at a physical object may have occasion to say later on that he is acquainted with it. The special use of the phrase is narrower. Though perhaps not as frequent as the other, it is yet perfectly clear. In this sense we are not directly acquainted with physical objects but only with the *sort* of things of which sense data are one kind. The characters exemplified by sense data, percepts and their characters, feelings, memory images are other kinds of this sort. There are still others. This is why the name, sense data philosophy, is misleading. Now for the metaphor. A philosopher "starts" from those things which he names by the undefined descriptive signs of his (implicit or explicit) ideal language. A sense data philosophy is one that starts with the sort of things sense data are, i.e., it takes 'direct acquaintance' in its special sense and accepts the formula with which I began. This is one of its strengths. Why this is a strength is clear to every one who understands the dialectic of the classical realism issue (irrespective of the position he takes on it). Most of those who now attack the sense data philosophy either unwittingly prejudge this issue or dismiss it, together with all philosophical questions, out of hand. In the main they use two arguments. Fascinated by a most extraordinary something they call ordinary language, they say that they do not understand the special meaning of 'direct acquaintance'. The more is the pity. The second argument is more serious. It claims that, even if we wanted to, we could not start from the sort of things sense data are. Or, what amounts to the same, it claims that literally accurate definitions of, say, 'chair' and 'stone' cannot be produced in a language which so limits the range of the things to which its undefined descriptive signs refer. This claim

is sound. The proper way to counter it is therefore to clarify how "definition" or, as one also says, reconstruction, ought to be understood in
this context.

A philosopher ought to start from what he is certain of. This, too, is a
formula. The metaphor is the same as before, except that this time it
involves not the simplest terms but the simplest sentences. For the
rest, I am much less impressed with this formula than with the first.
To my mind, many philosophers have gone astray in the quest for an
unreasonable kind of certainty. Even so, the explication of the several
meanings of 'certain' is among the major tasks of any serious philosophy. The very way I stated the formula takes account of one of these
clarifications. Things (states of affairs) are neither certain nor uncertain. They simply are (or are not). But there remains the question
whether there are not among the things (states of affairs) of which we
are in fact certain several kinds so different among themselves that
they give rise to different meanings of 'certain'. There are such kinds;
two are basic; the others are derivative. (A) We are certain of what we
have recognized as analytic. (B) We are certain of what is wholly
presented to us in one act of direct acquaintance (in the narrower sense).
For instance, we are sometimes certain (B) that a sense datum is red,
or loud, or sweet, as the case may be. If it were not for such cases, I,
for one, would not know what 'certain' means (except, perhaps, a de-
gree of belief). This is fundamental. The explication of (A), i.e., of
'analytic' has several parts and is very complex. One of these parts
rests on the explication of (B).[55] (Otherwise I wouldn't have said that
without (B) I wouldn't know what 'certain' means.) Sense data philosophies, since they recognize the sort of things sense data are, are
among those that can explicate 'certain'. This is another of their
strengths. They even "start" from things of this sort. But that is for
this purpose less important.

Sense data and the other kinds of their sort are not continuants. Some[56]
of these kinds are the only ones whose instances are named by particulars in the ideal language of a sense data philosophy. The particulars
of a sense data philosophy do therefore not name continuants. With
one exception to which I shall presently attend, sense data philosophies
are in fact the only ones whose particulars do not name continuants.
This is the third source of their strength. To appreciate it one merely
has to remember that, as we saw, one who insists on naming continuants by particulars of his ideal language, must accept either abso-

[55] See "Two Cornerstones of Empiricism," *Synthese*, 8, 1953, 435–52; reprinted in MLP.

[56] E.g., sense data, but not their characters; hence "some" and not "all."

lute space and absolute time or, at least, absolute time. Few, if any, contemporary philosophers are prepared to do that, least of all those who now so vociferously attack the sense data philosophy. Nor, for that matter, am I prepared to accept absolute time. The reason for this reluctance is, simply enough, that I do not know how to "point" at a moment as such, that is, as one says, at a moment in abstraction from everything that occurs "at" that moment.[57] Now for two more comments; then I shall be done.

The exception I just mentioned is the physicalism I ascribed to Carnap. Its particulars name "momentary cross sections of physical objects." One may think that this choice of individuals makes the task of reconstruction, i.e., the definition of, say, 'chair' and 'stone' easier. A little reflection shows that, taken literally, it is still more than we can do. In that respect this philosophy has therefore no advantage over a sense data philosophy. Its only "advantage," as I see it, is that it provides its proponents with a formulation of their unexamined realism which for some reason is acceptable to them. Conversely, the substance issue arises already, quite independently of the realism issue, if one tries to introduce continuants named by particulars into a succession of phenomenal fields.

One may wonder why this third great strength of the sense data philosophy has not been made more of by its defenders during this century. One answer which suggests itself is that during this period the advocacy of substance has been rather subdued, at least within analytical philosophy. Those who, like Moore and Broad, either explicitly or implicitly accepted or, at least, sympathetically considered the notion, have charmed us all by their caution as well as their learning. Those, however, who now so confidently decry sense data are neither very cautious nor, sometimes, very learned. It may therefore not be untimely to remind them that the gambit they propose has been tried before. This is the lesson.

[57] Notice that I do not use the argument according to which contemporary physics has disposed of absolute space and time. See "Professor Quine on Analyticity," *Mind*, 64, 1955, 254–58, and also pp. 139–43 of this book.

Some Remarks on the Philosophy of Malebranche*

APHILOSOPHICAL *system* purports to be a comprehensive account of the world and our experience of it. Some such accounts are very strange, or, to say the least, surprising. This, however, is not what I mean when I call a system *speculative*. The author of a speculative system is not as preoccupied as most of us are today with questioning how either he or anyone else could ever know that his account is true. Judged from without, the "self-evident" propositions on which a speculative system rests therefore sometimes themselves rest on nothing more solid than some unexamined metaphors. Some speculative systems are nevertheless of great intellectual interest. In these cases, any analysis or examination, to be worth while, must be mixed, partly from within the system and partly from without.

The philosophy of Malebranche is a speculative system of great intellectual interest. A comprehensive examination of it, however concise, is therefore a major undertaking. In this paper I shall limit myself to three points. I shall examine, partly from within and partly from without, Malebranche's account of perception as it relates to the realism-nominalism problem; I shall inquire what, if anything, he has to say about the related problem of individuation; and I shall analyze some aspects of the vision in God. These three topics will be taken up, in this order, in Sections Three, Four, and Five. The first two sections provide background. Section One deals, most concisely yet in an analytical fashion, with the realism issue. Section Two digests, in the same manner, what I shall need of Malebranche's system. Section Six contains some concluding remarks.

* The Review of Metaphysics, *10, 1956, 207–26. Reprinted by permission.*

The method I shall use is not only mixed, partly from within and partly from without, but also linguistic. That is, I shall try to make explicit what some now call the logic of the crucial terms, and shall call attention to the metaphors on which it rests. I adopt this method not just to curry favor with current fashion, but because I believe that this is the best way to find out what a speculative system is about. The best way to argue for a method is, of course, not to argue at all but to show it at work. Even so, it may help if I indicate in one instance what, I believe, this method achieves and what, as I also believe, cannot be achieved otherwise. Any system which, like Augustine's, Bonaventure's, and Malebranche's, appeals to the vision in God has a "mystical" core refractory to logic. This is evident. Malebranche's system is over wide stretches also one of the most minute and "rational." This, too, is hardly worth repeating. Yet, it may be worth while to show *accurately*, as I shall try to show, *that* and *how* the logic of the system breaks down where these stretches meet that core.

One more word to make my peace with the historical scholars, if that be possible. I make no pretense whatsoever of historical scholarship. Nor have I read all of Malebranche. I have read very carefully the *Entretiens sur la Métaphysique* and *De la Recherche de la Vérité*, including the tenth *Éclaircissement* to the latter. Because of my admiration for Arnauld, I have also examined his *Des Vraies et des Fausses Idées* and the exchange between him and Malebranche to which it gave rise. But I was not surprised not to find there anything that would shed further light on the three points with which I am concerned; for, what is there centrally at stake—presentative versus representative realism, as we would put it—is only tangentially, if at all, relevant to these points. My interest, then, I repeat, is logical or structural, not historical. The few "historical" remarks I shall permit myself concern structural rather than causal connections. With three exceptions, which I cannot resist, I shall therefore abstain from direct quotation. I merely mention that virtually everything I shall say about Malebranche can be documented from the eighth *Entretien* and the third book of the *Recherche*, particularly the sixth and seventh chapters of the second part.

I

I look at *two* cubes. Assume that they are alike in all nonrelational respects. For instance, they are both (the same shade of) green. Assume, furthermore, that while looking at these cubes I make two judgments, 'This is green', and 'That is green'. In one way these judgments differ; in another, they agree. In the two statements the difference is expressed by the occurrence of different words, 'this' and 'that', in the subject place; the agreement, by the occurrence of the same word, 'green', in the predicate place. For the judgments to be grounded, both the difference and the agreement must be grounded in the two states of affairs or situations that are judged. How, then, are they grounded? One possible answer has four parts. (1) Each of the two situations contains two constituents. (2) There are all together three constituents, named by 'this', 'that', and 'green' respectively. The constituents named by 'this' and 'that' are called *particulars;* the one named by 'green', a *universal.* (3) The universal, which is the constituent common to both situations, accounts for my judging both cubes to be green. (4) The two particulars being different accounts for my knowing the cubes from each other. This, I believe, is the simplest modern version of what is classically known as *realism;* (4) in particular solves what is classically known as the problem of *individuation.*

Classical realism has many variants. Two of them, or at least their gist, are easily stated in modern terms. One variant assumes that no two situations agree in all universals. That makes it possible to solve the problem of individuation without recourse to particulars. This is what Scotus does. Leibniz shares his assumption although, for reasons that do not concern us, he also introduces particulars. The other variant (roughly, moderate realism) claims that our two situations have four constituents, named by 'this', 'that', 'green₁', and 'green₂', respectively. This attack merely postpones the issue; for, whatever can be asked about the connections among constituents named 'this', 'that', and 'green' can *mutatis mutandis* also be asked about those among the constituents named 'green₁' and 'green₂' and a further one, named 'green', which rather obviously would have to be introduced in one way or another. Neither of these two variants is directly relevant to my purpose. Aquinas' is. It will serve my purpose best if, without paying attention to the subtleties of his moderate realism, I present this third version by contrasting it with a fourth, namely, Aristotle's. Both these precartesian versions, Aristotle's and Aquinas', reject what I called Scotus' assumption. Yet neither recognizes anything like the particulars which I introduced into the modern version. This makes individuation one of their major difficulties.

According to Aristotle, every *being* (synonymously, *existent*) except God is a compound of two constituents neither of which exists; or, at least, they do not exist in the same sense.[1] One of these constituents is

---

[1] Notice the shift from state of affairs or situation talk, which fits the modern version, to being or existent talk, which is more appropriate to the classical versions. Notice also that I ignore, as irrelevant for my purpose, the distinction between substantial and nonsubstantial forms as well as the problem of the so-called multiplicity of forms.

a *form;* the other is *matter.* In my example the form involved is the color green. Forms correspond to the universals of the modern version, except that a proponent of the latter might wish to say, as an Aristotelian would not, that both particulars and universals (forms) exist. This puts the burden of individuation upon matter. One would have to say some such thing as that each of my two cubes, for instance, is a compound of the same form (or forms) with different "parts" of matter. The difficulty, unresolved I believe, is that in this system matter is something so "formless" and so "unreal" that one cannot consistently within the system speak of its "parts."

To understand Aquinas' version, we must first attend to a second use or meaning of 'being'. Systems which introduce forms all recognize a hierarchy among them. This is of course the heritage of Plato. Each form is a compound of being and nonbeing. This is the second use of 'being'. The higher a form's place in the hierarchy, the less the amount or proportion or admixture—the notion remains rather vague —of nonbeing it contains. At the one extreme, only God is pure being. At the other extreme, there is now the possibility of attributing even to "matter" a form and a minimum of being. Some Franciscan philosophers availed themselves of this possibility, thus introducing a new use or meaning of 'matter'.

Aquinas invented a new kind of nonexistent and a third use or meaning of 'being'. The new nonexistents are called *natures.* Each nature is compounded of a form and of matter, the former corresponding to the proportion of being (second meaning), the latter to the proportion of nonbeing it contains.[2] These natures correspond in his system to the universals of the modern version. An existent in turn is compounded of a nature and something else. This something else is "being." This is the third use or meaning of 'being'. An existent is created whenever God through an individual or, at least, individualizable act of His will endows a nature with being. There is now a new possibility for at least a verbal solution of the problem of individuation. What distinguishes my two cubes, for instance, is that they are created by two decrees of the divine will which are, without further analysis, taken to be distinct or, at least, distinguishable. I said individualizable and I say now distinguishable because I do not of course wish to deny that in systems of this kind God's acts are in some sense one, just as he does not act in time but, rather, from eternity into time. This, however, belongs to the mystical core. Logically, one might say that the

---

[2] This is not true for angels. But I neglect, as throughout, what is of only theological interest. Notice also that I disregard the obscure doctrine of *materia signata.*

distinguishable acts of the divine will can be made to play the part of the particulars of the modern version.

II

Not considering God, there are, according to Malebranche, only two kinds of existents, namely, minds and bodies. Not considering angels, an existent is either a human mind (*esprit*) or a body (*corps*), human or otherwise. A body is a "part" of created extension (*étendue*), figured, configured,[3] and, at any moment, either in a determinate state of motion or at rest. Its extension is a body's *substance;* its figure, configuration, and state of motion are the *attributes* of its substance. To insist on this distinction, however, is, within the system, merely a way of expressing that though, say, figure cannot be conceived (see below) without extension, the ideas (see below) of all possible figures are contained in that of extension. The same thing is also expressed by saying that an existent's attributes are merely "modes of being" or modifications of its substance.[4] An existent's attributes are *in* it. I list this as the first use or meaning of 'in'. Even in the case of bodies this use is metaphorical, although in this case the metaphor is so inconspicuous that we somehow understand it. This metaphor pervades the whole system and, probably because it is so insidiously inconspicuous, is the only ground for some of its "self-evident" truths.

The substance of minds is awareness (*pensée*). When I feel a pain or see a color, what really happens is that the awareness which is I has either the one or the other of two attributes. One may wish to call these two attributes 'seeing green' and 'feeling a pain'. But one must not forget that, according to Malebranche, my seeing green does not, as the 'seeing' suggests, involve an act of my mind. To do justice to this feature, one may, with deliberate violence, call the second of the two attributes 'green'. In this case one must not forget that according to Malebranche there is literally nothing that is colored.

The divine reason, also called the Word, is cosubstantial with God. It contains the *ideas*. Numbers, for instance, are ideas. Ideas are not existents. Yet there are, among the ideas, the archtypes of all possible existents. Every existent is created in the image of its archtype or idea by a distinct or, at least, distinguishable act of God. The archtype of

[3] Configuration corresponds, in Cartesian physics, to what we now call the fine structure of matter. For my purpose it may safely be disregarded.

[4] In some other systems, e.g., Leibniz's, the distinction is made by allotting to attributes only "dependent" existence. Attributes, incidentally, correspond in my paradigm to "green₁" and "green₂"; "green" corresponds to the idea. In Malebranche's case, though, it will soon transpire, the paradigm is for this purpose singularly inept.

extension as such is called intelligible extension. It "contains" the ideas of all possible modes of extension, that is, the ideas of all possible kinds of bodies (not of all possible bodies). 'Contains', so used, is synonymous with 'logically implies', in the sense in which the axioms of a theory, say, Euclidean geometry, are said to imply its theorems. There is also created extension. One will not go wrong in thinking of it as physical space as long as one remembers that there is for Malebranche (and Descartes) no such thing as "empty space." Bodies are said to be *in* created extension. I list this as the second use or meaning of 'in' that occurs crucially in the system. I shall attend to it presently. At the moment I merely wish to call attention to three things. First: the divine reason is said to contain the ideas. Intelligible extension is said to contain those of, say, a cube and a sphere. One may ask whether these are two instances of the same use or meaning of 'contain'. Probably they are; I do not wish to pursue the matter; I merely mention in passing that in many natural languages, including ours, French, and Latin, the passive of '*A* contains *B*' is '*B* is contained *in A*'. Second: the ideas are also said to be *in* the divine reason. This use of "in" I shall examine in Section Five. Third: if God had created an existent in the image of intelligible thought as such, it would be the counterpart of created extension as such (physical space). There is, according to Malebranche, no such created thing.

Malebranche's world is emphatically nonrelational. There are no relations, not even in the sense in which there are attributes. This belief is of course not distinctive of Malebranche.[5] What distinguishes him is, rather, the consistency with which he infers from it that no created existent acts upon any other. The only agent is God. He acts by creating existents, by conserving them (in time), and by endowing them with (changing) attributes. Most of the logic of His agency, if I may so express myself, remains hidden in the mystical core of the system. Malebranche's rejection of relations provides the bridge that leads from his ontology, which is in the main Cartesian, to his epistemology, which is not Cartesian at all.

A mind is aware of or knows (*penser*, used generically) only what is either (a) *in it* or (b) what *it is in*. This is taken to be self-evident. Remembering that a mind's attributes are in it (first meaning of 'in'), we recognize in (a) one of the fundamental metaphors at work. Thus we conclude, correctly within the system, that a mind knows its attri-

---

[5] For an account of the role of relations in Leibniz's system and in substance philosophies generally, see "Russell's Examination of Leibniz Examined," *Philosophy of Science*, 23, 1956, 175–203, and also pp. 155–88 of this book. Also below, Sections Four and Six.

butes. Depending upon the circumstances, this species of knowing is called either sensing or imagining (*sentir et imaginer*). (b) requires explication. This part of the story is, for my purposes, best told in the context of my first point.

III

Consider *one* green cube. Its archtype is a figured and configured part of extension, say, at rest. When I look at the cube two things happen. (1) My mind acquires an attribute of the kind called 'seeing green'. (2) My mind conceives the archtype. Why and how this happens on the occasion of my seeing the cube is accounted for by the doctrine of secondary causes (occasionalism). This part of the system I propose to ignore, partly because I have nothing new to say about it, partly because Malebranche's own exposition of it is admirably lucid, detailed, and consistent.[6] What concerns me is, rather, the species of knowing mentioned in (2). Called conceiving (*concevoir*), it corresponds to (b) in the last paragraph of the preceding section. To conceive an idea is to see it "in" God. While I am not yet ready to analyze this use of 'in', I must prepare some material for the analysis. The 'in it' of (b) is merely a metaphor within the metaphor. Without this second metaphor, my mind and the idea it conceives are both said to be "in" God. What happens when I conceive it is that the two unite with each other (*s'unir*) or touch (*toucher*). Here we recognize an enlargement (contiguity instead of *in*ness) of the second use of 'in' (being *in* space) and, also, how in this case it assimilates the first (an attribute being *in* an existent). For, so we are told, a mind knows best the things that are in it (*a*); though these, alas, are not the best things (in the hierarchical sense of 'being') it may know. Next best known (b) to a mind are the things it "touches." All this is fairly obvious. But let us not rashly conclude that the two meanings of 'in' which I have isolated so far suffice, together with their enlargements and assimilations, for a complete analysis of the use of 'in' in 'seeing in God'.

Upon Malebranche's account of perception the archtypes of physical objects play the role of universals. More precisely, they can be made to carry the burden of what I called universals in my modern version of realism. Only, one must not forget that in Malebranche's world bodies have no other qualities than, roughly, those Locke called primary. With respect to these Malebranche's account of perception is therefore realistic. With respect to secondary qualities, or, rather, with

---

[6] This judgment does not include what Malebranche says about free will, sin, and grace. But then, much of what he says on these topics is only of theological interest.

respect to the attributes of mind which correspond to them in the system, it is not. This is my first point. Its negative half requires some explanation.

In the divine reason there is, as an idea among ideas, intelligible thought, the archtype of minds, the counterpart of intelligible extension, as well as, contained in it in the sense of implication, the archtypes of all possible attributes of human minds. Human minds, though, do not and cannot conceive these ideas. Yet, whenever a mind exemplifies an attribute, it also knows that it exemplifies it.[7] This is a third species of knowledge, called self-awareness (*sentiment intérieur* or *conscience intérieure*). Not being conceptual, self-awareness is, like sensing and imagining, neither clear nor distinct and, therefore, like sensing and imagining, inferior to conceiving. Even so, there is no doubt that whenever I exemplify an attribute, say, seeing green, I know, not only that I exemplify some attribute, but also that I exemplify one of a certain *kind*, namely, the kind called 'seeing green'. Malebranche himself insists on that, very wisely, I think. For, if it were otherwise, how could I ever know my seeing green from my being in pain? There is thus, within the system, a knowledge of kinds, even if it be only knowledge of an inferior sort, which is mediated neither by universals nor by what, within the system, corresponds to universals. For the kinds so known Malebranche's account of perception is therefore not realistic. For an example, take the two perceptual judgments expressed by 'This (or that) is a cube' and 'This (or that) is green'. Malebranche's account of the first is realistic. His account of the second is not. This is the point.

IV

In Section One the example was two green cubes. In Section Three I shifted to one such cube. The reason for the change must have been transparent even then. I contrived to reserve everything connected with individuation for a connected treatment in this section. Notice also that although explicating "individuation," I have not even once used the noun 'individual'. Remember, too, that I used 'substance' most sparingly and, when introducing it, insisted that for Malebranche (as for Descartes) there is one and only one difference between a substance and its attributes. The idea of the former can be thought without those of the latter; but not conversely. The distinction is thus al-most a matter of logic. (I put it strongly, for the sake of indicating a

---

[7] This raises the nice question whether, when a mind conceives an idea, it also has a *conscience intérieure* of this conceiving. One would think so. However, I have not found anything very conclusive on this point in either the *Recherche* or the *Entretiens*.

tendency; more strongly, I think, than could be justified.) Ontologically, therefore, one might say (with the same exaggeration), a substance is merely an attribute among attributes. But if a substance is an attribute, or like an attribute, what is it an attribute of? By the logic of the two terms within the system the question can be asked.[8] So it must eventually be faced.[9] This, however, is not the line of thought I wish to pursue.

Individuals are simple; they have no "parts." Individuals are the only existents, at least in the full, unqualified sense of 'exist'. Individuals are substances. These three sentences belong to the logic of 'individual', 'substance', and 'exist' in the systems of Aristotle[10] and Aquinas. What makes an individual a substance is, for Aristotle, a (substantial) form; for Aquinas, a nature. But forms as well as natures are generic. One and the same form, for instance, may "inform" several individuals. That is why in these systems the problem of individuation is so important.

For Malebranche, as for Descartes, created extension is a substance that has "parts." This is a radically different use or meaning of 'substance'. According to the older use, a substance, being an individual, has no "parts." The newer use came to the fore with Descartes.[11] Through his influence, the older one became submerged, at least outside of the schools, until it emerged again with Leibniz.[12] The most vigorous clashes between these two notions of substance, the one with parts and the one without parts, occurred, ever since Descartes, not explicitly in metaphysics but implicitly in physics. There the conflict was between the *particle* and the *stuff* models of matter. A particle, in

[8] I would much rather say "grammar," using the term not, as is now so often done, as a virtual synonym of 'logic' but as a handy idiomatic equivalent of 'axioms'. Thus it would be an axiom concerning substances and attributes that every attribute inheres in (is an attribute of) a substance. These distinctions, however, are not at issue in this paper. That is why I do not hesitate to use 'logic' as I do, or, for that matter, to identify "use" and "meaning." When the hare is safe, one may, if it proves expedient, safely run with the hounds.

[9] This is of course the point of structural contact with Spinoza. *Étendue* can, characteristically, be read as a past participle and is, perhaps, most accurately translated by "the extended." (*La chose étendue?* But then, what is *la chose?*) In English, the transition from 'extended' to 'extension' is more abrupt.

[10] I disregard that very special use of 'part' with which its form and matter are "parts" of an individual substance. Nor do I claim that there are no passages in Aristotle which could plausibly be taken to support the later doctrine of the multiplicity of forms.

[11] Within the medieval context, it would seem, Descartes was anticipated by Grosseteste and Bonaventure.

[12] This neglects Spinoza's unique substance which is mainly of theological interest. For an analysis of the older notion, see "Russell's Examination of Leibniz Examined."

the extreme, is punctiform. A stuff is spread out continuously, like a fluid. Atoms are of course particles. The various classical ethers are stuffs. The modern notion of a field can be traced to that of a stuff. The connection between the physics of "matter" and the metaphysics of "substance" (or, if you please, the logic of 'substance') is thus more intimate than some may think. Interesting as it is, I cannot and I need not here pursue it further.[13]

What was the impact of the new use of 'substance' on the problem of individuation? What happened is what one might expect. The problem faded into the background. There is of course more to be said. First, though, there is something else I must make as clear as I possibly can. I do not claim that either Descartes or Malebranche maintained either explicitly or implicitly anything as heterodox as that minds were divisible. On the other hand, I think it rather remarkable how little they worried about this glaring discrepancy between the only kinds of substance they recognized. Their unconcern is in fact part of what I mean by the fading of the problem. For the rest, it will be best if I treat the two kinds of substance separately.

The "parts" of created extension are points, lines, surfaces, and volumes. Points themselves have no parts. All other parts are collections of them. This makes points the heart of the matter and I shall therefore limit myself to them. The explication of this use of 'part' is set-theoretical. The area of the smaller of two concentric circles one draws on a piece of paper is in this sense a part of the area, or is *in* the area, of the larger. This, incidentally, is the only literal spatial use of "in" with which I am familiar. Our second use (a body being in space) is merely another insidiously inconspicuous metaphor. The reason for this is that there is no body called 'space'. Thus, when we say that a body is "in space" we merely refer metaphorically to the web of the (spatial) relations in which it stands to all other bodies "in space." Malebranche, of course, would disagree. Even so, he mentions this web of relations again and again when he insists, as he does again and again, that they and they alone exhaust the ideas of extension and of its attributes. In view of the fact that there are no relations in his world, that may seem a bit awkward. In Section Six we shall see that within the system it isn't. The crucial point, though, is that the idea of extension contains (in the sense of implication) those of its parts. In other words, this particular substance does not just happen to have parts; to be divisible is its very essence.

[13] For some detailed comments on the particle and stuff notions, particularly with respect to so-called action over distance, see the second chapter of *Philosophy of Science* (Madison: University of Wisconsin Press, 1957). I hardly need to mention that in this paragraph I use 'matter' as physicists use it.

How can bodies be individuated in such a world? The answer is by now obvious. My two cubes, for instance, occupy or, rather, they are different parts of extension equally figured and configured. Generally, the burden of the modern particulars is in this system carried by the points. What was not noticed is, *first*, that the points thus become, in the older use, the only substances, and, *second*, that there is within the system no answer to the obvious question of how two points are distinguished from each other. This is the heart of the matter. One very good reason why these two things may have been overlooked is, I submit, that the idea of extension, which as we saw is merely a glorified attribute, was held to contain those of its parts, in the sense in which the axioms of a theory contain (imply) its theorems. Yet axioms and theorems are propositions. An idea, one would think, is named by a term. This strange notion that one idea implies others is, one might say, the logical sleight of hand by which in this system the *quid* is produced from the *quale*. This is my second point, as it refers to bodies.

Malebranche, if he were faced with these criticisms, could in the case of bodies withdraw to a second position, which he has prepared for himself, by admitting that what eventually distinguishes my two cubes are the two distinguishable acts of God to which they owe their existence and nothing else.[14] Whether Malebranche would actually make this admission is of course a moot question. But it is by no means moot to point out that in the case of minds there is in his system nothing else that could carry the burden of individuation except these distinguishable acts of God, at least not from what has been said so far or, for that matter, from what is to be found in either the *Recherche* or the *Entretiens*. Structurally, though, there is another possibility. We conceive extension and, therefore, within human limits, all its possible attributes. But we cannot, we recall, conceive either mind or any of its attributes. For all we know, therefore, it could well be that no two created minds agree in all their attributes. If it were so, the problem of individuation for minds could consistently within the system be solved in the manner of Scotus. This is my second point, as it refers to minds.

Malebranche's views on individuation are, as I indicated, very much like Descartes'. Neither is greatly concerned. The problem has faded. Yet, it would seem that Malebranche's explicit concern is greater than Descartes'. In this respect Descartes is more modern. But I can also think of a likely reason for Malebranche's greater concern. Since he takes pain to place the ideas "outside" of all created existents, the problem of individuation imposes itself on him more forcefully, as does the problem of universals. Descartes, on the other hand, puts the ideas

[14] That I believe this "solution" to be rather verbal, in the pejorative sense of "verbal," I have indicated before.

"in" the existents that exemplify them as well as "in" the minds of those who perceive them. Thus he preserves, at least implicitly, a goodly part of the precartesian account of perception. In this respect Malebranche is more modern.

V

Now for the vision in God. We read: "*Dieu est très étroitement uni à nos âmes par sa présence, de sorte qu'on peut dire qu'il est le lieu des esprits, de même que les espaces sont en un sens le lieu des corps.*"[15] We also read: "*Les esprits, Ariste, sont dans la raison divine, et les corps dans son immensité.*"[16] Each of these two passages directs us to the mystical core of the system, the vision in God. Yet, when they are properly explicated within the system, they are seen to contradict each other. The first passage, it seems, is somehow adequate to the mystical core; unhappily, what it says cannot be consistently maintained within the system. What the second says can be consistently maintained within the system; unhappily, it does not do justice to the mystical core. This, in general, is my third point. I must now make it in detail. As one might expect, everything hinges on the *other* crucial uses of 'in' that occur in the system. I shall first review the two I isolated before, then with their help analyze the first passage. Next I shall introduce two further uses of 'in' and with their help analyze the second passage.

Attributes are *in* substances. Bodies are *in* space. These are the first and the second uses. Both, we saw, are metaphorical although the metaphor in both cases is insidiously inconspicuous. The first transfers the literal spatial use of 'in' to matters nonspatial; yet the case of bodies enables us to understand it somehow. The second is not really metaphorical, except for the container image it evokes, but rather a succinct way of referring to a body's position in the web of spatial relations. With this explication, we saw, Malebranche agrees. Nor is this agreement dependent on his agreeing with us, as he does *not*, that there is, literally, no such thing as (created) extension and, therefore, no container "space." The only difference made by that disagreement is that an alternative explication not open to us is open to Malebranche. He could take the second use to express that a body is, in the set-theoretical sense, a part of extension. As it happens, this difference, namely, his having two alternatives where we have only one, makes no difference for what I have to say.

The last clause of the first passage leaves no doubt that the phrase *être le lieu* corresponds to the second meaning of 'in'. The phrase *en un sens* I take, not to weaken the closeness of the comparison (*de même*

---

[15] *Recherche*, ed. J. Simon (Paris, 1871), I, 398.
[16] *Entretiens*, ed. J. Simon (Paris, 1871), p. 183.

que), but to indicate that Malebranche was aware of the inconspicuous metaphor involved in the second use of 'in'. The substitution of *la raison divine* for *Dieu* is supported, not only by the second passage, but also by countless others I do not quote. Remember, too, that the divine reason is cosubstantial with God. This yields, as an accurate transcription of the larger part of the passage, "Minds are in the divine reason as bodies are in space." Minds and the divine reason are not spatial. Thus the first 'in' of the transcription must be taken analogically. In this analogy the divine reason corresponds to created extension (space). This makes no sense within the system. What *would* correspond to created extension as such as minds correspond to bodies is, if there were such a thing, created thought as such. There is, as we saw, no such thing in the system. Nor, for that matter, is *la pensée intelligible* identical with the divine reason. It is, like *l'étendue intelligible*, just an idea among ideas. This is what I meant when I said that the first passage cannot be consistently maintained within the system. As we now see, I could have put it more strongly. The passage does not even make sense in the system.

The connection between a body and the space it is in is, poetically speaking, very close (*très étroit*) and intimate. Bodies are, as it were, immersed in space. This is what I had in mind when I suggested that the first passage does justice to the mystical core. The part I have not transcribed supports the suggestion.

God is *in* every existent. The ideas are *in* God (the divine reason). The two sentences exemplify the third and the fourth of the special uses to which 'in' is put in the system. Both are metaphorical. The spatial image controlling the third is closely akin to that which controls the first. Just as the attributes of an existent cannot be anywhere but in it, so an agent can only act "where" he is. The only agent, creating every substance, conserving it in time, causing its modifications, is God. God, therefore, is in every substance. That much for the third use of 'in'. Whether the ideas are in God in exactly the same sense in which the theorems of a theory are "contained *in*" its axioms is, as I said, a question I do not wish to pursue. Surely a good case can be made for the identity of these two uses in the more "logicizing" systems of the Platonic succession. Be that as it may, Malebranche himself explains the fourth use of 'in' very carefully. Take the idea of extension. It is not an attribute of God. But God himself has an attribute that contains it eminently, or in which it is, in the sense in which the less is in the more. God's attributes, however, are all unintelligible to us. The one "in" which intelligible extension is, as the less is in the more, is called His immensity. Intelligible time is in His eternity. Clearly, this is the neoplatonic pattern of negative theology. Which, then, we may ask, is the divine "attribute" that contains intelligible thought? The answer is: the divine reason, which is not an attribute but the divine substance itself.[17] There are two structural reasons to support this answer. For one, we saw that the precartesian gulf between substance and attribute has been narrowed in our system. I expressed this, with some exaggeration, by calling the distinction logical. For another, we must remember that Malebranche's notion of God is completely orthodox. Essence and existence, substance and attribute all coincide in the unity of unlimited being.

The context of the second passage leaves no doubt that we only make its sense more explicit if we replace *et* by *de même que*. "Minds are *in* God's reason as bodies are *in* His immensity." In this "proportion" bodies are to minds as God's immensity is to His reason. The passage thus confirms what has been said in the last paragraph. Yet there remains a question. Even though the archtypes are in God, it does not follow that the existents created in their image are. The answer is as follows. Every existent participates, in the Platonic sense, in its archtype. The archtype itself is in God. In this mediated sense every existent is itself in God. Strictly speaking, this is a fifth meaning of 'in', compounded of the fourth and Platonic participation. So explicated, the second passage can consistently be maintained within the system. The trouble is that in this sense not only minds but also bodies, trees, stones, and every grain of dust, are in God. This is what I meant when I said that the passage does not do justice to the mystical core.

I shall not show that the two passages contradict each other. This, I take it, is by now evident. I ask instead how within the system the damage could be repaired. The first passage would have to be repudiated or, what amounts to the same thing, it would have to be reduced to the status of a haunting image. The second passage, we just saw, though defensible within the system, does not do justice to the mystical core. To represent this core, a sixth use or meaning of 'in', as in 'seeing in God', would have to be distinguished. It remains unexplicated and inexplicable. This is quite proper. For it merely directs us onto the *via negativa* towards what surpasses understanding.

VI

1. Scholars quite naturally connect Malebranche with Berkeley. About causal connections I have nothing to say. Structurally, one may be tempted to say, from what we saw in Section Three, that while Malebranche was a realist with respect to some kinds, he was, like Berkeley, a nominalist with respect to some others. This is false. Since there are ideas of all kinds in the divine reason, Malebranche was not a

---

[17] Theologically speaking, the Second Person.

nominalist with respect to any of them. It is true, though, that his account of the perception of some kinds is nominalistic, or, more cautiously, that it has a nominalistic flavor. For, when I exemplify an attribute, I know, in a particular self-awareness, that it is of a certain kind; yet this case of self-awareness is not a case of my mind conceiving (being in contact with) the idea or archtype of the attribute. Even this partially nominalistic account of perception is, I submit, an intriguing structural similarity between Malebranche and Berkeley.

In one passage the nominalistic flavor is particularly strong. This is the third passage I shall quote. After having insisted that one in pain is always *"modifié par une douleur particulière,"* Malebranche continues: *"Et si vous pouvez penser à la douleur en général, c'est que vous pouvez joindre la généralité à toutes choses."*[18] One adds (the idea of?) generality to something! I wonder whether one who says this sort of thing and lets it go at that is still greatly concerned with the nominalism-realism issue. Or, to put it as I put it before, one may well wonder whether for the Cartesian philosophers this problem, too, has faded into the background. I believe it has. Nor is it difficult to suggest a plausible reason for its temporary eclipse. What these philosophers were primarily interested in is, not how this or that existent manages to be a cube or how I come to know that it is one, but rather, how we come to know the "general" (or "abstract," or "conceptual") truths of geometry. Their answer is, of course, that in such knowledge our minds make contact with (nonexistent) ideas. This fits well with the fact that when we wanted to understand how Malebranche used 'idea', we sometimes had to think of an idea as an axiom or a group of axioms rather than as what is ordinarily meant by a universal. Very generally speaking, what happened in this case is what, I believe, has happened several times. The fascination of an age with some science, in this case, geometry, obscures to its philosophers some fundamental philosophical problems, in this case, the problem of universals and that of individuation.[19]

2. The difficulties encountered by any ontology without relations are, I believe, unconquerable. If this is so, then one must not wonder that Malebranche, too, failed to conquer them. But he at least handled them more effectively than some others by concentrating them, as it were, in two areas, thus keeping the rest of the field free of them.

There is, first, the relation between a cause and its effect.[20] Since

[18] *Entretiens*, p. 37.

[19] Characteristically, Malebranche hardly ever uses the traditional technical term (*universel*).

[20] Upon finer analysis, it turns out that every non-Humean account of causation involves, not relations, but what I call pseudorelations. These modern subtleties, though, are not at issue. See also *The Metaphysics of Logical Positivism*.

God is the only agent, there are no causal relations among existents. This concentrates a large part of the difficulty in the "logic" of God's agency. About this logic we are told only two things; first, quite traditionally, that God's acts are identical with His volitions; and second, perhaps not so traditionally, that even He can only act "where" He is. This I had occasion to mention before.

There are, second, such relations as, say, that exemplified by one stick being longer than another. These relations, we are told, are relations among the ideas of the existents related. This concentrates the remaining part of the difficulty in the realm of ideas. What, then, one must ask, about relations among ideas, whether they be among ideas that are archtypes of existents, as in the case of the sticks, or relations among other ideas such as, say, one number being larger than another. Are there relational ideas corresponding to these relations among ideas? Platonizing systems may still differ in their answer to this question. Malebranche's answer is the most radical. There are no such ideas. Since he did not explore the matter very thoroughly, he did not get into trouble.

3. Aquinas and Scotus agree that we cannot perceive minds, our own or others', in the same way in which we perceive physical objects. The structural root of this agreement is that they both use 'being' also in the hierarchical sense which was mentioned in Section One. The point is, first, that the direction in which action flows in both systems, from the top downward, as it were, is determined by the hierarchy; and second, that perception is, in both systems, a transaction in which the perceiver is active. This provides the grammatical bridge for the proposition that an existent cannot (conceptually) know another existent unless the position of the latter's form (or nature) is lower in the hierarchy than that of the former. Malebranche's persistent emphasis on our not being able to conceive the ideas of either mind or any of its attributes is, therefore, very medieval. Descartes, at least explicitly, makes much less of this point. Certainly he does not set self-awareness apart as a special and inferior kind of knowledge. In this he is much more modern. Malebranche, on the other hand, pushes self-awareness as far as one possibly can after having denied it the status of conceptual knowledge. In this he reminds one of Scotus. As is well known, the yearning for self-knowledge is one of the marks of the Augustinian tradition. Probably it has something to do with the Augustinian concern for what, in ordinary parlance, is called the inner or spiritual life. It would seem that Descartes' system has not to the same extent been shaped by that concern. In this he reminds one of Aquinas.

Frege's Hidden Nominalism*

OME philosophical pieces are like symphonies, others like quar-
tets. This one is merely an ontological theme with variations.
After I have introduced the theme, it will be seen that *Exemplification versus Mapping* is a very good name for it. The phrase does not
signify, though, except to one already familiar with the theme. That is
why I did not choose it as a title. All but the last of the variations are
comments on Frege's ontology, though as such they are highly selective.[1] This is one reason for the title I chose. The other is that I hope
to draw expository advantage from its shock value.

I

In ontological discourse two clusters of very ordinary words are used
philosophically. First of all, therefore, I shall state how I propose to
handle these words. One cluster contains 'thing', 'object', 'entity',
'existent'. When I do not wish to indicate anybody's ontological commitment, I use *entity*. When I wish to speak of what philosophers,
speaking philosophically, assert to "exist," I use *existent*. Frege uses
both 'object' and 'function' philosophically; and he holds, either explicitly or very nearly so, that every entity (not, existent!) is either an
object or a function.[2] The other cluster contains 'naming', 'denoting',

* Philosophical Review, *67, 1958, 437–59. Reprinted by permission.*

*I have profited from discussions with Reinhardt Grossmann, who will elaborate some
of the points in this paper as well as some related ones in his doctoral dissertation.*

[1] An excellent detailed exposition may be found in R. Wells, "Frege's Ontology," *The Review of Metaphysics*, 4, 1951, 537–73. References to this study are
by page number, preceded by the letter *W*.

[2] In rendering Frege's terms I follow the well-known *Translations from the
Philosophical Writings of Gottlob Frege* by M. Black and P. Geach (Oxford:
Blackwell, 1952). References to this volume are by page number, preceded by
the letter *F*.

'designating', 'referring'. Nor are the philosophical uses of the two clusters independent. Some philosophers, for instance, maintain that an existent is what is or could be named (denoted, designated) by a word or expression. When I wish to speak without indicating ontological commitment, I avoid all these verbs and borrow instead Frege's *standing for*. If they followed this use, the philosophers just mentioned could say that a name is a word or expression which stands for an existent.

Consider 'This is green'. On one occasion, 'this' may stand for an apple; 'green', for its color. Some hold that, on another occasion, the two words could stand for what they call a sensum and one of its qualities, respectively. Others disagree. The difference makes no difference for my purpose. So I shall entirely ignore it in calling the sort of thing 'this' and 'green' stand for, on all occasions, an *individual* and a *character*, respectively. Also, I shall in this essay use the two words without ontological commitment even though, in the case of 'individual', that is admittedly unusual. For Frege, individuals are one kind of object; characters, one kind of function. But there are in his world still other kinds of objects and of functions.

Some ontologists, including Russell (and myself) though not Frege, make much of a distinction between simple and complex characters. For what I am about it is irrelevant, so I shall disregard it. There is also the distinction between types of characters and functions. Both Frege and Russell pay attention to it. But again, with one glancing exception, it is irrelevant for what I am about, so I shall virtually ignore it. This shows how selective I shall be in my remarks about Frege.

Even in ontological discourse the terms *realism* and *nominalism* are used in two ways; once strictly, once broadly. The ontologist's first business is to list all kinds of existents (not, all existents). If he discerns many kinds, perhaps too many, one calls him a realist. If he lists but few, perhaps too few, one calls him a nominalist. This is the broad use. In the strict sense, an ontologist is a realist if he counts characters, or at least some characters (for example, simple ones), as a kind of existent. A nominalist in the strict sense holds, conversely, that no characters are existents. In this essay, unless there be a qualification to the contrary, both terms are always used strictly.

Two things about Frege are beyond reasonable doubt. Had he used 'existent' as I do (as far as I know he did not use it at all), he would have agreed that everything he calls an object is an existent. This is the first thing. Of objects there are in his world many kinds. Nor are the distinctions among them "ordinary," like that between cats and dogs. They are even more sweeping than that between physical and phenomenal objects, which surely is sweeping enough and, according to some, anything but ordinary. His distinctions are so sweeping indeed that, if the word is to have any meaning at all, one cannot but call them ontological. This is the second thing beyond reasonable doubt. Specifically, Frege distinguishes (at least) the following (ontological) kinds (of objects): individuals, numbers, truth values, value ranges (classes of objects), senses, propositions (thoughts), concept correlates.[3] Many philosophers think that with the sole exception of individuals all these kinds are odd. Or, to say the same thing differently, they refuse to consider the odd kinds of entities as existents. Still differently, these philosophers (including myself) reject Frege's exaggerated realism (broad sense). It is not my purpose to rehearse their arguments, or to improve on them, or to invent new ones; even though I shall permit myself, *en passant*, to call attention to two oddities about truth values. As far as Frege is concerned, my purpose is rather to give some reasons for my belief that, for all his exuberant realism in the broad sense, he was in the strict sense at least implicitly a nominalist. My primary concern, though, is neither biographical nor textual. What I shall really argue, therefore, is that the structure of Frege's ontology though not, as will transpire, of Church's emendation of it,[4] is nominalistic.

Everything said so far is merely preliminary. I shall proceed as follows. In the next section the theme is introduced and used to exhibit what I take to be the root of Frege's nominalism. In the third section I shall show that in one case this very nominalism forces upon Frege that multiplication of entities (or rather of existents) which is so characteristic of his ontology. In the fourth section I shall show that what is, broadly speaking, the most serious as well as the most obvious intrinsic flaw of the system is but another consequence of its author's hidden nominalism. I say intrinsic because this flaw is of course not that exuberant realism (broad sense) which, as I said, I shall not question except once and incidentally. In the last section I shall vary my theme, very briefly and very sketchily, by sounding it as a background for the siren songs of a more recent nominalism.

II

Where one arrives depends in part on where he starts. A philosopher's starting point depends in part on his basic paradigm. Frege's is very different from the realist's. My theme builds on this difference or, rather, contrast. I present first the realist, because it helps to bring out

[3] As far as I know, the term is Wells's.
[4] A. Church, *Introduction to Mathematical Logic* (Princeton: Princeton University Press, 1957).

the contrast more forcefully. Some realists, including myself, propose an explication of the philosophical use of 'exist' upon which all individuals and (some of) their characters but no higher characters are existents.[5] The realist I present is of this sort. My case does not depend on the limitation. But again, it helps to bring out the theme more clearly by freeing it from some bywork that otherwise would have to be introduced.

The realist starts from individuals and their characters. That is, he starts from entities Frege calls objects (and from their characters), though not from those objects which with Frege's critics I called odd. 'Peter is blond' may thus serve as the realist's paradigm. What claims does it suggest to him? What do and what don't these claims imply? What reasons can he give for them? I shall take up the three questions in this order.

First. 'Peter' and 'blond' both stand for existents. Generally, both individuals and characters are existents. This is one major claim. Many realists, including myself, also hold that every existent is either an individual or a character; but for the purpose at hand that does not matter. What 'Peter is blond' stands for comes about if two existents, one of each kind, enter into a certain "relation," or, as I would rather say, nexus. This nexus the realist calls *exemplification.* Obviously it is a very fundamental feature of his world. This is another major claim. To see that it is not independent of the first, notice that to say of something that it does or may enter into a nexus is to presuppose that it exists. Notice also that when I spoke of a sentence "standing for" something, I quite deliberately paid with clumsiness for the agreed-upon neutrality of the phrase.

Second. (a) An individual may or may not exemplify a character. To say that a character exemplifies an individual is nonsense. The very nexus between the two kinds is thus asymmetrical. This alone shows that individuals and characters are not alike *in all respects* which concern the ontologist. Nor do the realist's claims imply that they are. Obviously not, I should say. For, if they were, what point would there be in distinguishing between them? (b) In the paradigm, the copula or, as I prefer to say, the predicative 'is' stands for exemplification. In a much larger number of cases, to say the least, the verbal image of this nexus between things is predication, that is, the grammatical rela-

---

[5] See "Elementarism," *Philosophy and Phenomenological Research,* 18, 1957, 107–14, and also pp. 115–23 of this book.

tion between subject and predicate. That follows from the realist's claims.

Third. An articulate realist has of course many reasons for the position he takes. Fortunately they do not all matter for my purpose. What matters is that every time he discovers *some respect* in which individuals and characters are alike, he has discovered *a* reason. I shall state two such reasons, the two which I think carry most weight. (a) Just as we are never presented with an individual that is not qualitied, that is, does not exemplify a character, so we are never presented with a character that is not exemplified by some individual with which we are also presented. Notice that I speak of entities being presented to us, that is, as one says, epistemologically. Had I not promised to keep out the distinction between simple and complex characters and had I limited myself to the former, I could have spoken ontologically: Just as there is no individual that is not qualitied, so there is no character that is not exemplified. This is one fundamental likeness. (b) Consider the three entities that 'Peter', 'blond', and 'Peter is blond' stand for. The differences among them are ontologically significant. With that Frege agrees. For, if he did not, he would not, as an ontologist, either distinguish concepts from objects or set aside truth values as a kind of object. The realist says the same thing differently. Neither an individual nor a character is the kind of entity (notice the noncommittal word!) a sentence stands for. This is a second likeness. (b') The reader is assumed to be familiar with Frege's distinction between saturated and unsaturated expressions. 'Blond' or, as he would really have to say, 'is blond', is unsaturated. 'Peter' is saturated. (So is, very importantly, 'Peter is blond'; but that does not yet enter into my argument.) Primarily at least, the dichotomy is between expressions, not between entities. If one wants to apply it to entities, one must specify what in this case the two terms are to mean. For instance, one may propose "Individuals and characters are equally unsaturated" as an alternative way of stating the second fundamental likeness. An unsophisticated realist may object to this on the ground that, since individuals and characters are both existents, they really are both equally saturated. We know that he merely proposes another meaning for one(!) of the two terms as applied to entities. But his proposal has the merit of showing not only that this application serves no purpose but also the dangers that beset it.[6]

The realist's gambit has a further consequence, which gives rise to

[6] See "Propositional Functions," *Analysis*, 17, 1956, 43–48.

an objection, which in turn leads to a clarification. It will pay later if in introducing this matter I change the paradigm to 'Peter is *a* boy'. The objector points out that one who takes the predicative 'is' to stand for exemplification ought to admit that the paradigm and the sentence 'Peter exemplifies *the* character of being a boy' stand for one and the same entity. After a fashion, the realist does admit that. He even admits it for the sentence 'The individual (object) Peter exemplifies the character (concept) of being a boy'; and, if he used the two words in parentheses, he would also admit it for the further variations they make possible. Now the objector taunts the realist with a Bradleyan regress. It seems, he says, that in order to grasp what exemplification is, he must first grasp what it means for the (relational) character of being exemplified to be exemplified. The realist answers as follows. Exemplification is a very peculiar character. (That is why I called it a nexus and only once, in quotation marks, a relation.) Its peculiarity is the same as that of such "characters" as being an individual or a character. To be an individual, for instance, is not to be of an "ordinary" kind, as is being a cat or a dog, but to be the sort of entity expressions of a certain grammatical kind stand for. The expressions for these peculiar kinds are therefore all expendable and the several alternatives for the paradigm need not be considered unless one speaks in a language containing them about another language and what its expressions stand for. I need not on this occasion endorse this answer. Nor would I on any occasion endorse it in this crude form. (That is why I said the realist admits what I made him admit "after a fashion.") I merely mention this answer because, being familiar and thus permitting me to communicate quickly about what does not matter for what I am about, it helps me to prepare the ground for what does. So much for the realist.

Frege starts from numbers and their functions. 'x^2' may thus serve as his paradigm. That numbers are objects and therefore existents he takes for granted. Questionable as that is, I need not question it. My concern is with functions, mathematical and otherwise. The current mathematical name for the crucial idea is *mapping*. The square function, for instance, maps each number onto another, namely, its square. Generally, given two classes of entities which may but need not coincide or overlap, a function is a mapping rule, mapping each member of one of the two classes upon one (and, in the paradigmatic case, only one) member of the other. Let me now for a moment speak as a poet might, using some very loaded words very freely. A rule is a thing totally different from the things to which it applies. A mapping rule, in particular, is a thing much more shadowy, much less real, less palpable, less substantial than the things mapped and mapped upon. This more and these less, rather than the questionable status of numbers, is the heart of the matter. So I shall try to state it, not as a poet but as a philosopher might.

Numbers and their functions differ from each other in the two fundamental respects in which, as we saw, individuals and characters are alike. (a) Just as there is no unexemplified character, so there is no unqualitied individual. But there are of course numbers whether or not they be either arguments or values of functions. (b) The two notions of an individual and of a character, containing or presupposing each other to exactly the same extent, are equally "saturated" or "unsaturated." The notion of a number neither contains nor presupposes that of a function. The latter, however, contains and presupposes that of the two ranges (of numbers). (c) The realist's basic paradigm involves two entities, an individual and a (nonrelational) character. So does a function of one variable, which is Frege's basic paradigm. Or, rather, this is so after an argument has been chosen and the corresponding value computed by means of the function. The need for this additional step, which Frege never tires of emphasizing, increases the "ontological distance" between objects and functions. In Frege's paradigm, moreover, though not in the realist's, the two existents involved, the argument and "its" value, are existents of the same kind. This further increases the impression of disparity between them and the entity which is the function.

Still another circumstance subtly undermines the ontological status of functions. What mathematicians say about the latter often has a *subjective* ring. As they speak, it is they who do the mapping or, as it is often put, establish the correlation. 'Rule' itself, in most of its uses, has the same ring or tinge. This is an occasion for comment. *First.* Dangerous as that subjective ring or tinge may be philosophically, it is of course quite harmless as long as the mathematicians attend to their own business. What makes it even more harmless is that in fact mathematicians are not at all busy establishing or making functions. The vast bulk of their work consists in demonstrating what further properties a function has, assuming that it has some others. *Second.* The realist pulls the fangs of this potentially dangerous talk by construing functional expressions as, in the *Principia* sense, indefinite descriptions,[7]

---

[7] '*The* father of x' is in this sense an indefinite description; '*a* son of Peter' is not, irrespective of how many sons, if any, Peter has. A. J. Ayer's "Individuals," reprinted in his *Philosophical Essays* (New York: Macmillan, 1954), makes one wonder whether he appreciates the distinction. What he calls indefinite descriptions seem to be predicative expressions which *happen* to be true for several subjects.

either mathematical or otherwise (the square of x, the father of x). Descriptions in turn contain expressions standing for characters. And there is nothing subjective about characters (including, of course, relations), least of all in the case of numbers. As Russell put it, in a justly celebrated passage about the order relation, "we can no more 'arrange' the natural numbers than we can the starry heavens."[8] Notice, though, that even if starting from numbers in one sense, one who accepts this clarification starts in another sense from the realist's paradigm. *Third.* I spoke quite deliberately of the subjective tinge or blur from which some of the mathematicians' phrases suffer. My purpose was to give an objector his opportunity. Frege, this objector reminds us, insists over and over again that not only his odd objects but also functions, though they are not objects, are yet *objective.* I know that this is one of his guiding ideas. And I admire the steadfastness with which he wielded it as a weapon against the psychologism rampant in the Germany of his day. One may appreciate all this, as of course I do, and yet consistently hold, as I also do, that while within his system at least Frege succeeded in securing full ontological status for his odd objects, he did not so succeed, even within the system, in the case of functions. That is what I mean by his hidden nominalism. Notice that I call it hidden or implicit. Remember, too, that in this section I merely undertook to state it and to trace it to what I take to be its root, namely, the contrast between exemplification and mapping. The evidence will be found in the next two sections. But I am not quite done with the business at hand.

Nominalism is a thesis about characters. Nothing will be lost if we limit ourselves to nonrelational ones. Frege calls them *concepts.* What, then, does he have to say about concepts? The realist, we just saw, construes functions in terms of characters (concepts). Frege, proceeding in the opposite direction, as it were, construes concepts as a kind of function. In this way, the nominalism I have shown to be implicit in any analysis that starts from mapping is spread to concepts (characters). This is the point. Or, if you please, this is the last bar of my theme.

Frege's execution of the idea is familiar. If 'Peter is blond' is to be construed in analogy to 'the square of 3', then we must look for an object that goes with Peter as the value 9 goes with the argument 3. This object is the truth value of the sentence. This is one motive for Frege's "creation" of the two odd objects T and F. It fits nicely with another. He wants every saturated expression to stand for an object;

---

[8] B. Russell, *Introduction to Mathematical Philosophy,* p. 30 of the 1919 edition. The whole page repays reading in this context.

sentences are saturated expressions; so the truth value of a sentence can serve as the object it stands for. Though Frege had still other motives for the "reification" of T and F, structurally these two are undoubtedly the most important. I should like to suggest that the first, that is, the need to make good the precarious analogy between concepts and functions, goes even deeper than the second.

I turn from things to words. The alleged analogy between characters and functions is not reflected in our language. If it were, we would have to say 'blond *of* Peter', just as we say '*the* square *of* 3', and not, as we do, 'Peter *is* blond'. (The reader who can anticipate the sequel will be struck by the irony of our propensity, if we consider such verbal violence at all, to say '*the* blond(-ness) of Peter'.) The culprit in the case is the predicative 'is'. From where the realist stands, we remember, it reflects very nicely the nexus of exemplification and is *a*, if not perhaps *the*, fundamental use of 'is'.[9] For Frege it is but a clumsily disguised 'of'. In 'Peter *is* the father of John', on the other hand, as in '$3^2 = 9$' and, alas, in 'Peter is blond $= T$', 'is' reflects very nicely, from where Frege stands, what it is used to speak about. To express identity thus becomes *the* or at least *a* fundamental use of 'is'. In the last section I shall give some reasons why I believe that all nominalists are forced to consider it, more or less covertly, *the* fundamental use of 'is'.

This is the place to call attention to two oddities about truth values. First, let '*P*' stand for a sentence and consider the series

$$P = T, \quad (P = T) = T, \quad [(P = T) = T] = T, \quad \ldots$$

If *P* is true, so are all members of the series. If the arithmetical analogue were to hold, the members of the series

$$3^2 = 9, \quad (3^2 = 9) = 9, \quad [(3^2 = 9) = 9] = 9, \quad \ldots$$

would also all be true. Yet they are not even well formed (except the first). This is odd. Second, senses and propositions (thoughts) are in the system two kinds of objects, kindred in that a proposition is, as it were, the sense of a sentence. This is familiar.[10] Now there is a passage (*F* 64) in which I take Frege to assert that '*P*' and '$P = T$' have (express) the same sense. If the arithmetical analogue held, so would therefore '3^2' and '$3^2 = 9$'. Yet the former denotes a number; the second, T. Thus they do not even denote the same kind of object. This, too, is odd. If one has already accepted the system, he will probably not boggle at such oddities. But if he hasn't, they may make him even more averse

---

[9] It becomes *the* fundamental use if the Leibniz-Russell explication of identity is considered adequate.

[10] See Sections III and IV.

to the reification of T and F and to what, as we saw, is at the bottom of it all, Frege's analysis of exemplification in terms of mapping.

III

A nodding acquaintance with Frege's work, or even with what is currently being said about it, leaves two impressions. The first is of the multiplication of entities due to his distinction between *reference* and *sense*, that is, between the objects *denoted* and the objects *expressed* by such saturated expressions as, say, 'the Morning Star' and 'Peter is blond'. The second impression is that *the* main intellectual motive for the multiplication is the hope that, by means of it, it will be possible to conquer the difficulties that arise in intentional contexts, that is, in contexts mentioning either modalities or propositional attitudes, such as believing, knowing, and so on. Considering the system as a whole, that certainly is *a* motive. But if the two impressions are as widely spread as I believe them to be, then it is probably worth pointing out that Frege was first forced into that business of multiplying entities by the very logic of his nominalism in a case much simpler and more fundamental, which has nothing whatsoever to do with either modalities or propositional attitudes. This is the case of *classes* (extensions, value ranges). Corresponding to each concept, which according to him is not an object and (if I am right) at least implicitly not an existent, Frege "creates" another entity, which according to him is an object, namely, the class of all objects which, as he says, fall under the concept.[11] In this section I shall give two reasons why his nominalism, made explicit, forces him to do just that. Such reasons, if sound, are of course the kind of structural evidence one must accumulate in order to establish that the system is, at least implicitly, nominalistic.

Consider the two functional expressions 'x^2' and 'x^2-x+x' and the equation '$x^2=x^2-x+x$'. After a fashion, we all know what the equation stands for. Practicing mathematicians, without giving the matter much thought, say either that the two functions have the same extension, that is, the class of ordered pairs $[(1, 1), (2, 4), \ldots]$, or, alternatively, that the two functions are equal (the same, identical). Strictly speaking, from where Frege stands, the second alternative makes no sense. A function is a mapping rule. Following one of the two rules mentioned, one obtains the value by squaring the argument. Following the other, one first squares the argument, then subtracts it from the square, then adds it to the intermediate result. Considered as rules, the two functions are thus not the same. Generally, two rules are never the same, in a

---

[11] The limitation to first-level concepts which this formulation entails does not affect my purpose.

sense both strict and intelligible, unless they are, as one says, two tokens of the same type. All one can mean by calling them so is, therefore, that they yield the same result (have the same extension). I conclude that, if he wants to be consistent, Frege cannot, as in fact he does not, specify conditions of identity for concepts and functions. Or, rather, he would have to hold that an assertion of identity between two (concepts or) functions is true if and only if the two expressions mentioned are different tokens of the same type. Of this more later. For the moment we notice that had he stopped at this point, Frege could not have preserved what as a mathematician he surely wanted to preserve, namely, the equation '$x^2 = x^2 - x + x$' and the truism for which it stands. His way out is to interpret it as an identity not between the two functions but, rather, between their extensions. (Technically, he introduces a special notation for the latter and rewrites the equation as a statement of identity between them.) The *possibility* of this interpretation he thinks is *indemonstrable*. So he appeals to a *fundamental law of logic*. The words and the phrase italicized are his (*F* 26). This is the first reason I undertook to adduce. It shows how the nominalism implicit in any analysis that starts from mapping creates the need for the new entities. The second reason will show that they must be objects.

Frege does not specify the fundamental law of logic to which he appeals. What then is it? Does he use the phrase merely to dignify what is done in this case? Or is there a general principle involved? Even though his words at this place seem to suggest the first alternative, the second is I believe the right one. Consider the following three propositions. 1. To be a name and to be an expression standing for an existent is one and the same thing. 2. For a statement of identity, '$\alpha = \beta$', to be true, 'α' and 'β' must denote existents. 3. For '$\alpha = \beta$' to be a statement (to be well-formed, or to be meaningful), 'α' and 'β' must denote (or purport to denote) existents. Obviously, 3 is stronger than 2. Many ontologists endorse either 2 or 3, depending on the stand they take on issues which do not concern us. I would not even endorse 2.[12] That, however, is beside the point. The point is that either 1 and 3 or, perhaps, 1 and 2 follow deductively from the way many ontologists tended and still tend to use 'existent', 'name', and 'identity'. Add now, as a fourth proposition, that every saturated expression is a name; in the first three propositions replace 'existent' by 'object', and you obtain four principles, or four aspects of one principle, which underlie, either explicitly or very nearly so, all of Frege's analysis. This, I believe, is

[12] To this point I hope to return on another occasion. See "Sameness, Meaning, and Identity," to appear in the *Proceedings of the Twelfth International Congress of Philosophy* (Venice, 1958), and also pp. 132–38 of this book.

quite uncontroversial. Assume now that this principle is the fundamental law of logic to which Frege appealed. It follows that extensions (value ranges, classes) must be objects. This is the second reason I promised to adduce. Moreover, I have made it plausible, to say the least, that Frege uses 'object' as many ontologists use 'existent'. Concepts and functions in general, we remember, though objective, are not objects. It follows that, at least implicitly, the system is nominalistic. This concludes the main argument of the section. I proceed to four comments.

First. Let a_1, a_2, . . . be all the objects that are blond; b_1, b_2, . . . all those that are not. The class one ordinarily associates with the character blond is that of the a, $[a_1, a_2, . . .]$. It can be argued that the class Frege associates with the concept blond is that of all ordered pairs (a, T) *and* (b, F). If so, in his world what sort of object is an ordered pair of objects? Probing deeply in some such directions, one is eventually led to the Russell paradox and the question as to what, if anything, Frege can do about it. I realize all that. Clearly, these subtleties do not matter for what I am about. That is why I proceeded as I did. But it may hurt my thesis if I appear ignorant where I am merely selective. That is why I mention the matter.

Second. Frege (*F* 50) feels the need to distinguish "the relation of an object to a first-level concept that it falls under . . . from the (admittedly similar) relation of a first-level concept to a second-level concept." So he proposes that in the former case we speak of falling *under*, in the latter of falling *within*. His purpose, he tells us, is to preserve the distinction of concept and object "with all its sharpness" or, as I would put it, to increase the ontological distance between them. Taken by itself, the passage may be read as merely a plea for pervasive type distinctions. In context it provides subsidiary evidence for my thesis.

Third. An objector might argue as follows: "True, Frege does not specify conditions of identity for functions. But, then, neither does he specify such conditions or criteria for senses. (I follow you in using 'sense' for propositions (thoughts) as well as for what is expressed by nonsentential saturated expressions such as 'the Morning Star'.) Yet senses are objects. This greatly weakens your argument." Wells (*W* 544) shrewdly anticipates part of the answer. Frege, he reminds us, had an additional reason, which does not, or at least not directly, apply to functions, for not specifying criteria for the identity of senses. To grasp this reason, remember that one of Frege's intellectual motives was to solve the problems of intentional contexts. In this enterprise the reification of senses is merely a first step. The decisive second step is to specify criteria of identity among senses. This second step Frege never took, simply because (or so I believe) he could not think of any that were acceptable to him and did the job. In any case, he examined and rejected two. By one of them, two expressions have (express) the same sense if and only if they are analytically equivalent. This criterion he recognized as too broad. By the other, two expressions have the same sense if and only if they are different tokens of the same type. If we accepted this criterion, logic, he thinks (F 46), "would simply be crippled," if only because "all definitions would then have to be rejected as false."[13] However that may be, Frege had an additional reason for not specifying a criterion of identity for senses. This is part of the answer I would give to the objector. For the rest, I would remind him of what was pointed out at the beginning of this section, namely, that its main argument is completely independent of what does or does not hold for senses.

Fourth. Frege, who started from mapping, was forced to reify classes. Does the realist who starts from exemplification find himself similarly compelled? If the answer were No, it would greatly add to the poignancy of my theme. The answer, I believe, is No. However, this is not the place to go into the reasons for that belief. So I shall merely hint at what is rather familiar. Our realist may so explicate the philosophical use of 'exist' that only what undefined terms stand for exists in this very peculiar sense. (This is an issue I promised to keep out of the main argument.) When Russell supported his contention that classes do not exist by defining the expressions standing for them in terms of predicative expressions, he was at least implicitly guided by this explication of 'exist'.[14] A realist who accepts Russell's analysis of the class notion together with the explication of 'exist' it implies or at least suggests need not therefore, like the Fregean nominalist, reify classes. The contrast adds depth to that between mapping and exemplification.

[13] I do not subscribe to the dogma. This, though, is another story. See "Intentionality," *Semantica* (Archivio di Filosofia, Roma: Bocca, 1955), pp. 177–216, and also pp. 3–38 of this book; "Elementarism," *Philosophy and Phenomenological Research*, 18, 1957, 107–14, and also pp. 115–23 of this book; and "Concepts" (jointly with Herbert Hochberg), *Philosophical Studies*, 8, 1957, 19–27, and also pp. 106–14 of this book.

[14] See "Particularity and the New Nominalism," *Methodos*, 6, 1954, 131–47, and also pp. 91–105 of this book.

IV

Consider the phrase 'the concept blond' and the sentence 'The concept blond is a concept'. As Wells points out (*W* 550), one would think that the latter is not only true but truistic. Frege, as he must, disagrees. Like every saturated expression beginning with 'the', the phrase is a name. A name denotes an object (existent). These two principles, we saw, Frege never questions. But a concept is not an object (existent). Hence, the supposed truism is false. Perhaps it is even nonsensical. That leaves two alternatives. One is to declare the sentence expendable. The other is to create a new kind of odd objects. Frege chose the second. The new objects are the *concept correlates*. A concept correlate "represents" its concept. Or it is obtained by "converting" the concept into an object. These are Frege's words. Nor must the correlate of a concept be confused with its extension. Starting with one entity, the concept, which as I argue does not exist, Frege thus ends up with two more which indubitably do exist, namely, the concept's correlate and its extension.

The need for the creation of this further kind of odd object is, to my mind, the most obvious intrinsic flaw of the system *as it stands*. By calling it intrinsic I indicate, as before, that I do not on this occasion wish to challenge the odd kinds merely because to some of us they seem odd. Nor do I call it a flaw merely because this particular reification is patently *ad hoc*. For so is that of the two truth values. My point is that, once the new kind, the concept correlate, has been introduced, one cannot escape answering the question in what relation, or connection— use any word you wish—it stands to the other two, the concept itself and its extension. Yet there is no answer. This is the flaw I have in mind. It is as obvious as it is serious. One cue to its being a flaw is the opacity of the two metaphors, representation and conversion. This is not to say that I blame Frege just for speaking metaphorically. Many philosophers sometimes do, and sometimes it helps. I merely wish to say that these two metaphors do not help me in the least. Nothing comes through.

The way I presented the matter leaves no doubt that the need for concept correlates is a consequence of what I claim is the implicit nominalism of the system. In this respect there is no difference between concept correlates and classes (extensions). But there is in another. Notice that I spoke of the system "as it stands." In the case of concept correlates, though not of classes, a very slight emendation eliminates the need for their reification as a further kind of objects. I shall next use this circumstance to argue that the nominalism which, if it were explicitly present in the system, would necessitate the reification, actually is present in it, at least implicitly.

Take (α) 'Peter', (β) 'Peter is blond', (γ) 'blond'. They exemplify Frege's three basic grammatical categories. Let the Greek letters stand for these categories. Every α and β expression has a reference and a sense. It denotes the former, expresses the latter. The reference of a β expression is a truth value, its sense a proposition (thought). Senses are objects. Hence they can be named. In the case of the paradigm, their names are 'the sense Peter'[15] and 'the proposition Peter is blond'[16] respectively. Being a name, each of these two expressions has in turn a sense. We have entered upon an infinite regress. Within the system, though, that is no difficulty. Nor does it disturb the lucidity of the pattern. The difficulty is, rather, that the pattern does not apply to the unsaturated expressions γ. There (I limit myself to concepts) it is disturbed by that dangling third entity, the concept correlate.

Assume now that concepts are existents. If so, they can be named and the pattern can be extended as follows. A γ expression, say, 'blond', denotes its extension and expresses its sense, which is the concept itself, which in turn is denoted by 'the concept blond'. With this emendation the same pattern applies to all three categories. Moreover, the need for concept correlates has disappeared.

The emendation is in substance the one Church proposed. With all the respect due to him, it does not seem very farfetched, at least by hindsight. Nor is it overdoing the respect we owe to Frege's ingenuity to believe that it was not, even by foresight, beyond his grasp. Why, then, one must ask, did he not take this almost obvious step? The answer I propose will not come as a surprise. He balked at the one assumption which as I have shown the step implies, namely, that concepts, though not objects, are yet full-fledged existents. This concludes the main argument of the section. I proceed to two comments.

First. Wells reports (*W* 546) Church to have argued as early as 1939, in a paper not generally accessible, that Frege's concepts are full-fledged existents. In other words, he disagreed sharply with my thesis. I am neither surprised nor disturbed. *As emended* by Church, the system is indeed no longer nominalistic in structure. That merely proves that Church is not a nominalist. It proves nothing about the system *as it stands*. I also grant and even insist that the emendation is nearly obvious. That explains why Church did not want to charge his master with what he must have considered a flaw. But it does not explain why Frege himself put up with an obvious and serious flaw rather than take Church's nearly obvious step. My thesis does explain that.

[15] Or, as one says rather, *the concept Peter*. It is obvious why I avoid that locution.

[16] Or, in intentional contexts, *that Peter is blond*.

Second. What can the realist do about Frege's problem? To answer, I first state the problem in the way it impressed itself upon Frege. Consider 'Fido is *a* dog'. If 'dog' and 'the concept dog' stood for the same entity, they would have to be interchangeable *salva veritate*. This is another principle Frege never questioned. Yet, 'Fido is *the* concept dog' is nonsense. (Frege, everyone knows, was tremendously and of course quite rightly impressed with the contrast between the definite and the indefinite article. That is why I changed the paradigm.) The concept correlates are an obvious way out of the difficulty. The realist does not need them. Admitting, for the sake of the argument, that 'dog' and 'the concept dog' stand for the same entity, he need not therefore abandon the principle. He merely adds the proviso, which I introduced in Section II, that whenever such a substitution is made, 'exemplifies' must, in the nature of things, be substituted for 'is'. In this way he obtains, quite smoothly, 'Fido exemplifies the concept dog'. The reason the realist finds this answer is that, unlike Frege who starts from mapping, he can do justice to that fundamental feature of our world from which he starts. Thus we are once more led back to the contrast between mapping and exemplification.

V

Consider 'This is red'. Frege and the realist agree that the demonstrative denotes an existent. By the realist's account, so does the adjective. Frege, we saw, disagrees, at least implicitly. The root of the matter, we also saw, is that he starts from mapping. The inspiration for this alternative to exemplification is mathematical. In this his nominalism is unique. All other varieties I know of—I am tempted to call them the ordinary varieties—operate with the doctrine of *common names*. Or, as I would rather say, there are really only two kinds of nominalism, Frege's and the doctrine of common names. The difference between the two is by no means negligible. Both kinds, though, in addition to being nominalisms, which to my mind is a weakness, share still another weakness. Neither does justice to the predicative 'is', which stands for exemplification. Both, therefore, more or less covertly take identity to be the fundamental meaning of 'is'. In Section II I showed this for Frege. In this section I shall show it for the doctrine of common names, first generally, then by analyzing an essay of Quine's.[17]

Assume that when I said 'This is red' I pointed at an individual, say,

[17] "Identity, Ostension, and Hypostasis," reprinted in *From a Logical Point of View* (Cambridge: Harvard University Press, 1953). References to this volume are by page number, preceded by the letter *Q*.

a red apple. The demonstrative and the adjective are both names of the apple. The only difference is that while the former is (serves as) a "proper name," the latter is a "common name." A proper name is a label arbitrarily attached to one and only one individual. A common name applies indifferently to each of several individuals, namely, all those sharing a character. This is the doctrine of common names. It runs into an objection and a difficulty.

A common name applies to an individual if and only if that individual has a certain character. Hence it is not an arbitrary label, in the sense in which a proper name is one, unless it be, as the realist insists and the nominalist denies, the name or label of the character itself. What, then, the realist asks the defender of the doctrine, is there "objectively" in or about each of the several individuals by virtue of which the common name is properly applied to each of them? Some nominalists answer (Q 68) that upon hearing and seeing a common name applied, we learn to apply it ourselves "by induction." The realist retorts that for such learning to occur, there must be a clue common to all individuals to which the learner hears and sees the common name applied. That leaves the issue where it was before. The doctrine of common names has no answer to this objection. Frege answered it, after a fashion, by insisting that functions, though not objects (existents), are yet "objective." That is why his nominalism is so superior to the other kind and, being superior, can remain "hidden." That much for the objection. The difficulty relates to what I am about.

Assume that an individual has two names, say 'Napoleon' and 'Bonaparte'. Consider 'Napoleon is Bonaparte'. In this sentence 'is' stands for identity. Generally, if an individual has two names, what way is there of combining them into a sentence except by the 'is' of identity? This suggests that proponents of the doctrine may be tempted to assimilate the predicative 'is' to that of identity. Notice that I just spoke of names, without distinction between common and proper ones. I did this because I do not really understand what it means for a word to be a common name. Or, to say the same thing differently, a name, in the only use of the term I understand, is a word attached as a label to one and only one entity. Or, still differently, in the manner of speaking I wish to discourage, every name, whatever it may name, is a proper name. Notice, second, that I spoke of suggestion. In other words, not every proponent of the doctrine asserts that in 'This is red' the copula stands for identity. To claim anything of the sort would be unreasonable indeed. For is it not the very purpose of the doctrine of common names to prevent this collapse of the two uses of 'is'? Only its proponents still somehow think of "common names" as "names." Therein, I claim, lies a temptation, or a suggestion, or perhaps even a compulsion in the direction of that collapse. This claim is not at all unreasonable. To substantiate it, I shall present two series of comments, the first about classical (Aristotelian) logic, the second about the essay by Quine.

1. For Aristotle, there is an important difference between 'This is green' and 'Socrates is a man'. For my purpose the difference does not matter. Even so, consider the second sentence, if only because everyone knows that classical logic cannot cope with it except by the device of subsuming it, rather artificially, under the A-sentence. To do that is to construe the predicative 'is' as the 'is' (or 'are') of the A-, E-, I-, and O-sentences. For Aristotle, this third use of 'is' is the fundamental one. It is, if I may so put it, the only one for which he can account. (Frege and the realist both construe it as a combination of two predicative uses with a quantifier.) Be that as it may, formally or logically the device does the trick. But it does not even touch the heart of the difficulty, which is ontological rather than logical. Within the hylomorphic scheme, the problem of individuation is insoluble.[18] One may of course abandon individuals. That is the way Scotus took. But it can be argued that in taking it he also abandoned hylomorphism. The original terminists did not wish to go that far. Yet they faced up to the Parmenidean illusion, which is one of the roots, if not perhaps the root, of the classical difficulty, that every occurrence of the copula indicates an identity. Moreover, they insisted, like Frege, that any two names of an individual must be substitutable for each other *salva veritate* in all contexts; and they noticed that, say, 'this' and 'red' are not so substitutable. Thus they were led to the distinction which is the core of their doctrine of signification. *Connotatively*, they held, the adjective signifies indifferently each of the several red things; *denotatively* it, or, rather, its abstractum 'redness', signifies the character itself. Deny now that characters are existents. Then there is nothing for the adjective (or its abstractum) to signify denotatively and you arrive at the doctrine of common names. This is the step Ockham took.

[18] This is by now at least a respectable opinion. See, for all this, "Some Remarks on the Ontology of Ockham," *Philosophical Review*, 53, 1954, 560–71, and also pp. 144–54 of this book; "Russell's Examination of Leibniz Examined," *Philosophy of Science*, 23, 1956, 175–203, and also pp. 155–88 of this book; "Some Remarks on the Philosophy of Malebranche," *The Review of Metaphysics*, 10, 1956, 207–26, and also pp. 189–204 of this book. Leibniz, it is true, manages to accommodate both kinds of existent. But he pays the price of having to maintain that in a sense every predication is analytic (*Predicatum inest subjecto*).

2. An apple is, in a familiar sense, spatio-temporally extended. Its color and shape, as the realist conceives them, are not. For Quine, to be an existent and to be spatio-temporally extended, or, as for brevity's sake I shall say, to be extended or an extension, are one and the same thing. This is the guiding idea of his ontology. It has an important corollary. The *sum* of any number of extensions is itself extended. Roughly, sum here means set-theoretical sum. Precisely, it is the function axiomatized in the so-called meromorphic calculus. This subtlety we can safely ignore. Notice, though, that the notion of a function, in the Fregean sense of the term, is needed to state the intuitive core of this ontology.

Assume now once more that, pointing at an apple, I say 'This is red'. Or for that matter, assume that, pointing at a certain volume of water, I say 'This is the Iowa River'. Quine holds (Q 69) that there is in principle no difference between the two "ostensions." Just as the Iowa River is the sum of certain watery extensions, so the color may be thought of as the sum of all red ones. Which extensions we are meant to sum we learn in either case "by induction" from watching what is being pointed at (Q 68). Pointing, however, is ambiguous (Q 67). Taking advantage of the ambiguity, Quine says that one who speaks and points as by assumption I do "identifies" for the purposes of the discourse what he points at with the sum in question (Q 71). Notice how subtle it all is. Quine does not tell us that the copula in 'This is red' stands for identity. Of course he doesn't. As a logician, he knows better than that. Yet he says obliquely, by means of the opaque metaphor of "identification," that what I really point at is the sum. If this were so and if the color could be conceived as the sum in question, then 'This is red' would indeed state an identity.

Quine is convinced that nobody in his right mind would "hypostatize" characters as the realist does. So he must explain why such hypostasis ever seemed plausible. The explanation takes the form of an anthropological fable. Its hero is misled by a faulty analogy (Q 73). As it happens, some adjectives may be thought of as standing for a sum of extensions. So he is led to hope that this is so for all adjectives. Quine constructs a simple universe in which the sum of all triangles coincides with the sum of all squares (Q 72). Negatively, this frustrates that hope. Positively, we are told (Q 75) that "in ostensively explaining 'square' . . . we say each time 'This is square' *without* imputing identity of indicated object from one occasion to the next." Again the metaphor is opaque. I do not really know what it means to impute identity. I do know, though, that we are left with two alternatives. Either 'square' stands for a character as the realist conceives it; or, even though there is no such character, we learn "inductively" how to use the common name. Quine rejects the first alternative, chooses the second (Q 75). Thus he lays himself open to the classical objection which I rehearsed earlier.

Quine's nominalism is clearly a doctrine of common names. That makes it very different from Frege's. Yet there are also two points of contact. The first is that, sums being functions, the Fregean notion of function is an ingredient of the intuitive core of the doctrine. The other point of contact seems at first rather verbal. Quine is fond of the formula that while sentences are either true or false, a predicate is either true or false *of* something. For Frege, we remember, the predicative 'is' is merely a clumsily disguised 'of'. Ofness, if I may coin a word, thus plays a crucial role in both systems. One may wonder whether this similarity is merely a chance product of the idiom.

Some Reflections on Time*

ONE who seriously philosophizes over any length of time inevitably weaves a *pattern*. These patterns used to be called systems. Today many philosophers, including myself, dislike the word. Some even deny the fact. I shall therefore simply speak of my pattern. Such patterns may in turn be arranged into patterns. These pattern patterns are the several *traditions* or styles. Traditions may be labeled. But again, within my tradition at least, it is nowadays considered bad strategy to make too much of labels. So I shall merely say that my pattern belongs to the analytical tradition and that, as I use this label, it applies not only to the patterns of Russell and Wittgenstein but also to those of Brentano and G. E. Moore and, reaching further back, to those of Locke and Leibniz.

Philosophical questions about time are as crucial as they are difficult. Since they are difficult, they cannot be answered while the listener stands on one foot. Since they are crucial, a serious philosopher must not dodge them. In trying to answer them, or some of them, even in a long essay, he will, therefore, if he is also prudent, insist on an assumption and a limitation. He will assume at least some familiarity with his pattern and he will limit himself to arguments and answers within it. In principle I shall make the assumption. In practice I shall mitigate its rigor by a hint here and a digression there. If these don't suffice, the reader will have to turn to what has been said elsewhere.[1] As it happens two of the most detailed expositions so far have appeared in Italy.[2]

---

* Il Tempo (*Archivio di Filosofia, Padova: Cedam, 1958*), pp. 49–82. *Reprinted by permission.*

[1] E.g., *The Metaphysics of Logical Positivism*, hereafter cited as MLP, followed by a numeral to indicate the essay referred to.

[2] "Logical Positivism, Language, and the Reconstruction of Metaphysics," *Rivista critica di storia della filosofia*, 8, 1953, 435–52, which is MLP3; and, particularly, "Intentionality," *Semantica* (Archivio di Filosofia, Roma: Bocca, 1955), pp. 177–216, and also pp. 3–38 of this book.

That much for the assumption. As far as the limitation is concerned, I shall throw all caution to the winds. Naturally, I shall speak within my pattern. Nobody can really do anything else. But I shall also try to exhibit the full dialectic of time within the analytical tradition. Such boldness, not to be sheer temerity, ought to have a compelling *motive* as well as some *hope* of success.

Each philosophy implies a metaphilosophy. Less succinctly, a pattern cannot be both adequate and fully articulated unless it contains an account of its author's *method*. Mine is the ideal language method. For brevity's sake I shall simply call it the method, just as in speaking of my pattern and the analytical tradition I shall often call them the pattern and the tradition. The tradition has always been method conscious. At present it is even more so. I provide therefore the first of the promised hints by stating the idea of the method.[3] A word or phrase may be used either nonphilosophically (commonsensically, ordinarily) or philosophically. All philosophical uses require explication. In explicating one, the practitioner of the method talks commonsensically about the structure and interpretation of an artificial language or schema. His goal is to find a schema, called the ideal language, L, by means of which all philosophical uses can be explicated, or, what amounts to the same thing, all philosophical problems can be solved. In choosing his L, a philosopher chooses the substantive part of his pattern. But he is not, merely by adopting the method, committed to the choice of any particular L. In this sense the method is neutral, or at least, it is more nearly neutral than others.[4] This is why I *hope* that I shall not utterly fail in the ambitious task I have set myself of exhibiting the full dialectic of time not only within the pattern but also within the tradition.

Some patterns of the tradition are antisubstantialist; some are not. Mine certainly is. If it were not, I could not within it answer certain questions about time. (This is one very good reason for calling these questions crucial.) Yet I am also convinced that, after a fashion, time is the substance of the world. Clearly, that is merely an aphorism; at

---

[3] For a defense of the method against its recent critics, see "The Revolt against Logical Atomism," *Philosophical Quarterly*, 7, 1957, 323–39, and 8, 1958, 1–13, and also pp. 39–72 of this book.

[4] I have myself applied the method to such apparently unlikely candidates as Leibniz and Malebranche. See "Russell's Examination of Leibniz Examined," *Philosophy of Science*, 23, 1956, 175–203, and also pp. 155–88 of this book; and "Some Remarks on the Philosophy of Malebranche," *The Review of Metaphysics*, 10, 1956, 207–26, and also pp. 189–204 of this book. Some of the points of the Leibniz study are briefly restated and further developed in the first part of this essay.

worst, it is a paradox; at best, a formula. Its sole purpose is to spot a certain tension. The desire to face this tension is the *motive* that compels me. It will indeed transpire that in a sense this essay as a whole is the explication of that formula.

Philosophical questions have a way of clustering. 'Ontology' and 'epistemology' are convenient labels for two major clusters. The first part of this essay deals mainly with ontological questions; the second, mainly with epistemological ones. In the third and last part I shall face that tension. In the first two parts I shall speak as an analyst. The third part is speculative, though not, of course, in the sense in which another tradition may be so labeled. (Plotinus' and Hegel's are important patterns in that tradition.) So, perhaps, I had better say that in the third part I shall present some reflections, anthropological ones, if you please, about the nature of the analytical enterprise.

I

Is time absolute or is it relative? This is the traditional wording of the main question. I would rather ask whether time is or is not relational. But I shall use the old words. Every relativist holds that moments do not *exist*. All relativists except one hold that (some) temporal relations do exist and that no nonrelational temporal character does. (The exception is Leibniz. Of him later.) Some absolutists may hold that, in addition to moments, some temporal relations and, perhaps, nonrelational characters also exist. Some others may hold that only moments exist. Call the former and the latter moderate and extreme absolutists respectively. Theirs is a family quarrel. The main issue lies between the relativist and the absolutist. This issue, or question, is inseparable from four others. What is an *individual?* Do individuals exist? What is a *substance?* Do substances exist? The uses I just made of 'exist', 'individual', and 'substance' are of course philosophical. (That is why I italicized their first occurrences. I shall continue the practice and as far as that is possible avoid the ordinary uses of these words.) Thus they require explication. That is my cue for a longish digression.

I begin by stating some features of L. (I reserve this abbreviation for the ideal language (IL) of my pattern.) 1. Each undefined (synonymously: primitive) sign (of L) is of one and only one of two kinds. It is either logical or descriptive. 2. L is a subject-predicate schema. That means two things. It means, first, that each sentence containing only undefined descriptive signs (uds) is of one of the forms $\phi^1(\alpha)$, $\phi^2(\alpha, \beta)$, $\phi^3(\alpha, \beta, \gamma)$, and so on; each Greek letter marking the place of a uds. It means, second, that after abbreviations have been eliminated, these are the only places at which uds can enter into sentences. The ϕ-place is called the predicate place; the others, subject places. ϕ^1 marks (the place of) a nonrelational predicate; the other ϕ's, relational ones. A world or pattern whose IL possesses this feature I call a subject-predicate world or pattern. 3. Some uds may occupy the predicate place in one sentence and a subject place in another. Some others never occupy the predicate place. These latter are called "particulars." 4. Each uds is attached to one and only one thing; as a label, as I prefer to say; or, as one also says, as a "proper name." 5. The IL of some patterns in the tradition is the schema of *Principia Mathematica* (PM), supplemented by classes of uds. L is not this schema. However, it contains a very large part that is. Call this part L_1. What must be added to L_1 to make it L, or, if I may so express myself, the difference between L and L_1 is needed for an adequate philosophy of mind and meaning.[5] For the ontology (not: the epistemology!) of time, however, this difference makes no difference. To say the same thing in another way, in the first part of this essay L_1 could stand in for L.

The fifth point is a rather general comment for which this is a convenient place. The fourth concerns the interpretation of L. All the rest of the preceding paragraph is syntactical. Accordingly, not a single word in the paragraph is italicized (used philosophically). 'Particular' is surrounded by double quotes because the sentence in which it occurs explains a rather technical yet purely syntactical and therefore nonphilosophical use. 'Proper name' might have been italicized; for it also has philosophical uses (as, by the way, has 'particular'). In some contexts these uses are crucial indeed.[6] But I do not and shall not so use either of these two words. Now for a string of explications. In presenting them I shall not argue for the adequacy of any I have proposed before. If I did that, I would not merely digress but rewrite what may be found elsewhere. Except for the word to be explicated, each sentence containing an explication will be italicized.

Ontology is a search for simples, i.e., for the kinds of things of which, in some sense of 'consist', all others consist. This idea controls the philosophical use of 'exist'. To exist or to be an existent, therefore, is to be an (ontological) *simple*. This use of 'simple' is itself philosophical. Its explication is syntactical. *A thing is* simple *if and only if it is or (by the rules for the interpretation of L) could be named by a uds.* Now we are

---

[5] See "Intentionality."

[6] Concerning *particularity*, see "Particularity and the New Nominalism," *Methodos*, 6, 1954, 131–47, and also pp. 91–105 of this book; concerning *names*, "Frege's Hidden Nominalism," *Philosophical Review*, 67, 1958, 437–59, and also pp. 205–24 of this book.

in a position to explicate 'existent'. *An* existent *is what is or could be named by a uds (of L)*. An *individual* is an existent that is *concrete*. Since this sentence contains two as yet unexplicated philosophical uses, it cannot qualify as the explication of either. *An existent is* concrete *if and only if it is or could be named by a particular (zero-level uds of L)*.[7] This explication I have not proposed before. So I shall argue it presently. *An* individual *is an existent that is concrete*. 'Substance' has a strong and a weak philosophical use. The explication of the strong use, which is also the classical one, has four parts. S_1. Substances are individuals. S_2. Substances are continuants. S_3. Substances are capable of existing *independently*. S_4. Substances have *natures*. In the weak sense (S_1 and S_2), *a* substance *is an individual that is a continuant*. My concern in this essay is with the weaker notion. So we need not tarry to explicate 'independently' and 'substance'. These philosophical uses are explored elsewhere.[8] Notice, finally, that I did not italicize 'continuant'. The word is a bit technical; that does not make every use of it philosophical. Commonsensically, and that is the way I mean it, a continuant is simply a thing such as a stone or an apple that persists in time.

These explications all rest on certain features of *L*. Yet I undertook to display the dialectic of time not only within my pattern but within the tradition. That calls for comment. The ILs of some patterns in the tradition share the relevant features of *L*. Some others don't. The point is that many, if perhaps not all, of these latter ILs have parts that do share those features and that only these parts matter for the ontology of time, just as within my pattern only L_1 matters. The coverage of the present analysis, if perhaps not complete, is thus much wider than it may seem. That concludes the digression. I shall next state the absolutist's and the relativist's position and show what each involves. Eventually I shall take sides. Of course I shall. But I shall postpone the decision as long as possible. For I know of no better way to find out what depends on what and on what grounds one may or must eventually choose.

Extensionless points are not existents but an invention of the geometricians. More precisely, they are entities (I use the word without

---

[7] The explication goes naturally with two others so obvious that they belong at most in a footnote. *A (relational or nonrelational)* character *is what is or could be referred to by a (relational or nonrelational) predicate expression. An existent is* abstract *if and only if it is not concrete*. It follows that primitive characters are abstract. The qualification, primitive, is necessary because upon our explication of 'exist' compound characters do not exist. For the key to the phenomenalism-realism issue which this distinction offers, see MLP6.

[8] See "Russell's Examination of Leibniz Examined," also for the involvement of natures (strong substances) with time.

ontological commitment) of axiomatic calculi. Or, at best, they can be defined in terms of existents, as Russell and some of his contemporaries tried to define them, by what they called the method of extensive abstraction. As with space, so with time. A moment is a specious present. Durationless moments or instants, as I shall call them, are on a par with extensionless points. Yet I shall for a while ignore the distinction and treat moments as if they were instants. And I shall employ the same strategy of neglecting temporarily what eventually must be attended to by proceeding as if every one were agreed that no nonrelational temporal character exists. The advantage of the strategy is the one just mentioned. It brings out what depends on what.

Moments are individuals. This is the absolutist's thesis. More precisely, it is the moderate half, the other half being that moments are the only temporal things named by uds. I omit the extreme half because I want to give the absolutist a run for his money. Moments are ordered. If one treats them as instants, then their order is linear. Such an order can only be generated by a precedence relation. If he knows what he is about, an absolutist will therefore be moderate. That is, he will hold that in addition to particulars naming moments, his IL contains an undefined descriptive predicate sign ('*pr*') which transcribes 'earlier than'. Or, what amounts to the same thing, he will admit that in addition to moments at least one relational temporal character exists. *The two relational characters of being earlier ('pr') and being simultaneous ('sim') are the only temporal existents.* This is the relativist's thesis. Whether or not the two relations can be defined in terms of a single one is merely a mathematical nicety with which we need not bother.[9]

An absolutist may or may not hold that there are substances (S_1 and S_2). Most, if not all, absolutists assert that there are. A consistent relativist is committed to holding that there are none. To see why this is so, consider a continuant (S_2), say, an apple. If it is to be a substance, it must be an individual (S_1). Its name, therefore, is a particular, say, '*a*'. Continuants at different moments exemplify different characters. Now, i.e., at a certain moment (t_2), the apple is red ('*rd*'); at some earlier moment (t_1) it was not red but green. The absolutist has no trouble in transcribing these two English sentences into a subject-predicate scheme. He writes '*rd* (a, t_2)' for the first, '$\sim$*rd* (a, t_1)' for (the crucial part of) the second. Call an individual that is not a moment, such as our apple, an ordinary individual. Notice that in this pattern no ordi-

---

[9] The absolutist naturally will define simultaneity as occupancy of the same moment. But, then, how about the analysis (transcription) of the occupancy relation?

nary individual exemplifies a nonrelational character. The color mentioned in the paradigm, for instance, has become a relation between an ordinary individual and a moment.[10] Similarly, the distance (at a moment!) between, say, two apples becomes a ternary relation; and so on. As we ordinarily speak and think, 'green' is a nonrelational predicate; 'this (apple) is green', a complete sentence, even though we may, if we wish, tack a temporal determination on to it by means of an adverbial clause. To one whose linguistic imagination cannot soar above his idiom the absolutist's transcription will thus seem odd. One not so limited understands that the alleged oddity is not a weakness but, rather, a strength of the transcription, namely, the strength or virtue of exhibiting a major consequence of the absolutist's gambit. The relativist, who knows no individuals that are moments, cannot possibly construe the color as a relational character. That makes, in his IL, 'red' a nonrelational predicate and '$rd\ (a)$' a complete sentence. Moreover, '$rd\ (a)$' and '$\sim rd\ (a)$' are the only transcriptions available to him for the two English sentences of the paradigm. Since the latter are both true their counterparts, too, ought to be true; otherwise the transcription is not adequate. But '$rd\ (a)$' and '$\sim rd\ (a)$' contradict each other as, of course, '$rd\ (a,\ t_2)$' and '$\sim rd\ (a,\ t_1)$' do not. The relativist, it follows, cannot consistently hold that there are substances. This is the connection between time and substance. It is as spectacular as it is, or ought to be, familiar.

There is also a dialectical tie between individuality and time. It is more subtle and not at all familiar. My next task is to explain this tie. That requires four preparatory steps.

First. While engaged on the task, I shall proceed as if the relativist were right. Quite independent of one's eventual decision, this is the only proper way to proceed. For, while all relativists are committed to the thesis that there are no substances, they are not at all committed to the quite different and much more radical one that there are no individuals. The only thing a consistent relativist must insist on is that individuals, if there be any, undergo no changes. (This tenet is often expressed by the formula that the relativist's individuals are momentary existents, or, what amounts to the same thing, that they are wholly contained in a specious present. To the blur here between moment and instance I shall attend later.) Such individuals do in fact occur in all patterns of

---

[10] This is of course not the occupancy relation mentioned in the preceding note. For the proper transcription of a statement that ascribes a "permanent" character (attribute) to an individual, see "Russell's Examination of Leibniz Examined."

the tradition. Even the left-wing patterns recognize, either implicitly or explicitly, the individuality of sensa. In a right-wing pattern such as mine, awarenesses are also construed as individuals.[11]

Second. Individuals are *in* time; characters are *timeless.*[12] The formula is familiar. No doubt it is also convenient. Presently I shall employ it myself. Yet, the two italicized uses are metaphorical. That does not necessarily make them philosophical uses. But the latter have a way of either springing from or hiding behind metaphors as rudimentary and therefore inconspicuous as these two. So we had better ask what literal sense the relativist can make of them. In all patterns of the tradition '*pr*' and '*sim*' are predicates of the first type. Individuals are therefore the only existents that could possibly exemplify them. This is the literal sense of the metaphor that individuals are "in time." Similarly, green ('*gr*') and red are in these patterns construed as first-level characters. That makes such expressions as '*pr(gr, rd)*' syntactical nonsense. Generally, characters, of whatever level and whether defined or undefined, cannot, on syntactical grounds alone, exemplify either of the two temporal existents. This is the literal sense of the metaphor that characters are timeless. So explicated, the formula is harmless enough. Only, the explication also shows how it may mislead us. Consider two sensa which are tones. Jointly they exemplify one of the two relations higher-in-pitch and equal-in-pitch. The transcription of 'green is a middle *c*' is ill formed (syntactical nonsense). If we followed the suggestion of the formula, we would therefore say that tones are "in pitch" and that colors are "pitchless." Yet we do not say this sort of thing. That shows how the formula may mislead by setting time spuriously apart. From where the relativist stands, the two temporal relations, no matter how pervasively exemplified, are just characters among characters, existents among existents. Thus, if the relativist looks for a formula, I suggest: Time (and space) are in the world. The absolutist, we shall see, willingly embraces its converse: The world is in time (and space). (I mention space because what goes for time in this respect *mutatis mutandis* goes for space.)

Third. (The relativist's) individuals are in time. Each of them is "wholly contained in" a moment. The phrase between quotation marks is another rudimentary metaphor. But it is harmless. The use of 'mo-

---

[11] See "Intentionality." For some observations on the differences between the two wings and their consequences, see "The Revolt against Logical Atomism."

[12] To be *eternal*, in the traditional sense of 'eternal', is not the same as to be timeless.

ment' is commonsensical. Thus the relativist need not avoid it. But it may help if I say instead that each individual is attached to one and only one segment (of time). Characters, being timeless, are not so attached. That is, they may be exemplified by individuals attached to different segments. Let now 'a' and 'f_1' name an individual and a character respectively, the latter not being exemplified by the former nor by any other individual attached to the same segment as the former. The sentence '$\sim f_1 (a)$' is well formed. Nor do we get into trouble by asserting it. In other words, we need not and do not hesitate to predicate, negatively, of an individual a character which it does not exemplify and which may not be exemplified at all in the individual's segment. Call this the *Principle of Negative Predication*.

Fourth. Could there be a world without individuals? If so, could it contain time? These are questions of pure or speculative[13] ontology. The method reconstructs them as questions about schemata. An individual (of a world), we remember, is what is or could be named by a zero-level uds of the IL (of this world). All one needs to do, therefore, in order to construct (the IL of) a world without individuals, is to modify PM so that the type hierarchy of the modified schema is of the order $\ldots -2, -1, 0, 1, 2, \ldots$, and then add to it classes of uds such that there is no lowest type level to which some of these uds are assigned.[14] Since all this can be easily done, the answer to the first question is Yes. The second question we reconstruct as follows: Can the schema just described consistently contain two relational uds—call them again 'pr' and 'sim'—which establish a linear order (with coincidence) among the expressions of *some* type? To obtain the answer, notice, first, that in such a world it would again make sense to say that the things ordered are in time, each being attached to one and only one segment (of time), while the things of all other levels, not being so attached, are timeless. Call the attached things 'a', 'b', and so on; assume, second, that their type number is zero. Since there is no lowest type, this is merely a notational convention. Notice, third, that in this world an attached thing cannot only, as in ours, exemplify a timeless thing, namely, one of type 1, but also *be* exemplif*ied* by a timeless thing, namely, one of type -1. Let f_1^{-1} be a thing of this latter kind, a and b two zero-level things attached to different moments. f_1^{-1} being unat-

[13] This use of 'speculative' is different from the two others that occurred before; one in 'speculative tradition', the other in 'speculative anthropology'.

[14] For details, see "The Revolt against Logical Atomism." The "logic" of such a world is the same as ours. For this, see "Analyticity," *Theoria*, 24, 1958, 71–93, and also pp. 73–90 of this book.

tached, 'a $(f_1{}^{-1})$' and 'b $(f_1{}^{-1})$' may both be true. Suppose that they are. Suppose, finally, that an inhabitant of this world wants to state what is presented to him in the segment of, say, b.[15] He will surely assert 'b $(f_1{}^{-1})$'. But if he relies on the Principle of Negative Predication, he will (or may) also assert '$\sim a$ $(f_1{}^{-1})$'. Thus he is up against a contradiction. The only way to avoid it is to exclude as ill-formed the negations of all sentences in which the name of a thing that is in time occurs in the predicate place.

The pending question can now be answered. A world without individuals cannot contain time. More precisely, it cannot contain time unless we are prepared, as of course we are not, to sacrifice the Principle of Negative Predication. This is the answer. It is also the explanation of the connection between time and individuality. Nor is that the only reward for having climbed the four preparatory steps. I am ready to gather another loose end by presenting the promised argument for the proposed explication of 'concrete'.

(1) Individuals are concrete; characters, abstract. (2) Individuals can be pointed at, characters cannot. Both formulae are familiar. In (1) all four uses are philosophical. Some students, having grown suspicious of such uses, offer (2) as an explication of (1). That is, they propose the following explication of 'concrete' and 'abstract': (3) What is concrete (abstract) is what can (cannot) be pointed at. Ignore (3) for the time being and attend to (2). As it stands, (2) fails of its purpose. To see that, assume for the sake of the argument that apples are individuals. Suppose that I looked and, as one usually says, pointed at a red apple. When I looked, I saw both the individual and the character, that is, two things and not one. How, then, will you decide at which of the two I pointed? If you can't, and I am convinced that you can't, then (2) has failed of its purpose. I suggest, therefore, that those who propose (2) as an explication of (1) use on this occasion 'pointing' so that a thing can be pointed at if and only if it is "in" (space and) time. (Ordinarily, one would rather say: occupies an area in space and time.) Consider now that the connection between individuality and time may be stated as follows. (4) If there is to be time (in a subject-predicate world), then there *must* be a lowest type; and the things of this level are the only ones which are "in" time. Recall next the proposed explication of 'concrete': An existent is concrete if and only if it is (or could be) named by a uds of the lowest type. Reflect on this proposal in conjunction with

[15] The sentence would benefit from explanation. This explanation, together with that of the connection between individuality and identity, may be found in "Individuals," *Philosophical Studies*, 9, 1958, 78–85, and also pp. 124–31 of this book.

(1), (2), (3), (4) and you will see that it does state commonsensically what those who struggled with the philosophical uses of 'concrete' tried to express. That concludes the argument I promised. But it will pay later if we pursue right now its line of thought a bit further.

In unexplicated philosophical use, we just saw, 'concrete' pairs off with 'individual'; 'abstract' with 'character'. There are other such connections or associations. I wish to examine two of them. (A) "The concrete exists, the abstract doesn't." This is one of the two. Joining it to (1) in the last paragraph, one obtains: "Individuals exist, characters don't." That rebuilds *one* verbal bridge which may lead one from the unexplicated use of 'concrete' and 'abstract' to nominalism. Nominalism is absurd, of course.[16] Be that as it may, there is still *another* such bridge. Its far or nominalistic end is the formula "To exist is to be in (space and) time," which happens to be the hidden, or, perhaps, not so hidden core of Quine's ontology.[17] To build the bridge, consider what was said in the last paragraph about the use of 'pointing' in (2). (B) "Individuals exist independently, characters dependently." This is the second association I wish to examine. It is more subtle, if only because we stand here at the point of confluence of two unexplicated uses. (B1) One of these occurs in S_3, i.e., in the explication of 'substance'. The idea is that, in some philosophical sense of 'create' or 'produce', individuals create or produce the characters they exemplify. To pursue this idea is one thing; to be a nominalist is another. The nominalistic slant, if any, is therefore more subtle in this case. To show that there actually is or was one, I make a historical comment. Patterns containing the idea also tend to contain the distinction between attributes, i.e., characters as exemplified, and characters as such. And, whatever the wording may be, in patterns containing the latter distinction, characters as such are not, or at least not in the relevant sense, existents. According to one classical wording, they "exist" as "eternal" things in the mind of God. (B2) "If there were no characters, there still somehow could be individuals; but if there were no individuals, there could be no characters." This is the idea behind the other philosophical use of 'dependent' and 'independent'. This time, the nominalistic slant is less subtle. The idea itself is irremediably confused. Using 'exist' as it has been and I believe must be explicated, I hold of course that both individuals and (simple) characters exist. That is not to say that they

[16] To see that, one merely has to consider what the nominalistic thesis becomes upon reconstruction: All uds of the IL are of type zero. The only serious attempt to meet this condition is Goodman's. For criticism, see MLP5 and "Particularity and the New Nominalism."

[17] See "Frege's Hidden Nominalism."

are alike in *all* respects which concern the ontologist. On the other hand, just as I have never encountered a character which was not exemplified, so I have never come across an individual which did not exemplify some character. Both alternatives are equally absurd. In *this* respect individuals and characters are alike. That is why I called the idea irremediably confused.

Let us take stock. I divided the analytical task by three stratagems. I left to one side the question of nonrelational temporal existents. I delayed the decision between absolutist and relativist. I treated moments as if they were instants. I shall now take up these matters in this order.

The full phrase, nonrelational temporal existent, is long and clumsy. I shall save breath and ink by speaking instead of temporal qualities (tqs). Their one great defender was Leibniz. In examining their case we may therefore as well start from his pattern. Tqs are the only temporal existents. That is his thesis. Being exemplified by individuals, tqs are of the first level. Any particular tq is the property of being-at-that-(particular)-moment.[18] Are there such things? Once more, I delay the decision, calling attention instead to two further propositions. (1) Temporal relations do not exist. (2) Moments do not exist. They are equally obvious corollaries. Yet their import, we shall see, is quite different.

Concerning (1). The proposition also follows directly from the more general thesis that no relation exists. The major intellectual motive for this thesis was undoubtedly Leibniz's concern with aseity (B1). Its major consequence was a logical error. Or, perhaps the error came first, lending credence to the thesis. That is beside my point. To discover the error, reconstruct the thesis: Relations can all be defined in terms of qualities. Hence, in particular, all temporal relations can be defined in terms of tqs. That is what Leibniz believed. That was his error. Since it is logical, or, if I may so express myself, since it is merely logical, one may want to correct it in order to see what then becomes of his ontological gambit. The only "correction" I can think of is thoroughly against the spirit of his pattern. But that is again beside the point. The alternative to which we are thus led is interesting in its own right. The correction itself is obvious. The tqs must be ordered in the familiar manner by

---

[18] Some may wonder whether I am here dismissing out of hand such alleged tqs as presentness, pastness, and futurity. In a sense I do; in a sense I don't. They do not at any rate belong in this context, at least not within my pattern. See Part Three. The statements about Leibniz are not only most succinct but remain here of necessity unsupported by evidence. For the latter, see "Russell's Examination of Leibniz Examined."

introducing two simple relations of the second level. That yields the following alternative: Temporal qualities as well as temporal relations exist; moments do not exist. Could there be substances in such a world? I have shown elsewhere that the answer is No.

Concerning (2). The alternative pattern we have come upon is remarkably similar to the moderate absolutist's. In the latter we find a class of zero-level things (moments) ordered by two simple first-level relations. In the former, we find a class of nonrelational first-level things, the tqs, ordered by two simple relations which are the "same" as before, except of course that they now appear on the second level. The only difference is in the type level. With respect to substance it is decisive. The moderate absolutist can have substances. In Leibniz's world, with or without the correction, one really can't. This, however, Leibniz did not know. With respect to time itself, on the other hand, the difference seems rather slight. Why, then, one must ask, did it seem so momentous to him and, surely, not to him alone. The key to the answer is in what was said about nominalism. Leibniz did not invent relativism, of course. But he was its most vigorous defender against the innovator Newton. This vigor, I submit, fed on a source even deeper than the manifest issue. To unearth it, remember that one not completely immune to the lure of nominalism will want to say that if there were no individuals there could be no characters, though not conversely (B2). What Leibniz actually said was that if there were no (ordinary) individuals there could be no time. So he had to deny that moments are (temporal) individuals. In this he may have been right or wrong. We shall see. But, whether he was wrong or right, if my diagnosis is correct, then he was, because of the implicit nominalistic slant of his pattern, at least implicitly wrong in another respect. Some (spatial and) temporal things are just existents among existents. This, at least implicitly, he denied.

Do moments exist? I am ready to state what I think are the only proper grounds for the decision. What exists, in the relevant sense of 'exist', is what is or could be named by a uds. When, then, may a uds appear in the IL? The rule here appealed to, in my pattern but surely not just in mine, is known as the Principle[19] of Acquaintance (PA): A uds must not occur unless it names a thing with which we are "directly acquainted." At this point everyone can and must decide for himself. I, for one, am not directly acquainted with any nonrelational temporal

---

[19] A "principle" cannot be defended directly but only indirectly. For what this means, see MLP, *passim;* also "Elementarism," *Philosophy and Phenomenological Research*, 18, 1957, 107–14, and also pp. 115–23 of this book.

thing, be it either individual or character, either physical or phenomenal. More simply, I would not really know what 'Now' meant if I could not so analyze it that it stands for being simultaneous with either this or that, as the case may be. This and this alone is the ground on which I take my stand with the relativist. Nor did I in stating it merely disclaim direct acquaintance with moments. Rather, I disclaimed any such acquaintance with all nonrelational temporal things, adding two clauses: be they either individuals or characters; be they either physical or phenomenal. The first clause expresses the opinion that as far as time itself is concerned, the issue is not so much whether moments exist but, rather, whether there are any nonrelational temporal existents. If this opinion is justified, then there is a sense in which Leibniz must be counted an absolutist. That may seem paradoxical. I don't think that it is. The analyses of time, substance, individuality and the nominalism issue are inseparably connected. What is so connected nonetheless can and must be analytically distinguished. The apparent paradox indicates that when Leibniz fought his great battle with the Newtonians these distinctions were not yet as sharp as we can now make them. That much for the first of the two clauses. I turn to the second.

'Directly acquainted', the operative phrase in the PA, has two uses. That is why I surrounded it with double quotes. Both these uses are commonsensical. That is why I did not italicize the phrase. In one use, we are directly acquainted with physical objects and some of the properties and relations they exemplify. This use, call it the first, is no doubt the most frequent. In the other use, phenomenal things are the only ones we are directly acquainted with. This use, call it the second, is more technical and less frequent. That does not make it a philosophical use. Which of the two yields a viable PA? That is a celebrated argument. Carried on according to the method, it reconstructs (part of) what is at stake between the traditional realists and the traditional phenomenalists. Hence the following two explications: *To select the first use as the one proper in PA is to propose a* realistic *IL. To select the second is to propose a* phenomenalistic *IL.* With these explications to fall back upon, let me for a moment speak traditionally. Realism[20] versus phenomenalism is a major issue. It cuts rather deep, as one says. The issues of time lie even deeper. This is a point of considerable importance. To grasp it firmly one merely has to inquire whether a realist and a phenomenalist can consistently agree that there are no nonrelational tem-

---

[20] This is of course not the use in which realism and nominalism are contradictories. The distinction is so familiar that I do not bother to mark it.

poral things, either physical or phenomenal, with which we are directly acquainted. The answer is Yes. This is the point.

Take a phenomenal field so simple that it contains only two color spots; one is red and in the center; the other blue and some way to the right. The blue spot grows brighter; otherwise nothing changes. Or, perhaps, the blue spot moves from the right to the left of the other; otherwise again nothing changes. In either case, the change occurs in a specious present. Consider now a phenomenalistic schema. (*L* is such a schema; though I am of course not a phenomenalist in the traditional sense.) Its particulars, '*a*', '*b*', and so on, name such things as color spots in a specious present. Attach '*a*' to the red spot, i.e., the one which does not change. There will be no trouble. But if you attach both '*a*' and '*b*', the former as before, the latter to the blue spot, you will run into the contradiction of the apple which was once green and is now red. I call it the contradiction of the apple because the logical difficulty is exactly the same. So I shall not bother to explain it once more. The situation calls for comments. I shall make four.

First. The relativist's individuals do not and must not undergo any change whatsoever. To ensure that they don't it does not suffice to make them entities wholly contained in a specious present. The reason it does not suffice is that moments are not instants. (That gathers up the last loose end.) But, then, couldn't one call a duration an instant if and only if, though not literally an instant, it is yet so short that no phenomenal change occurs in it? To do that is to jump from the frying pan into the fire. As I interpret the PA and as I think it must be interpreted, we are not directly acquainted with anything that is not "wholly presented" in a specious present. Hence, if no change could occur in a specious present, we would not be acquainted with the two characters of being earlier and being later.[21]

Second. The problem of change already arises in phenomenal fields. A careful phenomenalist (or a practitioner of the method whose IL is, like mine, phenomenalistic) therefore must not ignore it. To say the same thing more interestingly, the problem of change lies deeper than the phenomenalism-realism issue. It is of course part of the problems of time and of substance. It is indeed the exact overlap of these two. Specifically, it is the problem behind S_2. A continuant, however, as we or-

[21] To be "wholly presented" in a specious present is not the same thing as to be "wholly contained" in it. Otherwise we would not be directly acquainted with any character. See "Elementarism." Some other questions that may occur at this point will be taken up in Part Two below.

dinarily use the word, extends beyond a specious present. That is why I prefer to speak of the problem of change.

Third. Return to the case of the blue spot which moved from the right to the left of the red spot. Ordinarily we say (1) "It has moved." In *L* we must not say that. If "it" has moved then it is no longer "it." We just saw that. It follows that (1) must be reconstructed in *L*, just as (2) "This is a chair," where 'chair' refers to a physical object, must be reconstructed. This meaning of reconstruction is familiar. Its problems are shared by many patterns of the tradition.[22] Nor is there anything peculiar about (1) except that it is so much "simpler" than (2) or any other standard paradigm of the tradition that one may easily overlook that in one respect (1) and (2) are in the same boat. They must both be reconstructed. What goes for (1) goes for a large class of comparable statements. (Remember the spot growing brighter.) Let (1) stand for them all. Has (1) been reconstructed? Some analysts, the early Russell among them, gave a good deal of attention to the problem. Have their efforts been successful? Remember that all reconstruction is reconstruction in principle only. In principle, however, we may consider that the job has been done. The mathematicians have developed techniques by which the continuum (the curve) can be defined in terms of the discontinuous (the point). One merely has to transfer these techniques from their context to ours.

Fourth. If 'This moves' must be reconstructed, then the transcription of 'moves' in *L* is a defined expression. What holds for 'moves' holds for all other verbs of change. Let 'move' represent them all. It follows that, in the ontological sense of 'exist', movement does not exist. Yet movement is "phenomenally simple." More precisely, some instances of it are. We stand at the proximate source of the tension I shall eventually confront. For the moment I limit myself to two comments on phenomenal simplicity. (A) What is not simple (complex) can in some sense be analyzed (decomposed). But there is a sense in which every phenomenon is what it is and in which I literally do not understand what could be meant by decomposing it. In *L* (not: in *L₁*) this sense is reflected by the tautology governing '*M*', which is the transcription of the intentional meaning of 'meaning'.[23] 'Phenomenally simple' is thus mis-

[22] The first who tackled these problems was Berkeley, of course. For some explanations, see "The Revolt against Logical Atomism."

[23] See "Intentionality," also "Elementarism," and "Concepts" (jointly with Herbert Hochberg), *Philosophical Studies*, 8, 1957, 19–27, and also pp. 106–14 of this book.

leading. What the phrase intends is better expressed by 'introspectively simple'. This is a psychological notion. Given a phenomenal content, we can under the appropriate set produce a certain series of others. If this series satisfies certain criteria,[24] then we call it an introspective analysis of the original phenomenal content. What cannot be so analyzed is introspectively simple. (B) Do the uds of L all refer to introspective simples? The answer is Yes. However, this is not a principle like the PA. Rather, it turns out, as philosophical analysis proceeds, that a schema cannot serve as IL unless its uds are interpreted in this way. The case of movement is, as it were, the reverse of the coin. If the pattern is to be of a certain kind, then some (introspective) simples must not be named by uds.

The tradition has always paid a good deal of attention to science. As long as we are not spellbound by it, this is all to the good. So I shall conclude these ontological reflections on time by exploring how they relate to what the scientists have recently told us about time. The relational view is one thing; the relativity theory is another. The former vastly antedates the latter. Nor does it depend on the latter. C. D. Broad quite some time ago knew and explained all that very well. But there is a widespread belief that the relativity theory is in principle incompatible with the absolutistic view. As it is usually understood, this belief is in principle without ground. The argument has three steps.

First. A scientific theory of any complexity more often than not contains a "partially interpreted" axiomatic calculus (C). Perhaps it always does. Remember what was said about instants. Some terms of C are interpreted, not of course into any IL, but into the ordinary language the scientist speaks. Some others are not and by the rules for the interpretation of C cannot be so attached. Among the latter there may be and sometimes are some primitive (i.e., undefined descriptive) signs of C. That is where the phrase, partially interpreted, comes from.[25] The quantum theory as of now is logically so complex that it contains two partially interpreted C, one piled upon the other, as it were. One, the so-called quantum mechanics, is partially interpreted into the other, the so-called semiclassical model, which is in turn partially interpreted into ordinary language. Call quantum mechanics for the moment the last calculus. *Second.* The scientists tell us that they discover "what is

[24] See MLP17.

[25] For details see *Philosophy of Science* (Madison: University of Wisconsin Press, 1957); also "The Logic of Quanta," reprinted in H. Feigl and M. Brodbeck, eds., *Readings in the Philosophy of Science* (New York: Appleton-Century-Crofts, 1953).

really (objectively) there (exists)." If thereupon we ask them what, specifically, exists, they mention the entities referred to by the primitives of the present last C. Notice, in passing, how this indirectly confirms the proposed explication of the philosophical use of 'exist'. *Third*. Absolutism is false because the IL, whether realistic or phenomenalistic, does not and upon the PA cannot contain uds naming nonrelational temporal things. A C is not an IL. (Those who believe that it is, as Carnap and Quine do, are victims of scientism.) A philosopher who (like myself) could not make ends meet if his IL were not a subject-predicate schema can therefore cheerfully admit (as I do) that the last C need not be such a schema. If it is not, then it may well contain a class of nonrelational undefined primitives or parameters, as they are called in such calculi, which in it play very much the same role the absolutist's moments play in his IL. In principle there is no reason why the last calculus could not be of this kind, particularly if one considers how very different a partially interpreted calculus can be from what it interprets. In this connection it is not without interest that, if I understand the experts correctly, Milne's cosmological theory is a calculus of this kind and yet does justice to all the facts on which the relativity theory rests. If so, then the scientists, expressing themselves as they usually do, would have to say that "really" or "objectively" absolute time is there or "exists"; or, more cautiously, that as far as they now know it could exist.

II

What is the nature of our knowledge of the past? What is the nature of memory? One who can answer these two epistemological questions about time can answer all others. So I shall limit myself to these two. They are not independent, of course. Memory is one source of our knowledge of the past. But each of us also knows many things about the past which he does not remember. Historians and geologists know some no one remembers. Thus, if the first question is so understood that whatever also falls under the second is excluded, there still remains a question. This is the way I shall here understand it.

The method splits each of the two main questions into two. (1) What is the transcription (into L) of a statement about the past (about memory)? (2) Can one by talking commonsensically about this transcription reconstruct and solve all epistemological questions concerning our knowledge of the past (concerning memory)? Trying to answer (2) in general makes no sense. The thing to do is to get on with the job, not for all possible problems, which again makes no sense, but for some crucial and representative problems, which is all anyone can do. (1)

contains a preliminary question. Can statements about the past be transcribed at all (into the schema proposed as IL)? Statements about the past are commonsensical. Hence, if the answer is No, the schema cannot possibly be the IL. If the answer is Yes, it still cannot be the IL unless the answer to (2) is also affirmative.[26]

When I now say that it rained yesterday I am making a statement about the past. But I shall not attempt to transcribe (reconstruct) anything as complex as 'It rained yesterday'. Reconstruction is reconstruction in principle only; and "divide and conquer" is good advice in any analytical enterprise. Let us then search for a simpler paradigm. Consider (a) 'There was something green and square'. Take the two adjectives in (a) to refer to the phenomenal characters; the tense, to what is wholly beyond the specious present (of the utterance of (a)). So understood, (a) is as simple a statement about the past as I can think of. Thus I shall make it my paradigm.[27] Since the adjectives in (a) are taken phenomenally, the thing that was green and square is a sensum. Notice, though, that I do not undertake to transcribe 'There was a green and square sensum'. The transcription of this statement is considerably more complex than that of (a). Rather obviously, though, the increase in complexity is not due to its being a statement about the past, but to the occurrence in it of the psychological word 'sensum'.

Remember the difference between L_1 and L. What must be added to L_1 is needed only for an adequate philosophy of mind. That is why in Part One L_1 could stand in for L. What holds for the ontology of time, holds also for (the epistemology of our knowledge of)[28] the past (a). It does not hold for memory (b). Since remembering is a mental act, that is not surprising. This difference between (a) and (b) made a difference for the course of recent analytical philosophy, i.e., the movement which began about the turn of the century and had spent itself at the start of the second world war.[29] Not heeding the teaching of Moore, the recent analysts were all left-wingers, i.e., they all mistook L_1 for L. This mistake deprived them of the means for solving the problems of (b), but not of (a). Accordingly, while their contribution to (b) was negligible,

[26] Notice the negative formulation. The task of showing that any proposed schema actually is the IL is, in an obvious sense, unending.

[27] Why I have not picked the even simpler 'There was something green' will become clear as the argument unfolds. See note 49.

[28] Henceforth I shall suppress such tedious clauses and simply speak of the past and of memory, or, even more simply, of (a) and (b).

[29] The main figures of the movement are Russell and the Wittgenstein of the *Tractatus*. The most important figure in the immediate background is G. E. Moore. In "The Revolt against Logical Atomism," where the historical perspective is shorter, these philosophers are called the classical analysts.

some did very well by (a). Some others—for reasons that will soon be apparent I call them the *verificationists*—also made some other mistakes. Because of these mistakes they also bungled (a). The diagnosis suggests an order of exposition. First I shall attend to the past (A). Then I shall explain the mistakes of the verificationists (B). Finally I shall attend to memory (C). In A and C the concern is thus only with the thing itself; B is critical.

A. Whether (a) can be transcribed into L depends on L, or, as I shall say, on the *specification*[30] of L. The specification of an IL has two parts. First, one syntactically constructs the schema; second, one lays down the rules for its interpretation. Some points concerning the specification of L are contained in the longish digression near the beginning of Part One. Now another digression is in order.

An expression (string of signs) may or may not be "well-formed." To be a "sentence" is to be a well-formed expression of a certain kind. In L, for instance, if 'f_1' is a well-formed predicate expression, then '$(\exists x)f_1(x)$' is a well-formed sentence. The notion itself is purely syntactical (i.e., in the case of a written schema, geometrical). The definition of 'well-formed' is therefore an important part of the first stage. This seems obvious enough. Truisms, though, have a way of being overlooked, sometimes with disastrous consequences. The second stage requires the interpretation not only of the uds, but also of the primitive logical signs. This is another important truism. L (precisely: L_1) may be constructed with three logical primitives, two connectives ('$\sim$' and 'v') and the so-called existential operator ('$(\exists x) \ldots x \ldots$'). They are interpreted into the English 'not', 'or', and 'there is something such that $\ldots$ it $\ldots$', respectively.[31] Predication signifies exemplification. Predication and the operator either both are or both are not tenseless. (not: timeless). That is again obvious. L's gambit is that they are both tenseless.[32] The idea behind this gambit is that upon any adequate explication of certain important philosophical uses of 'logic', 'form', and 'content' exemplification will turn out to be a "logical" or "formal" nexus while (space and) time will be counted among the world's "content."[33] The existential operator, then, is tenseless. (Not "exist-

---

[30] This redundancy will soon be useful. As on some other occasions, the word is italicized for emphasis, not in order to mark a philosophical use. The context should leave no doubt which purpose the typographical device serves each time.

[31] This interpretation involves the familiar standardization of English to which Oxford now objects. See "The Revolt against Logical Atomism."

[32] For criticism of a scientistic and, therefore, wrong defense of this gambit, see "Professor Quine on Analyticity," *Mind*, 64, 1955, 254–58, and also pp. 139–43 of this book.

[33] The Kantian bias to the contrary was among the causes that propelled Wittgenstein on the road from the *Tractatus* to the *Investigations*. See MLP3.

ence is timeless"; for that, as follows from Part One, is mere gibberish.)
The operator's conventional name may lead to the misapprehension
that its occurrence marks a philosophical use of 'exist' (in L). There are
no philosophical uses in $L;$ otherwise L could not be the IL. And in
every nonphilosophical use (in English) 'exist' can without change of
meaning be replaced by 'there is (are)'.

Assume that Smith is asked what he is at the moment aware of. Call
the answer the actual text of Smith's awareness. The analyst assigns to
each awareness (of Smith) a sentence of L as its artificial text. This particular way[34] of describing the interpretation of L brings out that L is
not only not a language actually to be spoken but not even the so-
called language of the so-called inner monologue. The occurrence of uds
is regulated by the PA. Whether a uds occurs in the artificial text of an
awareness of Smith depends therefore on what Smith is directly acquainted with. But there is also an important difference between particulars and predicates. A particular may occur in the (artificial) text of
an awareness (of Smith) only if the individual it names is presented (to
Smith) in the awareness. This rule is a part of the specification of L.
Since it is a rule, it obviously cannot and need not be "proved." In
another sense, it must prove itself by the success of the IL it specifies.
But it may be well to mention the major motive for this particular rule
or gambit. The problems created by talk about the present king of
Portugal are as familiar as they are serious. The only way to solve them
is by Russell's justly celebrated analysis of descriptions. The rule
merely encodes, for a phenomenalistic language, the basic idea of this
analysis.[35]

I am ready to propose a transcription for (a). Let 'gr' and 'sq' be two
uds of the first type transcribing the phenomenal meaning of 'green'
and 'square' respectively. In terms of them a predicative expression,
'$grsq$', naming the property of being both green and square, can be
defined (in L). Let 'n' be a particular naming an individual presented
in the awareness of which (a) is the actual text. I transcribe (a) by

$$(\alpha) \qquad\qquad (\exists x)[pr(x,\ n)\cdot grsq(x)]$$

In words: There is something which (temporally) precedes this and is
green and square. Since the individual in question does not belong to
the relevant specious present, a particular naming it cannot occur in

---

[34] For details, see "Intentionality."

[35] For the troubles one courts by abandoning the rule see three papers by
Herbert Hochberg: "The Ontological Operator," *Philosophy of Science*, 23, 1956,
250–59; "Professor Quine, Pegasus, and Dr. Cartwright," *ibid.*, 24, 1957, 191–
203; "On Pegasizing," *Philosophy and Phenomenological Research*, 17, 1957, 551–
54.

(α); hence the need for the operator. '$grsq$' is unproblematic. Concerning 'pr' I shall entertain two objections. *First*, it may be objected that, even though '$(\exists x)pr(x, n)$' is well formed (as is (α)), the only exemplifications of the relation we are ever presented with are such that the two individuals exemplifying it are in the same specious present, while n and the thing which was both green and square by assumption are not. The import of the objection, I take it, is that the PA does not authorize the use made of 'pr' in (α). However, to begin with, consider a similar case. Assume I say about a green spot at the extreme left of my phenomenal field that there is another such spot to the left of it. (The spatial relation is taken phenomenally, of course.) My objector should consistently also object to this use of 'to the left of'. But he doesn't do so. Nor does he think that consistently he must. The reason he need not, he says, is a certain difference between the two cases. One merely has to turn one's head in order to be presented with the second spot (if there is one). But there is no way of procuring a presentation of the past. I grant the difference, of course. But I hurry to add that it is a difference in the kind of evidence available for statements and not, as it would have to be if the PA is appealed to, a difference in the meaning of words. If it were not for the specious present, I would indeed not know what 'earlier' meant. Once I do know that, however, then I can without change of meaning use the word beyond the specious present by means of the logical operator. This objection, I believe, would not be raised if one firmly grasps that the specification of the logical apparatus is an essential part of the specification of L. The *second* objection will not detain us as long. There is nothing in (α) to tell us that n and the thing which was green and square do not in fact belong to the same specious present. In some cases, therefore, (α) will be a statement about the past; in some others, it will not. I agree. Only, a little reflection will show that all my argument requires is the admission that in some cases (α) is a statement about the past.[36] I take it, then, that (α) does transcribe (a) into L. Is the transcription adequate? To show that it is, I shall put it to use in explaining and answering a representative series of crucial questions about the past. (A good deal of what will be said applies *mutatis mutandis* to statements about the future.)

1. *Are statements about the past "meaningful"?* 'Meaningless' and 'meaningful' have been discredited by the reckless way some recent analysts used them. Even aside from that, the question seems odd. It

---

[36] To make sure that the statement is in all cases about the past, it would have to be much more complex; obviously so, since the relevant notion of a specious present is psychological. Remember what was said earlier about the reconstruction of a sentence containing 'sensum'.

is odd. Nor would I raise it if it were not for the verificationists. Anyone who asks seriously whether (a) is meaningful, uses 'meaningful' in a peculiar way. The verificationists used it so that to be meaningful is to satisfy a certain meaning criterion. 'Meaning criterion' in turn was so used that to lay down a meaning criterion is to specify an IL. In other words, a statement is said to be meaningful (by a philosopher) if and only if it can be transcribed into (his) IL. Since (α) is the transcription of (a) into L, the answer to the odd question is Yes. The verificationists thought that there was a difficulty. Of that later.

Granted that statements about the past are "meaningful," can we ever know any one of them to be true? As it is usually meant, this is not just one question but an umbrella covering several. I shall take these up one after the other and when I am done with them return to the original question.

2. *Can a statement about the past ever be certain?* We are supremely confident of many statements about the past. If you replace 'supremely confident' by 'certain' you obtain a good example of the one and only unproblematic use of 'certain'. Literally, neither a statement nor a state of affairs is certain. Rather, we are certain of it. Or, what amounts to the same, certainty is a quality of an act. But there are also two philosophical uses of 'certain' that are relevant to the question. In the first use, *a statement (of L) is certain if and only if it is either atomic or molecular.* A statement is atomic or molecular if and only if after all abbreviations (definitions) have been eliminated it contains no operators. E.g., '$grsq(b)$' is molecular. Certainty in this very special sense has nothing to do with either truth or knowledge. In the second use, *a statement (of L) is certain if and only if it is analytic.* (α) contains an operator; and it is of course not analytic. It follows that if 'certain' is taken commonsensically, the answer to the question is Yes; if it is taken in either philosophical sense, the answer, equally obviously, is No.

One who asserts that it rained yesterday may be challenged to produce evidence. The production of evidence in all such matters[37] eventually leads to the invitation: Look and see! To look and see is to *observe*. One who observes in order to ascertain the truth (or falsehood) of a statement attempts to *verify* it (or to falsify it, as the case may be).

3. *Can statements about the past be verified?* Verification is either *direct* or *indirect*. The distinction is crucial. Nothing will be lost and much ink will be saved if in explaining it I return to the phenomenal context.

---

[37] That is, as one usually says, in all empirical matters. But I like to avoid this sadly overworked word.

In this context an observation is an awareness that is a seeing or a hearing or a smelling, and so on, and whose (artificial) text is an atomic or molecular sentence. Assume now that the green and square individual was once presented to me; that I then called it '*b*'; and that the text of the awareness I then had is '*grsq(b)*'. Those who assert that statements about the past cannot be directly verified assert that I shall not and cannot, either at the moment when (*α*) is the text of my awareness or at any later moment, have an awareness whose (complete or partial) text is '*grsq(b)*'. They assert a truism. Thus they are of course right. *Statements about the past cannot be directly verified.* Or, rather, that is the way the matter is usually put. There is a slight blur here. Strictly, a statement about the past must mention certain things *as past*, as (*α*) does and '*grsq(b)*' doesn't.[38] But we know what is meant. So I shall let it go. Indirect verification is a different story. Take 'lightning' and 'thunder' phenomenally. Suppose I now observe a thunderclap. (I would rather say that I hear it, but I adapt myself to the jargon.) From the statement of this observation in conjunction with the law, which I know, that thunder is always preceded by lightning, I deduce that there was a lightning stroke which, as it happened, I had not observed. This is the idea of indirect verification. All the rest is sweat and pedantry. The example involves a statement about the past. *Statements about the past can be verified indirectly.* Of course. How would we otherwise know anything past which we do not remember?

4. *If the world as it now is including ourselves as we now are had been created yesterday, could we know it?* One may accept the question as a colorful way of calling attention to what has been said so far, less colorfully, about the past. If so, then it is not really a question. As a real question it is fuzzy. Some recent analysts who should have known better nevertheless took it seriously and worried about it. To uncover the source of their worry, I shall ask a different question which is not at all fuzzy. To be able to ask it I must make an assumption. The assumption is fantastic, in the sense in which science fiction is fantastic, but again, it is not at all fuzzy. Nor will the answer be. Assume that we now make in a laboratory an adult man with a normal adult mind furnished with a good deal of knowledge of his personal past. This is

---

[38] One source of the blur is failure to distinguish clearly between *L*, which stands for what Smith might say, and the analyst's talk *about L*. The analyst knows of course that the green square thing is in the past. So he overlooks that '*grsq(b)*' does not say that it is. The blur is particularly noticeable in what the verificationists say about the past. But I shall not bother to point it out again.

the assumption. Could our homunculus know that what he knows, or believes, or believes he knows[39] about his personal past is in fact false? More precisely, could he know it now, at the moment of his creation, before he has had an opportunity to discover the truth? This is the question. The answer plainly is No. It seems to have worried those philosophers. I do not see why it should have. Is it, perhaps, that they were hard-core skeptics? If so, why didn't they also worry about whether they really heard or saw what they heard or saw, at the very moment they heard or saw it?

Remember the umbrella. Can we ever know a statement about the past to be true? What has been said since the question was first raised contains the answer. But it may help if I spell it out. In any reasonable sense of 'knowing' the answer is *obviously Yes*. If 'knowing' is so used that we know only what is certain in that very special sense of 'certain' in which only atomic or molecular statements are certain, and that only at the moment of the awareness containing what the statement refers to, then the answer is *trivially No*.[40]

B. The verificationists' analysis led them to conclude that we can know the past. Nothing is thus wrong with their conclusion. The trouble is that in arriving at it they made two major mistakes. They chose an unviable meaning criterion (MC) and they held that it is logically impossible to verify directly statements about the past. These two mistakes appear already in what they have to say about (a). When the statement about the past mentions physical objects, they make still other mistakes. These I shall ignore. For they are mistakes in the verificationists' analysis of our knowledge of physical objects rather than, specifically, of the past. To propose an MC, we saw, is to propose an IL. The verificationists did not explicitly practice the method. But I have no doubt that, had they practiced it, L_1 is the IL they would have proposed. MC does not succeed in specifying L_1. This is one very gen-

---

[39] I put no store in these idiomatic distinctions. At Oxford they now use the "linguistic truth" that one cannot know what is not true as a pretext for either ignoring or prejudging philosophical questions. Concerning "linguistic truths," see below.

[40] In view of the clause beginning "and that only," the sentence contains the explication of a third philosophical use of 'certain'. As I used 'observation', phenomenally, the only things thus certain are observations (or observation statements) at the moment the observation is made. Overconcern with this kind of certainty is the skeptics' Pandoran bequest to the tradition. It also misled the verificationists. That will become clear as the argument unfolds, even though I shall not bother to point it out again.

eral though, I think, illuminating way of stating what went wrong.

"A sentence is meaningful if and only if it is either (A) an *observation statement* (OS) or (B) one can deduce from it, in conjunction with premises belonging to certain specified kinds, an OS which cannot be deduced from these premises alone." This is the idea of the MC. I say idea because the most elaborate formulation of (B) so far proposed extends the scope of the "meaningful" beyond all reason and surely beyond the intent of its proponent. The flaw is logical.[41] But it is merely logical, if I may again so express myself, and the other mistakes of the verificationists are of considerable philosophical interest.[42] So I shall ignore that flaw even though, alas, it is fatal. To understand the intent of (A) further explanation is necessary. "A statement is an OS if and only if (1) it is an atomic or molecular statement (of *L*) and (2) it is *logically possible* to observe what it refers to." This use of 'logically possible' is philosophical. *What a sentence (of L) refers to is* logically possible (impossible) *if and only if the sentence is not (is) contradictory* (i.e., if its negation is analytic). The verificationists agree with this explication. Where they err is in the explication of 'analytic'. Of this more presently, after two orienting remarks. *First.* The crucial statement for our purpose is '*grsq(b)*'.[43] The verificationists claim that it is not an OS because it is logically impossible to observe what it refers to. Literally, this claim is patently false. So I shall restate it as it was meant, namely, that it is logically impossible to make the relevant observation in any specious present which does not contain *b*. That we cannot in fact make the observation in any such specious present (the interest is in the later ones, of course) is a truism. Remember what was said earlier about direct verification. That shows that the heart of the matter is indeed the alleged logical impossibility. *Second.* Turn again to the lightning-thunder paradigm. The second half (B) of the MC is meant to include among the admissible premises such laws as that thunder is always preceded by lightning (both terms still taken phenomenally). That is how the verificationists eventually manage to make statements about the past meaningful. The story itself is the one I told when discussing indirect verification. So I need not tell it again. Notice, though, that the statement thus eventually salvaged as "meaningful" is (α), which is literally about the past, and not '*grsq(b)*', which is not.

The stage is now set for four things. 1. I shall state one feature of the

[41] It was pointed out by the mathematical logician Church.

[42] For other criticism of these mistakes, see MLP7.

[43] I use the same notation as in A3. Remember also, here and to the end of the paragraph, what was said in note 38.

adequate explication[44] of 'analytic' and call attention to one of its consequences concerning time. 2. I shall state the gist of the verificationists' explication and call attention to its inadequacy as well as to one of its consequences for time. 3. I shall show that the verificationists' claim concerning '$grsq(b)$' stands with the wrong and falls with the right explication of 'analytic'. 4. I shall advert to another odd question about the past which would never have been raised if it hadn't been for the verificationists and which is most easily handled if one knows and understands their mistakes.

1. Properly explicated, analyticity is a purely syntactical notion. That has an important consequence. As it has been put, very aptly, in an analytic sentence descriptive expressions occur only vacuously. Take an example involving time: (γ) '$\sim(\exists x, y)[sim(x, y)\cdot pr(x, y)]$'. In words, 'There are no two simultaneous individuals of which one precedes the other'.[45] (γ) is true, of course. 'pr' and 'sim' are uds; replace them by (the transcriptions of) 'louder' and 'equal-in-pitch' respectively; the resulting sentence is false. If 'sim' and 'pr' occurred vacuously in (γ), this sentence as well as all other sentences similarly obtained would be true. It follows that (γ) is not analytic. Consider an objection. "Replace (the transcription of) 'simultaneous' by what it really means, namely, (the transcription of) 'neither precedes nor is preceded by' and you will see that the resulting sentence (γ') is even upon your own criterion analytic." To see why this will not do, notice first that the proposal amounts to introducing 'sim' as a defined expression. Notice further that, in some appropriate sense of 'means', the defined term and our 'sim' mean the same thing only because (γ') and a few related sentences can be deduced from a small class of sentences, containing no other uds than 'pr', such as (γ'') '$(x, y, z)[pr(x, y)\cdot pr(x, z) \supset pr(x, z)]$', which states the transitivity of pr. Thus, to make his case the way he intended, the objector would have to claim that (γ'') and all the other members of that small class are analytic. The wish to support this claim is indeed one of the intellectual motives behind the verificationists' (and Oxford's) explication of 'analytic'.

[44] For arguments in its support, see MLP, "Intentionality," and "Analyticity." Concerning the inadequacy of the verificationists' explication, which in different trappings is now being offered at Oxford, see also "The Revolt against Logical Atomism."

[45] Assume in this and the next two paragraphs that individuals are instantaneous; and, whenever the argument requires it, take 'precede' so that when one individual precedes another, there is no awareness that contains them both. All that merely brushes aside what in the context does not matter.

2. "A sentence is analytic (contradictory) if and only if its truth (falsehood) depends only on linguistic rules (i.e., rules for the use of the language)." This is the explication I reject. What it means depends on what is meant by 'linguistic rule'. The specification of an IL contains many sentences one may commonsensically call rules. I spoke of interpretation rules. There are also syntactical rules.[46] If you wish, call these two kinds of rules linguistic. This use of the phrase I understand. But I do not understand what it could possibly mean to say, as the verificationists do, that (γ), or (γ''), is true by virtue of linguistic rules and therefore analytic. Or, rather, what I do understand is absurd. (γ) is of course a true generality. But there are other such generalities which no one, except perhaps an embattled Hegelian, ever thought of calling analytic. By which criterion do we know the two kinds from each other? The verificationists have no answer. Is it perhaps that when we are supremely confident of a generality we issue a decree that makes every sentence contradicting it "ungrammatical"? Again, I do not understand this use of 'grammar'. Not even a real contradiction, such as 'It is and it is not raining' is ungrammatical in any sense of the word I understand. If it were, how would you know what it meant? And if you didn't know what it meant, how would you know that it was a contradiction?

3. Consider three sentences. (P) Of two simultaneous individuals neither precedes the other. (R_1) A particular (of L) does not occur in the text assigned to an awareness unless the individual it names is in (the content of) this awareness. (R_2) If an individual precedes another, a particular naming the former never occurs in the text assigned to an awareness in which the latter is. If one observes the rules for the interpretation of L, (R_1) will be a true (English) sentence (about L).[47] That is, (R_1) is true by virtue of a linguistic rule (about L) or, briefly, it is a "linguistic truth." A sentence deduced from premises which are all linguistic truths is itself one. (R_2) cannot be deduced from (R_1) alone. Grant, though, for the sake of the argument, that (R_2) can be deduced from (R_1) and (P); that merely neglects unessentials. Hence, if (P) were what it is not, namely, a linguistic truth, then (R_2) would be one, too. Since the verificationists hold that (P) is a linguistic truth, they conclude that (R_2) is one and that, therefore, it is analytic. But a little

---

[46] They are of course the only ones mentioned in the syntactical explication of analyticity.

[47] If one collapses L and English, as the verificationists do, one will easily overlook the need for the parenthetical clauses. That greatly adds to the confusion. The method forces one to pay attention. That is one of its obvious merits.

reflection[48] will show that to assert that (R₂) is analytic is to assert that it is "logically impossible to observe the past." That, we know, is the verificationists' thesis. They support it with the argument I dissected. Since neither (R₁) nor (P) is in fact analytic, even though (R₁) may intelligibly be called a linguistic truth, their argument collapses. The thesis itself would never have been proposed but for the confused notion of analyticity as "linguistic truth." Nor would the verificationists have been as preoccupied as they were with the rather arid question of whether or not it is logically impossible to observe the past, if they had not chosen a wrong MC. For if L is correctly specified, it is immediately evident that (α) and '$grsq(b)$' are both "meaningful," i.e., well-formed in L. That is how the verificationists' two major mistakes hang together.[49]

4. *Are statements about the past really about the present and the future?*
'Peter is blond' is about or refers to Peter being blond. 'The moon is a lantern' refers to the moon being a lantern. This is the commonsensical use of 'refer'. If one questions it on such grounds as that the moon is not a lantern (negative facts!), he starts the dialectical game, thus crossing the line between ordinary and philosophical use. 'Means' has *several* ordinary uses (meanings).[50] *One* coincides with the just illustrated use of 'refer'. Call it the reference use. The reference "meaning" of a sentence is, accordingly, what it refers to. The reference meaning of (α) is there having been a green and square thing. (α) thus is about (means, refers to) what one would naturally think it to be about, namely, the past. How, then, did the odd question ever come to be raised? To say what *"meaning"* is (upon *one* of the *several* uses of 'means') is one thing. To propose an MC, i.e., to specify an IL is another thing. If this difference is not clearly seen, as it wasn't, partly because of that unfortunate phrase, 'meaning criterion'; if it is not realized, as it wasn't, that reference is only *a* but not *the* meaning of 'meaning'; and if one is as preoccupied with verification as the verificationists were, then one may be tempted to say that the "real meaning" of a statement is the class of all those states of affairs which it is "logically possible" to observe and which, or at least some of which,

---

[48] In the notation I used before, the two individuals mentioned in (P) are b and n.

[49] The PA is a linguistic rule. One may want to argue from it that if 'gr' occurs at all in L, then (the transcription of) 'There was something green' is a "linguistic truth." That does not make it analytic, of course. But it makes it an awkward paradigm for a statement about the past. That is why I chose '$grsq$'. See note 27.

[50] For details, see "The Revolt against Logical Atomism."

one would want to observe when looking for evidence supporting the statement. These states of affairs are of course always either in the present or in the future, whether or not the statement to be verified is about the past. That explains why the odd question was asked. Some even answered it in the affirmative.

C. 'Knowing' has several ordinary uses. When I say that Smith knows how to swim, I refer neither to an awareness of Smith nor to the content of such an awareness. This is one ordinary use. Sometimes, when saying that I know something, or that Smith does, I do refer to an awareness of mine, or of Smith's. In other words, sometimes 'I know that it rained yesterday' is the actual text of an awareness. Its content is a knowing, not just what is known, namely, that it rained yesterday. In still other words, sometimes I am aware of my knowing something (not just: of something) in the manner some now call knowing-that. This is another ordinary use of 'knowing'. Philosophically it is crucial. A philosopher who ignores it or reconstructs it wrongly condemns himself to an inadequate philosophy of mind. As for 'knowing', so for 'remembering'. Sometimes, 'I remember that it rained yesterday' is the (actual) text of a characteristic awareness. Its content is a remembering, not just what is being remembered. Philosophically, this is again the crucial use. Ignoring all other uses and following the method, I shall therefore transcribe this crucial use and then answer some philosophical questions about memory by talking commonsensically about the transcription. Like the transcription of the crucial use of 'knowing' and unlike that of statements about the past, the transcription of 'remembering' requires the full resources of L and not just of L_1, which is the left-wingers' implicit or explicit IL. That necessitates a digression about L and the philosophy of mind it implies. First, though, for four preliminary comments.

First. As in the case of the past and for the same reason, namely, in order to exclude all problems which are not specifically problems of memory, I shall choose my paradigm among the simplest memory statements. Take again 'green' and 'square' phenomenally. Then (b) 'I remember that there was something green and square' is such a statement. So I shall make it my paradigm. *Second.* In (b) the clause following 'I remember that' is the sentence I called (a) and transcribed by (α). One may wonder whether by limiting myself to (b) I ignore such statements as 'I remember my mother's face', i.e., statements where the corresponding clause is (in English) not a sentence. The answer is that I don't. The content of every awareness is propositional. This I argued elsewhere.[51] *Third*. One may wonder whether the transcription and analysis of (b) also covers such statements as (b') 'Smith remembers that there was something green and square'. This time the answer is that it doesn't. The analysis of (b') is very complex. The analysis of (b) is but a part of it. The remaining part involves the problem of our knowledge of other minds. This, though a major issue, is not specifically one of memory.[52] That is why in this essay I can safely ignore (b'). *Fourth*. The Self is a continuant. Within the pattern it is therefore not an individual.[53] Awarenesses, however, are. The claim is, of course, that if names for these "mental" individuals and their characteristic qualities are included in the IL, then the Self can be reconstructed, i.e., the personal pronoun can in principle be transcribed and the philosophical questions about the Self be answered by talking commonsensically about the transcription. The answers, incidentally, are in the style of Locke. Technically, this means that the sentence I shall transcribe (and continue to call (b)) is not literally the one I called (b) but rather 'There having been something green and square is remembered'.

An awareness and a "mental" individual are one and the same thing. 'Awareness', in other words, is used generically. An awareness may be a knowing, a doubting, an imagining, a remembering, and so on. Some of these specifying characters may have to be referred to by uds. An awareness, though it may be in the content of another, is always distinct from its own content. It is an awareness *of* its content by virtue of exemplifying a character of the kind called propositional. One may call these characters thoughts. Only, one must not forget that a thought is then a universal. Each awareness of $2+2=4$, for instance, is an individual. But these individuals all exemplify the same propositional character (thought). That is why they are all awarenesses of $2+2=4$. Unlike certain patterns of sounds and of marks on paper, a propositional character (briefly, proposition) is thus a mental thing and not, in the only sense of the phrase I understand, a "linguistic thing." In L this analysis is reflected as follows. The text of an awareness refers to its content. Let 'a' and 'p_1' refer to an awareness and its text respectively.[54] The proposition exemplified by a is referred to by ' 'p_1' '; that a is an awareness of p_1, by ' 'p_1'(a)'. ' 'p_1' ' is a uds. This is as it ought to be.

---

[51] See "Intentionality."

[52] See MLP6.

[53] This is not either to assert or to deny that the Self is phenomenally simple. Remember what was said about movement in Part One. For details concerning what is said in this and the next paragraph, see "Intentionality."

[54] 'p_1' is of course merely an abbreviation.

For, when we are aware of one of our thoughts, though not when we are just thinking it, we are directly acquainted with it, though not necessarily with what it is the thought of. The quotes (' . . . ') and 'M' are the "*new*" logical primitives of L. 'M' transcribes the intentional meaning of 'means'. The sentence '$'p_1'$ Mp_1' is *analytic*. The italicized uses of 'logical' and 'analytic' are not just honorary but can be given precise and rich meanings. This is important because the analyticity of '$'p_1'$ Mp_1' reflects the nexus between a thought and its content.

How shall we now transcribe (b)? Use 'p_1' as an abbreviation for the sentence (of L) called (α). Obviously, 'p_1' will not do as a transcription of (b). For we may know (be aware of) something past without remembering it. Remembering, it seems, involves awareness of an awareness. To remember, one might therefore think, is to be aware of a past awareness. That suggests the sentence[55] '$(\exists x)\,[pr(x,\ n)\cdot'grsq(b)'(x)\,]$', which I shall abbreviate by 'p_2'. But, again, I may know on very good evidence that I was aware of something, not just that there was something, and yet not remember my having been aware of it. The objection is the same as before and again it is fatal. 'p_2' will not do either. But it will help later if I now show why another objection, which some may wish to raise against 'p_2', is mistaken. "The particular 'b' names an individual in the content of an earlier awareness; yet it occurs in the supposed text of a later awareness, namely, 'p_2'; that violates the interpretation rule for particulars." This is the objection. I reply first that 'b', being part of a quoted expression having all the syntactical properties of a uds, does not literally occur in 'p_2'. I reply, second, that since '$'grsq(b)'$ ', which does occur in 'p_2', is the name of a character which like all characters is timeless, the interpretation rule for particulars does not apply to it.

The idea that remembering involves the awareness of an awareness is sound. The trouble was only that 'p_2' did not implement it adequately. We must try again. In remembering the past one is aware not of a past awareness but of a present awareness of the past. This analysis will lead to an adequate implementation of the sound idea. It immediately suggests '$'p_1'(a)$' as the transcription of (b); a being the awareness we are aware of in remembering something. Once more, though, this will not do. The awareness a may be a knowing or a doubting or an imagining. Hence, if '$'p_1'(a)$' were the complete transcription of (b), we couldn't tell the text of a remembering from that of a knowing, a doubting, or an imagining. This time, however, the defect can be cor-

---

[55] 'n' and 'b' are used as before.

rected. Let '*mem*' stand for the specific character exemplified by all and only those awarenesses that are rememberings. I propose

$$(\beta) \qquad\qquad 'p_1'(a) \cdot mem(a)$$

as the transcription of (b). Presently I shall furnish evidence for its adequacy. That is, I shall by talking about it explicate and answer two philosophical questions about memory. First, though, I wish to examine an alternative to (β).

Consider (β') '$'p_2'(a) \cdot mem(a)$'. The difference between (β) and (β') corresponds to the idiomatic difference between 'I remember something' and 'I remember having seen (or heard, etc.) something'. Thus one may argue that (β) and (β') transcribe different actual memory texts. If so, then I stay with the simpler one, which is transcribed by (β). But one may also argue that, whatever the actual text may be, accurate phenomenological description[56] shows any memory to have the complexity revealed by (β'). Maybe that is so. But, whether or not it is so, this is, I am convinced, the wrong *kind* of argument. Phenomenological description is one thing. Reconstruction (transcription) for the purpose of philosophical analysis is another thing. The latter need not and often cannot retrace every detail of the former.[57]

Is memory fallible? The question has bothered several analysts. So I shall take it up, even though I do not think that its philosophical core is quite as impressive as the attention it has received might lead one to expect. Yet there is such a core and, such as it is, it needs unwrapping. Two extraneous matters, one purely verbal, one scientific, must be cleared away. If one wishes, one may so standardize the (ordinary) use of 'remembering' that one cannot remember what has not actually happened. Suppose I "remembered" some time ago that there was something green and square. By now I have found out that there was no such thing. If I accept the standardization proposal, then I shall now say that I did not "really" remember anything but merely thought or believed that I did. Memory is thus made infallible by verbal decree.[58] If the standardization proposal is mistaken for the discovery of a "linguistic truth," then it will do harm by preventing one from recognizing the philosophical core of the question. Otherwise, it is as harmless as it is trivial. The other extraneous matter is psychological. How reliable is memory? Or, to say the same thing differently, when

---

[56] For reasons I explained earlier I speak of phenomenological description rather than of phenomenological analysis.

[57] See "Elementarism"; also "Concepts."

[58] Compare what was said about knowing in note 39.

we remember something, how likely are we to be mistaken? Every now and then we are in fact mistaken. This is just common sense. To investigate the circumstances on which the likelihood of a mistake depends is the business of the science of psychology.

'(In-)fallible' and '(un-)certain' are kindred words. Not surprisingly, therefore, the philosophical core of the question involves the philosophical uses of 'certain'. Among these, we remember, two stand out. So we shall again not be surprised if we discover two questions, each connected with one of these two uses of 'certain', at the core of the original question. *First.* ' 'p_1' ' is a uds. So is '*mem*'; or, at least, I am strongly inclined to believe that it is. If ' 'p_1' ' and '*mem*' are both uds, then (β) is molecular. It follows that, in one philosophical sense of 'certain', (β) is certain (infallible). There is nothing very peculiar about that except, perhaps, that the certainty, in this sense, of (β) does not at all depend on the complexity of 'p_1' (not: of ' 'p_1' '). It may be that this peculiarity is in part responsible for the strange belief that memory is also infallible (certain) in the other sense. *Second.* Can 'p_1' be deduced from (β)? Or, what amounts to the same, is (δ) ' 'p_1'(a) $\cdot$ *mem*(a) $\supset p_1$' analytic? This is the second question. Its connection with the second philosophical use of 'certain' is obvious, I trust; for to be certain in this sense, it will be remembered, is to be analytic. As to the question itself, we know that memory is in fact not always reliable. That is, we cannot be as certain that what we remember actually happened as we are of remembering it. Thus we would be embarrassed if (δ) were analytic. Happily, it is not.[59] This is one of the virtues of *L*. Incidentally, what holds for (δ) also holds for the sentences obtained from it by putting in the place of '*mem*' (the transcriptions of) either 'knowing' or 'doubting' or 'imagining', and so on. Technically, the crucial question is whether ' 'p_1'(a) $\supset p_1$' is analytic. The answer is No. Or, if after these clarifications you still feel the urge to use the word, memory is not infallible.

It is instructive to speculate on one possible cause of the mistaken belief that memory is infallible (in the sense connected with analyticity). Remember (β'). It is at least a plausible candidate for the transcription of (b). Suppose now that one practicing the method actually fastens on (β'). Or, if he does not practice the method, suppose that he argues to this effect. (I.e., if he practiced it, he would propose (β').) Such a one may also argue, or be imagined to argue, that memory is infallible on the ground that 'b' occurs in (β'), even though only in a (doubly) quoted context, and that by "linguistic rule" it could not so occur unless there once actually was an individual called 'b'. With the gaps in

---

[59] That follows immediately from the (partial) explication of analyticity given in "Intentionality."

this argument we are already familiar. The verbal bridge leads from 'linguistic rule' over 'linguistic truth' to 'analytic'.

What is the role of memory images? Or, if you please, what is their nature? The question has exercised quite a few philosophers. That is why I take it up. I do not think that it has a philosophical core. That is why I shall give it short shrift. Under the appropriate set, I am aware of sensa and the characters they exemplify. But when I see a chair I see a chair and not sensa. Generally, the content of an awareness is what its text says it is. When I remember something, then I remember this thing, irrespective of (as the psychologists put it) how the memory is carried. Phenomenological description or introspective analysis—which are two things and not one—may or may not reveal memory images or introspectively simple feelings of familiarity or, perhaps, both. These are matters of phenomenology and psychology. As a philosopher I am not concerned with them. I should like to add, though, that I, for one, am not acquainted with a phenomenal character which, if exemplified by a nonmental individual, makes it a "memory individual," as some other character may make it a tone, or a pain, or a smell. Thus I cannot but believe that one claiming acquaintance with such a character deceives himself. In the pattern, awarenesses and their characters take the place occupied by mental acts in some classical patterns of the tradition. The cause of self-deception, I surmise, is the reluctance to give mind its proper place in the world.[60] Technically that amounts to this. If "being a memory" could be construed as a character exemplified by (nonmental) individuals occurring in memory images, then L_1 might be the IL. But L_1 cannot do justice to any of the problems of the philosophy of mind. Of these problems memory is but one. This increases my confidence that the analysis of memory here proposed is at least on the right track.

III

Trees do not grow into the sky. As with trees, so with men. Every human enterprise has its limits, causing unrest, dissatisfaction, and futile disparagement. When the limits are clearly seen, and seen to be grounded in the very nature of the enterprise, they no longer appear as limitations. We accept them and the tension ceases. I embarked on these reflections by calling attention to a certain tension, promising to confront it at the end. Now, having come to the end, I shall show that it is merely our response to the natural limits of the analytic enterprise. When I first mentioned this source of discontent, I spoke

[60] This reluctance clashes almost pathetically with the implicit phenomenalism of many of the recent analysts. See "The Revolt against Logical Atomism."

aphoristically. My pattern, I said, was antisubstantialist, even though after a fashion time is the substance of the world. I shall begin by unpacking the aphorism.

As before, my concern is not with substances in the strong sense but only with continuants. A continuant is an individual that persists in time. Literally, it therefore makes no sense to call time itself a continuant. Metaphorically, absolute time may be so called. For one, all the moments of a world with absolute time are linearly ordered by a unique relation which they and they alone exemplify. For another, every (ordinary) individual of this world is related to this series in a unique way which we explored in Part One. The metaphor aptly points at these two features. Its aptness is further enhanced by another result of Part One. *In a subject-predicate world* there can be continuants only if there is absolute time. The italicized phrase strikes the theme that will presently come to the fore.

In the world science constructs there may be absolute time. This, too, we saw in Part One. Science, however, is merely the long arm of common sense; and commonsensically there are also continuants. In the relevant sense, there is in our world no absolute time. Of this I am very certain, as certain as of my not being directly acquainted with any nonrelational temporal thing. But this is also the source of the tension. The point is that while I am not directly acquainted with absolute time (moments or tqs), I am so acquainted with change. Remember what was said about movement in the specious present. Also, such movement was merely our paradigm for the many kinds of change with which we are directly acquainted. Change, that is, unlike absolute time, is given to us. Yet there cannot be individuals that change in a subject-predicate world unless there be also absolute time. Why, then, cling to the idea that our world is a subject-predicate world? Or, as I would rather put it, why persist in one's attempts to solve all philosophical problems by means of an IL which, like *L*, is a subject-predicate schema? Before answering this question I wish to correct an omission.

Some philosophers have told us a good deal about pastness, presentness, and futurity. I take them to have spoken of three introspectively simple characters with which they claimed direct acquaintance. When I dealt with Leibniz's peculiar tqs, I proceeded as if there couldn't be any others. So I may have seemed to dismiss the claim of these philosophers out of hand.[61] That is the omission. Part Two should have left no doubt that I do disclaim direct acquaintance with either pastness or futurity. I do not even know what 'past' and 'future', so under-

[61] See note 18.

stood, could possibly mean. Presentness is a different matter. So I shall now say something about it. That requires a precaution. The phenomenal material is conclusive. Arguments about it often are anything but conclusive. This is no paradox. The source of the blur in the arguments is the tendency, apparently very hard to eradicate, of mixing phenomenological description with the two extraneous matters of either psychological or philosophical analysis. The philosophical analyst must not permit himself to be drawn into these arguments. That is the precaution required of him. The method shows why his refusal is legitimate. Let me then show it in the case at hand. Phenomenally, there is the "thrust" of the present; there is also change; there is perhaps even the Self of the specious present. But I shall not, because for my purposes I need not, inquire whether these three are one thing rather than three (or two) closely related things. I need not because, in case they are more than one, if one among them can be construed as an existent (in the technical sense, as explicated),[62] then clearly so can the others. For, if I may recall an earlier phrase, the heart of the matter is the paradox of the apple and nothing else. Remember, too, that while the method requires us to be directly acquainted with what is named by a uds—this is indeed the one and only connection between philosophical analysis and phenomenological description—it is not required that every introspective simple be named by a uds.

In a subject-predicate world without absolute time change does not exist. That spots the tension. The only way out is to drop the assumption that our world is a subject-predicate world. Yet this assumption is of the very essence of the analytical enterprise. To drop it is to abandon as insoluble one of the most fundamental problems of analytical philosophy. Let me explain why this is so.

1. This is red. 2. That is blue. 3. This is not blue. 4. This is red and that is blue. 5. All dogs are mammals. 6. It either is or is not raining. Assume 1 and 2 to be true; then so are the other four sentences. Being true, each refers to a fact, i.e., to a state of affairs which is the case. The examples throw further light on this use of 'fact'. Properly understood, 1 and 2 are atomic sentences. Thus they refer to what some call atomic facts.[63] In 3 the predication is negative. Thus its atomic constit-

---

[62] More precisely: if one of them can be construed as an existent which is not either what the psychologists call a feeling or a character thereof. In view of the vacillating terminology of the classical British philosophers I add that in this narrow sense of 'feeling' a sensum is not a feeling.

[63] Some now contend that the Wittgenstein of the *Tractatus* propounded an ontology of atomic facts. I disagree. The very idea of an ontology of facts is inherently confused. Nor does it have any ground in the tradition. Ontologists have always searched for simples which are things named by terms, not states of affairs referred to by sentences. See "The Revolt against Logical Atomism."

uent refers to what some philosophers (though not I) call a negative fact. The facts referred to by 4, 5, 6 may be called complex. Someone may insist that since 6 is analytic, it does not refer to a fact. We need not accept his standardization proposal for the (ordinary) use of 'fact'. Moreover, his use of 'analytic' is philosophical. So we may rule him out of order. What he says is nonetheless very important. In one sense, each fact is what it is, namely, a fact and they are all in the same boat. In another sense, there is a distinction. Some facts are necessary, some are not. The difference is clearly felt. Yet the idea of necessity[64] is anything but clear. If it were, no philosopher could have seriously asserted that whatever is (the case) is necessary. I do not agree with the philosophers who said this sort of thing. Of course I don't. But I take their error as a sign that the notion of necessity is very difficult and, being both philosophical and fundamental, needs explication. The necessary, in the relevant sense, is the logically necessary. The logically necessary is referred to by a sentence (of the IL) which is analytic. These are the first obvious steps towards an explication. But, then, how shall we explicate 'analytic'? The only explication that may be adequate is syntactical and, like all other syntactical explications that have been proposed, presupposes that the IL is a subject-predicate schema. Nor is that all. I do not know of and cannot even imagine any line of approach that might lead to an explication if the ideal schema is not of the subject-predicate kind. But the problem of analyticity (necessity) is *one* of the most fundamental problems of the tradition, i.e., it is crucial in the familiar sense that upon its solution the solution of many other philosophical problems depends. This is a matter of record. Philosophically, I have thus proved my case. Anthropologically, I shall go even further, showing that there is a close and intimate connection between the problem of analyticity and what is *the* most fundamental philosophical problem, in my opinion but surely not just in mine nor just within my tradition, namely, the nature (or, as one would rather say in my tradition, the analysis) of mind and its place in the world.

A fact is necessary by being what it is. Its necessity does not depend on anything outside itself. An explication that wouldn't bear out this idea wouldn't bear out what is clearly felt. Thus it could not be adequate. On this score, though of course not necessarily on all others, every syntactical explication of 'analytic' is adequate. It follows that a fact being necessary and our thinking or knowing that it is are two things and not one. Philosophically, that is, there is no connection whatsoever between necessity and the existence and nature of mental

---

[64] I limit myself to necessity. The explications of 'possible', 'impossible', 'contingent' flow in the familiar fashion from that of 'necessary'.

things. Anthropologically, however, the connection is close and intimate. The ability to think necessity is the very essence of thought or mind. To understand what that means, consider '$p_1 \vee \sim p_1$'. Of its two constituents, 'p_1' and '$\sim p_1$', one is true, one is false. Which of the two is the true one does not matter. One who thinks that it does is confused by the confused philosophical uses of 'fact'. What matters is, rather, that we can think what is false. For, if we couldn't, we could not, as we now see, think '$p_1 \vee \sim p_1$', which is the simplest of all necessary truths. Conversely, since we can think what is false, we can also think necessity. Thoughts (propositional characters) are existents. And there are of course no "negative existents," whatever that may mean, just as there are no "negative facts." But there are thoughts which mean what is not the case. Philosophically, the existence of such thoughts causes no difficulty, at least not upon our analysis of mind and meaning. Anthropologically, the ability to think what is false is the very essence of mind. This diagnosis, though penetrating, is anything but new. Recall what the scientific students of man have told us for quite some time. Language, they say, is the essence of mind. And we know ourselves that the possibility of saying what is false is the logical essence of language. Thoughts, of course, are not linguistic things. To believe that they are is to fall into the error of the philosophical behaviorists (materialists). But, then, I speak anthropologically. Besides, there are of course connections between thought and language that can be traced and clarified in the philosophical reconstruction.

Now the whole pattern lies before us. The ability to think necessity is the essence of mind. For this reason alone if for no other, the explication of the idea of necessity is the paramount task of analytical philosophy.[65] Depending on whether or not this task is soluble, analytical philosophy may stand or must fall. If our world is not a subject-predicate world, then it falls. But analysis also shows, irrefragably on its own grounds, that there is no absolute time. Hence, if analytical philosophy is not to fail, change must not (in the ontological sense, as explicated) exist. That is, while there are of course continuants, including minds, there cannot be any that are (in the ontological sense, as explicated) existents. Yet we are directly acquainted with change. That is the origin of the tension. Now we understand that it was merely our response to the natural limits of philosophical analysis. So we are at rest.

[65] The explication of analyticity in what I called the difference between L and L_1 is indeed tantamount to the analysis of the place of minds in the world. The crucial ideas are that 'M', which is the transcription of the intentional use of 'means', is a logical sign and that ''p_1'Mp_1', which reflects the traditional idea that an act intends its content, is analytic. See "Intentionality."

AUTHOR'S NOTE

The papers in this volume appeared originally as follows:

I   "Intentionality" in *Semantica* (Archivio di Filosofia, Roma: Bocca, 1955), pp. 177–216.

II   "The Revolt against Logical Atomism" in *The Philosophical Quarterly*, 7, 1957, 323–39, and 8, 1958, 1–13.

III   "Analyticity" in *Theoria*, 24, 1958, 71–93.

IV   "Particularity and the New Nominalism" in *Methodos*, 6, 1954, 131–47.

V   "Concepts" (jointly with Herbert Hochberg) in *Philosophical Studies*, 8, 1957, 19–27.

VI   "Elementarism" in *Philosophy and Phenomenological Research*, 18, 1957, 107–14.

VII   "Individuals" in *Philosophical Studies*, 9, 1958, 78–85.

VIII   "Sameness, Meaning, and Identity" scheduled to appear in *Proceedings of the Twelfth International Congress of Philosophy*.

IX   "Professor Quine on Analyticity" in *Mind*, 64, 1955, 254–58.

X   "Some Remarks on the Ontology of Ockham" in *Philosophical Review*, 53, 1954, 560–71.

XI   "Russell's Examination of Leibniz Examined" in *Philosophy of Science*, 23, 1956, 175–203.

XII   "Some Remarks on the Philosophy of Malebranche" in *The Review of Metaphysics*, 10, 1956, 207–26.

XIII   "Frege's Hidden Nominalism" in *Philosophical Review*, 67, 1958, 437–59.

XIV   "Some Reflections on Time" in *Il Tempo* (Archivio di Filosofia, Padova: Cedam, 1958), pp. 49–82.

Index

Ackermann, W., 78n

Acquaintance: and awareness, 6, 7, 18, 24, 50, 118, 256, 259; and improved language, 44–45, 58, 60, 116, 126–28, 186; objects of, 49, 50, 60, 116n, 126, 133, 238; principle of, 116–17, 118–19, 126, 186, 237, 245; and nominalism, 117

Act: and awareness, 4, 8–10; and meaning, 9, 135, 263n; as a relation, 10; and Newtonian science, 10; and interaction, 10–11; and psychology, 12–17; and 'certain', 58n, 247; of memory, 242–59; and knowing, 194–96, 254–55

'All': as infinite conjunction, 53, 173

Allaire, E., x, 57n

Analysis: philosophical vs. nonphilosophical, 42, 50; paradox of, 112

Analysts, classical, v, Essay II 39–72; and nominalism, 52, 57, 59; and mind, 51, 65, 248; and ideal language method, 51, 106, 247; presupposition of, 45; and analyticity, 45–46, 79, 86, 251–53; four weaknesses of, 51–52; and phenomenalism, 52n, 58, 62; and individuals, 57; and basic propositions, 59; and meaning, 64, 249–53; and verification theory, 40, 64–66, 247–53

Analyticity, Essay III 73–90; as basic problem, vi, 262–63; and mind, vi, 262–63; and meaning, vi, 30, 32–33, 70, 90, 113–14, 137, 251, 256; vs. demonstrability, 23, 75; and linguistic truth, 23, 33, 87, 252–53,

259; extended notion of, 26, 29–33, 40, 108, 137; explication of, 30, 75–90, 251–52; and truth, 30–31, 36, 81, 86–87; and validity theory, 30–31, 53, 76–85; and classical analysts, 46, 53, 79, 86, 251–53; and 'natures', 57; and 'certain', 58n, 78, 247; word used philosophically, 73–74; and axiom of infinity, 74, 75, 76–79, 82–83, 101; and tautology, 75–76, 79, 90; and truth-tables, 76, 79, 81; and possibility, 79–80, 90, 250–53; and logic, 81–87; and ideal language, 73–76, 100; and predication, 81; of arithmetic, 84; and identity, 111–12; and conceivability, 119; and space-time, 141–43; and Leibniz, 168; and 'grammar', 252; and subject-predicate schema, 262; and necessity, 262–63

Analytic-synthetic dichotomy, 70–72, 92, 139

Aquinas, Thomas, 151, 153, 167, 191, 192–93, 197, 204

Aristotle, 151, 167, 172, 191–92, 197, 222

Arithmetic, 73, 74–75, 83–84

Arnauld, A., 156, 171, 175, 190

Atomic: sentences, 46, 58–60; facts, 48, 54, 58, 261

Atomism: in physics, 41, 198; vs. instrumentalism, 45; psychological, 69. *See* Logical Atomism

Augustine, 190

Awareness: existence of, 4, 5, 15, 137–38, 263; is a particular, 4, 28, 107, 113, 118, 136, 232, 255; and mind, 4,